BERNARD MALAMUD

Bernard Malamud

A Centennial Tribute

EDITED BY
VICTORIA AARONS
&
GUSTAVO SÁNCHEZ CANALES

WAYNE STATE UNIVERSITY PRESS
DETROIT

ISBN 978-0-8143-4114-8 (paperback) / ISBN 978-0-8143-4115-5 (e-book)

Library of Congress Control Number: 2016930473

Designed and typeset by adam b. bohannon
Composed in Adobe Caslon

Wayne State University Press
Leonard N. Simons Building
4809 Woodward Avenue
Detroit, Michigan 48201-1309

Visit us online at wsupress.wayne.edu

For our children,
Aaron and Gabriel
and
Federico and Micaela

A smart man hears one word but he understand[s] two.

—Bernard Malamud, *The Assistant*

Contents

CONTENTS

Part II. European Voices

CONTENTS

Preface

Bernard Malamud (1914–1986), consummate storyteller, artful craftsman, and exacting stylist, is generally considered not only one of the three most influential postwar American-Jewish writers but also a writer holding a central place in the canon of twentieth-century American letters. Malamud came to prominence at an important moment in American social, political, and cultural history, writing at a time that saw dramatic changes in both America's self-assessment in the aftermath of World War II and in its ability to assimilate diverse sectors of its population. Along with the novelists Philip Roth and Saul Bellow, Bernard Malamud brought to life a decidedly American-Jewish protagonist and a newly emergent Jewish voice that came to define American letters and influence American writers for over half a century, an influence that continues. The Malamudian voice and characteristic urban landscape that define his fiction speak to the changing ethos in American life and thought at this pivotal, mid-twentieth-century moment in American history. Malamud's literary oeuvre reflects "a struggle to achieve order" in both life and literature, as well as a deep appreciation for the supple and elastic forms of the written word (Malamud, introduction vi). Malamud's legacy continues to be a hallmark of American literature, with the very best of his work—the novels and short stories that create the felt conditions of "what it means human" ("Idiots First," *Stories* 44)—an expression of the deep investment in an ethical life and in the rigors of "the human sentence" (Malamud, introduction xii).

While Malamud remains a major, formative voice in American letters, recent years have shown an emergent, burgeoning interest in Malamud among European scholars, who regard Malamud with growing interest not only as a central American voice but also as a writer whose fiction opens itself up to an exploration of stylistic technique, narrative voice, and the making of character. Thus, in recognition of this major voice in American literature, the editors of this volume have brought together both North American and European scholars in an attempt to show the range and depth of the possibilities for Malamud studies in the twenty-first century. In celebration of the one hundredth anniversary of Malamud's birth and in recognition of the thirtieth anniversary of Malamud's death, the editors of this tribute have attempted to bring together under one title a variety of approaches and responses to Malamud's central, defining works of fiction.

We have intended the essays gathered here to play off one another, to show differences as well as overlapping concerns and interests. In engaging scholars from the United States and abroad, we hope to establish a dialogue between the critical, traditional study of Malamud in America and the newly emerging one in Europe. Malamud's work lends itself to this cross-cultural engagement. Very much in the tradition of twentieth-century American writers, Malamud traveled to Europe, centering many of his stories there, a fertile context for looking back to the origins of America and its comparative cultural successes and failures. Many of Malamud's stories are set in Europe, especially the Italian stories. Europe was, for Malamud, a landscape for his characters' self-assessment against the backdrop of history. In, for example, "The Last Mohican," Malamud's recurring protagonist, Fidelman, in Rome, standing in the Eternal City, gazing at the remains of the Baths of Diocletian, whispers to himself, "Imagine all that history" (*Complete* 200). Europe figures in the Fidelman stories as a place of possibilities, opportunities, and self-reinvention. Abroad, Fidelman "experienced the sensation of suddenly seeing himself as he was" (201). And Henry Levin, in the story "The Lady of the Lake," travels "abroad seeking romance. . . . He liked the sense of foreignness of the city—of things different, anything likely to happen" (*Complete* 221). Paul Malamud's poem "Mediterranean," which is a part of this collection, speaks to his father's affinity and deep appreciation for a landscape and a history so different from his own, "a poor Jew from Brooklyn who had made good, walking under the olive trees."

The editors have arranged this book in an attempt to illustrate the richness and complexity of Malamud's work as a way of paying tribute to the writer and to the subtle utterance and perfection of the written word that is such a fundamental feature of Malamud's craft. Our hope is that including scholarly approaches from a range of countries—the United States, Spain, France, Germany, Italy, and Greece—will multiply the possibilities of study and appreciation of this important author and his work. And while our intention, initially, was to show an understanding of Malamud from two different perspectives—U.S. and European—the exchange among scholars demonstrates the enormous breadth and complexity in such a diverse perspectival reach. For ease of reading, we have structured this book in two parts: U.S. and European Voices. Each is introduced separately in order to set up, in general terms, the direction and focus for the evolving perspectives. What we find in such a dialogue is a kind of chiastic exchange, reflecting one of Malamud's major literary tropes, a relationship that has at its center the experience of an essential connection and consanguinity.

Bernard Malamud, Person and Writer

PAUL MALAMUD

(Address delivered at City College, New York, May, 2013)

Dad was known as a short-story writer and a novelist. The peak of his career was between the early 1960s and 1980 or so. He was known for his short stories, which began to appear in *Commentary*, the literary magazine, in the '50s. He was also known for his novels, such as the baseball yarn *The Natural* and *The Assistant*. The latter book was based in part on his own father's circumstances as an impoverished Jewish immigrant grocer living in Brooklyn, during the Great Depression. In the '60s, Dad wrote *The Fixer*, set in tsarist Russia, dealing in a fictional manner with the anti-Semitism of that time and place. A number of his books became best sellers, and most have been made into movies, including, famously, *The Natural*, starring Robert Redford.

Bernard Malamud was born in Brooklyn, New York, in 1914, into straitened circumstances. His family was Russian Jewish, immigrants who had virtually nothing, except their wits. His father, Max, owned a grocery store near the old Elevated Railroad. Since they lived in the back of the store, Dad's childhood was full of roars, rumbles, and fumes from the trains. When Dad was a small child, he contracted pneumonia and almost died. Upon his unexpected recovery, Max gave him a children's encyclopedia, though he could barely afford it, and that set Dad reading. His early life was not without frustrations and setbacks. His mother, Bertha, died early and under distressing circumstances, and Dad's younger brother, Eugene, was ill all his life. Dad and his stepmother never got along.

What salvaged Dad's ambitions were other relatives and Jewish families of the neighborhood, some of whom befriended him, and the New York City educational system of the day, which he came to esteem. As a child, he traveled alone a great distance each day to attend a good public school. He went on to Erasmus Hall high school and, as you know, received his bachelor's degree at City College. Like many ambitious kids of his day, he also had an instinct for ideas, philosophies, and the written word.

He began writing in high school. From then on, he had no goal except to write fiction and, later, to teach English. He did not seriously consider any other path in life, whatever the risk to his opportunities or his finances. He had an unswerving belief in his ability to prevail as a writer. His great break was being published in the 1950s by *Commentary* magazine. His second break came in the form of the celebrated literary editor Robert Giroux, who accepted *The Natural* for publication on behalf of Harcourt Brace in the early '50s. When Giroux moved on to a different publishing house, Farrar, Straus, he continued to publish Dad's work there.

After my father married my mother, Ann, another New Yorker, in 1945, he occupied college teaching positions, first in Oregon, then in Vermont. Two novels, *A New Life*, and *Dubin's Lives*, came out of those experiences. Throughout those years, they had many cordial community relationships, and my mother's deserved reputation as a cook and hostess helped cement those. By the early '70s, he and Mom had returned to Manhattan, this time uptown, and enjoyed such recognition and honor as comes the way of local boys who make good.

Dad was a very gentle man, who had great sympathy for the plights of others. Both my parents had an insatiable interest in whatever community they lived in, and in people's life stories and adventures. Dad had great flashes of geniality and warmth and an unusual sense of fantasy and humor. He also had a pessimistic Russian quality. He did not see himself as a writer in the Russian tradition or even solely in the Jewish tradition and felt happy to be accepted as an American novelist. He used to make up droll and funny fantasy stories to tell me when I was a small boy. He encouraged me to read constantly and to do well in school. He was extremely proud to be able to give me a set of *World Book Encyclopedia* and all kinds of other things his parents had not been able to give him. When I got into a good college in the 1960s, he was pleased. He and my mother bickered, yet theirs was a close and enduring marriage. At the beginning, she typed his manuscripts, read his early stuff, critiqued it, helped him proofread, and made them friends throughout. Dad always saw people as individuals—he had little serious interest in politics, took his centrist liberal opinions from his friends, and never ever had the slightest interest in systemic ideology or what came to be called political correctness.

Dad loved his college teaching. He admired intellect in his students, if he was sometimes scandalized by ignorance and humorlessness. He never questioned the premise that the teaching of literature was the core of civilized existence. His day was consumed by writing, teaching when he did it, and voracious reading and class preparation in the evening. As with all creative people, part of his mind was elsewhere—in his case, constructing plots, scenes, and dialogue. The great love of his life was the written word.

That is my memory of the person you are honoring here. Thank you again, on Dad's behalf, for this recognition of his achievement, from his alma mater.

Mediterranean

Paul Malamud

The olive groves, the wine-blush of the sea,
the salt air, looking down from ancient cliffs
on the Mediterranean, as if blood
of the old world turned to gold in the bright sun,

gold stones and gold rough grasses underfoot
on the Mediterranean coast in the sixties:
me a gangling teenager with my parents.
We walked towards a cafe with marble floors—

through olive trees, there, then, the plinth of coolness.
The sea like Lacoon's serpent, was coiled beneath
in compact sheathes, a cobalt blue, blood red.
We sipped wine—no-one knew we were alive.

My Dad said, this is Homer's wine-dark sea,
as the sun glinted on the crinkled sea,
thousands of feet below, beneath the cliffs,
He could say it without too much irony,

letting it go, past irony, the feeling,
walking uphill with his wife on the small path,
there in late middle age, a happy day;
in sunny southern France, the olive groves

past the dry yellow grass, rough olive trees,
black-clad women going up the cobbled hills,

turning to dusk— the sea, a cobalt jewel,
liquid, coiling like intertwined snakes.

That was his gift, the oddest gift, the feeling,
letting it go, past irony, the feeling
that all experience was real, sea,
both blue and red, deep, indescribable.

This is Homer's sea, my father said,
a poor Jew from Brooklyn who had made good,
walking under the olive trees,
in the hot sun, fifty years ago;

no-one could say it for me, then, like him,
so happy, self-assured, so full of life;
as I loped behind, in my penny loafers,
and my best checked summer short-sleeve shirt.

We walked on the streets of those medieval towns
sand in the rubber sandals, on our toes,
bitten to death by olive-fat mosquitoes,
laughing or shouting at the souvenirs,

walking towards the hillside cafe, laughing,
to eat a fish lunch in our relatively happy
discomfort and quarreling. See, that was it: feeling;
he had the gift of feeling—making it real

like the man in the play by Camus,
he made a coffee cup real when he touched it.

"Mediterranean" originally appeared in *Old Poems, New Translations* by
Paul Francis Malamud, 2013.

PART I

U.S. Voices

Introduction

"Moved by a Memory": Bernard Malamud's Literary Landscape

VICTORIA AARONS

> How past-drenched present life was.
> —Bernard Malamud, *A New Life*

The year 2014 marked the hundredth anniversary of Bernard Malamud's birth. Born in Brooklyn, New York, on April 26, 1914, to Russian-immigrant parents Max and Bertha (née Fidelman) Malamud, Bernard Malamud would become one of three major post–World War II American-Jewish writers to distinguish and authenticate the richly nuanced, urban voice of an emerging Jewish presence in American literature, a presence that has influenced generations of writers. In concert with Saul Bellow and Philip Roth, Malamud sanctioned the wide and fluid range of Jewish expression in American culture, a distinct ethos in the literature and life of postwar America that continues to speak to the felt experience of the changing culture of Jewish American life. In Malamud's fiction, one finds the possibilities, the promise and the failures, the small victories and the inevitable disillusions of self-reinvention and self-fashioning in the second half of the twentieth century, a transformative period in American history. For Malamud, such an undertaking is all a part of the arduous affair of making a life, which can become, as one of Malamud's characters ruefully reminds us, "a dreadfully boring business unless you think you have a future" ("The German Refugee" 106).[1] Imagining a future becomes the essential ordeal—both invitation and impediment—that drives Malamud's characters forward into the mercurial patterns of mid- to late-twentieth-century American life. Summoned into the future, Malamud's characteristically weary wanderers and petitioners, "moved by a memory," struggle against isolation and grief, all the while embracing their place in a long history of Jewish suffering and exultation ("The Jewbird" 154).

The blueprint of Malamud's literary landscape draws on the re-created worlds of Jewish history and his own much-more-proximate familial past. The son of a struggling immigrant grocer and mother whose suicide came to haunt so many of his characters, Malamud shapes his fictional settings by the circumstances of his own background and, at the same time, invokes the conditions of the Jewish-immigrant experience in America, the instabilities and vulnerabilities of immigrant life and the Yiddish-inflected English that in many ways defined that life. As the biographer Philip Davis has suggested, "Malamud was a time-haunted man" (Davis 6). Although his literary sensibilities and, for the most part, his terrain are distinctly American, his writing is informed by distinct moments in Jewish history. The 1966 novel *The Fixer*, a fictionalized account of the Beilis trial in which a Jew was accused of blood libel and for which Malamud received both the National Book Award and the Pulitzer Prize, reveals this preoccupation with Jewish history. The short story "The Lady of the Lake," in a similarly historicized way, evokes the suffering endured in the Holocaust. The trope of time is a fixture of Malamud's writing: the narrative present as well as the imagined future as informed by the past, a distinctly Jewish past of lamentation and celebration, one, as Frank Alpine, at the close of the novel *The Assistant*, discovers, "enraged and inspired him" ([1974] 297).

Malamud's characters, who straddle the dual worlds of Jewish and American and the requirements of brokering both, find themselves beholden to a cultural inheritance that shapes their experience of the juxtaposition of their worlds. In the introduction to *The Stories of Bernard Malamud* (published in 1983), Malamud explains about the early years of his writing career, "Almost without understanding why, I was thinking about my father's immigrant life—how he earned his meager living and what he paid for it, and about my mother's, diminished by fear and suffering—as perhaps matter for my fiction. . . . I had them in mind as I invented the characters who became their fictional counterparts . . . and felt I would often be writing about Jews, in celebration and expiation" (viii–ix). Thus, Malamud returns time and time again to stories about Jews, stories about impoverished grocers, *shadchonim* (marriage brokers), troubled rabbis, Jewish angels, *schnorrers* (beggars), lonely petitioners, mourners, and depleted refugees, those tragically for whom "broke what breaks" ("Take Pity" 6). Malamud is drawn to the past, and his fictive inspiration and landscape come instinctively from what he knows best, the daily sufferings of diasporic Jews. As the Soviet writer Feliks Levitansky, in Malamud's short story "Man in the Drawer," insists, "When I write about Jews comes out stories, so I write about Jews" (213). Jews and Jewish immigrant life become paradigmatic of both the success and failure of assimilation and also of the ways in which Jewish history and culture are grafted on American life. As Malamud explained, in "Imaginative Writing and the Jewish Experience," "Writing about Jews, for me at least, extends the area of imagination. I mean to say that the story of the Jews, of their history and culture, and the Jews themselves as people, are so rich in the ingredients of drama, so fruitful as a source of image, idea and symbol, that I feel I can at present more fully, even more easily, achieve my purpose as an American writer by writing of them" (184). Thus, as the novelist Cynthia Ozick puts it in her tribute to Malamud, "Remembrances: Bernard Malamud," "He wrote about suffering Jews, about poor Jews, about grocers and fixers and birds and horses and angels in Harlem and matchmakers and salesmen and rabbis and landlords and tenants and egg chandlers and writers and chimpanzees; he wrote about the plentitude and unity of the world" (27). And he did so in a language of the struggling immigrant Jew, the Yiddish of his background and his milieu, the sounds of home and of Eastern European Jewish life recreated in the voices of his characters and the very lives they embody— elegiac, plaintive, yearning voices, defining of the characters who inhabit them.

Indeed, Malamud's fiction, in particular the short stories that create the urgency and immediacy of a dramatic moment—as Philip Roth has said, some "of the best American short stories I'd ever read (or ever will)"—unfold to the sound and gestures of language ("Pictures"). In recreating the voice of the Jewish immigrant, Malamud captures the felt expression of the lives of the inheritors of dual histories, of those living in between worlds: the receding life of Eastern European Jewry and the accelerating exigencies of twentieth-century, post-Holocaust American life. This is, for Malamud's characters, a world of contradictions: insider / outsider; hope / despair, belonging / marginalization; comfort / disease; American / Jewish; English / Yiddish—poised in tense juxtaposition. In the very fluidity and malleability of the Yiddish-English that his characters, with great relish, speak, Malamud illustrates the pliability of that enormous representational project, the ways in which language defines experience as it is simultaneously shaped by that experience, signifying the past with the language, attitudes, and demeanor of Eastern European Jewish life grafted onto a volatile American cultural landscape. As Philip Davis has suggested, the voice of Malamud's characters is "the Yiddish-English amalgam that was in memory of the way his own father spoke. The second language of the son of immigrants with the original Yiddish still hanging around it" (117). Malamud skillfully re-creates the spoken tongue of the immigrant Jew, his signature idiom of the clatter of two worlds, his special brand of Yiddish-English: "It's not English and it's not Yiddish," explains Davidov, the census-taker in the short story "Take Pity," but rather "an old-fashioned language they don't use it nowadays" (11). And Malamud, in his skillful fusion of the languages of past and present, brings to life the sensations and dispositions of his Jewish characters, the condition, as one character puts it, of "what it means human" ("Idiots First" 44).

Reflecting a long and elastic tradition of Jewish linguistic fluidity and adaptability, Malamud celebrates the durability, the strength, and the resilience of his characters, those for whom the spoken word becomes an insistence on survival, the affirmation of self in a world that would prey on those who are most vulnerable. For the despondent transplant Oskar Gassner, a refugee of Nazi Germany, in the short story "The German Refugee," as for so many others, "the great loss was the loss of language— that they could not say what was in them to say" (97). Thus, Malamud creates an idiom that speaks to his struggling characters' attempts to shape, through language, the duality of worlds that they uneasily inhabit. The very language they speak provides a bridge to both worlds, a matter of clinging to the past and embracing an uncertain future. As Ozick has suggested, in giving life to his characters, Malamud "brought into being a new American idiom of his own idiosyncratic invention. . . . He not only wrote in the American language, he augmented it with fresh plasticity, he shaped our English into startling new configurations" ("Remembrances" 26). His characters speak their own intimate version of American English, drawing on the language of their forebears, the diasporic language of assimilation. In doing so, Malamud reshapes the linguistic structures and patterns, as Roth puts it, so "to make them dance to his sad tune" ("Pictures"). The Yiddish-English that defines Malamud's characters evokes the contradictory impulses of their lives; it comes to represent ambiguous moments of exile and home. A language of assimilation and accommodation, their characteristic speech patterns—the idiomatic inversions and linguistic blending and recanting—create, as Davis suggests, "the powerful intermingled language of thirst and hunger; the need for magic, or if not that, at least, a second chance" (7).

As Saul Bellow wrote in a eulogy for the novelist following his premature death on March 18, 1986, at the age of seventy-two, "Malamud in his novels and stories discovered a sort of communicative genius in the impoverished, harsh jargon of immigrant New York ("Memory" 436). Indeed, without question, Malamud was a wordsmith, a masterful craftsman of the carefully turned phrase, whose scrupulous, exacting prose becomes the measure of the painstaking construction of his characters' lives. In the tribute, "In Memory of Bernard Malamud," Bellow poses that for first-generation Americans, "language is a spiritual mansion," expansive and with room for experimentation (436). The Yiddish-English of the sounds and utterances, the shape of the language in the mouths of Malamud's characters—the linguistic tropes and turns of phrase—bend ordinary expression into extraordinary cadences. We find in Malamud's fiction the perfect sentence—perfectly balanced, perfectly poised, as is the character of Teddy in the short story "The Letter," a man who stands at the gate of a psychiatric hospital with a worn, "finger-soiled" letter in his hand. Standing in place, Teddy is poised as sentry with his letter in hand, a letter on which nothing is written, addressed to no one. Nonetheless, "he held it as he always held it, as though he had held it always" (156). Here the phrases are balanced by the chiasmus—"always held it . . . held it always"—and thus suggest the inversion and cessation of time, creating both timelessness and anticipation. Teddy waits for the reluctant Newman—the son who unwillingly comes to visit his father in the psychiatric hospital—to take from him his letter and, in something like a leap of faith, place it in the mailbox, for, as Teddy enigmatically cautions Newman, "it won't do you any good if you don't" (157). Clinging to his letter, Malamud's guardian of time and irrevocability will remain poised at the edge of possibility.

The troping of language as a signifier for its own production of meaning makes imperative, as Malamud once put it, the "struggle to achieve order" through fiction (introduction vii). The very texture of the language for Malamud makes emphatic the desperation with which his characters attempt to contain and mediate their lives. A writer of contradictions, Malamud captures the paradoxes and tensions of the lives his characters live in the linguistic push/pull and contrasting elements of his tightly constructed syntactical design. Consider, for example, the following antithesis from the short story "Talking Horse," a line that, in its paradoxical apposition provides a choice: his character wonders, "if I'm Abramowitz, a horse; or a horse *including* Abramowitz" (329; emphasis in the original); and this from "Rembrandt's Hat": "Each froze the other out of his life; or froze him in" (273). These structural antitheses offer choices that are not really choices but a refashioning of the lens through which his characters mark their place in the world. The syntactical antitheses have the effect of simultaneously pushing out and pulling in, holding characters in the balance but also in an inseparable and irresistible alliance with each other. They are allied in their juxtaposition, mirror images of one another. As the beleaguered grocer Morris Bober, in the novel *The Assistant*, tells Frank Alpine, the man who came to rob him and now labors alongside him in the store, "I suffer for you. . . . I mean you suffer for me" (150). In such figuring of speech, Malamud creates the condition of antithesis, balanced by contradiction: perfectly aligned—perfectly precarious. We are presented with such paradoxes in, for example, the rabbinical student Leo Finkle's mystification about his own motives and shortcomings: "He had never loved anyone. Or perhaps it went the other way, that he did not love God so well as he might, because he had not loved man" ("The Magic Barrel" 135); and this from *The Assistant*: "The right thing was to make the right choice but he made the wrong. Even when it was right it was wrong" (249). After all, in Malamud's fictional world, "nothing meant yes or it meant no" ("The Letter" 155). The language of his utterance takes back just at the moment it gives.

Such shaping of the language creates a kind of stasis, possibility held in abeyance in the sharply constructed linguistic reversals and arrangements. Of Rubin regarding himself in the mirror wearing the hat that is the source of such *tsouris*, Malamud's narrator says, "He wore it like a crown of failure and hope" ("Rembrandt's Hat" 276). And of the chastened tailor Manischevitz, seeking God, bewilderingly "cursing himself for having, beyond belief, believed," and later, having acknowledged that the black man sitting in his living room was, in fact, a disincarnated angel of God, he wonders, "If you said it it was said. If you believed it you must say it. If you believed, you believed" ("Angel Levine" 285, 289). Here the reversal—"if you said it it was said"—is arrested at the moment of the repetition ("it it") whose proximity holds the utterance at its center, thus creating a momentary suspension, a stark exposure of desired surety in an otherwise unstable and inscrutable condition of living. In Malamud's fictive enterprise, there are no such guarantees. Such tropes of contradiction in an otherwise static world offer possibilities, second chances for Malamud's characters. For, after all, "second chances" is the language of the immigrant, as we find in the short story "The Jewbird": presented with an open window, "the skinny bird flew in. Flappity-flap with its frazzled black wings. That's how it goes. It's open, you're in. Closed, you're out and that's your fate" (144). His characters' confusions about their futures and insecurities about place and identity are revealed in the balanced sentence, in the syntactical complexities, Malamud's Yiddish-inflected English itself becoming an opening of possible meanings and permutations. We can see this anxiety about the opening up of possibility in the recurring pattern of the polyptoton, a repetition of the root of a term with different prefixes or suffixes: "I'm frightened of the world. . . . It fills me with fright" ("My Son the Murderer" 91). And even when up against the harsh reality of finalities, closures, as the narrator of "Man in the Drawer" discovers, "there comes a time in a man's life when to get where he has to—if there are no doors or windows—he walks through a wall" (225).

In Malamud's fiction, one hears the voices of his literary predecessors, establishing his place in the long and rich oral and written tradition of Jewish literature, storytellers attempting to fill in the gaps, to explain and adjudicate, to live in the world among others. When a character in the story "The Mourners," for example, experiencing a shattering moment of mirroring, uncanny clarity, we are reminded of I. B. Singer's host of dybbuks and dreamers, who pursue life beyond the material realm: "Then it struck him with a terrible force that the mourner was mourning him: it was *he* who was dead" (34; emphasis in the original). So, too, in a Kafkaesque occasion of disorientation, a character such as the lonely, frightened son in "My Son the Murderer" stands "staring with shut eyes in the mirror" (85). And we hear the narrative assurance of Sholom Aleichem's Tevye when Malamud's character simply but aptly appraises life: "Everybody that don't die by age fifty-nine gets to be sixty" ("My Son the Murderer" 88). And reaching back further into history and myth, a Malamudian character laments his forlorn and hapless condition in the elevated language of lament: "Baring his chest, he smote the naked bones" ("Angel Levine" 285).

Reading Malamud is, at times, sheer poetry, as in the following lines from some of his short fiction: "The wind white-capped the leaden waves and the slow surf broke on the empty beaches with a quiet roar" ("My Son the Murderer" 91); "All that can be seen is the white shawl luminously praying" ("Man in the Drawer" 236); "Albert, wearing a massive, spike-laden headache, rushed down the booming stairs" ("The Silver Crown" 328); "The thick ticking of the tin clock stopped" ("Idiots First" 35); and "violins and lit candles revolved in the sky" ("The Magic Barrel" 143). The sharp crispness of the sentence, the sound and sensations and implied gesticulations, the figures and figuring of speech, and Malamud's affinity for the texture of language create the balanced feat of making sense of experience. And, one might well suggest, as does the novelist Ehud Havazelet, that Malamud's true mastery is realized in the short form: "His genius is in the stories. Nobody will ever write stories like he did. That's his crowning glory" (Wasserman).

The spoken utterance becomes for Malamud's characters a means of combating the solitary condition of grief. "To his anguish, loneliness," as one character imagines, might come the momentary reprieve of human connection ("My Son the Murderer" 85). The minimalist, elliptical construction of the lament—"To his anguish, loneliness"—suggests the cumulative effect of suffering. What's left out in the implied ellipsis makes emphatic the additive effect of sorrow: on top of anguish, for this character, is piled loneliness, misery accumulated, extended, endless, the weight of suffering. Enjoined together, anguish and loneliness will define his isolated experience. Standing alone, this singular, stark, minimal expression of grief foregrounds the aloneness of this character's anguish, lonely because silenced, unacknowledged, and thus unrequited. This is why the imperiled writer-turned-taxi-driver in "Man in the Drawer," with determined perseverance, attempts to have his stories smuggled out of the Soviet Union: "I feel I am locked in drawer with my stories. Now I must get out or I suffocate" (214). After all, as the Soviet writer of stories about Jews tells the reluctant narrator, "Imagination makes authority" (213). The voiced imagination here is—in keeping with a long tradition of Jewish storytelling—the measure of a life, as we find in this, a sentence to fall in love with: "He could, with a little more courage, have been more than he was" (*The Assistant* 278). As Malamud himself has expressed, "Working alone to create stories . . . is not a bad way to live our human loneliness" (introduction xiii). Malamud's novels and short fiction conclude with a perfect sense of closure—we know they are coming, we anticipate them, and at the same time we do not want them to end because we are invested in the lives of his characters and the tenor of their unsettled futures.

The editors of this collection have divided the volume into two sections: the first composed of Malamud scholars from the United States, the second, European scholars. In doing so, we hope to show the wide range of approaches—international in scope—in response to this influential and enduring writer. The essays that follow show the immense fluidity and range of possibility in Malamud's fiction, from his first publication of *The Natural* in 1952 to his late fiction. In doing so, we try to capture the rhythms and stylistic designs of genre and thematic arrangement, the leitmotif of voices aching to be heard, but also of the age in which Malamud wrote and lived. The essays gathered in this collection try to show the ways in which Malamud reaches back in history—his own and that of both American and Jewish histories—illustrating the myriad ways in which the past comes to inform present conditions and future possibilities. The relevance of Malamud's fiction in the twenty-first century cannot be overstated. His fiction has helped shape both Jewish and American letters. The chapters that follow pay tribute to the influence and originality of this major postwar literary figure whose characters and uniquely idiosyncratic voices speak to a distinctly Jewish and American experience. It is in the intersection of Jewish and American that Malamud's voice is most distinctly and exceptionally heard. The subsequent chapters thus demonstrate the breadth and complexity of this masterful storyteller, exploring the many directions that his rich body of work takes us. In touching on both the early and late works, the short fiction and the novels, the points of departure for these foci include the Malamudian protagonist's relation to the urban/natural space; the tensions between American and Jewish; Malamud's *menschlichkeit* and midrash; the Malamudian hero as modern schlemiel; suffering and the law; autobiography; comparative analyses; the complexities of gender, race, and ethnicity; anti-Semitism; and the function of the fantastical in his work.

Unlike the few other existing scholarly volumes devoted to Bernard Malamud, this collection has, at its center, an international emphasis, bringing together under one cover essays by leading Malamud scholars from across the globe, demonstrating Malamud's enormous, far-reaching, and continuing influence both in the United States and abroad—an American writer, to be sure, but one whose narrative weight transcends borders.

Leah Garrett, in "The Beard Makes the Man: Bernard Malamud's *A New Life*," discusses Jewish male rebellion and reinvention in the character of the protagonist S. Levin, an urban Jew in exile in the Pacific Northwest. In doing so, Garrett places the novel's dramatic center within the context of an American masculine ethos cultivated in the late 1950s, a postwar posture of self-reinvention and experimentation. Based loosely on Malamud's own professional upheaval, S. Levin responds to the changing conditions from urban Jewish life to his existence as a lecturer at the fictive college of "Cascadia" in the Pacific Northwest. The protagonist's quest for "an authentic self," as Garrett suggests, ironically exposes the intellectual and cultural landscape of the postwar years. As Garrett poses, in *A New Life*, Malamud shows his protagonist's attempts to navigate "four simultaneous cultural spaces that connote different visions of America in the postwar era: the *city*, the *country town*, the *West*, the *broader America*." Here in the portrait of the Jew as "other," Garrett shows Malamud's critique of the anxious promise of self-reinvention in midst of America reinventing itself.

Both Jessica Lang and Timothy Parrish approach Malamud's 1971 novel *The Tenants* but from very different perspectives. Timothy Parrish, in "Malamud's *The Tenants* and the Problem of Ralph Ellison's Second Novel," provocatively shows *The Tenants* to be a response to Ellison's own career, "a version of Ellison's own authorial life, which twenty years after

Ellison's death we are only beginning to fully comprehend." In thoughtfully aligning these two major twentieth-century writers, Parrish poses that "*The Tenants* tells the drama of Ellison's long-anticipated sequel to *Invisible Man* that he was unable to complete in his lifetime." In reading the one in relation to the other, Parrish evokes the underlying complexities in their literary kinship, demonstrating the ways in which Malamud refers to the situation of the black American writer in the politicized late 1960s–early 1970s to reflect on the aesthetic situation of the Jewish American writer during that same culturally and politically fraught era. In this way, Parrish's chapter sets the scene for further discussion of *The Tenants*.

Lang, in "Unbound and Un-bodied: Reading Race in Malamud's *The Tenants*," approaches the novel from a fresh perspective, one that redirects the focus from more traditionally held assumptions about Malamud's politicized novel that pose its central dramatic tension in the antagonistic relationship between two writers. Instead, Lang shows the novel's central characters, Willie Spearmint, an African American, and Harry Lesser, a Jew, to be consanguineous, "in partnership with one another, learning from one another, and even being or passing as one another." Instead of posing the two figures as murderous adversaries, Lang shows them to be deeply entwined, dependent on each other. Thus, the final, violent death scene, Lang argues, might be read as a suicide, as well. In demonstrating the characters' complex relationship—as writers, as African American and Jew, as literary rivals—Lang historicizes the political climate of New York in the late 1960s, especially with regard to race relations. Another pairing of essays looks at Malamud's 1966 novel *The Fixer*, recipient of both the Pulitzer Prize and the National Book Award. Both Andrew M. Gordon and Holli Levitsky explore Malamud's literary resurrection of the 1913 Beilis affair, in which a Russian Jew was accused of blood libel. Levitsky, in "'I Shit My Death': From the Providential to the Excremental in *The Fixer*," examines Malamud's "revision" of the Beilis trial. As Levitsky shows, in Malamud's imaginative reinvention of the events that provide the backdrop to his novel, the fate of Mendel Beilis in the guise of Malamud's Yakov Bok is far more ambiguous. The historical Beilis was exonerated, but Malamud leaves his readers with no such clarity regarding the fate of Bok. Levitsky proposes that Malamud's novel chillingly suggests a correspondence between the blood libel and the events of the

Holocaust. Malamud, thus, recontextualizes the suffering of "the fixer" to reveal the ongoing, historical pattern of atrocities against Jews. The Holocaust consciousness that informs the novel, according to Levitsky, speaks to a potent legacy of anti-Semitism and opens up a potential space where a similarly tortured protagonist-victim might reflect on fundamental questions of faith in extreme circumstances.

Gordon turns to the history of the Beilis trial and the myth of blood libel as dramatized in *The Fixer*. In "The Jew as Vampire in Bernard Malamud's *The Fixer*," Gordon examines the accusation of blood libel and ritual murder brought against the Jews, providing a psychoanalytic reading of this complex anti-Semitic phenomenon that, as he suggests, "mixes together several primitive fantasies: that the Jews were supposedly responsible for the crucifixion of Christ and that therefore they periodically repeat the crucifixion by the ritual murder of saintly, helpless Christians, using the blood to make Passover matzoh." Gordon argues that, ultimately and ironically, Malamud's portrait of Yakov Bok, based on the historical figure of Menahem Mendel Beilis, "is mistreated like Christ, imprisoned, chained, and beaten. At the end of the novel, he is bloody but unbowed."

Victoria Aarons, in "Midrash, Memory, and 'Miracles or Near-Miracles': Bernard Malamud's All-Too-Human Project," moves us in a different direction, focusing primarily on the short stories that, she argues, are at the center of Malamud's thematic and stylistic oeuvre. Aarons argues that Malamud typically positions each of his small yet persistent characters at an instant of moral reckoning: their own or that of others. At such moments of exposure, Malamud's "*kleyne mentshelekh*" insist existentially on their responsibilities as "human being" in a world that would pitilessly conspire against them. Aarons suggests that the short story, in particular, for Malamud might be seen as contemporary midrash, a genre of possibility, of second chances, of the making of character.

NOTES

1. All of Malamud's stories that are cited in this chapter are included in Malamud, *Stories.*, except "The Lady of the Lake," which is included in Malamud, *Complete.*

Novels

CHAPTER 1

The Beard Makes the Man

Bernard Malamud's *A New Life*

LEAH GARRETT

MONASH UNIVERSITY, AUSTRALIA

In 1950s America, the rise of the Cold War and McCarthyism meant a cultural shift toward conservatism and conformism. As the country entered an economic boom time, American life in the growing suburbs and small towns seemed to offer a place of escape from the bustling, chaotic city. Here individualism was less important than fitting in with one's neighbors' cultural and religious practices. Yet at the same time, as conservative trends dominated, a culture of rebellion sprung up, mostly centered on young, disaffected white men who sought to reinvent themselves as rebels. In popular culture, be it in the figures of James Dean, Marlon Brando, or Elvis, the angry sneer against mainstream America was a central meme of the day. These men were not rebelling against the vast range of current inequities—racism, sexism, economic disparity— but were rebelling for its own sake. In literature, Beat writers such as Jack Kerouac asserted that hitting the road and refusing the stagnating trends of suburbia was an effective act of rebellion against the status quo.

For Jewish authors, Allen Ginsberg's groundbreaking poetic Beat masterpiece *Howl*, written in 1955 and published one year later, showed that Jewish themes could be merged into masterful ballads undermining and challenging the set world, and that drugs were a positive tool for bringing oneself into an altered, poetic state. Norman Mailer's 1957 groundbreaking yet problematic essay "The White Negro: Superficial Reflections on the Hipster" asserted that white people should turn to African American culture as a way to infuse energy and rebellion into their mundane lives. Clearly there was a generation of Jewish young men who found themselves disaffected with the current, conformist climate and sought a means of self-reinvention, be it through hitting the road, becoming immersed in African American culture, or taking drugs.

Bernard Malamud's fourth major work, *A New Life* (1961), explored the idea of Jewish male rebellion and reinvention in the character of the protagonist, Seymour Levin. The novel was published after Malamud had become a prominent American writer who had recently won the National Book Award (1959) for his short-story collection *The Magic Barrel*. The work takes place in the fictional Pacific Northwestern state of Cascadia at Cascadia College in the town of Eastchester. It was based on Malamud's years from 1949 to 1961 working as an English instructor at Oregon State University in Corvallis, Oregon.[1] As Malamud's biographer Philip Davis notes, this was the first of Malamud's oeuvre that did not focus on the "world of his fathers"—the Jews of eastern Europe and New York City—and instead the novel is set in a location with no Jews except the protagonist (166).

While Malamud did not like the public to read his writings as disguised autobiographical works, there were numerous similarities between the protagonist, Seymour, and the author: Malamud, like Sy, got the post after sending out hundreds of job letters to a range of schools across the United States; both he and Sy only had master's degrees, so they could only be assigned composition courses; the English department focused on composition and grammar above all else; the faculty was more interested in playing and watching sports than in teaching; the head of the department grew tired of the liberal ways of Malamud/Sy and wanted to get rid of him; and so on (Davis 75–80). Like Sy, Malamud was the "odd man out" in his department, but there was a stark and important difference between the men: whereas Sy was generally ineffective in fighting the power structure, Malamud by contrast won concessions from the university, such as when he persuaded the dean and the president of the university to reinstate a young English lecturer whom they had fired for joining a protest against the Korean War, and Malamud also set up evening creative-writing workshops (Davis 77–78). Also unlike Sy, who tries to be a good and inspiring instructor, Malamud was viewed as a bad teacher, perennially angry at his students and doing the bare minimum required in his lectures. Also, he apparently enjoyed upsetting his students by discussing sexual topics with them (Davis 93).

Whereas Malamud was bold, cocky, and able in a way to get things done, Sy was his weak, "schlemiel" version who was comically inept. In other words, while Sy aimed to take on the role of the angry young rebel, he was unable or unwilling to truly upset the status quo. His beard, resonant of Karl Marx, an orthodox rabbi, or Allan Ginsberg, was his sole form of rebellion. Yet as an icon, the beard's ability to merge Marxist, Jewish, and Beat notions suggests a deep uncertainty about the pathways of rebellion for the Jewish urbanite. As a member of a group already "other" to mainstream culture and whose urban roots and intellectualism evinced a deep internal strain of liberalism and questioning, what one was rebelling against was seemingly the very thing that other "rebels" were gravitating toward. As Sy slowly realizes, the city that he is fleeing from also offers positive things that the country town's conformist culture negates and squelches.

The novel describes Sy Levin's quest for an authentic self. He is a born and bred New Yorker who has taken up this academic position after many fruitless years as a habitual drunk employed as a high school teacher at different schools around the city. Although academic jobs are competitive, he has somehow managed to snag the lectureship at Cascadia College even though he has barely begun his graduate studies. Besides his being an alcoholic, the reader knows virtually nothing about the protagonist except that he has a Jewish name, eccentrically sports a beard although all the men he meets are clean shaven, and aims to save his aimless life with this new job. The novel begins with his comical arrival in Cascadia, where he is picked up at the train station by the bland "yes man" Professor Gilley and introduced to his awkward, pretty wife, Pauline. Sy quickly realizes that he has made a huge mistake: he expected to be employed at a liberal arts college with a similar name (the University of Oregon in the real version), and he is instead at an agricultural college that has only a utilitarian interest in the humanities and where his main job will be teaching college composition to farming students. The department chair explains the aims of the English faculty: "Our main function, as I always tell everyone we employ here, is to satisfy the needs of the professional schools on the campus with respect to written communication. . . . We need foresters, farmers, engineers, agronomists, fish-and-game people, and every sort of extension agent. We need them—let's be frank—more than we need English majors. You can't fell a tree, run a four-lane highway over a mountain, or build a dam with poetry" (*A New Life* 40). In the postwar boom economy, the head of an English department believes that the humanities need to focus on the best ways to build up the country's infrastructure and capital, even if it means labeling intellectual pursuits as a waste of time. This is a remarkably cynical portrait but probably accurate of the postwar intellectual landscape at such institutions.

The department that Sy lands in is almost entirely staffed by men (as was typical of the time), most of whom feel no particular desire to teach their students more than English grammar and who are dominated by the soon-to-retire chair of the department. The department head has become rich through the countless reprints of his highly popular grammar textbook, but he is intellectually poor. Sy has a doppelganger, Leo Duffy, who was the departmental "disagreeable radical who made a lot of trouble" and was eventually fired (*A New Life* 35). Toward the end of the book, it comes out that Duffy, like Sy, cuckolded Gilley with his wife, Pauline, and in the end he committed suicide. Throughout the novel, Sy is obsessed with Duffy and judges the people around him by how they treated the man with whom he feels a deep affinity as a fellow "liberal."

Sy, whose beard marks him as a radical with a dangerous edge, is highly attractive to women, and he has illicit encounters, first with a waitress, a rendezvous that comically ends with his jealous friend stealing their clothes while they are attempting to have sex, and then with one of his students. Finally, he establishes a relationship with Mrs. Pauline Gilley following a chance encounter in the local forest, where they have sex under a tree. Their relationship is intense and secretive, and Sy grows to despise her husband for being a sellout and yes-man whose only concern is to win the upcoming election for the new English chair. Eventually, Sy grows sick of their affair and tries to end it but gives up when Pauline tells him that she is pregnant. The novel concludes with Sy and Pauline and her two adopted children driving to San Francisco to start (another) new life.

In *A New Life*, there are four simultaneous cultural spaces that connote different visions of America in the postwar era and that Sy must navigate: the *city*, the *country town*, the *West*, and the *broader America*. As Sy reacts to each of the locations, we see the impact of these cultural outlooks on a perennial American outsider: a young, lost, Jewish urbanite. The novel is comedic and uses the fish-out-of-water setup of the city Jew in the country town to deliver its comic punch. In fact, Sy is such an urbanite and everything is so strange and new that he is amazed the first time he watches a fire burn in a fireplace (11).

The first cultural space is the *city*, New York precisely, which exists entirely in Sy's memories and is a dark, lurid underbelly where one encounters all the things that drag down an ideal American selfhood: alcohol, filth, poverty, hopelessness. New York is the place from which Sy escapes, a landscape imbued with his Jewish past and the immigrant's desires and disgraces. It is loud and chaotic and manmade and the opposite of the western location he arrives at. It has a premodern flavor to it, undeveloped and unenlightened, versus the ordered country town that Sy calls "civilized" (74).

However, the longer Sy spends away from the city, the more he begins to miss its energy and promise and rebellion that is in contrast to the town, which is ordered and "civilized" but boring and uncreative:

> But at night remembrance of New York City struck him like a spear hurled across the continent, adding weight to his body and years to his age. . . . At night he missed the movement and mystery of people in dark city streets. The anticipation of adventure next block—walk one more and meet your fate among strangers—a bag of thousand dollar bills dropped at your feet, or a wise and beautiful woman waiting for you at the corner. In Eastchester, an hour after supper, although lines of cars were parked tight along the downtown curbs, the streets were weirdly deserted. (75)

The city becomes the place that the young Jew must flee from in order to reinvent himself but that in the end shows itself to have its unique, positive characteristics such as energy and promise. Sy is thus moving through two, opposing Americas: the chaotic, creative, unsettled, open city and the postwar country town, which is ordered and quiet and deserted of energy.

The second space is the *country town* that Sy escapes to. Here nature dominates: the smells of the trees and blooming flowers, the shifting weather patterns, the birds in the sky. Those who live in the town, even the academics who one would expect to spend their time pursuing intellectual pursuits, instead fill their days with sports or outdoor endeavors: farming, horse riding, hunting, fishing. As Gilley tells him, "This is a small town, Sy, ninety-seven hundred, and there isn't much doing unless you get outdoors or are interested in football and such" (9). For Sy, the natural world is wondrous, exotic, and enticing, and he is overwhelmed the first time he steps outside: "Levin went outside with him and almost cried out. In the amazing night air he smelled the forest. Imagine getting this for nothing. He drew in a deep wavering breath as he gazed at the stars splashed over the immense dark sky" (22).

For the first time in his life, Sy connects with the outdoors and finds his soul refreshed. However, as the novel ironically notes, his experience of the natural world is limited to the surrounding university-owned forests that ring the town. And when he attempts to escape from Eastchester to experience the broader surroundings, his car breaks down, and the farmer who assists him views Sy's dark, bearded self as suggesting a "Russian spy" (151). In other words, the country town, like the city, is a constructed space rather than a wild one undominated by civilization, and it is imbued with a range of cultural beliefs. We see this in the oppressive manner in which all the people there try to make their home and lawn match in their cult of the lawnmower:

> Leaves were raked—speared almost as they fell—into piles on parking strips for the town truck to haul away. . . . Lawn mowing went on and on. Let the sun shine a minute and Ed Purtzer, whose house was two blocks to the college side of Mrs. Beaty's, changed into shorts and sweatshirt, rolled the mower out of the garage, oiled and adjusted it, then shaved his lawn, raked the cut grass, edged and combed the one-inch turf until it resembled his own stiff haircut. If a shampoo for grass were on the market he would have used it. (99)

Culturally, the world of the country town matches the obsession with lawn tidiness: everyone is overwhelmingly white and Christian and conformist, and Sy comically sticks out merely by having a beard. There is little that is intellectually stimulating, and it is a comfortable, middle-class world that resonates with the American suburb where conservative political and cultural practices dominate. As a plainspoken New York Jew, Sy finds himself extremely lonely and unable to find friends and spends much of his time by himself. Yet beneath the middle-class veneer, women are cheating on their husbands, premarital sex is common, and office politics take on great stock.

The third cultural site in *A New Life* is the *West*, which the great critic Leslie Fiedler labeled as "goyish images in our Jewish heads" (124). Fiedler, like Malamud, spent many of his formative years as a transplanted New Yorker in a western university in an English department (in this case at the University of Montana), and his observations on Malamud's novel evince his personal insights into what that type of move meant for young, Jewish males of his generation. Fiedler reads the novel as reflecting Malamud's intention to add to the corpus of western discourse by writing of that location through a Jewish American lens (124). Whereas the West typically connotes an American space for exploration, self-reinvention, and boldness, *A New Life*'s take on it is the "particular Westward migration" (131) of Jewish urban academics, often schlemiel types, relocating to small-town colleges and trying to infuse into them (and largely failing) their own brand of liberalism. And as Fiedler notes, ironically these migrations were occurring during the heyday of McCarthyism, when the Jewish migrant would be rendered as suspicious merely for being a Jew, which is why it is so strange that in Malamud's novel Sy's Jewishness is only noted in the final pages. As Fiedler labels it, *A New Life* is about a "failed westering" (128), with our protagonist unable to really change things either internally or externally, because in the end he aims simply to transpose his eastern, liberal ethos on the "barbarian West" rather than really exploring and internalizing this new location (127).

The final cultural site in the novel is the *greater America* of politics and culture that the characters discuss and respond to. The United States at the time is in the grip of McCarthyism, and Cold War panic and conservative and conformist principles dominate the cultural arena and impact everyone. This larger climate is felt in the university, where the academics undergo pressure not to challenge authority, to conform, and to distance themselves from anything that reeks of "radicalism": "Intellectuals, scientists, teachers were investigated by numerous committees and if found to be good Americans were asked to sign loyalty oaths. Democracy was defended by cripples who crippled it. At Cascadia College the American fear manifested itself, paradoxically, in what was missing: ideas, serious criticism, a liberal position" (*A New Life* 229).

American intellectual life has seemingly undergone a full lobotomy during the postwar era, and discussion and thoughtfulness are dead. As a beard-wearing New York Jew, Sy is immediately spotted, and he identifies himself as a "radical" following the tradition of the man who previously held his job, Leo Duffy. The beard marks him both as a Jew and as a radical, since, as Gilley tells Sy his first night in the town, "This is a sort of beardless town. No one on the faculty wears one that I know of. The administration is clean shaven. . . . The president's wife was saying the other day every time she lays eyes on a beard the thought of a radical pops up in her head" (23). By wearing a beard, the requirement of a religiously practicing Jew, Sy's selfhood conflates the otherness he represents as the Jew and the radical-as-other. And since this is a conformist, Christian town, McCarthyism has meant that any of the political machinations in the English department resonate with the larger political landscape, and the dominance of yes-men on campus suggests the climate of repression. All of the infighting in the office, the paranoia, the spying, and the squelching of individualism become an allegory for the McCarthyist politics of the time. Sy's rebellions against authority, however, are small and generally yield few results. For instance, his attempt fails to have a fellow member of the department called out for letting the university football team know which classes are the easiest. Or when he runs to be the next head of the department against Gilley, he gets no votes. Sy only ends up making an impact after he has fled the college when a few of his ideas are put into place, such as allowing some of the staff to teach literature courses.

In small ways, Sy seeks to improve the department and have it push students toward greater intellectual achievements. Yet every step of the way, the mediocre, conformist climate means that no one supports him, and he lacks the dedication and courage to truly challenge the system:

> Although thoughts of "making things better" continued to arrive by inspiration, at Cascadia College he restrained them. He did nothing to resist the status quo. He was, after all, a newcomer

here; of the same race as the Cascadians, true, but a distant relative. And if not abysmally timid, not terribly courageous. Too often, in the midst of discussions with those who found his liberalism distasteful, Levin—as though his nervous system voted conservative—broke into hot sweat and his knees softened; lockjaw set in. (*A New Life* 229)

And by having the novel set in a university, where one would expect to find a center of intellectual, liberal resistance but instead encounters a den of conformism, mediocrity, and conservatism, Malamud levels a sharp attack on the United States at the time. Even in the cultural spots that should be the pinnacle of the thoughtful life, the conformist conservatism has saturated the landscape. There are no spots of resistance left (if there ever were). Moreover, having the protagonist be Sy Levin, the prototype of the urban, intellectual Jew, makes the stakes even higher. Will the leftist Jew manage to challenge the power structures that have even weakened the institutions of higher learning, the last bastions of the leftist, intellectual elite? Or will he in the end decide to conform?

As a New York Jew, Sy therefore becomes a subversive catalyst upsetting the social patterns and conformist world around him. Although he is largely ineffectual when he tries to change things—to rebel against things—his mere existence shakes things up. In fact, much of the novel centers on the tension between Sy's vision of himself as a liberal radical and his inability to do anything overtly radical. For instance, rather than confront the power plays and mediocrity being espoused by Gilley and others, as his predecessor Duffy would have done, Sy instead has an affair with Gilley's wife. Sy wants to be like the radical Duffy but is unable to: he looks the part but has a hard time playing the part of campus radical.

Much of the stress felt by Sy as he negotiates the four spheres of the city, the country town, the West, and broader America relate to his struggles to be a "real man." As a Jew, he is a figure typically ascribed with more intellectualism and thus more "feminine" gender traits as compared with the idealized American male. Moreover, as an urbanite, more at home indoors, he is the opposite of the stereotypical western male: the stoic, outdoors, tough man. In the postwar era, when the main icon of masculinity is the returning soldier, Sy represents everything that must be suppressed in the aim for self-reinvention in the masculine, western mold.

As a subversive force, Sy sheds light as well on the manner in which women are left empty by the demands that they be perfect wives and mothers and give up their own dreams for the sake of their families. In this way, *A New Life* presents and then challenges the ideal of the postwar suburban/small-town wife. This depiction is conveyed in particular in the relationship between Sy and Pauline, with Sy struggling to be the ideal western man and Pauline the ideal suburban/small-town wife. Both Sy and Pauline unwittingly challenge gender constructs that demand certain types of behavior from American women and men in the postwar era.

The couple's challenge to the idealized domestic, suburban portrait is immediately evident during their first highly comic interaction. Pauline, the housewife who should be the masterful mistress of the domestic sphere, when serving Sy dinner finds that "she missed Levin's plate and dropped a hot gob of tuna fish and potato into his lap" (*A New Life* 10). And later, one of her adopted children urinates all over Sy, making him leave the dinner in disgrace. At a time when the wife generally, and the professional's wife specifically, would be expected to entertain her husband's work colleagues, Pauline fails miserably. Moreover, the fact that her children are adopted, in an era when birthing one's own children would have been culturally preferred, marks that she has failed on this front as well. Not only a failure as a mother and as a domestic mistress, she is a failure as a wife by having affairs with her husband's work colleagues. She is a deeply unfulfilled and unhappy person, and the suburban domestic dream is shown to make her soul feel empty and restless rather than fulfilled.

Whereas Pauline evokes the unhappiness of the female gender pressures of the era, the men, by contrast, except for Sy, evince a comfort with their masculinity and the roles that have been prescribed for them. It is thus only the women throughout the novel who continually come off as unhappy. This is not to suggest that Malamud was intentionally doing a feminist critique. Rather, he was painting a landscape where the women often appear lost and bewildered, while the men, except for Sy, seem comfortable in their conformist, intellectually mediocre pursuits. Nevertheless, Malamud's portraits of women other than Pauline are at times problematic, playing into stereotypes of the shrill, loveless old maid or the oversexed country bumpkin. Yet the portrait of the deeply conflicted and empathetically drawn Pauline roots Malamud's gender portraits as critiques of the pressure on intellectual men (Sy) and women (Pauline) to fulfill certain gender stereotypes. In both realms, the cultural climate sublimates intellectualism and individualism to enable the individual to fit into the herd. It also means that whereas in the city the focus was on intellectual and cultural pursuits, in the country, where the aim is to be physical and strong, sexual needs are central. Or as the waitress Laverne, whom Sy attempts to have sex with in a barn, notes, "You gave up the Metropolitan Museum of Art and got love in a haystack" (80). For Sy, this means that although he has arrived as an intellectual whose "two hands are practically useless," by the end of the book, he is hiking through the woods and becoming at home in the country (34). He, like the good suburban man he is transforming into, even learns to drive and begins to explore the surroundings to try and understand this American world he has landed in: "Here too America; you learned as you lived, a refreshing change from books" (145). By having a Jewish urbanite as the protagonist, Malamud can delve into the contradictory roles prescribed by the times. Sy is a perennial outsider who can point out the aspects of mainstream life that those who are enmeshed in it do not see, but he is not a complete outsider such as an African American would be.

In the last chapter of the book, Sy transforms into the ideal, suburban husband when he decides to move to California with the pregnant Pauline and her two adopted children. He has stepped into his new role as a family man with wife and kids for whom he will be the main provider. His beard has been shaven, and he has chosen to face his responsibilities. Yet it is not a joyful decision but the one that seems the path of least resistance for him. In the end, we see that the liberal, leftist, radical Jew has conformed and become the family man, although there is still hope for him since they are moving to the last stronghold of rebellion, San Francisco, which Fiedler labels as "the East of the West" (128). Perhaps there Sy will regrow his beard and finally find a way to become a real radical. Or perhaps he will continue to conform. We do not know which path he will take, although Duffy's ending in suicide suggests that the path of the disaffected radical is tumultuous.

Strangely, although Sy is clearly Jewish, no one comments on this fact or makes note of it until the very end of this thinly veiled autobiographical novel, even though Malamud was outed as a Jew from his first days in Corvallis (Davis 76). This absence may reflect Malamud's personal dislike of labeling himself or his characters as Jewish, as is evident in an exchange on the topic in the *Paris Review*:

INTERVIEWER: Are you a Jewish writer?
MALAMUD: What is the question asking? . . .
INTERVIEWER: Thus S. Levin is Jewish and not much is made of it?
MALAMUD: He was a gent who interested me in a place that interested me. He was out to be educated. (Stern 63–64).

Only in the final pages of the book does Sy become actualized as a Jew when Pauline asserts that she "chose" him for the position from her husband's stack of job applications because of his Jewish name and her sense that he could somehow save her:

"You looked as though you needed a friend."
"Was that the reason?"
"I needed one. Your picture reminded me of a Jewish boy I knew in college who was very kind to me during a trying time in my life."
"So I was chosen," Levin said. (*A New Life* 361)

He has been handpicked for this role of shaker-upper and saver of Pauline from an unhappy marriage. In other words, Sy's "Jewishness" is his otherness and ability to upset the set patterns. His Jewishness also is found in his urbanity and radical tendencies. There is nothing religiously or culturally Jewish about him, and the only suggestion that he is Jewish, besides his name, is the couple of Yiddishisms sprinkled in his dialogue: "*goniff*," the Yiddish word for "thief," which he uses to describe his father, and "*luftmensh*," or head-in-the-clouds, to describe himself (229, 217). He is an angry young man but with little power or ability to change things. However, in the final scene, as he drives away with his new family in tow, Sy fully transforms into "A New Man," even using the new (non-Jewish-resonant) name Sam. Instead of bringing Pauline around to his otherness, his Jewishness, his rebelliousness, he transforms into her Anglicized partner.[2]

The ending of the book can therefore be read in two very different ways. Either one can read it as the Jewish urban, outsider, liberal who has transformed into the suburban man, driving to his new locale with his wife and kids in tow. Or one can note that this ideal portrait is marred by the fact that his future wife is a serial cheater, his kids are really her adopted ones, and he has no job and no future. Is he fulfilling the American dream, or is he pointing out its impossible ideal? Does the Jewish outsider corrupt, accept, or merely uncover the falsity of the American dream?

While Richard Astro views Sy's leave-taking as "distinctly pathetic" (150), Chiara Briganti's feminist reading of the novel describes it positively: "for the first time in his life he accepts the burden of his responsibilities and chooses an active role" (177). The *New York Times* review by David L. Stevenson similarly sees Sy's departure as the moment of his "salvation" (1). Malamud's own view was that it was an optimistic ending, since Sy decides to take control of his life and to do the right thing rather than continually flip-flopping, as is evident when he responds to Gilley's query of why he was doing this: "Because I can, you son of a bitch" (*A New Life* 360).

Bernard Malamud's 1950s-set novel *A New Life* presents a strong critique of the social trends dominating at the time: the conservatism, the conformism, the anti-intellectualism. Creating an outsider New York Jew, whose beard connotes both his Jewishness and his avowed radicalism, Malamud shows Sy Levin to interrupt and shake up the status quo. Yet in the end, as Sy leaves town, nothing has really changed. Gilley is still stepping in as the new head of the department, and the academics and the university will continue to have a utilitarian, anti-intellectual mandate. Sy has served to shed a certain light on the system but has barely upset it. The novel's conclusion is a highly pessimistic portrait of conditions after the war as America entered a boom economy and began the Cold War.

Malamud also shows how troubling the new era was for American Jews who had much to lose by embracing the bland conformity and shedding their ties to the urban, creative, intellectual, and essentially chaotic strands of their prewar city life. As Sy, now Sam, moves even further westward to take up "a new life," we see the shaky foundations on which the promise of self-reinvention in the postwar era are built. When Sy confronted the four cultural spaces that made up the novel, the city, the country town, the West, and greater America, he kept butting up against himself and his "sadness of spirit" (*A New Life* 256), where he could not find fulfillment, deep friendships, or true love. He was alone and adrift. Whereas other angry young men found clear pathways of reinvention, such as hitting the road, taking drugs, and immersing themselves in African American life, Sy instead finds that his rebellions are empty, and they leave him bereft. Unlike Mailer and Kerouac, who have drugs and the arts, all Sy really has is his beard, and once it is shaven and his mark of rebellion is gone, he is the same as any other young man.

In Sy, we find a dark portrait of the loss of footing felt by young men after the war who were seeking truth and meaning and often discovering a range of empty answers in diverse arenas. As Gilley labels him during one of their showdowns, "an outsider looking in" (*A New Life* 288), Sy represents the countless disaffected young men of the era who felt outsiders to the postwar, conservative climate and discovered that however much they may travel across the United States looking for answers, as Horace noted millennia ago, "they change their skies but not their souls those who run across the sea."

NOTES

1. Philip Davis's biography, *Bernard Malamud: A Writer's Life*, describes those years in his chapter "Oregon" (71–112).
2. When asked by a reporter for the local Corvallis newspaper what became of Sy and Pauline after they set off for San Francisco, Malamud replied, "I honestly don't know what happens to them. . . . All I can do is bring them to the last page; what they do after that is their business." Interview with John Marshall for Corvallis's *Gazette-Times*, May 5, 1977, in Malamud, *Conversations* 78.

CHAPTER 2

"I Shit My Death"

From the Providential to the Excremental in *The Fixer*

HOLLI LEVITSKY

LOYOLA MARYMOUNT UNIVERSITY

It is widely acknowledged that Bernard Malamud's 1966 novel *The Fixer* provides, to some extent, a fictionalized account of the 1913 Beilis trial in tsarist Russia that caused an international uproar. How much of Malamud's Yakov Bok resembles the historical figure Mendel Beilis remains to be seen. So, too, does the resemblance between each man's ordeal remain to be considered. In an extensive study of *The Fixer*'s debt to Beilis's own memoir, "Mendel Beilis's *The Story of My Sufferings* and Malamud's *The Fixer*: A Study of Indebtedness and Innovation," Michael Tritt notes that "Malamud has suggested many—and diverse—sources and influences" (73), but the connection to the historical incident is primary. In the novel, Malamud draws on Beilis's own memoir "extensively" (Tritt 59), and the correspondence is so specific "as to leave little doubt as to Malamud's fundamental reliance upon Beilis's memoir in the composition of *The Fixer*" (61). Indeed, the chilling blood-libel context that is so central in both the memoir and the novel highlights, in the latter, a correspondence to the even more chilling facts of the Holocaust. Malamud could, from his vantage point in history, recontextualize the suffering of the fixer so that the additional atrocities against Jews resonated.

Written twenty years after the Holocaust, the novel offers an even more potent legacy of anti-Semitism. The Russian pogroms against the Jews are there, of course, stemming in part from deep-rooted anti-Jewish feelings and reflecting a Judeophobia prevalent among many non-Jews. But after the even-greater prevalence of Jew-hatred that resulted in the Holocaust, the legacy of anti-Semitism fattened, sweeping across all of Europe. In these ways, we might agree with Lillian Kremer, who concludes, as others do, that Malamud's "tales of postwar Jewish life are informed by Holocaust consciousness" (*Witness* 82). Not surprisingly, Holocaust survivors had no language with which to express the broad slaughter of innocents and the prolonged dehumanizing atrocities committed against the Jews. The Holocaust had to be described by drawing on other ordeals, such as pogroms, or identified as indescribable. The author and Holocaust survivor Charlotte Delbo writes of trying to speak to nonsurvivors about her ordeal in Auschwitz: "They expect the worst—they do not expect the unthinkable" (4). Yet atrocities reported by survivors and uncovered by historians and other scholars reveal just that—the unthinkable. Victims experienced meaningless physical and emotional suffering, leaving an imprint of symptoms that we know they would continue to experience even after liberation. Moreover, an additional level of consideration added a profound sense of loss of religious faith for many victims. This became torture of a different sort. How does one pray or speak to God in such instances? In the camps or in hiding, reflection, prayer, and choosing what to believe were luxuries that few inmates had time for. Survival was often the only motivating factor for behavior.

Informed by Holocaust consciousness, *The Fixer* opens up a potential space where a similarly tortured protagonist-victim might reflect on such fundamental questions as these: Can I sustain a relationship with God in a state of extreme suffering? Can I remain merciful even as suffering consumes me? Malamud does not create the space as a fixed moment in the novel; rather, he uses the idea of "waiting" as a metaphor for unfinished or nonactualized time. Its most particular characteristic is its liminality; as an intermediate area between life and (potentially) death, it acts as a threshold or indeterminate area, where one no longer holds a before status but is not yet part of the after. Though *The Fixer* is certainly influenced by the earlier blood-libel case, the novel is absent of the trial and sentencing portion of the story, and in its place one finds only an indeterminacy in which the reader must imagine the prisoner's fate. The potential—or liminal—space is experienced as a kind of waiting, where, rather than reaching the trial, the novel concludes presumably moments before. Thus, the prisoner awaits, rather than receives, his fate. The novelistic deferral of his sentencing, and thus fate, terrifies but also animates Malamud's reimagined prisoner, offering also a way to retrieve some agency over his fate. It is as though he has discovered a new and final strength. But the novel is no more redemptive than the historical reality was; the only salvation it offers is to give the protagonist, Yakov Bok, a chance to defer his fate, which is really no salvation at all. Like many premature endings in Holocaust fiction, the fact that this novel concludes before the protagonist's sentence is issued can be seen as a mechanism to invoke the many unknown horrors of the Holocaust.

The Fixer is informed by the Holocaust on many levels; through the inconclusiveness of the protagonist's suffering, and the novel's lack of redemption, we can be sure the Holocaust is more than a shadow. The Holocaust inhabits the fixer and *The Fixer*. Like the untold victims who lived liminally, in concentration camps and other targeted spaces, waiting for death but not knowing the "when" and "if," Bok too does not know these final facts of his fate. The arc of his suffering is broad and long, with no end in sight. The painful tale of the fixer's woes offers a narrative that sweeps across centuries of anti-Semitism to land on a systematic and violent dehumanization drawn in an essential way from the befouled universe of the concentration camps. Bok, living in his own filth and offered no compassion or salvation unless he lies about his innocence, adapts to a new reality, one in which defilement of the body is more real than is faith in the providence of God.

What is known about the historical account of Mendel Beilis is this: On March 20, 1911, the mutilated body of thirteen-year-old Andrei Yushchinsky was discovered in a cave on the outskirts of Kiev, then a part of Russia. Police investigations found evidence pointing to the guilt of Vera Cheberyak, the leader of a criminal gang in Kiev and the mother of one of the boy's friends. However, following the discovery of the boy's body and during the investigation, a right-wing anti-Semitic group called the Black Hundreds began disseminating information claiming that the murder was an act of "blood libel," the pernicious (and persistent) myth that first developed during the Middle Ages alleging that Jews kidnapped and murdered Christian children to use their blood as part of religious ritual acts (a specific version of the blood libel focused on this use for the creation of the Pesach matzo). Tsar Nicholas II and the minister of justice, I. G. Shcheglovitov were well-known anti-Semites (Turtel 267). In accordance with the anti-Semitic efforts of the Black Hundreds organization and the support of the government, the search for the murderer turned toward the Jews of Kiev.

On the basis of the testimony of a lamplighter claiming to have seen Andrei kidnapped near a Jewish-owned brick factory located close to the site where the body was found, the superintendent, thirty-nine-year-old Mendel Beilis, was arrested on July 21, 1911. He remained in prison for over two years until his trial in the fall of 1913. The trial lasted thirty-four days, from September 25 through October 28, and attracted international attention. The jury was filled mostly with peasants, who were asked to deliberate on two charges put forth by the case's prosecutors: first, essentially whether the murder was indeed a "ritual murder" in accordance with the mythical Jewish rite, and second, whether Mendel Beilis was guilty "of committing the crime 'out of motives of religious fanaticism'" (Levin). The prosecution's witnesses included individuals who were bribed, drunk, or criminals, as well as one Catholic priest. The defense's witnesses included the rabbi of Moscow and several Russian professors. The jury ultimately found Beilis not guilty but also voted in agreement with the charge that the murder as described by the state was characteristic of Jewish ritual murder. Beilis and his family left Russia for Palestine and then in 1920 moved to the United States, where he died in 1934.

Extensively influenced by Beilis's memoir, Malamud nonetheless heightens the crudity of the language and, frequently, the treatment of the prisoner, in order to "intensify his alienation and misery, his introspective questioning, and the sense of his dogged perseverance" (Tritt 63). In Beilis's account, he reports the guard threatening him with this sardonic and terrifying pronouncement: "we'll feed you blood and matzos to your heart's content" (Tritt 63). The allusion to the blood-libel myth would not have been lost on the prisoner, who would know well that generation after generation of Jews in Europe were tortured and Jewish communities massacred or dispersed and broken up because of this pernicious myth. In 1960s America, when the novel was composed, the blood-libel myth was not commonly invoked. Malamud's revised line, "Here we'll feed you flour and blood till you shit matzos," offers more than a slightly altered version of the scene (*The Fixer* 144). It reimagines it as a way to expose the blood-libel myth as a complex of deliberate lies, trumped-up accusations, and popular beliefs about the murder-lust of the Jews and their bloodthirstiness, based on the conception that Jews hate Christianity and humankind in general. The crudely yoked-together blood-libel accusation with the elimination of bodily waste references the more modern and systematic massacre and defilement of Jews in the Holocaust, which recalled the myth. In line with this reference, Malamud makes Bok's pain "unbearable" (Tritt 64); for Beilis, it is only "almost so" (64). And most importantly, the historical figure Beilis was exonerated, while Malamud leaves his readers with no such clarity regarding the fate of Bok.

Malamud introduces Bok as a decent, if doubting, Jew whose faith is wavering—even eroding—in the face of personal devastation. He is orphaned at an early age and left without a loving caretaker. He survives a miserable childhood only to find marriage also impossible. His wife, apparently unable to produce a child, leaves him for another man. He knows he is smart but has no means to acquire a formal education. He lives from hand to mouth, bitter toward God for his loss and poverty. For most of the novel, Bok is a passive figure who "can only think, feel, and resist. He cannot act upon his surroundings to create a sense of dynamic emotion" (Marcus 89). But I would suggest that the lack of clarity regarding his fate begins to open up this dynamic space. As his character slowly unfolds and is tested by acts beyond his comprehension, so too does his faith begin to transform. In the underlying story of his suffering, we find a development that moves Jewish suffering away from a partnership with God to a platform absent of God. By creating new meaning and implications from the historical story, Malamud carefully manipulates our understanding of an extreme moment in the history of Jewish suffering, a moment that has already been claimed as inexpressible, unspeakable, indescribable, incomprehensible, inconceivable, unthinkable, unimaginable, and incomparable.

The blood-libel accusation at the heart of the Beilis story transforms, in *The Fixer*, into an existential crisis from which the fictional prisoner suffers excrementally. In a classic essay about exposure to human filth in Auschwitz, "Excremental Assault," Terence Des Pres explores in depth the assault of human waste that the prisoners experienced daily. His close reading of survivors' accounts of experiencing and witnessing such acts shows what it took to survive the most horrifying level of suffering: the attack on human dignity. Auschwitz "revealed not only the depravity of human existence, but also the grandeur that can be found in the refusal to despair and die" (Des Pres 201). As deliberate targets of both literal and symbolic "excremental assault," the Jewish prisoners were "systematically subjected to filth" (207). Des Pres quotes from a description in one of the survivors' memoirs of the interior of a locked boxcar holding eighty to a hundred people on their way to the camps in Poland: "We were to live for days on end breathing these foul smells, and soon we lived in the foulness itself" (203). With prisoners having little or no control over their natural functions, they soiled themselves and others. In the so-called anus mundi, they had no toilet paper, no sanitary facilities, and no way to keep themselves clean. Des Pres writes of the ones who were too weak to move that they "were slowly enveloped in their own decomposition" (205). From the beginning, subjection to filth is also an aspect of Bok's ordeal. With no access to hygiene, he urinates and defecates in a can kept in his cell. At first, he is subjected to strip-searches twice a day; they grow to six times a day by the end. A detailed description is given of these searches: "Yakov had first to raise his arms and spread his legs. The Deputy Warden probed with his four fingers in Yakov's armpits and around his testicles. The fixer then had to open his mouth and raise his tongue; he stretched both cheeks with his fingers as Zhitnyak peered into his mouth. At the end he had to bend over and pull apart his buttocks" (*The Fixer* 194–95). Even as Bok's cell is filled with human waste and foul smells, filth seems to cover the landscape of the novel, in the form of shit, vomit, urine, blood, and pus. It is as if the whole world around Bok is enveloped in its own decomposition. These conditions were not accidental; as in the camps, Malamud deliberately creates a universe in which the Jewish prisoner is humiliated and debased. And yet, in the face of systematic, ongoing, endless degradation, Bok resists being obliterated.

The novel itself opens as Yakov Bok sees through the "small crossed window of his room" a worrisome street scene (*The Fixer* 3). People coming from different directions are heading together toward one direction.

Notwithstanding the Christian imagery of the crossed window, Bok does not expect the "excitement" on the street to include him—he feels safe (and anonymous) in a fictionalized Christian identity in Kiev. Yet he is terrified without knowing exactly why. Within a day, he reads an anti-Semitic leaflet that charges the Jews with the ritual murder of a Russian child to use his blood for religious purposes. His concern deepens and leads him to a memory of the drunken soldiers who randomly killed his young father and the pogrom that he himself lived through as a child. This brief opening scene concludes with a final memory: he recalls being led out of a hiding place with a group of children and sighting "a black-bearded Jew with a white sausage stuffed into his mouth, lying in the road on a pile of bloody feathers, a peasant's pig devouring his arm" (5). Contrast this with the earlier description of the murdered Russian boy, "covered with stab wounds, his body bled white" (4). Read through the Christian iconography of the "cross," the boy's dead body, open and pure white, casts the memory of the dead Jewish body as impure, unclean, blackened, and filled with shame—and clearly transgressive. These first few pages introduce and frame the shift from personal suffering to what we might call excremental suffering: the Jew is force-fed the profane pig, while a peasant's live pig eats his arm, suggesting a later elimination—or double shitting—of the Jew's death. The Jew shits his own death by eating the unkosher pig (white sausage), and the pig shits the Jew's death by eating his flesh and eliminating Jewish waste. Recalled in the final section of the novel when Bok curses the tsar for his suffering, the image is a powerful statement of the retrieval of human agency when he says, "I shit my death on him" (269).

Perhaps it is history itself that seeks to reimagine this story. Is Bok the "suffering servant" of the prophet Isaiah? Certainly not in its interpretation and use by Christian theologians and missionaries, many of whom would identify the servant to be Jesus Christ. Malamud was concerned with Jewish suffering; he wrote, "To the goyim what one Jew is is what they all are. If the fixer stands accused of murdering one of their children, so does the rest of the tribe" (*The Fixer* 273). Indeed, Jews have a long history of documenting the particular suffering of anti-Semitism. But the history of Jewish life also tells us that Jews suffered for more than their religion. Given the broad history of such suffering, and in light of both the pre-Holocaust and Holocaust-era landscape of pain and suffering inflicted on Jews, it is useful to examine such a history. What do the religious texts teach about suffering? Is personal suffering (of a physical, emotional, or mental nature) to be understood differently than persecution as a Jew? For Bok, the ordeal begins as anti-Semitism, but the procedures used against him become more and more sadistic. As the sadism inflicted on him increases, he feels the burden of Jewish history on his shoulders. The burden forces him to consider what agency he still has left—what action does this moment in history offer him? He pities the Jews for their fate in history, but his suffering has given him a new strength. At this point, Bok the revolutionary emerges. The story becomes proleptic, a prefiguration of Hitler as a mad killer demanding Jewish blood: "Overnight a madman is born who thinks Jewish blood is water. Overnight life becomes worthless. . . . A person is shit" (274). Bok makes a covenant with himself to protect his people, because "if God's not a man he has to be" (274). He must endure, but he will do it on his own terms. He thinks, "Suffering I can gladly live without, I hate the taste of it, but if I must suffer let it be for something" (273). Human beings must resist being obliterated, even in the face of systematic and ongoing degradation. History offers this moment to him.

The particular "something" or "someone" that Bok imagines suffering for is his father-in-law, Shmuel, the one person who cared enough about him to warn him against leaving the *shtetl*. In fact, he begs Bok not to go to Kiev, to wait longer for his wife to return, to stay with the Jews, not to walk into the hands of the anti-Semites, to stay away from the impure, to go to Palestine instead. He insists that in leaving the *shtetl*, Bok is looking for trouble. Shmuel is also nearly penniless and suffers from the loss of his daughter; yet as a believer, he treats her desertion differently than Bok does: "I've cursed her more than once but I ask God not to listen" (10). Shmuel's noble suffering notwithstanding, Bok "cannot quite see the point of redemption by suffering" (Fisch 164). Shmuel's final warning, that "here at least God is with us," does not just go unheeded (*The Fixer* 12); Bok uses the warning, more than once, to curse God for his absence. He thinks, "What do I get from him but a bang on the head and a stream of piss in my face" (17).

For Bok, Shmuel, Raisl (the wife and daughter who abandoned them both), and the other suffering Jews of the *shtetl*, life is a trial. "What's in the world . . . is in the shtetl—people, their trials, worries, circumstances"

(12), Shmuel observes. These few pages of dialogue between Bok and Shmuel as the former is about to depart for Kiev, give us an overview of how suffering has been, and continues to be, understood as part of God's plan for the Jews. It is neither a clear-cut plan nor one without contradiction. For example, suffering is seen as a punishment for sin, but pain is also simply part of being human. Similarly, one should accept suffering with humility, but if possible, it should be prevented or resisted. Finally, it is imperative to offer compassion to the sufferer.

Raised on Jewish teachings, like Shmuel, Bok should accept suffering with humility and know that he is protected by his faith. He should also do what he can to alleviate suffering. But he curses his situation, refusing to forgive his wife, his wretchedness clouding his faith. He feels persecuted by God's absence. His reflection on his own wretchedness calls to mind the story of Job, who struggles with tension over theodicy and faith in God despite personal suffering and experiences with evil. And yet, in the Hebrew Bible, suffering is acknowledged as a defining part of humanity in both Genesis 3:19 and Job 5:7. Since the story of Job, Jewish history has tried to understand and codify suffering. Personal suffering may be for unknown reasons—Satan's back-room deal with God—or for committing a sin under the influence of some evil. Persecution as a Jew amps up the existential consequences; it is less delicately but more vividly considered excremental suffering—that is, the understanding that one's value is less than shit, that commitment to faith comes at the expense of a death that is an excretion formed by a diet of existential threat. Indeed, the story of Job is the *ab origine* story of suffering and redemption. It illuminates all of the ways one can suffer while offering an example of how to respond in the face of that suffering. Moreover, it offers a substantive story of good versus evil—a real living adversary named Satan who roams the earth, causing all the suffering in the world, while God waits. Bok does not know what kind of suffering will befall him, just as Job did not know about the argument taking place between God and Satan. Shmuel's faith, his love and trust in God in the face of such suffering, sides with Job, who exemplifies the correct (Jewish) response; Bok's faithlessness does not. Bok does not trust that God will help him; he questions God, though it is beyond his full comprehension to understand the reasons why suffering is allowed.

The story of Job suggests that faith in times of suffering is crucial. While Bok cannot fully understand why he suffers, faith would allow him to be comforted. Faith would convince him that the creator is a loving protector and victor—but these are things Bok never experienced; he was never parented or truly loved. The story of Job—with its behind-the-scenes action—also offers a powerful lesson about the intersection between faith and free will. Humans can freely choose to do evil or to do good. Thus, human free will allows for the existence of suffering. Some innocents suffer at the hands of those who choose evil because freedom requires that evil be allowed to occur without interference or punishment—"with all the undeserved suffering which this implies" (Gottlieb). Indeed, it is even said that "sometimes the future good to which the suffering contributes is for the sufferer himself" (Gottlieb), since some people argue that suffering can reform the sufferer for the better. The bottom line is that justice will prevail.

Although commonly accepted beliefs about suffering include the notion that God uses pain to test our faith or to punish us for sin or that it is required for a good afterlife, these assumptions characterize God as unkind and vindictive. So, for example, Abraham was tested by God when God commanded him to sacrifice his son, Isaac. Within this mode of thinking, the idea of a compassionate God still prevails. God allows suffering as a test of spiritual strength and divine faith, and its acceptance is itself an affirmation of faith. "The Rabbinic attitude towards sufferings is . . . one of humble resignation to the will of God. . . . The convinced faith in a future life of blessedness and happiness enabled the Rabbis to face sufferings, not indeed, for the most part, with pleasure, but with fortitude, and even *sometimes* with joy, because they were regarded as sure passports to 'heaven'" (Montefiore and Loewe 541; emphasis in the original).

Of the rest of the suffering, it is undeserved in terms of the past but "justified by the good it serves to create" (Gottlieb). The reasons why people deserve such suffering may not be apparent to others. Sufferers may have failed with respect to human responsibilities, for example, deserving suffering because they are intentionally not living up to their fullest potential; that is, the sufferer may be held to a higher standard because of greater abilities than others have. A second personal benefit of suffering is seen in the development of abilities that might otherwise lie dormant. A person with the capacity for heroism may never develop that ability if his or her life is completely tranquil. Through suffering, we discover and develop new strengths and capabilities. The arc of life resembles the arc in the story of Job; one struggles through for a better future.

Bok's struggle is more than a literary imitation of the trials of Mendel Beilis, the hapless Jewish peasant who suffered through pogroms and random acts of anti-Semitism to end up charged with a crime he did not commit. Bok's struggle also includes the six and a half million murdered Jews and the many more victims of Hitler's madness. Was any of this suffering deserved? Very few people would argue such. Rather, with Beilis exonerated and the Holocaust rightly seen as the murder of innocents, it is a struggle for anyone to imagine this suffering as justified. If it is not justified, what happens to faith, the providence of God, which would normally empower us to react to tragedy with dignity and humility? Bok's legacy is so inclusive, so ineffable, that he can be neither strengthened nor comforted by faith. Instead, Malamud elides Bok's faith, and in its place Bok finds shit.

Perhaps personal pain and existential suffering can be understood in these terms. But how do we respond to the suffering of others, especially with such visible symptoms as illness and poverty? Is there a difference between our own and others' suffering? Jewish doctrine dictates that one should sympathize with those who are suffering and try to help alleviate their pain. "God Himself is often described as suffering with man. Man is challenged to remedy suffering wherever it can be remedied and to endure it without complaining wherever it is irremediable" (Schwarzschild). Jews can neither ignore another's pain nor simply witness it. Rather, one must actively engage in compassion: "Judaism demands that man extend active sympathy toward the suffering of others. . . . Man is admonished to share in the suffering of the community and not enjoy himself while others are suffering" (Schwarzschild).

Even to the end of the novel, Bok continues to face terrifying obstacles. These ordeals, during which he receives little or no pity, compassion, or mercy, move him further from God. His final thoughts beg the question about the Jewish concept of compassion, even as they draw our attention to his extended suffering: in poverty, as a childless and abandoned husband, and of course, imprisoned, tortured, humiliated, and shown no justice in the course of the novel. Bok understands the imperative to show compassion toward others; it was through an act of great compassion that his troubles began (saving the life of Nikolai Maximovitch Lebedev).

Though abused, assaulted, tortured, and murdered, individually and as a people, Jews have always been capable of extending compassion even as they suffer. In the face of extreme circumstances, they feel ordained to show mercy, charity, and kindness toward others. Often described by the Yiddish word *rachmones* —derived from the Hebrew root word (*rechem*) meaning "womb" (S. Friedman 76)—it is a concept born in the human, central to Jewish belief; the Jews are "raḥamanim benei raḥamanim— 'compassionate scions of compassionate forbears'" (Silberman 123).

What is especially revolutionary, in Malamud's universe, is the development of Yakov Bok's lack of compassion. Yet this development replaces his faith and is what gives him some important measure of agency over his fate. On the way to his trial, escorted by prison officials, a bomb explodes on the street just outside where the carriage is passing. Chaos ensues, and in the pause to his fate, the resolute prisoner is overcome by yet another prolongation of the systematic and ongoing pain and abuse he has suffered. In his degraded state, he imagines a final conversation with the tsar. In it, the tsar sits naked in a cell, holding an icon of the Virgin Mary, forced to defend his rule. Now the interrogator, Bok sits opposite him, revolver by his side, listening to the tsar's litany of obligations and burdens. When the tsar asks Bok if his suffering has not taught him the meaning of mercy, as the tsar feels his has, Bok is clear: he flips the Jewish notion of *rachmones* and tells the tsar that suffering has only taught him "the uselessness of suffering" (*The Fixer* 333). Instead of feeling redeemed, tempering his hatred with mercy, the Jewish Bok imagines that something deep within him has changed: "I fear less and hate more," he says (319). He feels "overcome by hatred so intense his chest heaved" (331). He then shoots the tsar dead: "Better him than us" (334), he thinks. Still on the way to the trial, these final thoughts and imagined conversations conclude the novel.

Bok's relentless suffering has provided him with a manual for contempt rather than mercy. The novel's brilliance lies in its slow and steady development of a post-Holocaust reimagining of the Jewish concept of *rachmones*—Bok uses the Yiddish term—not as an opportunity to show mercy, compassion, or pity for the other, thereby creating a redemptive moment. Rather, it allows a Yakov Bok to whom no pity has been shown to identify the most Jewish of Jewish suffering and to imagine it as his own; as he was fed contempt and repulsion, so too he excretes it. As he imagines the tsar dead, Bok sees the uselessness of all suffering. As the final moments of the novel come to an end, Bok declares himself a revolutionary, but not as a result of triumph over misery and suffering. Rather, Malamud posits the revolutionary position in the way Bok answers the question posed by Victoria Aarons. She writes, "In one form or another, Malamud's short fiction implicitly asks the question: in what should human beings believe?" ("In Defense" 67). This longer novel asks the same question. Answered in the final scenes, Bok declares himself without mercy or compassion for the sufferings of the tsar. His beliefs have turned from the providential—acting as a Jew protected by God's mercy—to the excremental, a devolutionary (rather than evolutionary but still revolutionary) position shaped by a prolonged, literal defilement of the body.

The Fixer is not unique in the Malamudian universe in providing a setting for such trials of humanity. Malamud's characters are often tested under conditions in which they must prove that they are compassionate humans, who show, as L. Lamar Nisly points out, "a commitment to the intrinsic value of humanity" (40). Aarons highlights how deeply Malamud's characters defend their humanity. Within Malamud's world, "it is human compassion that can bring about redemption" by pleading for, and expecting, compassion from other humans ("In Defense" 59). Indeed, in the history of Jewish literature, "such pleas are not uncommon"; they arise as "appeals to a human moral conscience, without which there can be no meaning to suffering" (58). Even prolonged suffering can be seen as meaningful in this way if the story itself is based on a narrative of suffering, like *The Fixer*'s Yakov Bok. Bok's many inner monologues and external dialogue relay to the reader stories of his misery and persecution or of God's—and humanity's—denial of compassion. Aarons writes, "Talk becomes a commitment, an admission even, to all that is human" (58). Like other Malamud characters, Bok addresses his words to those whom he believes have some control over his suffering. And yet, from the first pages of the novel, we learn that Bok's suffering is ongoing and relentless and that he himself sees it as meaningless—that God is not watchful over him.

Bok's fantasy conversation with the tsar tells us much about who he has become: a man in control of his destiny. His decision to stay true to his story and to do this for the Jews, rather than as a result of his faith in

God, positions him as both a victim to whom no mercy has been shown and a merciful Jew. In the prolonged final scene, his Jewishness is reconfigured into a defiance of suffering, articulated as a revolutionary stand against it. If the character of Yakov Bok does seem to evolve, it is a movement from victim to revolutionary.

CHAPTER 3

The Jew as Vampire in
Bernard Malamud's *The Fixer*

ANDREW M. GORDON

UNIVERSITY OF FLORIDA

Bernard Malamud's 1966 novel *The Fixer* won both the Pulitzer Prize and the National Book Award for fiction and was adapted into a successful movie. The novel concerns Yakov Bok, a poor handyman who grows alienated from his wife because she cannot bear him a child. Eventually, she abandons him for another man. Bitter and ashamed, Bok leaves the *shtetl* for a Russian city, where he adopts a less Jewish-sounding name to get a better job. But soon he finds himself falsely accused of the murder of a Christian child, although the evidence points to his accuser, the boy's mother. The luckless Bok's only crime is that he is a Jew, a convenient scapegoat, and he languishes in prison for years, suffering cruel treatment, awaiting trial.

The story was inspired by the most infamous case of blood libel in the twentieth century, that of Mendel Beilis, accused in Kiev in 1911 of murdering a Christian boy in a religious ritual. The case drew international attention. Despite the desires of the tsarist government, Beilis was ultimately acquitted by a jury of Russian peasants. The novel, however, ends ambiguously, with Bok on his way to trial.

Originally Malamud wanted to write about American injustice at the time of the civil rights movement. He looked for a story set in the past: "So I could invent it into myth. . . . I wanted to show how recurrent, almost without thought, almost ritualistic, some of our unfortunate historical experiences are" (Malamud, *Talking Horse* 88). To Beilis's prison term, Malamud added "something of Dreyfus' and Vanzetti's, shaping the whole to suggest the quality of the afflictions of the Jews under Hitler" (89). The novel is a kind of Holocaust parable in which a single victim symbolically represents the entire Jewish people.

The Fixer is the best exploration in modern fiction of the historical "blood libel," an anti-Semitic myth that has persisted for almost nine hundred years. The libel originated in England in the Middle Ages and then spread across Europe and into the Muslim world. In 1144 in Norwich, England, Jews were accused of killing a Christian boy for ritual purposes, and a mob killed one of the leading members of the Jewish community. The boy was beatified as a martyr, St. William of Norwich. In 1255, nineteen Jews were hanged in Lincoln, England, accused of crucifying a boy named Hugh. It became the basis for a ballad, and Chaucer wrote about it in "The Prioress's Tale" in *The Canterbury Tales* (see Langmuir; Jacobs). In fact, *The Fixer* is prefaced with two epigraphs, the second from Chaucer: "O yonge Hugh of Lyncoln—slayn also / With cursed Jewes."

From England, blood-libel accusations spread to France and across Europe, despite being decried as a falsehood by various popes. Over the centuries, there were over a hundred cases of trials for ritual murder in many European countries. According to the anthropologist Alan Dundes, "Although one might have logically assumed that this strange medieval legend might have died out over time . . . this does not appear to be the case at all." Instead, the myth flourished: "between 1887 and 1891, there were some twenty-two indictments in Europe alone with some fifty cases of blood libel reported between 1870 and 1935" (340).

The blood libel was exploited by the Nazis and is still spread today by some Muslims. As recently as 2014, Osama Hamdan, the top representative of Hamas in Lebanon, stated, "We all remember how the Jews used to slaughter Christians, in order to mix their blood in their holy matzos. This is not a figment of imagination or something taken from a film. It is a fact, acknowledged by their own books and by historical evidence" ("Top Hamas Official").

The blood libel, also called blood accusation and ritual murder, is based on the power of myth. It mixes together several primitive fantasies: that the Jews were responsible for the crucifixion of Christ and that they periodically repeat the crucifixion by the ritual murder of saintly, helpless Christians, using the blood to make Passover matzoh. It is a legend taken as a historical reality: the warped, paranoid fantasy of the Jew as bloodsucker.

Anti-Semitism is a complex phenomenon that has many explanations: religious, historical, political, and economic. But obviously there is a psychological dimension as well to the weird and persistent blood-libel legend. Dundes analyzes the legend as a species of folklore that depends on the psychoanalytic concept of projective inversion: "Projective inversion refers to a psychological process in which A accuses B of carrying out an action which A really wishes to carry out him or herself" (353). Since blood is central to Christianity—the eating of the body and blood of Christ, the notion of being washed in the blood of the lamb, and so on—this fascination with blood is projected onto Judaism, so that Jews are seen as vampires who survive by drinking Christian blood. "It is the underlying Christian guilt for orally incorporating the blood and flesh of their god, commonly perceived as the Christ child, which makes them project their guilt to the convenient Jewish scapegoat" (Dundes 357). "So the Christian hatred of Jews is neatly transformed into the Jews' hatred of Christians" (355).

An alternative psychoanalytic explanation of the blood-libel legend is offered by Jacob A. Arlow: "Historically, as aliens and strangers, Jews evoke in their neighbors deep-seated, primitive, unresolved hostilities directed originally against younger sibling figures and against any others whom they might regard as encroaching upon what they consider their rightful, proprietary domain. The typical fantasy of older siblings consists of destroying the newborn child by eating and incorporating it. . . . The blood libel legend, I would suggest, originates from the projection of these infanticidal and cannibalistic wishes from the Christian upon the Jew" (291-92).

The central symbol of the novel is blood, beginning with an epigraph from Yeats: "Irrational streams of blood are staining earth." As Yakov Bok thinks, "After a short time of sunlight, you awake in a black and bloody world" (Malamud, *The Fixer* 274). Writes the critic Iska Alter, "The imagery of blood runs through the novel like a red thread, from the accusation of ritual murder to the hemophilia of the young Tsarevitch, from the menstrual flow of Zina Lebedev to Bok's visions of bloody pogroms, as a constant reminder of history's poisoned inhumanity to man" (158). Malamud uses blood in all its possible range of meanings: from the positive, suggesting compassion, the ties of kinship, and life, to the negative, implying rage and violence, bloodshed. As Bok thinks, "there is no getting rid of the blood" (*The Fixer* 297).

The first mention of blood comes in the opening chapter as Bok leaves the *shtetl* to find work in Kiev. As he leaves the village for the last time, "a big-wigged Jewess . . . plucked a bloody-necked hen between her knees," and "a pool of blood in the ditch marked the passage of the ritual slaughterer. Farther on, a bearded black goat with a twisted horn, tethered to a post, baaed at the horse and charged, but the rope around his neck held and though the post toppled, the goat was thrown on its back" (*The Fixer* 15). The bloody hen and the pool of blood of the ritual slaughterer remind us that all civilization, even that of the Jews, is based on the slaughter of animals, so that no one is free of bloodshed. The angry goat tethered to a post foreshadows the later role of Bok (whose name is German for "goat") as ritual scapegoat.

Next, Bok mistreats the tired old horse that pulls his cart. A passing Russian peasant advises Bok, "A horse understands a whip," so Bok beats the poor animal "until he drew blood" (*The Fixer* 18). This continues the pattern of cruelty in the novel, of man against animals and of man against man, as Bok listens to a brutal Christian and takes out his frustration and rage against the horse. Soon Bok gives the horse to the ferryman to pay his passage. "The nag, tethered to a paling, watched from the moonlit shore. Like an old Jew he looks, thought the fixer" (28). The tethered horse that Bok mistreats and abandons has now become identified with the Jews, whom he also abandons, and with the tethered scapegoat. Bok's rage against the horse is a projection of his rage at this early point in the narrative against his fellow Jews and against himself, which makes him abandon the *shtetl* to live in the city among gentiles and take a gentile name.

Much later, when Bok is in prison and fears he is losing his sanity, he has a vision of the horse accusing him: "A bloody horse with frantic eyes appeared. . . . 'Murderer!' The horse neighed. 'Horsekiller! Childkiller!

You deserve what you get!' He beat the nag's head with a log" (249). Bok's guilt about mistreating and abandoning the bloody horse is connected to his guilt about his wife, himself, and his fellow Jews. Although Bok is innocent of the charge for which he is imprisoned, the murder of a Christian child, he feels guilty for the murder of his own child. Perhaps Bok remained childless because he was unkind to his wife, which drove her away. Thus, yet another meaning of blood is kinship: by leaving his community and denying his identity, Bok cut his ties with his fellow Jews, with his own flesh and blood. "A father-in-law's blood was thicker than water" (10). In the course of the novel, he must learn the value of those "blood brothers."

Imagery of blood is also associated with the rage of vicious anti-Semites. Bok meets a ferryman who gives a chilling speech about his desire to murder all the Jews. The ferryman's right eye is "streaked with blood"; literally, he has blood in his eye (26). One of Bok's fellow prisoners is a man with "bloodshot eyes" (105) who "pounced on the fixer and with his rotten teeth tried to bite his neck" (107). This anti-Semite is literally bloodthirsty: he is a vampire who, through projective inversion, sees the Jews as vampires. And the prosecutor Grubeshov, in charge of Bok's case, who delivers a vicious anti-Semitic harangue like the ferryman, has "his face darkened by blood" (226). Yet blood is also associated with Bok's own anger. As he is mistreated in prison, "he felt his rage growing. The blood roared in his ears" (325).

On the other hand, the lack of blood is seen as a sure sign of guilt. One of Bok's fellow workers denounces him to the police, saying, "I had my eye on him. When I met him in the brickyard the blood ran out of his face and he couldn't raise his eyes at me" (114).

Yet blood also signifies compassion, our common humanity. When Bok's wife comes to visit him in prison and weeps, "he felt, as he watched her, the weight of the blood in his heart" (288). In a vision, Bok accuses the tsar of lacking humanity: "Your poor boy is a haemophiliac, something missing in the blood. In you, in spite of certain sentimental feelings, it is missing somewhere else—the sort of insight, you might call it, that creates in a man charity, respect for the most miserable. You say you are kind and prove it with pogroms" (334).

As Shylock says in Shakespeare's *The Merchant of Venice*, "If you prick us, do we not bleed?" Yet Malamud demonstrates that Jewish blood is considered of less worth than Christian blood, as if Jews were less human. Bok thinks, "Overnight a madman is born who thinks Jewish blood is water" (274). One of his guards says, "It's no secret why Jews won't eat pig. You're blood brothers and both live on shit" (275). The warden says, "If you have any more letters to write you'll write them in your own blood" (135).

Not only is Jewish blood considered less human than Christian blood, but also Christians believe that Jewish men are not men but women because they menstruate. "The days were passing and the Russian officials were waiting impatiently for his menstrual period to begin. . . . If it didn't start soon they threatened to pump blood out of his penis with a machine they had for that purpose" (139).

Malamud is well aware of the history and the political and psychological roots of the blood libel. As the investigator Bibikov tells Bok in the novel, "Alexander I, in 1817, and Nicholas I, in 1835, by official ukase prohibited blood libels against Jews living in Russia," but later the libels were revived to "provoke pogroms for political purposes." Ironically, Bibikov tells Bok, "The very same blood accusation made against the Jews was used by pagans of the first century to justify the accusation and slaughter of the early Christians. They too were called 'blood drinkers,' for reasons you would understand if you knew the Catholic mass. The blood mystique arose in a belief of primitive people that there is a miraculous power in blood" (172). Bibikov, a Russian Christian, knows "the prohibition in Leviticus that Jews may not eat any manner of blood" (174).

But the liberal, rational Bibikov is soon himself arrested and dies in prison, a victim of suicide or perhaps murder. The authorities prefer to inflame the populace with the blood libel because the tsar needs the Jews as scapegoats, a distraction to keep them from overthrowing his rule.

The Fixer shows that the Jews actually shun blood, avoiding it in kosher meat. Bok refuses to sleep with a woman because she is having her period, saying, "But you are unclean!" (52). Meanwhile, the Russians are shown as bloodthirsty and obsessed with blood. They desecrate the Torah, giving Bok pages of the Old Testament in Hebrew. "Half the book was missing and some of the pages were covered with muddy brown stains that looked like dry blood" (237).

Bok at first rails against his fate as a Jew, just as he had left the *shtetl* and changed his name. "His fate nauseated him. Escaping from the Pale he had at once been entrapped in prison. From birth a black horse had followed him, a Jewish nightmare. What was being a Jew but an everlasting curse? He was sick of their history, destiny, blood guilt" (227). Only later is Bok's rage turned against the appropriate targets, the tsar and those Russian Christians who persecute him (169). By the end, Bok has undergone a moral transformation in prison. The years of suffering have led him to accept his fate and to identify with the Jews. As he faces his trial, he realizes that he is not alone

Ironically, as the novel continues, Bok is mistreated like Christ, imprisoned, chained, and beaten. But his tormentors cannot break him, and they cannot make him sign a false confession. At the end, after two and a half years in solitary confinement, as he heads to the trial, he is bloody but unbowed. *The Fixer* deconstructs the vicious superstition of the "blood libel" legend, not only exposing the lie but also revealing the true blood brotherhood that binds all people together.

CHAPTER 4

Malamud's *The Tenants* and the Problem of Ralph Ellison's Second Novel

TIMOTHY PARRISH

VIRGINIA TECH

In 1983, the American Academy and Institute of Arts and Letters awarded Bernard Malamud its Gold Medal for Fiction. Four years earlier, Malamud had suffered a stroke that had damaged his speech and impaired the movement of his arm. Although he had managed to recover to the point where he was writing again, he remained in frail health. In three years, he would be dead. His peers wished to honor him while he was still alive, and the Gold Medal was the highest award they could confer on him. As of this writing, only eighteen American writers have been so honored, among them William Dean Howells (the first recipient in 1915), Edith Wharton, Willa Cather, William Faulkner, Eudora Welty, Saul Bellow, I. B. Singer, John Updike, and Philip Roth. It was both a humane tribute to an ailing writer whose work had placed him at the forefront of American writers of his era and a summary recognition of his achievement. As part of the ceremony, one of the members of the Academy gives a speech praising the recipient's achievement. Malamud received his medal and speech from Ralph Ellison.

On the face of it, Ellison may seem a peculiar choice to have given a speech characterizing the nature of Malamud's achievement. Why would

Saul Bellow or Philip Roth, two writers so often grouped with Malamud that Bellow remarked the three of them were "the Hart, Shaffner and Marx of American literature," not give the presentation (Benedict 135)? Yet, of the three other writers, it was Ellison who perhaps most clearly saw his own work being of a piece with Malamud's. His admiration went back to 1959, when he had been on the committee that gave Malamud's *The Magic Barrel* the National Book Award in fiction. In 1964, he and Malamud both were elected to the American Academy of Arts and Letters. Nearly twenty years later, Malamud's achievement was still sufficiently important to Ellison, though, that the latter was willing to risk social opprobrium to make the speech. According to Arnold Rampersad, one of Ellison's biographers, Ellison's remarks that evening went on long enough that he risked testing his audience's patience.[1]

What did Ellison see in Malamud other than that he was one of the best writers of his generation? I think it is not too much to say that he saw a version of his own life. As successful American artists, the two writers lived a similar story, despite their disparate origins. Like Ellison, Malamud came from humble circumstances outside the mainstream of American culture to make a name for himself though his work. Both writers drew on folklore in constructing their fictions. Perhaps most importantly, Malamud had to defend his work from the charge of being "merely" ethnic writing. Ellison's defense of himself as a black writer who writes as an American from black experience was replicated in Malamud's defense of himself as a Jewish writer who writes as an American for the benefit of anyone who wishes to read him. And there was perhaps another reason why Ellison was so intent on giving his tribute to Malamud. In *The Tenants*, Malamud dramatized the conflict of Ellison's career and, in the process, told a version of Ellison's own authorial life that twenty years after Ellison's death we are only beginning to fully comprehend. Twenty years before Ellison's death, *The Tenants* tells the drama of Ellison's long-anticipated sequel to *Invisible Man* that he was unable to complete in his lifetime. In order to understand the surprising ways in which *The Tenants* clarifies the meaning of *Three Days before the Shooting*, we must return to the critical debates about cultural identity that to this point have helped to define each writer's career.

Let us return to Bellow's oft-quoted joke. The main thrust of it is that they are Jews assumed to be working in the same business. It implies that

Malamud, Bellow, and Roth have gotten out of the *shtetl* and set themselves up for business in the New World on the strength of their wiles and what they know from the Old World. The joke's happiest implication is that they are expert tailors intent on dressing up the staid wardrobe of American literature. Its less happy implication is that their notoriety as writers is a consequence of the surprising anomaly that they are Jewish. For many readers, the differences between them as artists were less significant than their shared cultural heritage was.

Ellison's remarks both acknowledge and undermine this grouping. "In the popular mind," Ellison notes in his Gold Medal address, Malamud "is readily identified as one of a quartet of novelists whose very names—Bellow, Mailer, Malamud, and Roth—convey an aura of authorial glamour" (*Collected* 463). Here he adds a name to the firm, a Jewish one, but then and now Mailer was not usually identified as a "Jewish writer." Of this grouping, Ellison acknowledges "two basic facts" concerning Malamud: he comes from "a background of the American Jewish experience, and like them he is successful in a highly difficult art" (463). Taken together as writers, one is most struck by their differences, since "an attempt to impose an easy unity upon such a prickly diversity of talent is superficial" (463). What makes Malamud "successful" in his art, Ellison suggests, has nothing to do with his being Jewish, with his heredity, and has everything to do with countless decisions he makes as an artist in composing his work. Being a Jew has nothing more to do with writing well than being black or white does.

In 1975, Daniel Stern asked Malamud the question that Ellison's tribute tacitly undermines: "Are you a Jewish writer?" "What is the question asking?" Malamud replied (63). In other words, why the question? It seems to imply that there are writers who are simply writers, and then there are writers whose writing requires a qualifying adjective to know who, or what, they are. Ellison, one of Malamud's most devoted readers, was also deeply interested in such questions since he was asked it so often himself—though the wording was slightly altered. In Ellison's case, the qualifying word changed as the times did. At different points in his career, Ellison was asked what it meant to be a "Negro" writer, an "Afro-American" writer, an "African American" writer, and a "black" writer. The fluidity of the label suggests at once the slipperiness of history and potentially the futility of pinning a writer's work to what only seems to be an immovable abstract noun.

Ellison likewise was a writer subject to racial profiling from critics. "Isn't it going to be difficult," the *Paris Review* asked Ellison in 1954, "for the Negro writer to escape provincialism when his literature is concerned with a minority?" (Ellison, *Collected* 212). As Malamud did with Stern, Ellison challenges the premise of this question. Ellison says simply, "All novels are about certain minorities: the individual is a minority." For Ellison, "the universal" in writing is "reached only through the depiction of the specific man in a specific circumstance" (212). In other words, if one writes well, the "Negro writer" is a Jewish writer, and vice versa.

Malamud ultimately was even bolder in his claims for his writing. He tells Stern, "I'm an American, a Jew, and I write for all men" (63). Categories are limiting, he explains to Stern, and writing need be only as limited as its reader. Malamud might have pointed to the narrator of Ellison's *Invisible Man* for an example of his assertion. That novel ends with perhaps the most famous question of American literature—one that throws the premise of "black writer," "Jewish writer," or "white writer" back into the face, or mind, of its reader. The unnamed black narrator, invisible seemingly to everyone but his reader, having completed the story of his life, directly confronts his reader with the meaning of his story: "Who knows, but that on the lower frequencies, I speak for you?" (Ellison, *Invisible* 572). Why does he end his story by confronting his reader? He wants to challenge that reader to see beyond the limitations of history, of skin color, of gender, to see him as a part of a shared humanity. Can you, reader, see your story in my story? If you can, then a bond more powerful than culture or history has been revealed.

When Stern asks Malamud if he is a Jewish writer, the question also tacitly asks what it means to write about Jews for readers who are not Jews. "I write about Jews, when I write about Jews," Malamud says, "because they set my imagination going" (63). Note that he says "when I write about Jews." In *The Assistant*, he writes about a character, Frank Alpine, who is not Jewish but chooses to become Jewish. Does such a choice not imply that either you are not what you have chosen to be or you were not what you thought you were? And why would Malamud imagine such a plot twist? Is it that he can believably make a non-Jewish character become Jewish only because all of his heroes are in effect already Jewish whether he identifies them as Jewish or not? Does this mean that even when writing about non-Jews, he creates them through eyes that are irremediably Jewish? Or is the novel suggesting that his readers, even if they do not realize it, become Jews through the act of reading Malamud?

"All men are Jews except they don't know it," Malamud once remarked to Leslie and Joyce Field ("Interview" 11). The reader of *Invisible Man* might say that "all readers are Negroes." Ellison acknowledged that "the white reader" of *Invisible Man* may not "identify himself with Negro characters in terms of our immediate racial and social situation" but that "on a deeper human level, identification can become compelling when the situation is revealed artistically" (Ellison, *Collected* 212). But what is this "deeper human level"? Is there a "deeper" level than being black if one is black? Is there a "deeper" level than being white if one is white? And on which levels does one find the Jew? For Ellison and Malamud, these categories merge. Each of them is a subset to being human, but perhaps just as importantly, they are subsets to becoming a reader. When the reader engages a work of art, a consummation occurs. The imaginative synthesis that happens between writer and reader through the story they share creates a truth that dissolves whatever separates them before this meeting in the text.

When Malamud was asked if he was a Jewish writer or when Ellison was asked if writing by blacks was by definition provincial, each might have simply answered, who cares? The text does not know the color or gender of its reader or maker. A writer works in words. He or she arranges words in patterns that the reader may recognize and enjoy or not depending on the reader's taste, capacity for comprehension, and level of interest. "The universal in the novel," Ellison remarked to his *Paris Review* interviewers, "isn't that what we're all clamoring for these days?" (Ellison, *Collected* 212).

Because fiction, to make its own reality, remakes the world at large through its representation, questions of history and identity will invariably be a part of what it means for readers to engage a novel, story, play, or poem. By the time Bernard Malamud published *The Tenants* in 1973, Ellison's remarks concerning "universality" seemed to many people misguided. In the wake of the civil rights movement, black writers in particular were advocating for an aesthetics that was specifically, essentially black. The prospect that a white author or even a white reader could imagine or comprehend the point of view of a black writer or black character was questioned. Many black writers began to wonder to what extent the truth of their experience and work would be compromised by subjecting them to the influence of models they deemed to be white. Amiri Baraka's "Black Art," a crucial work of the Black Arts Movement, speaks of putting "dagger poems in the slimy balls of the owner-jew" and of "another bad poem cracking steel knuckles in a jewlady's mouth" (142). Asserting the need for "poems that kill," the voice says, "We want a black poem," and offers itself as an instance of what it proclaims. Black writing and white writing were conceived of as separate, opposed entities (142).

In *Invisible Man*, Ellison dramatized the costs of being one who is constantly misinterpreted, misused, and finally unseen on account of one's skin color (and the history associated with it). On one level, the novel was an anatomy of most white readers' race-based prejudices; on another, it was a call to black artists to come out and be seen and heard by the sound of their own voices. As Ellison was writing the novel, he told Albert Murray that his work would not "mean much in the long run" if it was "seen only by whites" (*Trading* 7). After the novel was published, Ellison cautioned that "too many books by Negro writers are addressed to a white audience" (*Collected* 213). By the early 1970s, though, Ellison was attacked by many black writers for having aligned his work with the "owner-jews" in writing a novel that could be praised by a predominantly white social and literary structure, despite the fact that the Black Arts Movement was arguably a logical extension of *Invisible Man*'s narrative. Literary history often progresses through cruel irony: Ellison writes, from his own "Negro experience," a novel that is later attacked by subsequent black writers for being insufficiently "black" in its achievement. As Ellison and Malamud well understood, once you use a word such as "black" or "Jew" or "white" to modify the word "writer," an inevitable question arises: how black or Jewish (or white) are you?

Such questions became a millstone around Ellison's neck. Malamud, by contrast, never had to validate, or have validated, his credentials as a "Jewish writer." Ellison, however, repeatedly had to defend himself as a black writer. That is, he had to defend himself as a writer, and he had to defend himself as a black person. The most famous instance occurred in 1963 when Irving Howe criticized his work for being insufficiently political, when compared with the works of Richard Wright. Ellison's reply, "The World and the Jug," claimed for the black writer the same aesthetic autonomy that any other writer might claim: "I can only ask that my fiction be judged as art; if it fails, it fails aesthetically, not because I did or did not fight some ideological battle" (*Collected* 182). Reviewing the Howe-Ellison exchange, Rampersad says that "probably for the first time in modern American history, a black intellectual had fought a public duel against a white intellectual and won" (402). Although Rampersad speculates that "many blacks probably took pleasure in this besting of a white man," the premise that a work of art may be judged by its formal properties is precisely what a poem such as "Black Art" denies (402).

One admirer of Ellison's essay was Malamud, who wrote Ellison to say that his argument was "beautifully and nobly written" (Rampersad 402). Ten years later, Malamud published *The Tenants*, which is in many ways a fictional replaying of the Howe-Ellison debate. "I have not found it possible to think about *The Tenants*," Cynthia Ozick noted at the time of its publication, "without turning Howe-Ellison round and round" ("Literary" [*Art & Ardor*] 102). Malamud's novel opposes two writers, one Jewish and one black, who fight each other over what makes writing worth reading. In particular, they fight about the meaning of the black writer's text. Although the Ellison-Howe debate is a touchstone for the novel, Malamud restages the debate so that Ellison occupies both sides. In effect, Malamud pits Ellison against himself.

In the Howe-Ellison exchange, Ellison claims the high ground of artist and places it above questions of racial politics. In *The Tenants*, it is the Jewish writer, Lesser, who copies Ellison's argument and insists that any artist, regardless of origins, must master one's form in order to create lasting work. For the artist, form is prior to content. Lesser's writer counterpart, Willie Spearmint, insists on the primacy of his experience as a black man as the guiding spirit of his writing. The content of his life matters beyond form's capacity to render it. Throughout, Spearmint speaks in the terms Howe did to Ellison. "How could a Negro put pen to paper," Ellison quotes Howe, "how could he so much as think or breathe, without some impulsion to protest, be it harsh or mild, political or private, released or buried? The 'sociology' formed a constant pressure on his literary work, and not merely in the way this might be true for any writer, but with a pain and ferocity nothing could remove" (*Collected* 158). Howe's argument seems to suggest that there is an appropriate subject and mode for writing by blacks: political anger.

Howe's argument suggested to Ellison that it was misguided for the black writer to write something that would appeal to readers whom he should be eager to affront or at least aggrieve. Must the work of a black writer expect different responses from the reader than the work of a white writer does? "White fiction ain't the same as *black*. It can't *be*," Malamud's Willie asserts (*The Tenants* 74). At times, Spearmint even rejects Lesser's capacity to read and understand his work. Yet, as we have seen, the Howe-Ellison debate resulted in many people declaring Ellison the winner precisely because the black writer claimed a universalism that the white, Jewish critic questioned.

Ellison may seem to define a realm where art and not skin color reigns, but he does not in fact surrender the position of writing as a *black* artist. Previously, he had said, "I recognized no dichotomy between art and protest" (Ellison, *Collected* 212). At the end of "The World and the Jug," Ellison mentions "the Negro Freedom Movement" in the context of defining his role as a writer (*Collected* 187). Observe that he says "Negro Freedom Movement" instead of "civil rights movement." His phrase makes of his immediate historical period a drama of *blacks freeing themselves* rather than blacks being recognized as having the same rights as whites. There is a touch of Malamud's Willie in this formulation. "I write for Black Freedom," Willie remarks to Lesser (*The Tenants* 60). Ellison further says he is enlisted in this movement "for the duration" (*Collected* 187). This fight with Howe, in other words, is one among many to come and is fundamentally a claim by Ellison to control the meaning of his art.

It is worth noting, then, that after Ellison defines his work in terms of its formal achievement, his conclusion flips the argument's terms. He claims for his work precisely the political impact that Howe demands of black writing. In making this claim, he points not to *Invisible Man*, which he certainly could have done, but to his then-unpublished novel that he spent the next thirty years writing without publishing. At the same time, he entertains and then refuses the role of "Negro leader" since blacks hardly need any more "would-be Negro leaders cluttering up the airways" (Ellison, *Collected* 187). He acknowledges only that his role is "to publish more novels": "and here I am remiss and vulnerable, perhaps" (*Complete* 187). Thirty-one years later, Ellison died without ever having published another novel. This lack came to dominate perceptions of his career almost as much as the fact that he was the author of *Invisible Man*.

What happened to Ellison? Why did his promised novel not emerge during his lifetime? How *does* a novelist master his form and advance the Negro Freedom Movement at the same time? Did he leave the novel unfinished because he simply could not write it or because he set himself an impossible task? Or did he not finish it because he was afflicted by the same tensions that prevent Malamud's Willie Spearmint from completing his novel?

Some answers to these questions are provided by the "black" novel written by Ellison's Jewish American novelist friend. In *The Tenants*, Malamud explores to its limits what we might call the Ellison-Malamud position, which insists that all people are Jews—or Negroes—and which insists that writing allows people to understand that which they have not experienced. The novel pits the everyman Jew, Lesser, against the clannish black writer, Spearmint. When they meet, both are struggling writers. Lesser labors to finish his third novel, which he has been working on for nearly ten years. The novel is complete except for the ending. He is revising it but cannot settle on how to finish it. The reader is left to wonder if it is a task he can ever complete.

The setting where Lesser writes seems to reflect on his position as writer. He lives in a building consigned to destruction. Everyone has moved out but him. He remains because he wants to complete the novel in the place he began it—to preserve its mysterious gestalt. Generous laws for tenants allow him to continue to live there even while the building is falling in all around him. The landlord offers him one better deal after another to leave, but Lesser insists he can only finish his book there. Writing the book virtually requires the destruction of the man he is and the environment that sustains him. Only the completed artifact need survive its creation. Life, the artist, the environment—everything is subservient to the work of art.

One day Lesser hears the sounds of a typewriter that is not his own, as if a double has sought him out to mock him. The "other" writer is Willie, who has occupied the building to write his novel. He is stealing space to fashion his story—like the narrator of *Invisible Man*, who also lived and wrote in a place off the city grid. The two writers become wary friends. When Lesser realizes that each "feels the anguish of the other" (*The Tenants* 230), he enacts what Ozick calls the "Malamudic assumption," that is, the "anguish of the other" ("Literary" [*Art & Ardor*] 92). To be true to himself, Lesser experiences Willie as a moral debt he must acknowledge and try to pay to the best of his ability. He struggles to help the apprentice writer achieve his vision in prose. In the end, though, the Jewish writer and the black writer square off and kill each other because neither can accommodate the other as a writer or as a man.

I suggest that Malamud is less pitting Howe against Ellison than he is pitting Ellison against himself. That is, if the terms of this self-confrontation come from "The World and the Jug," as Ozick suggests, this is because the issues that the Howe-Ellison debate raised had by the end of the 1960s become the battleground for how cultural difference in American writing was understood. They became the visible, burning ground of the Black Arts Movement and the Black Panther movement. The same "anger" that Howe presumed must characterize black writers seemed to explode into the streets as racial riots rocked Newark, Boston, and Detroit. At the same time, arguments that "literature" is universal and open to meanings anyone might construct or understand yielded to claims that "literature" is made up of a constellation of inassimilable particularities available only to writers and readers who share the same history, cultural context, and, in some cases, skin color.

In *The Tenants*, the black writer, Willie, is not interested in being equal to Lesser—or with Lesser being equal to him. "No ofay motherfucker can put himself in *my* place," he informs Lesser. "This is a *black* book we talkin' about that you don't understand at all" (74). Willie wants to tell his story and, in telling it, be true to it. His position pointedly refutes Malamud's claim that all men are Jews or Lesser's claim that "art is the glory and only a schmuck thinks otherwise" (50). When Willie asks Lesser if he is "an expert of black experience," Lesser replies, "I am an expert of writing." Willie responds, "I hate all that shit when whites tell you about black" (36). In the Howe-Ellison debate, though, Ellison occupies both positions. Although Ellison couched his argument in terms of art, Ellison's speaks for the black writer when he refutes Howe's prescription of what manner of writing is appropriate for the black artist.

When *The Tenants* was published, it clearly responded to the end of the 1960s, the Black Arts Movement, and the sense of black anger that flourished after the success of the civil rights movement. In the *Paris Review* interview, Malamud mentioned "black activism" as one of the triggers to his writing the novel, and he noted that he was an avid reader of black writing (Stern 66). During the civil rights movement, American Jews and blacks were generally seen as allies in the struggle for greater freedom for all in American life. After the assassination of Martin Luther King Jr., however, some black intellectuals were accusing Jews of being as racist as anyone. As we have seen, Baraka's "Black Art" dramatically asserts this perspective by calling for the murder of former allies. Baraka's art tried to stake out a true cultural, aesthetic, and psychological autonomy and to create a single and united black nation.

Likewise, Malamud's Willie Spearmint hopes to heal himself by writing a true black book. In *The Tenants*, Malamud gives full voice to this position: "You want to know what's really art?" Willis says to Lesser. "*I* am art. Willie Spearmint, *black man*. My form is *myself*" (75; emphasis in original). Although Willie claims for himself a unique expression, he also writes "a black book" for all those who feel what he feels but have also been blocked by a racist society. The "Jewword" called "art" does not describe, Willie says, what he is doing (50). Willie writes for himself, but he also writes for those who lack the capacity to express what they also feel. Because Ellison limits his aesthetic vision to that of a single novelist, however, "The World and the Jug," even given its most militant reading, cannot be mistaken for a cry of black independence. Yet the aim he describes to Howe is virtually the same as the one Willie describes to Lesser.

"You can deny universality," Lesser answers, "but you can't abolish it" (75). Without surrendering the assumption that the experience of American blacks was singular, Ellison also expected a story could be true to that experience and resonate for others. As a social critic, Ellison frequently argued that blacks were already united by their folklore and shared historical experience. Their task was to transform the strength required of them to survive American slavery and its aftermath to take on leading roles in shaping American society. Although he never finished his second novel, as an essayist, a teacher, and the author of *Invisible Man*, he aspired to fulfill the very role he attributes to Malamud in 1983: "to speak to the whole of American experience when the diversity of the whole is so much greater and more unavailable than its parts" (*Collected* 464).

This is perhaps why Ellison took it so personally when, according to Rampersad, others tried to move him off the stage while he was giving his address to Malamud (538–39). In that speech, Ellison speaks of the American writer enduring a "symbolic state of civil war" because one's "democratic faith" is "bedeviled" by the "undemocratic contents" of American "attitudes and actions" (*Collected* 465). Speaking of *The Tenants*, Malamud told Stern, "All I know is that American blacks have been badly treated. We, as a society, have to redress the balance" (66). Ellison uses the occasion of Malamud's honor to posit a democratic artist, Malamud, who would critique without rejecting the promise of equality embedded in the nation's origins. Ellison admits that such a promise made by slaveholding white men could only be understood as a "future fiction" that must be earned and even created by its inheritors—black and white. Arguably, *Invisible Man* performed this function by imagining an angry black man willing to risk visibility among people used to not seeing his full humanity. *The Tenants* performed this function as well by giving voice to the anger that blacks felt as a consequence of a history that could not turn overnight and make them "equal" when for hundreds of years they had not been.

What will be the outcome of this anger? Can it fade as the nation's democratic conditions become truer to its ideals? Or is such an ideal impossible, in which case black anger must be irredeemable? With the 2010 publication of *Three Days before the Shooting*, a mostly complete version of Ellison's massive unfinished novel, we now know that these were the questions that Ellison was asking in the second novel. Many people thought that Ellison did not publish his novel because he was suffering from writer's block. He was not. Through art, he was seeking answers that only history can provide and in many ways was undoing the kind of argument he had made to Howe. It was not that Ellison ever questioned whether an individual black artist could render formally, and beautifully, his or her particular vision. Rather, Ellison's novel questioned whether black Americans and American society could ultimately accommodate each other. In public, he took an optimistic stance. In private, writing, it seems, for his own desk drawer, he absorbed himself in a story that he could not resolve because it could not be resolved. He was Willie, and he was Lesser too. And not one of them ever finished his book.

Ellison's position as the writer who lives at the intersection of universalism and provincialism reveals how alike Lesser and Willie are. Each is writing a novel that he cannot or will not finish; "each, thought the writer, feels the anguish of the other" (*The Tenants* 230). *The Tenants* has three endings—the most recalled one perhaps being where Lesser splits Willie's head with an axe, and Willie severs Lesser's testicles from his body. Why the three endings? Malamud was asked. "Because one wouldn't do" (Stern 66). In other words, there was for him no certain way to resolve the conflict between Lesser's and Willie's stories. Nor did he did want the grisly ending to be the only ending. The book's final words are actually a prayer for mercy.

In Ellison's second novel, the unsolvable conflict is between adopted father and adopted son. The father is Alonzo Hickman, a former jazz musician turned preacher. As a musician and a preacher, he exemplifies the two major types of black vernacular expression. The son is Bliss, a boy of indeterminate race whose birth causes the lynching of Hickman's brother. From the beginning, Hickman has had to swallow pain to love Bliss. Hickman raises Bliss as his own among a black community that is segregated—it takes place in "the territory," that region of what would become Oklahoma where Huck Finn disappeared at the conclusion of his story—but sufficient unto itself. Regardless of the child's indeterminate origins, he is raised as one of the black community. As the novel portrays in the long section that looks backward to this time and was first published as *Juneteenth* (1999), Bliss learns to speak, think, and even walk as those who raised him did. Whatever his skin color, he was "black." At some point, however, he leaves the community. He becomes a filmmaker and eventually a powerful northern U.S. senator, Adam Sunraider, whose power derives largely from his cynical manipulations of racism. The novel begins with the attempted assassination of the senator on the floor of the U.S. Senate. The assassin is Sunraider's illegitimate son, Severn, whom Sunraider fathered with a black woman of Indian descent. Bliss/Sunraider is literally dying through the whole course of the more than one thousand pages of the novel.

From different narrative perspectives, the novel tells Bliss's story and explores its meaning. Bliss looks white but is not definitively white because neither is American history. America has been built on murder, dispossession of peoples, and racial hatred. The Civil War did not end it. The civil rights movement, during which time Ellison was trying hardest to finish the novel, may not either. Can Bliss's story be redeemed into a future when its conflicts are healed? Hickman hopes so. No other character does. Hickman sits by his adopted son's bed hoping for a sign that his faith in his son will be rewarded. None definitively appears.

In *Invisible Man*, Ras the Exhorter is the eloquent voice of black rage. In the second novel, that eloquence belongs to the assassin's gun and Hickman's parishioners, who object to Hickman's faith that Bliss can be saved. Except for the shooting, though, anger erupting into violence is not present. There is no Ras in the second novel. There is no Willie—on the surface anyway. But, like *Invisible Man*, the novel is inconceivable without the historical black rage that Ellison the artist works to give form. In part 1 of the novel, a white Kentucky journalist named McIntyre seeks to understand Bliss's story, which is also Hickman's. Whether this white man can understand the story he seeks is doubtful. Although he once wanted to marry a black woman, the woman's family rejected him. One sees in this rejection a version of Willie's declaration, "White fiction ain't the same as *black*. It *can't* be" (*The Tenants* 74; emphasis in original).

As a critic, Ellison denied such a claim. As a writer, though, he seems to have given up McIntyre as a narrative device. Originally, it was McIntyre who was to explore the meaning of Bliss's story. In the later versions of the book, Hickman, the black character, is the one left to sift through its fragments and seek conclusions. Hickman, like King, is practically a saint as he confronts acts of violence directed toward him and his people with acts of love and forgiveness. Whether his ethic of sacrifice is part of an action that will help to change history the novel leaves unclear.

"Bliss" in the novel occurs in those moments when Hickman and Bliss have come together. These moments cannot be sustained, just as in *The Tenants* the friendship between Lesser and Willie cannot withstand their doubts about each other. "We groove on art, dad," Willie says in a good moment to Lesser. "You and I are gonna be real tight" (54). They were tight, and they could not bear it. As Bliss lies on his deathbed, he and Hickman look back to when they knew together "our kind of time" and when they were one (Ellison, *Three* 323). It is a mythic dream, at best. At the heart of their story is the rage that Willie represents, to which Ellison never gives full voice.

That rage, apparently, is a story Ellison does not want to specify, yet the story he does tell cannot exist without it. Had he let it out more obviously, would he have finished his novel? It is perhaps a question not worth asking. By rewriting the Howe-Ellison debate into one in which Ellison takes both sides, Malamud tells that story for Ellison. Malamud, it seems, does not care what interpretation the reader puts on his fable. Ellison, I hazard, did. It seems that such was the scope of Ellison's aim that his unfinished novel addressed all Americans: past, present, and, future. In the future, and only then, will Bliss's meaning be resolved. So the novel is unfinished—just as Malamud's novel is unfinished in the sense that the question it raises can yield no definite ending.

Malamud's novel, however, explicitly raises the question that Ellison's novel represses. What if Willie is right? What if universality can be abolished? What if American history, despite its promise of equality, is just another version of this abolition that blacks have to live through? What if what Ellison calls this "political fiction" cannot be realized in any "future condition" that Thomas Jefferson, Abraham Lincoln, or Ralph Ellison can imagine?

The Tenants leaves this question open, and so does Ellison's second novel. One answer, though, is unremitting violence. In Malamud's novel, one ending is that the Jew and the black man kill each other. Ellison's novel contemplated a violent revolt on the U.S. Senate floor. Ellison's novel begins with revolt and then spends a thousand pages trying to undo it. Though conceived in the 1950s, it anticipated the violence and the assassinations of the 1960s. Ellison told John Hersey that he was unnerved when events depicted in the novel suddenly seemed to appear again in the news of the day—as if he were writing history before it happened (793). As he went deeper into the story, and perhaps became lost in it, it seems this sense of anxiety never left him. Did he really want to publish a novel that many people might read as a concession to violent revolt as the only logical conclusion to the African American quest to be free in America? Was this the "Negro Freedom Movement" he was in for the duration? Was he, like Baraka, writing "A Black Poem," whatever his public pronouncements about democratic progress seemed to say?

In the address to Malamud, Ellison says, "we are all at some point secessionists" (*Collected* 465). Knowing this, how can the democratic artist render America whole? "I can't always be certain that what I write is going to be understood," Ellison told John Hersey, "because as an American writer I have a problem of communicating across our various social divisions" (*Collected* 798). Nonetheless, the writer puts into the writing "all what he cannot understand, cannot say, cannot even admit in any other way" (*Collected* xxviii). For Ellison, as well as Lesser, the mastery of form is what makes the incommunicable communicable. The finished novel, he says, "is the completion of personality" (*Collected* 794). Isn't this what Willie seeks through his fiction? *The Tenants* asks, first, whether Willie or anyone needs a work of art to justify his existence: "Art can kiss my juicy ass," Willie says. With Walt Whitman, Willie says, "my form is *myself*" (*The Tenants* 75). He seems to stop short of saying with Whitman that he contains multitudes. If Willie must finish his "Black Book" to complete his personality, though, then why cannot any of the many books that Willie essays be the form that he seeks? They fail because Lesser says so? Lesser could be like the "Jew publishers" who Willie says will not publish him. Is the case that Willie's truth is too much for white readers to bear? Even Willie acknowledges that his white Jewish girlfriend has learned from his art (99).

Of the work Lesser cannot finish, he thinks, "It was as though the book had asked him to say more than he knew; he could not meet its merciless demands. Each word weighed like a rock. If you've been writing a book for ten years time adds time to each word; they weigh like rocks the weight of waiting for the end, to become the book" (*The Tenants* 106). By 1971, Ellison had been writing his book for nearly twenty years; he kept writing it until his death. Lesser often recalls his dead painter friend, Lazar Kohn. For years, Kohn worked on a painting he could not finish. His friends persuaded him to sell it anyway. Its unfinished state was part of its aesthetic. The painter released the painting, and it became known as a masterpiece.

Lesser, the writer who cannot bring himself to settle on an ending, though he has written several, cannot follow his friend's example. Without a suitable ending, he has only "form unachieved." Such a thing does "not deserve to be a book" (*The Tenants* 112). He tells Willie the same thing, and Willie for a time believes him. Willie's efforts to write become more difficult when he accepts Lesser's advice that his story requires a different form: "You tryin to kill off my natural writin by pretendin you are interested in the fuckn form of it though the truth of it is you afraid of what I am goin to write in my book" (165). Willie curses himself for listening to Lesser, but he never finishes either: "I have got to write better," he tells himself. "Better and better. Black but better. Nothing but black. Now or never" (201). His blackness and his form are elusive to him.

Neither Lesser nor Willie can let go of the search for form that oppresses both of them.

Ellison was Malamud's friend. Presumably, Malamud wondered when Ellison was going to publish his second novel and had his theories regarding the matter of successful completion. Whether he did or not, though, *The Tenants* beautifully elucidates Ellison's predicament. "What's the distant dark mountain in my mind when I write?" Lesser asks himself. "It won't become diaphanous, radiance, fire, Moses himself climbing down the burning rock. . . . The writer wants his pen to turn stone into sunlight, language into fire" (*The Tenants* 184). Ellison wanted such a transformation; so did Malamud. What ambitious writer does not? Malamud, however, did something that Ellison, Lesser, and Willie could not bring themselves to do. Although his novel lacked a definitive ending, he followed the painter's example: he published his novel.

The Tenants does not take Willie's side. It does not take Lesser's side. Its theme is not, as Ozick suggests, "pogrom" ("Literary" [*Art & Ardor*] 111). It is not a Jewish novel any more than it is a black novel. It does not ask what it would mean to write a black novel. Malamud's conception of the novel required him to fabricate plots for Willie's black novels—to pretend to be a black writer as he gives voice to his voice seeking form. What of Malamud's presumption to imagine a black writer? (Willie tells Lesser that "the sister" in one of his novels is unbelievable as a black character.) Arguably, Malamud does not even allow himself that invention. Because of the multiple endings, and the narrative's tendency to move back and forth between the book that the reader is reading and the book that Lesser is writing, *The Tenants* could be read as the book Lesser himself is writing—as *Invisible Man* was also the book its protagonist was writing. If so, then Willie Spearmint is doubly illusory. He does not exist except as a character in the mind of another character, Lesser. His "blackness" is a measure of the reader's ability to recognize—or reject—it through the prism of Lesser's prejudices.

"We are in fact a nation of minorities," Ellison said to Malamud when defining the task of the democratic artist, "and if the reality of one is neglected, the common truth of experience is done incalculable violence" (*Collected* 467). *The Tenants* imagines violence but ends with a blessing. Willie is the mechanism by which Malamud completes the personality of Ellison's ideal American writer. Whether Malamud was telling Ellison to publish his own novel so that it might find its readers cannot be said. What can be said is that Ellison identified with Malamud's achievement and affirmed it as his own.

NOTES
1. For a discussion of how some who attended apparently tried to rush Ellison from the stage, see Rampersad 538–39.

CHAPTER 5

Unbound and Un-bodied

Reading Race in Malamud's *The Tenants*

JESSICA LANG

BARUCH COLLEGE, CITY UNIVERSITY OF NEW YORK

As odd as it might seem to those who are familiar with Malamud's 1971 novel *The Tenants*, the novel is perhaps at its most powerful when read and understood as a passing novel, a story that examines race as a tense combination of powerfully fluid imagined self-identity rooted in the destructive stereotype of otherness. Initially defined as a means by which an individual concealed one identity by assuming another, passing was understood in the early twentieth century within an empirical framework as a means to gain admission or access—deceptively—to a social institution that would otherwise have been off-limits.[1] This binary definition of passing—belonging or not belonging—which was often packaged together with a sense of moral misgiving, has evolved dramatically in more recent decades to one that recognizes more readily the performative element found in passing, one that separates it from former conceptions of passing as tied to being in a more absolute sense of the word: "In the postmodern context it is useless to speak of authentic as opposed to false ethnic culture, implying that only one deserves cultivation" (Boelhower 132). Passing has been interpreted as unsettling established understandings of racial identity; as a means to recognize and define humanity; as part of an American tradition of reinvention and self-making; and as social invention (Kawash; Hobbs; Pfeiffer; Sollors). More contemporary interpretations of passing, instead of regarding it as a choice between two modes of representation and a move only in one direction—upward—complicates its role and function thematically by identifying it as multiplying, rather than reducing, possibilities of representation and self-definition (Belluscio 9–10).

Malamud's *The Tenants* participates in this evolving and complicating understanding of passing by moving beyond what is perhaps its most basic premise: that passing, whether regarded as performance or as being, is rooted in the physical body. In contrast, I suggest here that Malamud experiments with what I call rhetorical passing, an effort to document art and imagination as a process of racially informed exchange and acquisition between two protagonists, one Jewish and one black. The word "exchange" bears a great deal of meaning here. I do not intend for it to convey a sense of evenhandedness. Rather, the exchange that takes place in *The Tenants* is often violent and imbalanced. What it does do very effectively, however, is convey a sense of mutuality. Ultimately the novel presents a story, both the one it describes and the one it is, that can be read and understood as a commingling of black and Jewish aesthetics, with the boundaries separating the two not always discernable—this being precisely the point. Malamud accomplishes this new form of passing in a range of ways, and here I examine two of them that reverberate throughout the novel: form and character. These two components are the areas of weakness that the two writer protagonists of *The Tenants*, the Jewish Harry Lesser and the black Willie Spearmint, recognize in the other: Harry criticizes Willie's literary form, and Willie criticizes Harry's inauthentic characterization of blackness. Not content merely to describe these features as an abstraction, a part of another (fictional) writer's oeuvre, Malamud inserts himself into the experiment of rhetorical passing in the novel, becoming an illustration of his own fictional representation. In terms of character, he is a Jewish author creating a black character deriding a Jewish character's portrayal of race. In terms of form, *The Tenants* is perhaps the most experimental of all of Malamud's novels because of its three imagined endings found within the text and its fourth actual ending. All four endings shift the novel from a story rooted in realism to one exploring fantasy and, specifically, fantasies around both the limitations and boundlessness of racial representation. Taken together, Malamud's experimentation with characterization and form from within the novel and of his own making invites readers to consider and reconsider the concept of literary invention and its relationship to race.

What does rhetorical passing do for reading? Why is conceiving of Malamud's novel in these terms important? I suggest here that Malamud's purpose in positioning rhetorical passing as central to the meaning of *The Tenants* is to present an intellectual device or method toward racial and social companionship, one that was painfully and bleakly absent in the environment in which he wrote. James Baldwin, a writer who is mentioned in *The Tenants*, makes the following statement in his 1962 book *The Fire Next Time*: "The white man's unadmitted—and apparently, to him, unspeakable—private fears and longings are projected onto the Negro. The only way he can be released from the Negro's tyrannical power over him is to consent, in effect, to become black himself, to become a part of that suffering and dancing country that he now watches wistfully from the heights of his lonely power and armed with spiritual traveller's checks, visits surreptitiously after dark" (96). In *The Tenants*, Malamud gives an imagined vision to Baldwin's sentiments. He voices both Jewish and African American positions, histories, and aesthetics, combining them in a violent death that is mutually destructive and mutually redemptive. Baldwin writes that "one ought to rejoice in the fact of death. . . . It is the responsibility of free men to trust and to celebrate what is constant—birth, struggle, and death are constant, and so is love" (92) Creating a community of Americans, Malamud acknowledges, is bloody and violent; it demands relinquishing superiority and acknowledging a deep need of one another. *The Tenants* investigates this possibility through terms that are both familiar (racial tension) and unfamiliar (a recognition and elevation of rhetorical passing through the imagination).

In Malamud's reflections on the motivations that led him to write *The Tenants*, he creates a succinct list: "Jews and blacks, the period of troubles in New York City; the teachers' strike, the rise of black activism, the mix-up of cause and effect. I thought I'd say a word" (Stern 61). The brevity of his statement belies the complexity of New York City's social and political environment throughout the 1960s, especially in the latter part of the decade. Paul Buhle and Robin D. G. Kelley note that "the grand alliance" between black and Jewish liberalism came to an end in 1967, when "Black leaders in the Student Nonviolent Coordinating Committee (SNCC) adopted 'Black Power' as their slogan and asked white members to devote their energies to fighting racism in white communities" (214). Those "white members," mostly Jews who did not identify with the "white communities" that their onetime partners identified them with, "felt . . . exiled from the organization they helped to build" (214). While other largely political events exacerbated the growing tensions between the two communities, none was more devastating than the dispute between community and union control of local schools. In 1968, the union representing New York City's fifty-five thousand predominantly white public schoolteachers, the United Federation of Teachers (UFT), locked horns with the local school board representing the predominantly black Ocean Hill–Brownsville district. The local school board, in an effort to wrest control from the UFT over what it regarded as its community school, dismissed a group of teachers and administrators working at the school, almost all of whom were white and Jewish. The UFT, angry that community control over schools limited its ability to protect teachers' positions, initiated a series of strikes that shut down New York City's public schools for nearly two months (Buhle and Kelley 216). As noted in a *New York Times* article written nearly thirty years later, when legislation was making its way through the state senate to undo some of the legacy of the decentralization effort that initiated the 1968 strike and, with it, the downward spiral of relationships between neighbors and neighborhoods, the "impact [of these events] on the city and beyond is hard to overstate" (Kifner).[2] The Ocean Hill–Brownsville dispute and the consequent teacher strikes poisoned long-cultivated relationships between the black and Jewish communities in New York for decades to come; even at the time it took place, those who were involved recognized that the relationship between the two communities was profoundly and adversely changed.

The Tenants is not Malamud's first attempt to address the tangled web of race relations through fiction, but it is his most sustained and complex. Many critics read the novel as his most dysphoric, understanding its bloody ending as approaching the apocalyptic. While the novel is certainly more violent than are many of his earlier stories involving race, my reading of *The Tenants* is as a confrontation of difference that is rooted in violence and, at the same time, projects a powerful image of unity. In Malamud's story "Angel Levine," written in 1955, the title character is a black Jew who has been told that in order to prove his worthiness as an angel, and thus earn his wings, he must inspire the faith of a Jewish tailor, Manischevitz, who in all things would not be considered a skeptic but who is astounded and perplexed, to the point of rejection, that a Jewish angel could be black. Manischevitz remains unconvinced, his lack of faith not only furthering his own worldly troubles but also impacting Levine's future as a full-fledged angel. Just as lack of faith proves detrimental to them both, Manischevitz undergoes a conversion of sorts, acknowledging Levine's holy status and bringing redemption to them both.

A second Malamud story that takes on Jewish-black relations, titled "Black Is My Favorite Color" (1963), centers on Nat Lime, a Jewish New York liquor-store owner who recounts a number of attempts to befriend members of the black community. His attempt as a child to draw near Buster, a black boy living in his neighborhood, ends with him being punched in the face. "What did you hit me for?" Nat asks. "Because you a Jew bastard," Buster responds. "Take your Jew movies and your Jew candy and shove them up your Jew ass." The blow that Nat suffers at Buster's hands foreshadows the end to his love affair, years later, with a black woman whom he wishes to marry. She ends the relationship, going so far as to leave town, when, as the two walk through her neighborhood one night, three black men assault Nat in an effort to turn him away. "If there's a ghetto," Nat declares, "I'm the one that's in it."

"Angel Levine" and "Black Is My Favorite Color" trace Malamud's commitment to and growing despair regarding what he calls "the efficacy of American democracy." This includes "guaranteeing blacks what they deserve as human beings—a larger share of our national wealth, equal opportunity under the law, their rights as men." Taken together, Malamud continues, these guarantees will mean that "the relationship of blacks and Jews and other minorities are bound to improve" (Field and Field, "Interview" 14). In a widely cited essay titled "Literary Blacks and Jews," Cynthia Ozick examines Malamud's investigation, over the course of a decade, into the relationship between the two communities. She declares that while by the end of the 1950s the fact that to Malamud "black and Jew are one is no miracle," the publication of *The Tenants* renders this same proposition "hollow" ([*Art & Ardor*] 91). Malamud, Ozick explains, once again "offers a parable of black and Jew culminating in fantasy," as he does in "Angel Levine," but in *The Tenants*, the fantasy is "a passionate bloodletting," a pogrom (91). Ozick objects to what she declares is Malamud's rapid about-face on race relations in America: it "took the narrowest blink of time for Malamud . . . to come from 'Believe me, there are Jews everywhere'"—the concluding sentiment to "Angel Levine"—to the "merciless" plot of *The Tenants* (92). She asks, "How was the transmutation from magical brotherhood to ax-murder wrought? Is it merely that society has changed so much since the late 1950s, or is it that the author of 'Angel Levine' was, even then, obtuse?" (92) And yet it is Ozick's initial assessment of Malamud's perception of blacks and Jews—namely, that they are one—that clearly carries through *The Tenants*. The final bloody scene between them, the one Ozick calls a pogrom, allows and predicts their simultaneous coexistence or their simultaneous self-destruction—that is, it can and even should be read as a demonstration of unity. Fed by the murders of civil rights leaders, by the burning of urban centers, by Vietnam, and by the more immediate and pressing social issues between blacks and Jews in New York City, Malamud reframes his vision to reflect the intervening two decades—but the vision itself remains largely the same. In this sense, I agree with Andrew Furman's recent assessment that the stakes are too high "for African and Jewish Americans to go their separate ways. African and Jewish-Americans . . . will always remain inextricably bound to one another in America, if for no other reason than historical accident" (146). The perception of commonality in fact fuels African and Jewish Americans' mutual appropriation of each other's voices, culminating in a shared (fantasy) murder ending. Passing is typically thought of as a method of concealment or hiding. In *The Tenants*, however, it is a tool of brutal revelation and violent discovery. As much as awe and delight colors "Angel Levine" and love permeates "Black Is My Favorite Color," *The Tenants* explores the production and loss created through mutual rage.

It is no simple task to summarize the plot of *The Tenants*—the plot is disjointed and confusing, deliberately so—but here I attempt to sketch it out briefly before moving on to examine its multiple endings. The novel opens quite simply: Harry Lesser, a forgotten secular Jewish novelist struggling to complete his third novel, which has taken almost a decade to write, lives in a squalid and virtually abandoned tenement building.

The building's landlord, Irving Levenspiel, an Old World Jew, is desperate to demolish and reconstruct the space into a row of shops with flats over them. Levenspiel effectively haunts the decaying building, begging Lesser to "hab rachmones" (have mercy) on him, to think of his "sick wife and knocked-up daughter, age sixteen" (Malamud, *The Tenants* 18). "Outside of your $72 monthly rent, which doesn't half pay for the oil I use on you, I have no income coming from here. So if you're really a man, Lesser, a reasonable being, how can you deny me my simple request?" (19). Lesser refuses in the name of art, determined, he says, to "write this novel exactly as I should" (21), an intent that includes not interrupting nine and a half years of labor by moving. For Lesser, physical dislocation is tantamount to intellectual dislocation; the idea of leaving the cocoon that has both nurtured his writing and witnessed his inability to bring it to fruition feeds the insistent possibility that the work will remain permanently undone. Lesser's physical stasis reflects an emotional inflexibility; while he worries that relocating may hinder his efforts to complete his novel, in fact it is his inability to be moved at all—emotionally (his cold response to Levenspiel is but one example) or physically—that prevents him from completing his work, a novel ironically titled *The Promised End*. The conclusion to this opening chapter marks the first fictional ending found within the novel.

Lesser discovers a black man pounding away at a typewriter in one of the abandoned apartments in his building. The man, who initially introduces himself as Willie Spearmint, an aspiring and as-yet-unpublished writer, changes his name toward the end of the novel to Bill Spearmint and then modifies it again to Bill Spear. In spite of these changes, the narrator persists in calling him Willie throughout. Using the apartment only during the daytime to write, Willie takes up Harry's offer to store his typewriter in his apartment, and the two strike up a tentative friendship that becomes increasingly subject to competition, suspicion, and jealousy. Willie invites Harry to a party, where Harry meets a black woman, Mary, whom he sleeps with, as well as Willie's Jewish girlfriend, Irene Bell, with whom Harry eventually begins an affair. Several months after Irene and Harry begin secretly seeing each other, Harry confronts Willie with the truth, revealing their plans to marry. Willie responds by burning Harry's book manuscript; Harry destroys Willie's typewriter. The two begin to keep close tabs on each other through discarded drafts and snooping, continually circling round each other through the decay of the old building. It is here that the second fictional ending takes place.

The two men finally face off, each with a weapon in hand, and strike mutually fatal blows. This is the third fictional ending. The final words of the novel, a plea for mercy initiated by Levenspiel in which the word "mercy" is repeated 115 times and concludes with no period or other punctuation, is both liturgical and song-like, a prayer and a statement, emphatic and dream-like.

The Tenants is a novel that concentrates on endings. The opening chapter concludes with the following statement centered just under its last line: "end of novel" (23). This is the first of three declared endings that take place within the novel and the most circumscribed of them all: Lesser, who "shuts his eyes and reads through the last pages of his ms.," dreams of Levenspiel starting a "tiny fire in a pile of wood shaving in the cellar" (23). The building burns while the author writes until the fire "with a convulsive roar flings open Lesser's door" (23). This ending, as with the other two fictional endings (they are as pronounced as this one), contributes to the distinctive narrative technique that Malamud employs throughout the novel, a point acknowledged by a number of critics regarding *The Tenants* and other stories by Malamud, in which realism abuts fantasy.

And it is here that I wish to make the first connection between the novel *The Tenants* and the trope of passing—at a moment when race has not asserted itself explicitly in the text: through the adoption of multiple endings, Malamud experiments with one of the primary conventions of text, namely, the idea that a story and its (singular) ending are tied together. Instead, Malamud presents us, as Alvin Kernan suggests, with a "conception of literature as a social institution," one that responds "in a dialectical manner to what takes place and is believed in that society" ("*Tenants*" 196). Malamud's experimentation with multiple endings in *The Tenants* reflects the social and moral upheaval of his environment, a sense that the understanding generated by traditional conceptions of art, form, and society is no longer sufficient, that the mirror separating art and society has cracked. Malamud's response is to say, effectively, that multiplying endings increases possibilities of understanding and interpretation, not only in the largest sense possible—in society and in art—but also in its most intimate form: ourselves. If the trope of passing has come to be understood as a means of self-invention—or selves-invention—the literary form that adopts multiple endings does much the same thing.

Moving us toward the second fictional ending, Lesser hears the typing of a writer making steady progress and searches the building to find him. And, indeed, setting up camp in one of the building's vacant apartments is Willie Spearmint, an aspiring black writer intent on authoring a personal narrative emblematic of the African American experience in the late 1960s, the time in which the novel is set. "Man . . . Can't you see me writing on my book?" Spearmint asks Lesser, annoyed at the disruption. Lesser then follows a moment later with his own self-identification—"I'm a writer myself"—before inviting Willie to come to him for any needs. Willie accepts Lesser's invitation and stores his enormously unwieldy typewriter, a symbol of the heavy lifting found in writing, in Lesser's apartment. The two enter into an uneasy relationship that is part rivalry, part apprenticeship—on both sides—discussing topics as wide-ranging as art, writing, music, the black experience, love, and sex. While initially Lesser claims the upper hand as a published novelist, Willie supersedes him in love. The competition between them is ratcheted up notch by notch: Willie's artistic talents develop, and Lesser feels threatened by them; Lesser seizes every opportunity to become closer to Willie's Jewish girlfriend, Irene Bell (née Belinsky). Before long, Lesser declares to Willie his intention to marry Irene. Willie retaliates by burning Lesser's manuscript; Lesser responds by smashing Willie's typewriter. The relationship between the two writer protagonists devolves, and they begin circling around each other menacingly, spying on each other, and rooting around in the trash trying to catch glimpses of discarded drafts.

In a dream-like state that echoes that found just before the first ending, Harry imagines a double marriage ceremony taking place in an African village. Officiating the ceremony is an old "black-eyed skinny chief" and a "nervous rabbi in grizzled beard and fedora" (207, 208–9). The chief marries Lesser to a pregnant Mary Kettlesmith, the black woman whom Harry has met through Willie and whom Harry rejects in favor of Irene, in a traditional tribal ceremony; the rabbi marries Willie and Irene in a traditional Jewish ceremony. Irene asks Lesser after the ceremonies have concluded, "How do you account for this, Harry?" Harry responds, "It's something I imagined, like an act of love, the end of my book, if I dared." "'You're not so smart,' says Irene . . . the end" (217). Unlike the first ending, which is a description of solitary destruction, this ending is populated by nearly every character in the novel and centers on production. There is the production that is the wedding itself, the production marked by Mary and Lesser's unborn child, and the production of dance and prayer that demarcates both foreignness and belonging. Looking at Lesser dressed in little more than a raffia skirt and ankle bands and holding a spear, Lesser's elderly, wheelchair-bound father remarks to his son, "You should be ashamed to dance like a shvartzer, without any clothes on. . . . It's my own fault because I didn't give you a Jewish education" (213). At Willie's marriage ceremony, Willie repeats the Hebrew words that legally bind him to Irene: "Hare at mekudeshet li betabaat zu, kedat moshe veyisrael." In keeping with the central image of the scene, with Lesser preparing to become the father of a black child while Willie is able to anticipate fathering a Jewish child, most critics read this ending as a redemptive fantasy that challenges the realism found elsewhere in the novel. Kernan notes that the ending comes at a moment when Harry recognizes his limitations and failings as a writer. But he "is still capable of dreaming of a promised end to both his life and his book in which he is married to a beautiful black girl by an African chief, while Willie is married to Irene Bell by a rabbi" ("*Tenants*" 205). Sheldon Hershinow focuses on the rabbi's proclamation as he marries Willie and Irene that "someday God will bring together Ishmael and Israel to live as one people" (*The Tenants* 216). That is the dream, Hershinow remarks; the reality "can not happen in Malamud's book any more than it can happen in Lesser's" (96). In a similar vein, John Alexander Allen and M. Rajagopalachari both note that the "miracle that will bring Ishmael and Israel together obviously hasn't happened in Malamud's book" and, indeed, reflects "the bitter reality of strained relations of the blacks and whites" (Allen 108; Rajagopalachari 166).

Even by critics who praise Malamud's experimentation with multiple endings in *The Tenants*, the endings themselves have been widely viewed as disconnected from the text as a whole. In part, this is a consequence of readers identifying the endings as fantasy and other parts of the novel as realism—and this is certainly one way of reading and understanding the novel. But, as is often the case with experimental fiction, the novel can and should be read and understood in more ways than one; indeed, I suggest that Malamud deliberately brings fantasy and realism closer and closer together as the novel progresses until it is not really possible to discern one from the other and in this yet different way again presents us with a model of rhetorical passing. In looking at the first ending, the phrase "shuts his eyes and reads" is itself quite clearly a gesture of fantasy or dreaming—Lesser reads not the text in front of him, his manuscript, but his own interiority and the prediction of his own failure or death as an author. The break indicated by the end of the chapter and the words "end of novel" are reinforced by the awakening of the senses with which the second chapter opens: "A wet dog with a bleeding eye hopped up six flights the next morning, and clawed and yelped at Lesser's door" (*The Tenants* 24). The fiery conflagration of the fantasy has been replaced—extinguished—by a wet dog needing attention, and with this creature, another story begins, one in which Willie and Lesser meet and do battle.

But here is perhaps the most important aspect of this first fantasy ending: it never completely ends. The fire that "surges its inevitable way upwards" anticipates the fire that Willie sets to burn Harry's manuscript: "Willie privately burns the vellum manuscript and its foolscap copy in a barrel in the outhouse, his eyes tearing from the thick smoke—some heartburn. The hot ashes stink of human flesh" (178). Critics for the most part read *The Tenants* as a text that moves between a binary of fantasy or realism, black or white. In fact, though, it never abandons one for the other, instead allowing and predicting their simultaneous coexistence. The most complicating aspect of this plurality involves the totalization of the reader's position: in terms of reading, *The Tenants* is a novel best understood in retrospect. That is, because of its focus on endings, it is only when readers reach *their* ending of the novel that we can begin to map out the scope and implications of the novel. This may sound obvious and a feature of all texts, but in fact the bucolic world of Wordsworth (Lesser mentions him early on in the first chapter) is at least in part bucolic because it *can* be read linearly and does not demand that the reader cope with the confusion of multiplying structures and tropes that Malamud employs in *The Tenants*. "The House of Fiction has been invaded by the world and has degenerated into a fearsome place of decay and terror" (Kernan, "*Tenants*" 197); and yet an elusive promise of some vague future, as offered in the second ending, still exists.

This idea of retrospective understanding, of reading both forward and backward, is perhaps the most salient feature of rhetorical passing present in the novel. In a novel that focuses so obsessively on endings, this demand on readers basically ensures that the novel has no end, that in fact it is the possibility of various endings that becomes the most vivid ending of all, encompassing—as it does—unity and fracture, art and violence, racism and love. All are part of an un-ending that is reflected in the world in which Malamud writes, one that he identifies with and is very much a part of. Instead of regarding passing as a choice between two modes of representation, Malamud's *The Tenants* moves beyond the most basic premise behind passing: that, whether regarded as performance or as being, passing is rooted in the physical body. In contrast, Malamud's experiment with "rhetorical passing" is an effort to document art and imagination as a process of racially informed exchange and acquisition between two protagonists, one Jewish and one black. Rhetorical passing is divorced from the human body; it holds at its heart a body of words, language, and textuality. If passing as we typically understand it urges us to reflect carefully on selfhood and identity, rhetorical passing demands that readers consider multiple modalities of form in the interpretive process.

Passing and rhetorical passing are not unknown to each other in *The Tenants*; they sometimes operate in the same arena. Willie Spearmint criticizes Harry Lesser's presentation of the "black sister" in his second novel: "She's not like anybody real I know, leastways nobody black. In some of the ways she does things she might be white under that black paint you laid down on her" (*The Tenants* 80). It is impossible not to think of Spearmint's words in connection with Ralph Ellison's *Invisible Man*, where the Optic White of the Liberty Paints plant, the purest white that can be found anywhere, both is composed of a milky brown substance and a black chemical and is a "white that is so white you can paint a chunka coal and you'd have to crack it open with a sledge hammer to prove it wasn't white clear through" (217). Lesser's paint job is significantly less sturdy and appears to melt away under the gaze of Willie Spearmint. And while Willie is critical of Harry's characterization of blackness, he is generous in his praise of the character's femininity: "I like her attitude. I wouldn't mind laying some pipe in her pants" (*The Tenants* 74). As an author, Lesser's constructions in gender are more convincing than those around race. This exchange goes to the heart of Malamud's understanding of race, not only because of what it reveals about Harry

Lesser's limitations with regard to passing in terms of voice and character but also because of what it reflects on these very qualities with regard to Malamud's ability as a Jewish author to effectively present through rhetoric and style a black author critiquing a Jewish author's poorly executed representation of blackness. The point that Malamud makes here is that the rhetorical passing that readers see (it is enunciated by Willie) and the rhetorical passing that readers fail to see (which would be Malamud, operating behind the scenes) depend on racial difference. And more broadly, it is these differences that are necessary to art.

Harry Lesser claims his own moment of critical advancement when Willie asks him to read and comment on his manuscript. Lesser is moved by it "for two reasons: the affecting subject of the work, and the final sad feeling that he has not yet mastered his craft" (66). What Lesser finds flawed about Willie's writing is its technique, its form, which he believes has to be built more carefully. The criticism turns, in Willie's mind, on race: "This is a *black* book we talkin about that you don't understand at all. White fiction ain't the same as *black*. It *can't* be" (74; emphasis in the original). Harry's patronizing response is to tell Willie that he "can't turn black experience into literature just by writing it down" (74). Willie angrily responds, "Art can kiss my juicy ass. You want to know what's really art? *I* am art. Willie Spearmint, *black man*. My form is *myself*" (68; emphasis in the original). Kernan notes that Spearmint's "writings directly reflect his own feelings, his self-disgust, his hatred for whites, his fears and furies; and their ends are as primal as their origins, self-expression, advancing the cause of black revolution, and a desire to make a lot of money and use it to enjoy a lot of sex" ("*Tenants*" 202). To this, I would add the deep sense of dependency toward whites and about whiteness that Willie Spearmint only implicitly acknowledges. Part of this dependency stems from a social hierarchy that privileges whiteness, as Baldwin so eloquently notes. But in order for Spearmint's art to have the impact he desires, he is also dependent, at least in part, on a white audience and a white readership, as his relationship to Harry Lesser depicts in micro form. While Lesser can publish weak illustrations of black character, presumably a reflection of his audience's like-minded limitations, Spearmint's art, in part because of its authenticity, is unable at this point to achieve the same reach and, indeed, deteriorates in form and concept by the end of the novel. Like Harry, Willie links rhetorical strategies to race, but he, the black author, rejects the premise of rhetorical passing. If Lesser's weakness is that he cannot convincingly write the character of a black woman, Spearmint makes clear that any perceived "weakness" in this direction is deliberate. Spearmint's statement "my form is myself" establishes blackness as a legitimate rhetorical position that does not need to be hidden, moderated, or constructed. Standing behind the alternating failures and successes of Lesser and Spearmint is Malamud himself, who, in an interview that took place shortly after the publication of *The Tenants*, noted, "If I'm not afraid to invent God in my fiction—or kinds of Jews I've never met—I don't see why I shouldn't invent Willie Spearmint" (Shenker). Authenticity and invention, the core (if at times contradictory) motivations behind racial and rhetorical passing, not only inform development of his fictional characters but are indeed the key to all artistic representation. That is, Malamud's work stresses the degree to which Jewish and black art depend on each other.

The second ending creates less of a conscious, realizable break between realism and fantasy within the text. Lesser gives up "poking around in the can in the snow" for discarded drafts of Willie's work. What "settle[s] in his mind" is a "double wedding" (*The Tenants* 206). The fantasy of the double wedding is not something that takes place with his eyes shut; it is a deliberate construction and evocation of racial stereotypes—and their inversion. The trappings of racial stereotype are plain to see: the garb, the dancing, the benedictions. It is Irene's final words, laden with skepticism and completely in character, that force the reader back into a finite world of realism. But, in a gesture that furthers the mirroring effect that only intensifies as the novel develops, Irene's final words resonate with the final fictional ending, one that is perhaps the most surreal of all. In short, the pronouncement of "The End" comes only after the reader has reentered a fictional world of realism in which fantasy becomes a means of understanding realism. Here is the multiplying effect that Malamud initiates with his first ending and continues to build, develop, and complicate as the novel progresses.

Approaching the third fictional ending, Harry and Willie track each other through the empty apartments and through scraps of revisions, their paranoia mounting, until one evening they stand before each other, not seeing but sensing the other. In an oddly twisted version of the wedding scene—single, not double—they exchange vows with each other in the form of epithets:

"Bloodsuckin Jew Niggerhater."
"Anti-Semitic Ape." (229)

Then they aim "at each other accurate blows. Lesser felt his jagged ax sink through bone and brain as the groaning black's razor-sharp saber, in a single boiling stabbing slash, cut the white's balls from the rest of him. . . . Each, thought the writer, feels the anguish of the other" (230). The simplest understanding of this scene is to read it, as many critics have, as something of a sellout, "an attempt by Malamud to resolve literary tensions by using a 'mirror trick'" (Hershinow 97). Alternatively, though, we can think of the brutality of this ending as rooted in its unifying effort to merge two into one. They murder each other but also, importantly, feel "the anguish of the other." The resolution carries with it a finality that, according to Baldwin, is necessarily bloody, as the novel's—and society's—binary structure is destroyed: it is (almost) The End. It is an ending that plays with binary structure, in form (fantasy and reality), in character (Lesser and Spearmint), and in race (black and white). While the novel has been built around duality, the brutality of this third fictional ending stems from its unifying effort to merge two into one—the violence and bloodiness found in unity.

This move, presented by both a separation and a bringing together, resonates with Malamud's use of the rhetorical device chiasmus—yet another instance of duality and one that consciously puts form into play—and plays with form. Coming from the Greek root meaning "crossing," chiasmus is a device in which clauses relate to each other through a reversal of structure: Lesser "lives to write, writes to live." In a rich piece on Malamud's use of chiasmus, Victoria Aarons notes that its usage reveals "Malamud's complex, deeply ironic moral sensibilities, the rhetorical complexities of his moral vision. And, like his complex and varied moral vision, the chiasmus offers, not simple equivalents, but intertwined, reflexive, and often self-contradictory inverse structures, shapes of perception that refractively define both character and action" ("Kind" 178). Chiasmus is a figure of repetition and reassertion, but it is also a declaration of opposition: its center is created through a crossing of direction and meaning, connection and disconnection. The final fictional ending is initiated by a verbal and visual chiasmus: "Willie's going up, Lesser, ready to spring if he is sprung at, on his way down" (The Tenants 223). It is an ending that enunciates difference just as it pronounces sameness. Most critics read the blows to brain and groin as an effort to eviscerate powers of thought and passion, as a "fantasy of violent confrontation between Jew and black" (Kellman, "*Tenants*" 466). Perhaps. But the violence the two enact—"they aimed at each other accurate blows"—is self-referential, a single suicide of a single man, as much as it is life affirming, uniting Lesser and Spearmint by taking them from two to one: what remains after their bloody encounter is one mind, one passion, one conception of art.

The Tenants, though, carries on for a bit longer after the words "the end" separate this third fictional ending from Malamud's ending, which comes in quick succession and is a single paragraph. "Hab rachmones," Levenspiel begs. "Mercy on me. Mercy mercy mercy mercy . . ." (*The Tenants* 230). The word is repeated 115 times. That sentence, and the novel, concludes without a period or any statement regarding an ending. The repetition of a single word is a complete abandonment of the duality on which the entire novel is based. And this is in keeping with the idea of violent unity that the final fictional ending offers: it is one word, spoken with one voice, one thought, one plea, one prayer, which emerges from a contested narrative set in a postapocalyptic, nearly inhuman environment. The repetition of a single word recalls Gertrude Stein's idea, made in "Portraits and Repetition," that there is no such thing as repetition; rather, repetitive motifs need to be understood as emphasis or insistence. Instead of diminishing meaning, repetition transforms it, inviting readers over and over again into the process of making meaning (Kirsch 67). These final words shift from the prayer of one man, Levenspiel, to the idea of prayer in Jewish liturgy, which is filled with pleas for *rachmanut* (mercy); these words echo with numerous Negro spirituals that plead, "O Lord, have mercy"; these words echo with the Buckinghams' 1967 hit "Mercy, Mercy, Mercy" and Marvin Gaye's 1971 hit "Mercy Mercy Me." This final reiterative word brings together the fractured foundation of the novel, accepts the many and varied identities that are invented, donned, or cast off, and suggests, at the very least, that a single path forward exists.

NOTES

1. One of the most well-known studies that illustrates this understanding of passing comes from Gunnar Myrdal's *An American Dilemma* (1944),

in which he defines passing as follows: "For all practical purposes, 'passing' means that a Negro becomes a white man, that is, moves from the lower to the higher caste. In the American caste order, this can be accomplished only by the deception of the white people with whom the passer comes to associate and by a conspiracy of silence on the part of other Negroes who might know about it" (683).

2. For a comprehensive history of the strike, see Podair,

Short Stories

CHAPTER 6

Midrash, Memory, and
"Miracles or Near-Miracles"

Bernard Malamud's All-Too-Human Project

VICTORIA AARONS

TRINITY UNIVERSITY

"Is this what a Jewish angel looks like?" He asked himself.
"This I am not convinced."
                    —Malamud, "Angel Levine"

When I write about Jews comes out stories, so I write about Jews.
                    —Malamud, "Man in the Drawer"

It always amazed Levin how past-drenched present time was.
                    —Malamud, *A New Life*

Bernard Malamud's desperate character Mendel, in the short story "Idiots First," demands from Ginzburg, the story's intractable incarnation of death, an accounting of the seemingly merciless motives of covenantal design. In the face of impending death, Mendel implores Ginzburg to reconsider "what kind of law is it" that would prevent him from fulfilling his obligations as a father before he dies. In doing so, Mendel insists on the fundamental imperative at the heart of all of Malamud's fiction: "what it means human" ("Idiots First" 44).[1] Malamud's despairing Mendel, a forlorn and frantic father, must, before he dies, *do for* his son: he must secure the means to dispatch the defenseless Isaac to his Uncle Leo in California and thus resist death's persistent entreaties, despite their inevitability, a little longer. He will do everything in his limited power to stave off the inevitable in order to perform small, if vital, acts of miracles. Like Mendel, the host of Malamud's muddled, bamboozled, forlorn, and disheartened characters find themselves—in story after story—poised at an aching, cataclysmic threshold. Like Mendel, "sitting at the edge of the bed" at the opening of "Idiots First," Malamud positions each of his small yet persistent characters at an instant of moral reckoning: their own or that of others ("Idiots First" 35). At such moments of exposure, Malamud's teetering characters insist existentially on their responsibilities as "human being" in a world that would pitilessly conspire against them ("Man in the Drawer" 215). As the silenced Soviet writer Feliks Levitansky, in Malamud's short story "Man in the Drawer" avows, the essential creed, the fundamental declaration of faith, is modest, if deceptively simple: "We are members of mankind. If I am drowning you must assist to save me" (222). Malamud's characters are, in other words, asked to be more than they are or more than their seeming limitations would prescribe them to be. Like Sholom Aleichem's *kleyne mentshelekh mit kleyne hasoges* (little people with little ideas), Malamud's *kleyne mentshelekh*, ordinary, stumbling Jews, given moments of reprieve, become transformed. They, with no little daring, show themselves to be extraordinary, capable, against all the odds—"what it means human."

Astonished and at times astonishing, Malamud's "little people" go up against the intransigence of the "cosmic, universal law, goddamn it," the one that would stand in the way of the basic Jewish ethic of *rachmones*, mercy, the compassionate embrace of others, which is shown to provide a momentary reprieve from suffering ("Idiots First" 44). In insisting on *rachmones*, on moments of clemency and affinity, Malamud's characters face their worst fears about themselves and others. Even Ginzburg, in "Idiots First," the anthropomorphized embodiment of "death," enacts the sensitivity to the suffering of others. "Who, me?" the astounded Ginzburg wonders, in an ordinary human way, seeing in the eyes of his antagonist, the anguished father, "the extent of his own awful wrath" ("Idiots First" 45). At such moments of moral clarity, Malamud's characters refuse to concede to an arbitrary, faceless, tyrannical law of indifference, a law designed providentially to "make happen what happens" ("Idiots First" 44). Rather, surprising even themselves—choosing to believe, as does the beleaguered tailor Manischevitz in the story "Angel Levine," far "beyond belief"—they rearrange, realign, and reassign this oppressive business of living, making accommodations for the impaired and imperiled (285). Characteristically, Malamud invests his fiction in the business of ordinary existential crisis, and all his characters find themselves mutually engaged in the vulnerability to seeming cosmic indifference. They are all in this project of being human, this transaction, together, "a dreadfully boring business unless you think you have a future" ("The German Refugee" 106). All the defeated grocers, crafty marriage brokers, cunning rabbis, enraged tailors, talking Jewbirds, and black, disincarnated angels that auspiciously people Malamud's fiction are offered the opportunity to make imperative and urgent their responsibilities as "human beings" in the midst of conditions spiraling out of their control. In their acknowledgment of shared suffering—"I suffer for you . . . you suffer for me," Morris Bober tells the small-time hood Frank Alpine, his unlikely compatriot in misery—they defy the deterministic conditions of their lives that would make compassion and responsibility inconsequential (*The Assistant* 150). In this way, Malamud's prescription for both the literary and human endeavor is a deeply moral enterprise. Art, Malamud maintained, "values life. Morality begins with an awareness of the sanctity of one's life, hence the lives of others" (Stern 61).

In drawing on both secular and scriptural conventions of Jewish storytelling, Malamud reconfigures the possibilities for *rachmones*, for compassion and for the suspension of isolated suffering, if only imagined for the moment of narrative intervention. "Imagination makes authority," the resilient Soviet writer Levitansky impresses on the reluctant traveler Howard Harvitz, in the short story "Man in the Drawer" (213). Like the unshakable Levitansky, motivated by the promise of reimagined worlds—"When I write about Jews comes out stories, so I write about Jews"—Malamud, in story after story, reconceives the possibilities for imaginative "authority" in the reinvention of the possibilities of choice and second chances (213). In invoking both the long-standing scriptural convention of midrash and the secular narrative conventions of late-nine-teenth, early-twentieth-century Yiddish storytelling, Malamud makes emphatic the imperative to acknowledge and to act on one's obligation to others—in the simple words of his paradigmatic protagonist Mendel, a most unlikely custodian of morality, "Be so kind, Mr. Ginzburg" ("Idiots First" 44). For it is the most vulnerable among us in whom Malamud is most interested, those for whom, as the menacing figure of death in "Idiots First" tells his forlorn petitioner, the train "just left—in one more minute" (43). But all it takes is "one more minute," a single moment in which Malamud's *kleyne mentshelekh* might reinvent themselves and alle-viate—if only momentarily—their immense suffering and the anguish of others. In Malamud's short fiction, these moments of midrashic per-formance arise when individual characters must project themselves, as agents of mercy and of the acknowledgment of otherness, into a world of impending loss. The midrashic moment, then, in Malamud's fiction, is a moment of choice and the extension of a narrative, both with the poten-tial to redefine a future. Malamud's *kleyne mentshelekh* are metonymies in his stories for his habitually midrashic, interpretive engagement with the intersection of the moral dilemmas posed by Hebrew scripture and the quotidian focus of his characters' untidy lives.

Thus, the seemingly inconsequential Mendel, in "Idiots First," seizes on the time he has left to rearrange "the cosmic universal law" that would render him helpless and would make meaningless—"a mockery"—the life bequeathed to him ("Idiots First" 44; "Angel Levine" 280). Mendel, like his fellow sufferer Manischevitz, in "Angel Levine," is a "man who never stopped hurting" ("Angel Levine" 285). The host of Malamud's characters suffer under the weight of both wayward circumstance and the "law": the impoverished tailor Manischevitz in "Angel Levine"; the former coffee salesman Rosen, existing uneasily somewhere in limbo, in "Take Pity"; the German refugee Oskar Gassner, suffering the immense loss of country, language, and family in "The German Refugee"; Yakov Bok, in the novel *The Fixer*, scapegoated and imprisoned for a crime he did not commit; the embittered Albert Gans, in "The Silver Crown," dying alone; the anguished grocer Morris Bober, in the novel *The Assistant*, who "made himself a victim" (278). Mendel, although ordinary, unexceptional, and vulnerable both to the vagaries of the external world and to his own limited capabilities, alters the unrelenting course of fate—his own and that of his son—just long enough to give meaning to the life of suffering he has unremittingly led. Like Manischevitz, whose life of suffering, "in sheer quantity of woe," has been crushing ("Angel Levine" 278), the bewildered Mendel's life has been one long performance of misery and failure: "All my life," Mendel laments, "what did I have? I was poor. I suffered from my health. When I worked I worked too hard. When I didn't work was worse. My wife died a young woman" ("Idiots First" 44). Left alone with an aging, vulnerable son who cannot care for himself, Mendel, like the interminably miserable Morris Bober, "felt every schmerz," every pain (*The Assistant* 5). Mendel, the embodiment of suffering, gives meaning to the extent of such suffering. He fulfills his obligations to his son, Isaac, and achieves what his unhappy cohort Morris Bober, who "with a little more courage" might "have been more than he was," could not (*The Assistant* 278).

At the opening of "Idiots First," the exhausted Mendel awakens "in fright" to the surety of death's approach (35). Conscious of the looming cessation of time—"the thick ticking of the tin clock stopped"—Mendel summons the fortitude necessary to don his "embittered clothing" and go in search of the money necessary to secure his son a future without the stewardship of his father (35). Mendel, recognizing that his time is up—"To tomorrow I said goodbye already. I am a dying man"—in his final hours, attempts to secure safe passage for his son (41). Isaac, "with small eyes and ears, thick hair graying the sides of his head," who, "like this all his life," lacks the mental capacity to care for himself, is vulnerable not only to his own mental deficiencies but to the indifference of both fate and the neglect of others (35, 38). But his father, who for thirty-nine years has "wait[ed] for him to grow up, but he don't," insists on compassion in the face of cold, unfeeling indifference (44). Mendel, recognizing that his own days are numbered, does not refuse his own destiny—"For what I got chicken won't cure it" (39). He accepts his own fate, but only after he has fulfilled his responsibilities as a father. He must put Isaac on a train to California, his last refuge, where "this poor boy" might be cared for by his aging Uncle Leo, who Mendel fantasizes opportunely lounging "under the sky in California . . . drinking tea with lemon" (44, 41). And despite the fact that Leo is eighty-one years old and Isaac's future uncertain, Mendel refuses to sacrifice his son to an unbending law of arbitrary design. As a modern midrash on the *akedah*, the binding of Isaac, Malamud's reconceptualization of ancient text shows Mendel, as Abraham, given another chance. He is unwilling to bend to the capriciousness of motives unknown and inconceivable to him. Rather, Mendel, a father asked to perform the impossible, refuses the call of certain destiny for higher obligations, demanding of the appointed, if peculiar, messenger of death, "For myself . . . I don't ask a thing. But what will happen to my boy?" (43).

Mendel, like Abraham before him, is summoned by the voice of authoritative intervention, a messenger of providence who comes for him with a writ of decree: "The law is the law" ("Idiots First" 44). Despite the haunting sense of inevitability, like all divine messengers, Malamud's herald of destiny appears unpredictably, an unforeseen and unanticipated courier: "That's how it goes" (44). Not entirely unlike his biblical predecessors—burning bushes, voices from the whirlwind—Malamud's herald is a most peculiar messenger from God: "a bulky, bearded man with hairy nostrils and a fishy smell" (43). Here Ginzburg, the incarnation of death's injunction, seeks out the lone wanderer. Mendel, like Abraham, is called to the task. In doing so, Malamud midrashically complicates the already impossible test summoned forth in the scriptural passage. In Genesis, God, suddenly and without seeming cause, calls on his servant Abraham, with whom he is mutually bound in the reciprocal strictures of the covenant: "Take your son, your favored one, Isaac, whom you love, and go to the land of Moriah, and offer him there as a burnt offering" (Gen. 22:2). The willing Abraham, as legend would have it, compliantly obeys God's injunction: "So early next morning, Abraham saddled his ass and took with him two of his servants and his son Isaac," the son he loves, to the place where he will arrange for the sacrifice, an offering to God (Gen. 22:3). The readiness with which Abraham complies with God's seemingly unreasonable and unprovoked request has been the source of much commentary. In some ways, it is the unquestioning "*so* early next morning" that, of all things troublesome in this brief but unsettling narrative, is most arresting: the readiness with which Abraham obeys God's command and moves events toward their unspeakable conclusion. In Malamud's revision of this difficult story, Abraham—prefiguring Mendel, the broken, fearful, and suffering Jew—is summoned by arbitrary and omniscient law.

While in Malamud's story, of course, it is not Isaac who is meant for death but rather Mendel, nonetheless it is indeed Isaac who will be sacrificed to an uncertain and threatened destiny without the stewardship of his father. But Mendel, made of surer stuff perhaps than Abraham, will not sacrifice his son. To die now is to fail in his obligation to his son's care. It is only after putting Isaac on the train to California, after, that is, seeing to Isaac's future, that Mendel substitutes himself at the sacrificial altar constructed by Malamud, at the train turnstile; he will be the sacrificial ram as he ascends the station steps in search of Ginzburg and his own death. Mendel, like Abraham, responds to the inevitability of divine command, to the inevitability of the covenant—"Here I am" (Gen. 22:1)—but for Mendel, such a declaration of self has been performatively transformed into a pronouncement of will and of challenge. Mendel's "Here I am" is implied by his going in search of Ginzburg after putting Isaac on the train, after, that is, he has interceded into the divine plan by preventing injustice and mercilessness to himself and his son. Mendel's version of the Abrahamic "Here I am" is a declaration of "I," of insistence and mercy, in the face of the cosmic, unfathomable law of no "favors" ("Idiots First" 43). In resisting a death-too-soon, before he can satisfy his obligation to his son, the persistent, defiant Mendel, breathless and depleted, will not yield, will not, unlike his biblical predecessor, surrender his son to blind, uncompromising law. Unlike Abraham, who as a demonstration of faithfulness to God had not "withheld [his] son, [his] favored one," Malamud's servant shows himself faithful instead to the human imperative, in Malamud's world a higher demand (Gen. 22:12).

In defiance of death's unacceptable edict, Mendel initially takes desperate steps to elude the shape-shifting figure of death. But despite Mendel's frantic escapades as he goes from place to place in search of money to buy Isaac's train ticket, always "after them noiselessly ran Ginzburg" (43). In running from death's inevitability, Mendel attempts to buy not only a train ticket for Isaac but also enough time to secure his son a future and give meaning to his own solitary life of suffering and abject fear. Mendel, like Abraham before him, summons his son—"Come, Isaac"— taking him not to be bound at the altar but instead to seek assistance and intercession from heartless fate (35). In imploring those from whom one might expect relief—the philanthropist Fishbein and the rabbi—Mendel, instead, comes up against coldhearted resistance. Mendel, sinking "to his creaking knees on the rug" of the rich Fishbein's palatial home, pleas for mercy: "If you will kindly give me thirty-five dollars, God will bless you" (39). Rebuked by the ultimately self-serving prevarications of the philanthropist—"Private contributions I don't make. . . . Take him to an institution"—Mendel and Isaac are cast out, cold and hungry, to further wandering, "buffeted by winds" that "blew mournfully" in the night sky (39–40). Arriving late at the home of the rabbi, the frantic Mendel—both pursued and in pursuit—finds once again the doors barred, this time by the rabbi's wife. Both the philanthropist and the rebbetzin show themselves to be callous and self-serving incarnations of the very figure of death pursuing Mendel. For help is found neither from the rich man, like Ginzburg, with "hairy nostrils," nor the rabbi's wife, whose mean "eyes glittered," both characters manifestations of the tyrannical figure of death and of the unwillingness to show compassion when most needed (38, 42). Unlike the callous philanthropist and the merciless rebbetzin, however, Mendel does not "turn away," does not avert his face from his son's naked and undeserved privation (42). And even the rabbi's meager and patently fraudulent apologies—"God will give you"—cannot make up for what is so blatantly missing, because, in Mendel's fruitless supplication, the weakness of a beneficent providence is exposed: "In the grave," Mendel retorts (42).

The biblical Abraham lived under the "protection" of the covenant. "Fear not," he is told, for, as the voice of the divine promises, "I am a shield to you; Your reward shall be very great" (Gen. 15:1). There is, of course, plenty to fear both in the stories set forth in Hebrew scripture and in Malamud's haunting narratives. The pronouncement of the deity is precisely the cultural mark of that fear. For Mendel, however, there are no such promises. For Mendel's world has been circumscribed to only this: a meager, narrow existence suffered with his only son, an imperfect man-child to whom Mendel devotes his life: "To me, for my boy, is everything," Mendel avows to the heartless Fishbein ("Idiots First" 39). To Mendel, it makes no difference that Isaac is flawed, functioning, as the unfeeling Ginzburg puts it, only "on one cylinder," a "halfwit," as the callous Fishbein declares, to Mendel's outrage (44, 39). To be sure, Mendel ultimately goes in search of Ginzburg, but only after he has provided for Isaac, protected his only son from the arbitrary hands of fate, preventing him, that is, from being symbolically a sacrifice. Mendel and Isaac's descendants may not be, as bequeathed to Abraham, "as numerous as the stars of heaven and the sands on the seashore" (Gen. 22:17). Nor, no doubt, will their "descendants seize the gates of their foes" (Gen. 22:17). Indeed, Malamud's Isaac may well be the end of the line. For him, no future is guaranteed. And in this way, Malamud's Jews are suspended, without a clear vision of a future, between immigrant European identity, with all the anxiety of marginalization implied by it, and a sense of a future, a next generational step. This suspension is manifest in Malamud's representation of the *akedah* in "Idiots First."

In recompense for Abraham's compliance, his willingness to unquestioningly sacrifice that which he loves most, he will be blessed, rewarded, as the voice of the angel, speaking on behalf of his divine benefactor, assures him, calling "to Abraham a second time from heaven": "Because you have done this and have not withheld your son, your favored one, I will bestow My blessing upon you" (Gen. 22:16). Here the angel stays the knife-wielding hand of Abraham and spares Isaac, but, we are to understand, because of Abraham's willingness to obey God and give up violently that which he loves most. However, in Malamud's narrative, it is the messenger, significantly, who antagonizes Mendel, rather than relieving him, and who must be resisted, defeated. Malamud's midrashic response to the unacceptable and preposterous demand of the *akedah* for the blood of one's own and for the future of a next generation rewards Mendel's obdurate and recalcitrant refusal to go along with a bargain not of his own making and unquestionably not in his or his son's favor. The outdone and momentarily flummoxed Ginzburg, whose "grip on the old man loosened," in an ironic reversal of the narrative of the *akedah*, yields to one singular man's petition for mercy. The issue of the "human" is foregrounded against the scriptural foregrounding of divine authority, and the existential moment of Mendel's resistance forms the center of Malamud's midrashic reading. Mendel's victory, small but courageous, is the typical Malamudian condition. Mendel's act of courage and his insistence on his own obligation is paradigmatic of the way so many of Malamud's characters give meaning to their shared, if lonely and impoverished, lives, the way they struggle to provide a momentary stay against suffering. For who can ask, finally, any more than that?

For Mendel and the host of Malamud's wandering supplicants, not unlike Abraham's unstable position in the wilderness, there is no time for hesitation, equivocation, or evasion. Whether, like Mendel, they are running from the persistent tentacles of death or dangling in limbo, as Rosen,

the former coffee salesman in "Take Pity," or walking "the streets in sorrow," as does Albert Gans in "The Silver Crown," or, like Manischevitz,
searching the honky-tonks of Harlem for the wayward, misplaced angel,
in "Angel Levine," all Malamud's forlorn, frantic characters must choose,
as does Manischevitz, finally and in exasperation—"Was ever man so
tried? Should he say he believed a half-drunk Negro was an angel?"—to
commit themselves to others ("The Silver Crown" 307; "Angel Levine"
288). In story after story, Malamud sets the stage for his characters to
demonstrate their responsibilities to others, to cast their lot with fellow
sufferers, a matter, more often than not, of "having, beyond belief, believed"
("Angel Levine" 285). Thus, Malamud's characters begin their journeys at
a precipice: Mendel, in "Idiots First," perched at the side of his bed on
what will surely be the onset of his final day on earth; Manischevitz, in
"Angel Levine," surprised by the black, Jewish angel who appears unbid-
den in his living room; Newman, in "The Letter," given the simple behest
to mail a letter from the inmate of a psychiatric ward, an envelope thrust
on him, on which there is no message, no address, and no stamp; Albert
Gans, given the opportunity to save his dying father by believing in the
mysterious healing powers of "the silver crown"; Martin Goldberg, the
perplexed, disconcerted translator for Oskar Gassner in "The German
Refugee"; Henry Freeman, beseeched by the enigmatic "lady of the lake"
to acknowledge his Jewish heritage; Fidelman, in "The Last Mohican,"
asked by the stranger Susskind, the Jewish refugee from Israel, "always
running," for the gift of a suit of clothes; Howard Harvitz, "passing tour-
ist," "marginal Jew," implored by the Soviet writer Feliks Levitansky, in
"Man in the Drawer," to smuggle prohibited manuscripts out of Russia;
and Morris Bober, made responsible for his most unlikely and unsolicited
clerk, the "Italianer," Frank Alpine, in the novel *The Assistant* ("Man in
the Drawer" 415, 195; "The Last Mohican" 202). Time after time, characters are asked to do what for them is seemingly impossible, beyond their
emotional, intellectual, or logistical capabilities, and, in the smallest of
ways, they rise to the moral challenge.

For Malamud's *kleyne mentshelekh*, the receipt of the strangely unexpected, though more often than not modest, behest—a suit of clothes, "a
piece of herring with a crust of bread," an inconsequential sum of money,
a job in a run-down grocery—is no less than an affirmation of faith in the
transformative potential of beneficent human intervention ("The Jewbird"

145). As the novelist Cynthia Ozick has argued, "For Malamud, trivia has no standing as trivial, everything counts, everything is at stake" ("Judging"). Such quotidian acts of compassionate reckoning and accountability are, for Malamud's characters, self-defining, startling moments of reinvention. Standing at an abyss of indecision and uncertainty, Malamud's "little people," frightened by the unknown but possibly retributive consequences of their actions—why, after all, should the future be any different from the past?—finally, if reluctantly, must declare themselves. As the chastened Manischevitz, pushed to the limits, concedes, "Believe, do not, yes, no, yes, no. . . . If you said it it was said. If you believed it you must say it. If you believed, you believed" ("Angel Levine" 289). And despite the rabbi Lifschitz's caution in the short story "The Silver Crown" that "for those who believe, there is no magic," and the angel Levine's insistence in the short story "Angel Levine" that he "cannot perform either miracles or near-miracles," such acts of compassion and faith are, indeed, small miracles ("The Silver Crown" 326; "Angel Levine" 281). For, to be sure, the challenge met by Malamud's frightened, cowed array of characters produces miraculous moments of wonder—"a dark figure borne aloft on a pair of strong black wings"; "a shining crown"; "violins and lit candles . . . in the sky"; "a shimmering, starry, blinding light"—astonishing moments of recognition in which, as Mendel discovers at the close of "Idiots First," the "crowd parted," a moment of empathetic intervention and reprieve ("Angel Levine" 289; "The Silver Crown" 319; "The Magic Barrel" 143; "Idiots First" 45).

For Malamud, human compassion is nothing less than a miracle and something of an act of protest against the essentializing forces of conventional religious morality. As Philip Roth has said of Malamud, "What it is to be human, and to be humane, is his deepest concern" ("Writing" 183). Thus, at the end of "Idiots First," the temporarily vanquished Ginzburg gives the decree "Let pass," and Mendel and his son, Isaac, enter the turnstile that will take them to the train that has been suspended in time long enough for Isaac to board (45). Isaac and his father will be given a "pass," leniency in response to Mendel's selfless petition for mercy. Just as the biblical Isaac is unshackled, liberated from capricious death, so, too, Malamud's Isaac is set free, given a future. But in Malamud's midrashic revision of the *akedah*, Isaac is not rewarded for his father's acquiescence and quiet surrender but, on the contrary, because of his father's determined will and courage and refusal to submit to conditions that fail to recognize the necessity of human compassion in the face of an otherwise unyielding and uninviting universe. Mendel cannot—will not—accept that "what will happen happens"; he cannot accept an indifferent or merciless, pitiless universe, an absolute law, without the possibility of redemption or intervention. He insists on reframing the god of wrath as a god of mercy. Thus, Malamud invokes the ancient *akedah* as an occasion to make emphatic the mutual engagement of "what it means human."

When Malamud's characters, anxious, fearful, and in flight, hesitate for an instant too long, when, in other words, they fail to act on behalf of the human enterprise of shared suffering and accountability, the consequences are thunderous and irreversible, if only in terms of daily life. The willful and largely self-serving failure to fulfill one's obligations, in Malamud's fictive universe, brings down a deafening wrath on them, as when Albert Gans, brought to admit his malevolent disaffection from his dying father, "in an explosion of silence . . . wearing a massive, spike-laden headache, rushed down the booming stairs" ("The Silver Crown" 328). His headlong retreat—his tumbling flight from the censuring rabbi and his reproachful daughter, but even far more so from his exposure as a failed, unloving son and human being—propels him once again out onto the lonely embittered streets of his misery, denied the embrace of community and kinship. Such characters find themselves, like Harry, in "My Son the Murderer," "who made himself into a lonely man," and Leo Finkle, in "The Magic Barrel," cast out, "unloved and loveless," feeling the "bitter but somehow not fully unexpected revelation" of their failures as "human being" ("My Son the Murderer" 92; "The Magic Barrel" 135; "Man in the Drawer" 215). The failure to enter the fray, that very messy business of consorting with others, of seeing their otherness, is, for Malamud, an inexcusable act of transgression. When his characters fail to see themselves in others and others in themselves—"Who, me?" asks the startled Ginzburg, "staring at himself in Mendel's eyes"—they are cast out to uneasy wandering, like Cain, without shelter, "to his anguish, loneliness," lonely and alone ("Idiots First" 45; "My Son the Murderer" 85).

Thus, such reiterative and impassioned petitions for empathy and accountability that we encounter over and again in Malamud's fiction—"Do you love [your father]?"; "What then is your responsibility?"; "My son, have mercy on me"—are points of departure, moments of exposure and reckoning ("The Silver Crown" 317; "Idiots First" 44; "My Son the Murderer" 91). And when his fearful, wavering characters do not meet the challenge, when they refuse to recognize their responsibilities to others, and ultimately to themselves, the consequences are disastrous, as with Henry Levin in "The Lady of the Lake," their wretchedness ensured. Levin, who renames himself Henry R. Freeman at the opening of the story, flees America for the romance and foreignness of Europe. Naively anticipating something of a self-reinvention, Levin, who "hoped for what he hadn't, what few got in the world and many dared not think of," now with a small inheritance "free" to remake himself, pursues a vague "expectancy. Of what, he wasn't sure" (222). Drawn to the Italian islands off the shore of Stresa, Freeman is cast back into a prelapsarian landscape that predates the very history he desperately tries to repudiate: "the vegetation lush, wilder, exotic birds flying around, . . . the place . . . bathed in mist, . . . the sense of awe and beauty, . . . orange and lemon trees, . . . magnolia, oleander. . . . Everywhere were flowers in great profusion, huge camellias, rhododendron, jasmine, roses in innumerable colors and varieties, all bathed in intoxicating floral fragrance, . . . luscious, . . . mellow sunlight" (223, 225, 232). The island has for him "a sad memory of unlived life" and thus the promise of possibility and transformation, "his own" (223). On Isola del Dongo, among the marble statuary, fountains, and gardens, Levin-Freeman encounters "his fate" in the form of the beautiful, desirable, and enigmatic Isabella, who asks him the one question to which he cannot abide: "Are you, perhaps, Jewish?" (226, 227). Because he believes his past to be "expendable," the fraudulent Levin-Freeman, unable to "tell the fake from the real," fails to recognize in Isabella the opportunity to be more than he is or, sadly, to admit to being himself, Henry Levin, Jew-in-flight (235, 233). And even when she gives him one more chance to admit to their shared, if still secreted, past, to come clean, he cannot bring himself to accept his faith, his identity, or his fate.

To "the soft, inevitable thunder: 'Are you a Jew?'" Levin-Freeman can only protest, "How many no's make never?" ("The Lady of the Lake" 240). Because of his fear, his refusal to admit his connection to history, to suffering, to his consanguineous relationship and obligation to others, he squanders his future. His blind refusal to see in this enigmatic woman of "opaque mystery" another suffering victim of Jewish history casts him out of paradise, an orphan of history, yet ironically mortgaged to the past he so desperately, cowardly, repudiates: "he felt time descend on him like an intricate trap" (232, 229). In reproach, she defiantly exposes her past, "tattooed on the soft and tender flesh a bluish line of distorted numbers. Buchenwald . . . when I was a little girl. . . . The Nazis did it" (240). While her body bears the stain of ruthless brutality and control, her face "holds the mark of history. . . . In her eyes [was] a hidden hunger, or memory thereof" (226). But such exposure, such striking recognition, comes to Levin-Freeman too late. For Levin-turned-Freeman, in an act of petulant renunciation of his name and heritage, "tired of the past— tired of the limitations it had imposed upon him," the consequences of abdicating his past and his obligations leave him bereft, clutching, at the story's close, not the woman of his dreams but "only moonlit stone" (221, 240). Henry Levin-Freeman, the assimilated American Jew, in denial of history and a legacy of suffering, is expelled, condemned, once again, to uneasy wandering. In this strange and disturbing story, Malamud has invoked a secular midrashic commentary on American-Jewish assimilation, on indifference to the Holocaust, and the emptiness and dangers that come from turning one's back on history and on those for whom the "past is meaningful" (240). As Isabella chastises Levin, now finally, irretrievably a "Freeman," "I treasure what I suffered for" (240). Malamud's midrashic lament on the willed absence of history, on unresponsiveness and a fear that would exempt one from the human endeavor, thus extends the memory of the Shoah and those who suffered. In Malamud's project, such abdication is an unconscionable act of cowardice, a refusal to participate in mutual suffering and mutual relief.

Routinely, Malamud invents scenarios in which his characters are asked to confront and put a stranglehold on their fear, as does the paradigmatic Mendel, who, in the face of that which most frightens him, "lunged at Ginzburg's throat and began to choke" the embodied shape of dread ("Idiots First" 44). Malamud consistently poses conditions in which his characters must reassess their worth and, in doing so, are offered the opportunity to mediate and thus temper their fear by acts of compassion, will, and courage. Such opportunities, for Malamud's characters, are occasions of arresting self-exposure. Unlike Mendel, who recognizes something unexpected in himself, Levin-Freeman succumbs to fear; he wears it like a hoped-for shield that does little to disguise his cowardice and self-loathing. Like Malamud's evasive and dissembling protagonist in the short story "In Retirement," Levin-Freeman, despite his hasty retreat and name change, "felt powerless to be other than he was" ("In Retirement" 168). Malamud's characters are frightened, anxious, deeply apprehensive, and uneasy petitioners. And they have reason to be so. The Malamudian prototype is both "a victim of circumstance" and that of constricted vision, misplaced chances (*The Assistant* 233). As with the defeated grocer Morris Bober, "What fate didn't do to him he had done to himself" (*The Assistant* 249). More often than not, for Malamud's exhausted protagonist, "The right thing was to make the right choice but he made the wrong. Even when it was right it was wrong" (249). Vulnerable to the vagaries of time, comportment, and chance, assailed by ill fortune, shattered hopes, and diminished prospects, "soured expectations, endless frustration, the years gone up in smoke," Malamud's ordinary and injured characters come to providence belatedly (29–30). "Something is missing in me," Frank Alpine admits, "in me or on account of me" (42).

But in between a litany of misery, missed opportunities, and impossible conditions, Malamud creates moments of promise, small but extraordinary occasions for the kind of moral reckoning that produces a momentary stay against suffering. "How much feeling have you got in your heart?" is the question not only asked by his characters but posed by Malamud of the writer and thus primarily of himself (Davis 97). As Bober instructs Alpine, his wayward assistant, "This means to do what is right, to be honest, to be good. This means to other people. Our life is hard enough. Why should we hurt somebody else?" (*The Assistant* 150). But stepping into the fray is risky business. "Was it worth taking a chance?" Howard Harvitz asks himself in the grip of indecision and uncertainty when asked to assist the dogged Russian writer ("Man in the Drawer" 219). And this is the question that all of Malamud's characters ask. In the face of impossible conditions, countless "years gone up in smoke," for Malamud's resolute characters, who serve as foils for those who, ultimately defeated and depleted, fail the test, fail, in other words, to show their faithfulness to higher principle, suffering is temporarily arrested (*The Assistant* 29–30). Thus, Mendel, with "a piercing anguished cry," protests the merciless conditions of fate and thus, rewarded, fulfills his obligations to his son ("Idiots First" 40). Such moments are small miracles of pardon and relief and wonder: "Isaac . . . at the edge of his seat, his face strained in the direction of his journey"; Fanny, wielding "a dust mop under the bed, and then upon the cobwebs on the wall" ("Idiots First" 45; "Angel Levine" 289). "I believe in miracles but who can make them?" one of Malamud's characters wonders, with deep misgivings ("Behold the Key" 243). But for Mendel, temporary victor in "Idiots First," the miracle here is not of divine intervention but human agency brought about by decency, generosity, and compassion—much harder gifts to bestow. "It's not easy to be moral," Cronin, another of Malamud's chagrined characters, admits to himself ("A Choice of Profession" 380). Thus, Malamud seems to ask, if human beings can accomplish such feats of the imagination, then why not God?

For Malamud, these midrashic moments, from both Hebrew scripture and Jewish history, are openings for instants of reckoning and insist on the interlocking of generations, the requirements and obligations to perpetuate and care for the future, all the while keeping alive the memory of the past, a history that, like the covenant, connects those who are linked by mutual comportment and inheritance. Thus, the final grappling between Mendel and Ginzburg in "Idiots First" starts as a wrestling match, like that of Jacob with the angel, a wrestling match not simply between the divine and the human but also between, more importantly, the human and the projection of the divine. Mendel is insistent on fulfilling his obligations to his son, and Ginzburg is equally insistent on upholding the law of absolutes, of no allowances. That Mendel prevails over this anthropomorphized figure of death suggests that the moment of moral struggle is irreducibly human for Malamud. This is Malamud's midrashic turn, his refocusing of the *akedah* on human-centered struggle. And so their grappling becomes ironically an embrace, a tableau of the "cosmic universal law" of human struggle and human need that would bend the strictures of the old law through a dialectical struggle for agency. The moment of awareness comes to Mendel when he recognizes the consequences of the extent of his failures and incapacities—"Now I die without helping Isaac" ("Idiots First" 45). Thus, steadfastly clinging to Ginzburg, Mendel insists on their mutual intercession, a joint project between the human and the law, both equally flawed, both equally empowered when joined, intertwined in embrace, in thrashing out the possible conditions of mercy (45). In acting in seeming defiance of the law, Mendel, enabled by his stunned, now-intimate coconspirator Ginzburg, secures the covenant. Their struggle and their resulting accidental embrace redefines but does not obliterate the law of inevitability and chance—in other words, "to make happen what happens"—but together they negotiate it (44). At the story's close, Mendel and Ginzburg, whom the old man has been eluding all along, become intertwined. They are in this together, like it or not: human will and cosmic law. It is, as the title of another story would have it, "the cost of living." Thus choreographed, Mendel, in an act of extreme courage, calls the law into question, exacting accountability: "You bastard," he demands of Ginzburg, "don't you understand what it means human?" (44).

Malamud's stories of thwarted promises, haunted relationships, desperate, agonized, and agonizing connections and antipathies—husbands and wives, parents and children, fathers and sons, humans and divine messengers—become, in Malamud's craft, parables of conscience, cautionary tales. The ordinary stories of Malamud's characters—stories of grocers, tailors, taxi drivers, marriage brokers—small people, smaller expectations, stand, in Malamud's fiction, for something morally larger than themselves. These delicate, finely tuned, economically precise narratives of skirmishes, misunderstandings, betrayals, and promises, in which Malamud's characters struggle to define themselves in relation to others, become, in both their simplicity and their complexity, metonymic reminders of the ethical imperative of human self-invention. Malamud writes, as the novelist Boris Fishman, puts it, "with an inimitable melancholy wryness, . . . the truest voice of Jewishness." Deceptively simple in scope and action—a father escorting his son to the train; a bird entering an open window, "flappity-flap with its frazzled black wings"; a barrel of names of the lovelorn; a falling-down grocery; a father and son standing at a gate; a tailor scanning the newspaper in his living room—Malamud's stories and the "little people" who warily inhabit them are extraordinary measures of courage and resolve ("The Jewbird" 144).

This life is complicated enough, as Malamud's characters know all too well, "in sheer quantity of woe, incomprehensible, . . . ridiculous, unjust, . . . an affront to God" and to humankind ("Angel Levine" 278). Why make all the more impossible that which is already impossible enough? Imperfectly armored against the confusions and indignities of life, Malamud's characters call on this most basic of imperatives, as voiced by Mendel, antagonist to the impassiveness and unresponsiveness of "cosmic" design: "With my whole heart I beg you this little favor" ("Idiots First" 43). Such importunity of "favor," small enough, can create a momentary hiatus, a small-enough parting in the narrative to allow for traces of miracles. As Malamud suggests in his introduction to the 1983 collection of his short stories, the endeavor "to create stories, despite serious inconveniences, is not a bad way to live our human loneliness" (xiii). "Literature," Malamud posits, "since it values man by describing him, tends toward morality in the same way that Robert Frost's poem is 'a momentary stay against confusion'" (xiii). Richly figured, Malamud's craft is governed by the overlay of simplicity and intricately hewn texture. In the face of the inconceivable, the irretrievable, and the incredible, Malamud's stories, like his characters, are small gems, magic barrels of mystery and chance.

NOTES

1. "Angel Levine," "Idiots First," "In Retirement," "The Jewbird," "My Son the Murderer," "The Last Mohican," "The Letter," "The Magic Barrel," "Take Pity," "The Cost of Living," "The German Refugee," and "The Silver Crown" are included in Malamud, *Stories*; "Man in the Drawer," "The Lady of the Lake," "Behold the Key," and "A Choice of Profession" are included in Malamud, *Complete*.

PART II

European Voices

Introduction

Encountering Bernard Malamud through an I-Thou Relationship

GUSTAVO SÁNCHEZ CANALES

All men are Jews except they don't know it.
—Malamud, in Field and Field, "An Interview with Bernard Malamud"

[Suffering] teaches us to want the right things.
—Malamud, *The Natural*

I

In order to open this introduction to part 2, "European Voices," of *Bernard Malamud: A Centennial Tribute*, I cannot think of a better name than that of Martin Buber to address Malamud's fiction here.

In *I and Thou* (1923), the Jewish Austrian philosopher talks about what he calls the "I-It"/"I-Thou" relationship. In the former, the relationship that the "I" establishes with the surrounding world is similar to the one the individual has with an object. The "I-It" turns into an "I-Thou" relationship when the encounter of the "I" with the other occurs through dialogue—hence his statement that "I require a You to become; becoming I, I say You. All actual life is encounter"[1] (*I and Thou* 62). It is also important to point out that unlike the "I-It" relationship, that of the "I-Thou" is subject-to-subject, and, as such, it is an act of choosing—and of having been chosen. For this reason, also unlike in the "I-It" relationship, the "I-Thou" encounter is direct and interpersonal, and because of this, it does not admit any intermediaries. In Paul Malamud's address to City College, included in this volume, the novelist's son says something about his father that sounds truly Buberian to me: "Dad always saw people as individuals." And he adds, "he had little serious interest in politics, took his centrist liberal opinions from his friends, and never ever had the slightest interest in systemic ideology or what came to be called political correctness."

This idea of the "I-Thou" relationship as a direct, interpersonal encounter is crucial to understanding one major theme in Buber: his approach to the issue of love—and that of love for the other. His explanation is timely and accurate:

> Jesus' feeling for the possessed man is different from his feeling for the beloved disciple; but the love is one. *Feelings one "has"; love occurs. Feelings dwell in man, but man dwells in his love. . . . Love is a cosmic force.* For those who stand in it and behold in it, men emerge from their entanglement in busy-ness; and the good and the evil, the clever and the foolish, the beautiful and the ugly, one after another become actual and a You for them; that is, liberated, emerging into a unique confrontation. *Exclusiveness comes into being miraculously again and again—and now one can act, help, educate, raise, redeem. Love is responsibility of an I for a You.* (*I and Thou* 66; emphasis added)

Buber's belief that "feelings one 'has'; love occurs. Feelings dwell in man, but man dwells in his love" makes me think of a part of Paul Malamud's poem "Mediterranean"—also included in our tribute to his father—which helps me confirm my reading of the novelist's works from a Buberian standpoint.

> We walked on the streets of those medieval towns
> sand in the rubber sandals, on our toes,
> bitten to death by olive-fat mosquitoes,
> laughing or shouting at the souvenirs,
> walking towards the hillside cafe, laughing,
> to eat a fish lunch in our relatively happy
> discomfort and quarreling. *See, that was it: feeling;*

he had the gift of feeling—making it real
like the man in the play by Camus,
he made a coffee cup real when he touched it (lines 37–46; emphasis
added)

Clearly, Bernard Malamud's "gift of feeling—making it real" (even if
it was "a coffee cup") and "love [as] responsibility of an I for a You" are
at the core of Morris Bober's philosophy of life "I suffer for you" (Malamud, *The Assistant* 150). Love as responsibility of a subject for another
subject implicitly entails a lot of suffering, suffering that, from a Malamudian perspective, leads to an eventual commitment with the other.
That other, in his or her turn, commits him- or herself with the suffering
"I." Undoubtedly, this is the great lesson that Frank Alpine finally learns
from the grocer. If we can apply the Buberian idea of love as responsibility of the I for the Thou, we can make Buber's statement "*one can act, help,
educate, raise, redeem*" extensible to the Morris-Frank relationship before
the grocer dies.[2]

II

When, in late 2013, Victoria Aarons and I discussed the idea of preparing
a tribute to Bernard Malamud, we were inadvertently coming up with
a book conceived of in a Buberian/Malamudian fashion. The reason is
easy to understand. Although the purpose of this volume is to interpret
Malamud's fiction from two different perspectives—U.S. and European
approaches—there have been direct, interpersonal encounters through
what I would call a *single-carriageway dialogue* without any intermediaries. I am convinced that all of us are aware that "I require a You to
become; becoming I, I say You" because, as explained earlier, ours has
been "an act of choosing—and of having been chosen."

One interesting way to read the chapters of *Bernard Malamud: A Centennial Tribute* is by establishing a kind of "I-Thou" relationship between
those scholars who address the same Malamud novels and/or short stories from different perspectives. To give just two examples, it is possible to
establish a dialogue, on the one hand, between Andrew Gordon's "The Jew
as Vampire in Bernard Malamud's *The Fixer*," Holli Levitsky's "'I Shit My
Death': From the Providential to the Excremental in Malamud's *The Fixer*,"
and Martín Urdiales Shaw's "Fixing Bernard Malamud's *The Fixer* through

Translation: From *El hombre de Kiev* (1967) to *El reparador* (2011)," and, on the other, between Victoria Aarons's "Midrash, Memory, and 'Miracles or Near-Miracles': Bernard Malamud's All-Too-Human Project," Emilio Cañadas Rodríguez's "Seeking the Man behind the Text, or a Biographical Approach to Bernard Malamud's Short Stories," and Félix Martín Gutiérrez's "Malamud's Short Fiction: Angels and Specters." (Interestingly, in the introduction to part 1, Victoria Aarons also proposes what I interpret as a Buberian reading of Malamud's fiction—for example, in the case of *The Tenants*, Jessica Lang's "Unbound and Un-bodied: Reading Race in Malamud's *The Tenants*" and Timothy Parrish's "Malamud's *The Tenants* and the Problem of Ralph Ellison's Second Novel"; and in the case of *The Fixer*, Holli Levitsky's "'I Shit My Death': From the Providential to the Excremental in Malamud's The Fixer" and Andrew Gordon's "The Jew as Vampire in Bernard Malamud's *The Fixer*.")

For the sake of clarity and ease of reading, part 2 has been divided into two sections arranged in chronological order. As in the case of part 1, the first section is devoted to the analysis of Malamud's novels; the second focuses on the study of his short stories.

The first section opens with Pilar Alonso's "Rethinking the Discourse of Suffering in Bernard Malamud's Fiction," in which the author proposes a conceptual approach to Bernard Malamud's discourse of suffering on the basis of the Theory of Conceptual Metaphor—Lakoff, Lakoff and Johnson, Lakoff and Turner, Turner, and Fauconnier and Turner. According to Alonso, suffering is central to understanding the global unifying dimension represented by the concept of Jewishness as a metaphor for life in Malamud's fiction.

In "'What's in a Name?': Aptronyms and Archetypes in Bernard Malamud's *The Assistant* and *The Fixer*," Gustavo Sánchez Canales starts from Franklin P. Adams's concept of "aptronym" (a name that fits some aspect of a character because it gives a physical description and/or a psychological profile of its bearer) and Carol Meyers's concept of "archetype" ("the characters in the creation story present the essential (archetypal) features of human life, not the first (prototypical) humans in a historical sense"; *Discovering* 80–81) in order to analyze the names of Frank Alpine, Morris Bober, Yakov Bok, and Raisl and Shmuel Rabinovitch from a religious perspective in an attempt to better understand their behavior.

Martín Urdiales Shaw's "Fixing Bernard Malamud's *The Fixer* through Translation: From *El hombre de Kiev* (1967) to *El reparador* (2011)" aims to discuss comparatively these texts against the sociopolitical and cultural backgrounds in which *The Fixer* has been brought to Spanish readerships at different periods of time. According to Urdiales Shaw, *The Fixer* poses very thought-provoking issues in relation to its translation and adaptation into Spanish, Spain being a country with a historical— albeit remote—legacy of Jewish culture and religion but also deep-seated Christian roots.

Rémi Astruc's "Dostoevsky, Lawrence, Malamud: Malamud's Heroes, Heirs of *Sons and Lovers*, Facing the Twin Rejection of Identity and Sensuality," which addresses *The Tenants* and *Dubin's Lives*, advocates the idea that Malamud's narratives follow a cardinal rule whereby the heroes discover their identity by discovering sensuality. Two figures—woman and the "double" (at once mentor, rival, and image of the hero)—emerge as privileged actors in the dramas of the slow discovery of love and self depicted in Malamud's novels. Astruc thinks that the quest for sensuality and the quest for self are at the heart of two novels key to understanding Malamud's oeuvre: Fyodor Dostoevsky's *The Double* and D. H. Lawrence's *Sons and Lovers*.

As for *God's Grace*, the last novel under study in this part, in spite of some negative comments it has received—for example, Harold Bloom's laconic reference to Malamud's 1982 novel as a "disaster"—Till Kinzel's "Writing on the Edge of Doom: Theological Reflections on Bernard Malamud's *God's Grace*" ponders the possibility that this narrative was not the "disaster" that Bloom, among other critics, thinks it is but Malamud's vision of a story about "the end." With the intention of addressing this theme, Kinzel explores some of the theological and philosophical implications of Malamud's rewriting of old stories, particularly biblical ones.

The second section opens with Emilio Cañadas Rodríguez's "Seeking the Man behind the Text or a Biographical Approach to Bernard Malamud's Short Stories." Although the approach to a writer's life through his or her works has been a major concern among scholars for a number of years, this has not been the case with Malamud's short stories. In order to address the interrelation between writing and life, Cañadas Rodríguez takes *Dubin's Lives* as a starting point and then focuses on the novelist's short stories "Armistice" and "The German Refugee."

By resorting to the question "Can Jews haunt people?" which opens Malamud's "Alma Redeemed," Félix Martín Gutiérrez offers in "Malamud's Short Fiction: Angels and Specters" a fresh approach to Malamud's short stories by showing that many of them—among others, "The Last Mohican," "The Lady of the Lake," "Angel Levine," "The German Refugee," *Pictures of Fidelman*, and "Alma Redeemed"—display a fictional mirage of depths and surfaces, an intertextual fictive body of "spectral" attraction. What is more, Martín Gutiérrez reads Malamud's short fiction as a process whereby textual traces rooted in Jewish cultural history weave a haunting narrative that helps to keep the past alive and illuminates the present.

In "Bernard Malamud's and John Updike's Art Stories: The Act of Creation in 'Still Life' and 'Leaves,'" which explores the issue of art in fiction, Aristi Trendel makes a comparative study between Updike's short story "Leaves" and Malamud's "Still Life." Theories of reception (Iser, Jauss, Holub) and of the act of creation (Freud, Koestler, Anzieu) serve as the theoretical basis for this chapter, which points to the idea of the act of creation as it is constructed by the artist and as it is construed by the reader/viewer.

In "Arthur Fidelman's Aesthetic Adventures and Malamud's Poetics of Creativity," Theodora Tsimpouki investigates the ways in which *ekphrasis*—that is, a literary description or commentary on a visual work of art—functions in *Pictures of Fidelman*. According to Tsimpouki, in this collection of short stories, ekphrastic narration is multifunctional: on the narrative level, Malamud's insertion of the visual element in a verbal text is used as a way to advance narrative and to articulate the protagonist's otherness. And on a metanarrative level, the novelist's engagement with art addresses issues of representation and originality while it reenacts the infinite dialogue between art and life.

III

In conclusion, I would like to retrieve Martin Buber's well-known "all actual life is encounter," which I used at the outset to this introduction to part 2. The reason is easy to understand: it is my abiding conviction that—in our case, greatly facilitated by Bernard Malamud's son, Paul—this is what Victoria Aarons, Pilar Alonso, Rémi Astruc, Emilio Cañadas Rodríguez, Leah Garrett, Andrew M. Gordon, Till Kinzel, Jessica Lang, Holli Levitsky, Félix Martín Gutiérrez, Timothy Parrish, Gustavo Sánchez Canales, Aristi Trendel, Theodora Tsimpouki, and Martín Urdiales Shaw have attempted to do. On behalf of our contributors and ourselves, Victoria and I do hope our goal has been successfully achieved.

NOTES

1. "Ich werde am Du; Ich werdend spreche ich Du. Alles wirkliche Leben ist Begegnung" (Buber, *Ich und Du* 18).

2. Shear (216), Abramson (*Bernard* 33–34), and Beer (80–81) have analyzed (a part of) Bernard Malamud's fiction from a Buberian standpoint. Apart from this, for a study of Bellow's *The Victim* (1947) and Chaim Potok's *The Chosen* (1967) in light of Buber's "I-It" and "I-Thou" relationships, see, respectively, Sánchez Canales, "Alienation" (183–184) and "Significance."

Novels

CHAPTER 7

Rethinking the Discourse of Suffering in Bernard Malamud's Fiction

PILAR ALONSO

UNIVERSIDAD DE SALAMANCA, SPAIN

This chapter proposes a conceptual approach to Bernard Malamud's discourse of suffering. It claims that suffering is central to understanding the overall unifying dimension represented by the concept of Jewishness as a metaphor for life in Malamud's fiction. Following the Theory of Conceptual Metaphor (Lakoff and Johnson, *Metaphors We Live By*; Lakoff, "Contemporary Theory of Metaphor"; Lakoff and Turner, *More than Cool Reason: A Field Guide to Poetic Metaphor*; Fauconnier and Turner, *The Way We Think* and "Rethinking Metaphor") and taking into account the historical background in which Malamud lived and wrote, connections are drawn between the values of suffering, which Malamud sees as a builder of happiness, and the allegorical function that he concedes to Jewishness in his narrative re-creations of human experience. The present study thus reconsiders and explores further the conclusions reached in a previous publication (Alonso, *Tres aspectos de la frontera interior*) on the role of Bernard Malamud's fiction within the context of what Ethan Goffman has called "The Golden Age of Jewish American Literature."

In 1987, I published a book on Jewish American fiction focusing especially on the figures of Saul Bellow, Bernard Malamud, and Philip

Roth, three leading writers of the moment who were united by their Jewish origins and differentiated by their literary response and position in relation to the double context, Jewish and American, that helped to shape their work. At that time, they shared the heritage of the destabilizing inner experience of the Second World War and the horror of the Holocaust as well as a convinced awareness of unconditionally belonging to the American social sphere of life and culture. Mainly as a consequence of the suffocating climate arising from the need to balance the notions of death, survival, and everyday life, the three writers were forced to develop their own codes and modes of writing and imagining, partially as an answer to the tensions between conflicting aspects of personal and general history that were for them essential components of their daily concerns. In that book, I concluded that Malamud's attempt to make sense of his environment oscillated between the double polarities of Jewishness and humanity, intermediated by his perception of suffering as a way to develop, express, and improve a person's temperament and selfhood. Equally important was his conception of love and art as productive means of reconstructing the individual and collective identity at a time of critical transition. The dramatic elements of the surrounding history interfered with Malamud's comprehensive observation of life and supported his gradually formed conviction that Jewishness could be converted through art into a metaphor that favored his and everyone's understanding of and reconciliation with the world. In this sense and in Malamud's postwar literature, the concepts of Jewishness and Americanness become compatible, complementary, and interchangeable, as well as mutually enriching and clarifying. For Malamud, there is no separation between this personal and literary double affiliation and its all-embracing projection. His words "I'm an American, I'm a Jew, and I write for all men," pronounced in an interview he gave to the *Paris Review* in 1975 on the very day he turned sixty, reveal the key principles of his writing (Stern 63).

Here I focus on the notion of suffering and the centrality it acquires in Bernard Malamud's fictional discourse. Although, given the chronological context, it seems legitimate to expect that suffering should be primarily related to the Jewish condition in Malamud's conception of life, the truth is that the healing effects that Malamud assigns to all kinds of painful experiences exceed the limits of his Jewishness to impregnate the totality of his narrative. In fact, suffering is already a decisive theme in his first novel, *The Natural*, which happens to be a non-Jewish novel and is instead devoted to baseball, the defining American sport. There, the enigmatic and ephemeral but crucial character Iris Lemon spells out what will result in the author's literary credo. She says, "Experience makes good people better. . . . Through their suffering. . . . We have two lives, . . . the life we learn with and the life we live with after that. Suffering is what brings us toward happiness" (*The Natural* 158). Lemon's words summarize and anticipate how, in Bernard Malamud's world, life and suffering are made to be completely intertwined and fused, so much so that the pursuit and achievement of a better self and a freer life are conceived as dependent on a person's capacity to accept and recognize the centrality of suffering.

CONCEPTUALIZING LIFE THROUGH THE DISCOURSE OF SUFFERING

As Malamud's fiction progresses and turns, at times, more and more Jewish, we learn that, in the author's ideology, suffering and humanity often become personified in the figure of the Jewish man. This is a straightforward thought partly rooted in Jewish tradition, which is openly acknowledged by the author and traceable through much of his literary production (*The Fixer*, "Rembrandt's Hat," "The Magic Barrel," and *The Assistant*, to cite but a few). As Robert Gibbs says, in Jewish tradition a singular man "represents the people—the singularity of the community" (227). For Malamud, the transposition from personal to communal is meant to embrace humanity. A good example of this thinking is provided by his well-known words "all men are Jews, except that they don't know it," reproduced by Samuel Irving Bellman in his article "Women, Children and Idiots First: The Transformation Psychology of Bernard Malamud" (127). Similarly, in his fiction, Leo Finkle, the afflicted protagonist of the short story "The Magic Barrel," included in the collection published under the same title in 1958, describes himself as "unloved and loveless" (143),[1] a tragic state of mind in Malamud's universe, and initiates his redemption by drawing "the consolation that he was a Jew and that a Jew suffered" (143). Such a conviction is in consonance with the views of the time. As Marcus Klein puts it in his chapter "Bernard Malamud: The Sadness of

Goodness," during the middle decades of twentieth-century America, there seemed to be the extended belief that Jews "are chosen to suffer" (267).

These assertions, which tended to mark the post-Holocaust Jewish American people as representatives of all Americans, on the one hand, and as symbols of suffering, on the other, emerge from the historical consequences, feelings, and realities of the period after the Second World War, which transformed the Jewish American writer into a spokesperson for a whole generation. In this respect and in reference to Malamud, Sheldon Norman Grebstein says,

> The Jewish movement responded to an urgent cultural need, in short, and this is now a truism, the Jewish writer was made the beneficiary of Hitler's death camps. We, Americans, spared the war's worst horrors, had to know about those piles of corpses, teeth, shoes, we saw in the newsreels. Whether out of guilt, morbid curiosity, or both the Jew became important to us. In the Western imagination the Jew had always played a special role as a wizard, magician, possessor of secret knowledge, but never before until Auschwitz and Buchenwald, had such moral authority been conferred upon him. From hatred, fear or ridiculed figure lurking on the fringes of culture, he was transformed into the Man Who Suffered, Everyman. (19)

There is no doubt that even the poorest and more disgraceful of Malamud's characters are conscious of this undesired protagonism. For example, in *The Fixer*, a novel based on the Beilis case, Yakov Bok says, drowning in misery, "we are all in history, that's sure, but some are more than others, Jews more than some" (314). His words are not an exception—much to the contrary. In Malamud's work, suffering is a defining trait, so much so that it becomes prototypical and representative of Jewishness and by extension of humanity. In this respect, Allen Guttmann in his book *The Jewish Writer in America* defines Malamud as "the most Jewish of American Jewish writers" (112). It is after all true that, despite the context and the shared desperation, not all postwar Jewish American writers convert the practice of suffering into a healing component of their characters' fictional lives and a means to achieve personal liberation, nor do they necessarily seek a coincidence between the Jewish man and Everyman.

In Bernard Malamud's literary creations, suffering embodies and enfolds the properties sought for in a human being and acts as a metaphorical builder of meaning. The author actually declares his taste for metaphor in the construction of his imaginary worlds. In the *Paris Review* interview and while talking about *The Natural*, his baseball novel mentioned earlier, he says, "I love metaphor. It provides two loaves where there seems to be one. Sometimes it throws in a load of fish." And a few sentences further on, he claims, "I am not talented as a conceptual thinker but I am in the uses of metaphor" (Stern 61). Although he does not seem to establish a connection between metaphorical writing and conceptual thinking, later research on both conceptualization and metaphor has come to show that "metaphor is not just a matter of language but of thought and reason" (Lakoff 208). This current of studies has also proved that together with other conceptual projections, metaphor lies at the basis of most human manifestations and actions and is key to the elaboration and invention of "both everyday meaning and exceptional human creativity" (Fauconnier and Turner, *Way* 6). On these grounds, I argue in this chapter that Malamud's love of and expertise in the use of metaphor give him the power and the tools to build and offer a new conceptualization of the existing universe. I also claim that this reconceptualization process entirely gives a purpose to his characters' fictional experience and to their sense of endurance. It is from this perspective that I (re)consider the complex role played by the notion of suffering in Malamud's work in the following section.

SUFFERING AS A BUILDER OF METAPHORICAL MEANING

In the article "Bernard Malamud: The Old Life and the New," Theodore Solotaroff affirms that "Malamud uses Jewishness as a type of metaphor for anyone's life, the one of the spirit, and for a code of personal morality and salvation that is more psychological than religious" (73). The all-comprising thought that, as Solotaroff states, underlies Malamud's fictional world involves an integrating conceptual projection based on a complex type of metaphor that conceives of Jewishness as humanity and of life in terms of personal salvation. This means, as George Lakoff and Mark Johnson explained in their seminal work *Metaphors We Live By*, that there is an experientially grounded conception of the author's (invented) reality that systematically affects the thoughts, the language, and the action that pervade his production.

Lakoff and Johnson claim "that most of our normal conceptual system is metaphorically structured; that is, most concepts are partially understood in terms of other concepts" (56). According to the authors, this implies that underneath much of our everyday understanding of life and the surrounding environment, there coexist millions of conceptual domain projections that allow us to extend, develop, clarify, and/or elaborate our perception of experience. Later research on the subject, especially that undertaken by Gilles Fauconnier and Mark Turner ("Rethinking Metaphor") has established that metaphorical systems of conceptualization are powerful enough to interact with other mental processes and are able to produce new emergent structures of thought, beliefs, events, and emotions through compression. The emergent structure is based on the blending of preexisting conceptual units or domains but differs from them insofar as their construction draws from the selection and combination of only those properties that, coming from the various interacting domains, are of relevance to the person or the collectivity. Furthermore, Fauconnier and Turner argue that the newly created conceptual structure may be stable or unstable, predictable or unconventional, contextually dependent and narrow scope or wide scope and universal. That is, the construction resulting from those mixed processes of the mind acquires autonomy and develops a new map of content and relations that can integrate aspects related to culture, social or individual history, and collective or subjective experience.

From this perspective, Malamud's literary compositions and the double relation he establishes between humanity and Jewishness, on the one hand, and life and suffering, on the other, may be seen as representations of the conceptual mappings generated by the confluence and clashing of contexts, cultures, personal idiosyncrasies, and historical events sculpted in his individual mind. For Lakoff and Johnson, "when two metaphors successfully satisfy two purposes, then overlaps in the purposes will correspond to overlaps in the metaphors" (97). This is the case for Malamud's reconfiguration of reality, whose double metaphor of men as Jews and life as suffering causes him to focus on a selection of overlapping personal and contextual traits that revolve around the metonymic part-whole relation that holds the two pairs of concepts together: Jews as a part of humanity, suffering as a part of life. Fauconnier and Turner contend that mental phenomena such as metaphor or metonymy are never separate: "[They] are consequences of the same basic human ability for double-scope blending. More specifically, these phenomena are all the product of integration networks under the same general principles and overarching goals. They are separable neither in theory nor in practice: the majority of cases involve more than one kind of integration. The resulting products can belong simultaneously to any (or none) of the surface types 'metaphors'" ("Rethinking" 54).

The extent to which this metaphorical thinking is a central element in Malamud's fiction is made manifest by the salience given in his writing to the Jew as representative of a human being who suffers and the equally constant reference to suffering as an essential part of life redemption. Thus, the Jewish person and his or her capacity to incorporate suffering into his or her vision and experience of life are foregrounded in Malamud's fiction; they become prototypical features with which to make sense of the surrounding world. One of his contributions to the scene is that the redeeming and self-liberating quality of suffering is sometimes achieved through the generosity of love and, at others, through the transcendent and central effect that he concedes to art. As will be seen shortly, there are numerous examples in his narrative that support this assertion.

UNFOLDING THE BLEND

In *The Assistant*, Malamud traces a circle and describes a path that unites Jewishness with life, and suffering with love and humanity. At one point in the novel, Morris Bober, the protagonist, says, "that's what [Jews] live for . . . to suffer" (81). At another point, he adds, "If you live you suffer, some people suffer more, but not because they want. But I think if a Jew don't suffer for the Law, he will suffer for nothing." Along the same lines, when his interlocutor, Frank, asks him, "what do you suffer for, Morris?" he answers, "I suffer for you. . . . I mean you suffer for me" (150). In "The Magic Barrel," the author emphasizes the grounds for this complex metaphor when he maximizes the role played by the love component in the blend he has created among Jewishness, life, and suffering. This becomes evident when the "unloved and loveless" (143) protagonist, Leo Finkle, a Yeshiva student and future rabbi, finds love in the face of the daughter of Saltzman, the matchmaker he has visited to procure himself a wife, and not because she is beautiful but because her look transmits suffering:

> Her face deeply moved him. Why, he could at first not say. It gave him the impression of youth—spring flowers, yet age—a sense of having been used to the bone, wasted; this came from the eyes, which where hauntingly familiar. . . . It was not, he affirmed, that she had an extraordinary beauty—no, though her face was attractive enough; it was that *something* about her moved him. . . . [She] had *lived*, or wanted to—more than just wanted, perhaps regretted how she had lived—had somehow deeply suffered. (145)

In *The Fixer*, the tragic loss of life by suffering that the protagonist, Yakov Bok, fears so much is only accepted if it serves to save others, in this case his dear Shmuel: "Live Shmuel . . . live. Let me die for you" (272). This is his reasoning: "If I die I die to fuck them and end my suffering." But the consequence seems devoid of purpose if it is devoid of love: "What do I get by dying, outside of release from pain? What have I earned if a single Jew dies because I did? Suffering I can gladly live without, I hate the taste of it, but if I must suffer let it be for something. Let it be for Shmuel" (273). In *The Fixer*, Malamud also integrates the consideration of freedom as an essential part of a human being's life and his or her sense of humanity, and once again he fuses it with Jewishness and suffering: "Where there is no fight for it there is no freedom" are Yakov Bok's words after killing the tsar in an allegorical dream (335). Like Spinoza, Bok declares himself "a freethinker" (99). And although he hardly understands the philosopher, he knows "that [Spinoza] was out to make a free man out of himself" (76) and stresses the need to "keep in mind that the purpose of freedom is to create it for others" (319). In William J. Handy's terms, "what [*The Fixer*] finally affirms is that the freedom to live is not merely the freedom to experience, but also ironically the freedom to struggle and even to suffer" (142).

Freedom through suffering is a key concept in Malamud's short story "Man in the Drawer." The narrative shares with his novel *The Tenants* that in both of them the foregrounded element of the life-as-suffering metaphor and its concomitant central axis for the human condition is the struggle among life, freedom, and literature. In both works, there are two kinds of self-imprisoned writers who share the anguish and hardships of *The Fixer* but this time through the subtle filter of art. Art is often present in Malamud's fiction in its visual or writing modalities (think, for example, of *Pictures of Fidelman*, "Rembrandt's Hat," or *Dubin's Lives*). He shows an inclination to explore and conceptualize human experience through the imaginative territories of the fine and the literary arts, and he does not disdain creativity in other genres such as architecture, crafts, biographies, magazine writing, criticism, or translation as a means to approach or evaluate life. "Art, in essence, celebrates life and gives us our measure" is Malamud's maxim in his sixtieth-birthday interview for the *Paris Review* (Stern 61); it is also the final statement engraved on his gravestone in beautiful, landscaped Mount Auburn Cemetery. In Malamud's fiction, art is the mirror image of life as freedom; it is valued as a way to achieve, affirm, perpetuate, or lose freedom, and more often than not, the hope for freedom is inherently joined to suffering.

In "Man in the Drawer," the issue at stake is inner freedom in a sociopolitical context lacking freedom. The narration develops around Levitansky, a persecuted and clandestine half-Jewish Russian writer who drives a cab for a living and cannot follow the official advice of burning his non-Soviet Jewish stories because, he says, "if I stop my writing I may as well be dead" (431). He asks his American alter ego, Howard Harvitz, a Jewish American freelance writer struggling with identity and life choices who visits Russia for a short vacation after the death of his wife with the purpose of getting closer to his true self, to smuggle his manuscripts out for him in a desperate attempt to have them published, and hence secure their survival, in the free world. The reason for the uncertainties and qualms that the petition raises in both characters builds around the damage that performing or not performing the act of freedom for the book would cause to "my interior liberty" ("Man in the Drawer" 429, 436; "my" referring to each of them, depending on who uses the words to express his worrisome thoughts of the moment). Thus, in this story, art preservation competes, alternates, and gradually fuses with life preservation, and the suffering that this blend causes transcends the particularities of the Jewish or non-Jewish condition of both men: "We are members of mankind," says Levitansky. "If I am drowning you must assist to save me" (435). The salvation of the manuscript is finally confronted and resolved in the name of "human freedom" (441), but the travel of freedom for the book triggers the moment of "trial and suffering" (442) for Levitansky. Harvitz is well aware of that when he too moves beyond his fears and accepts the share of suffering that is required of him to complete the mission.

LIFE'S DESTRUCTION IN A CONCEPTUAL CLASH

The same struggle around art, life, and freedom underlies *The Tenants*; but here the death fight involves two American writers: one is Jewish, the other black. The tragic confrontation they invent for themselves is personal and nonimposed, racial and ethnic, physical and self-defeating. Malamud links his writing about Jews and blacks to "experience and books" and claims nonexisting differences between the two communities at the time of his childhood: "I lived on the edge of a black neighbour-hood when I was a boy. I played with blacks in the Flatbush Boys Club. I had a friend Buster; we used to go to his house every so often." He acknowledges, however, that "what set off *The Tenants*" were "Jews and blacks, the period of the troubles in New York City; the teachers strike, the rise of black activism, the mix-up of cause and effect" (Stern 66). As Cynthia Ozick puts it, "the corrosion of relations" between blacks and Jews began "fundamentally out of the responsiveness of America itself: The Jews had been lucky in America, the blacks not. . . . America felt simultaneously as Jewish Eden and black inferno" ("Literary" [Field and Field] 83). It is in this frame of social conflict that Malamud's conceptual metaphor for Jewishness as humanity, life as art, and love as freedom is dissected to reveal other thoughts and other ways of doing.

In *The Tenants*, experience becomes a hellish experiment for the two American writers who remain voluntarily imprisoned together in two apartments of a ruinous New York building where they set themselves to write their books. Their concepts of life and art are as different and as identical as their historical and social selves. Harry Lesser, the Jewish man, is closer to Malamud's creative credo. For him, art is his life and his action: "I've got to get up to write, otherwise there's no peace in me" (*The Tenants* 3). He feels that he is part of tradition: he quotes Twain, Wordsworth, Coleridge, Shakespeare, Keats, and Dryden. His novel is about love (48); it is "called *The Promised End*, title and epigraph from *Lear*" (192). And he seeks "redemption in another book" (21) and "immortality"

(50). Willie Spearmint, the black writer, embodies his people's heritage and activism: he follows Richard Wright, Claude Brown, Malcolm X, and Eldridge Cleaver. For him, life is "true action" (166), "revolution is the real art," (178) and art is his individual experiential blackness: "I *am* art. Willie Spearmint, *black man*. My form is *myself*" (75; emphasis in original). His writing is at the service of his life, and what he seeks is "green power" (50).

The two writers also differ in the boundaries they set to the nature and scope of their art, which they both conceptualize as a metaphorical projection of themselves and their people. For Spearmint, "White fiction ain't the same as *black*. It *can't* be. . . . Black ain't white and never can be. . . . It ain't universal" (74; emphasis in original). Lesser, like Malamud, values the transcendence of writing: "If the experience is about being human and moves me then you've made it my experience. You created it for me. You can deny universality, Willie, but you can't abolish it" (75). As the story develops, the two writers undergo a deep transformation that fuses and separates them; they end up living each other's lives, loving and not committing to the same woman, obsessively trying to write their works. The kaleidoscopic construction of the story in *The Tenants* helps to unfold the complexity of Malamud's thinking project as it fragments and separates it into its minimal components: there is suffering, art, love, and freedom, but they are not conceived as a means to achieve a better life or to improve humanity. On the contrary, they pivot around the characters' selfish individual actions and serve only to provoke personal annihilation. For Spearmint, "being human is shit, it don't give you any privileges, it never gave us any." Submerged in the flow of the moment, he thinks that "the way to black freedom is against [the Jews]" (220). For Lesser, the inner conflict causes oscillations between writing and life as opposed to death and freedom: "One thing about writing a book you keep death in place; idea is to keep on writing" (198). But, on the other hand, reaching the book's end would have, he says, "freed it from me, freed me. Freedom favors love" (227).

The Tenants is a book of deep suffering, but it is not the fruitful universal suffering that Malamud pursues. In "Man in the Drawer," the transcendent nature of art gives suffering a purpose, just as love for the "dear other" as representative of humanity is the only morally acceptable reason for Bok to embrace suffering in *The Fixer*. The problem with *The Tenants* is that it contains two opposing conceptualizations of art and life that in the book appear as irreconcilable. If we follow Richard Wright, there is another metaphorical conceptualization representing the complexities of the American condition: "The Negro is America's Metaphor," he says (quoted in Hassan 74). And the black man speaks only for himself and his own, if we follow Willie Spearmint: "I write black because I am black and what I got to say means something different to black people than it does to whites" (*The Tenants* 82). The clash between the two conceptions of life and art alter the balance of Malamud's thinking system and breaks the overarching metaphor that expands through his work, thus annihilating all possible expectations of love and freedom to redeem the characters in this novel. Malamud creates alternate endings of union and hatred to resolve the unbearable tension between Lesser and Spearmint: a double mixed wedding, a U.S. pogrom, turning blacks into the Chosen People, the physical destruction of each other's work and selves. All endings are possible because the blending of the two men only causes confusion to humanity. As someone says at one point in the novel, "The whites are black. The blacks are the true white" (129). Writing unites the two characters, but their self-centered concepts of life, art, freedom, and suffering separate them and bring in hopelessness. The weight of Malamud's contemporary reality thus becomes evident in *The Tenants*, in which he shifts the story away from his imaginative construct to reveal the disquieting signs of the outer world.

THE SCOPE OF THE METAPHOR

In order to restore the metaphor, it is helpful to turn to other works in which the myriad of concepts that integrate Malamud's literary universe are spelled out. For example, in his short story "My Son the Murderer," there is a father obsessed with his son's despair while waiting to be drafted. The father's words, when he sees his lonely child standing on the beach on the verge of committing suicide, recover the author's conceptualization of life to its fullest extent: "All I can say to you is who says life is easy? Since when? It wasn't for me and it isn't for you. It's life, that's the way it is—what more can I say? But if a person don't want to live what can he do if he's dead? Nothing is nothing, it's better to live" (453). The same message is given in the title of his short story "Life Is Better than Death," in which a widowed man and woman oscillate between fidelity to their unfaithful dead spouses and to themselves. In "Suppose a Wedding," a story that represents a scene of a play, Feuer, a retired Jewish actor who suffers "for those who suffer . . . for all the injustice in this world" (303), tells his interlocutor, Leon Singer, "A writer writes tragedy so people don't forget that they are human" (303).

But the metaphor shows its power to capture the complexity of Malamud's mental design, when the reading of his works reveals that his conceptual order also functions in the opposite direction. For example, in *The Assistant*, the non-Jew Frank Alpine fuses human condition with Jewish suffering: "Suffering, he thought, is like a piece of goods. I bet the Jews could make a suit of clothes out of it. The other funny thing is that there are more of them around than anybody knows about" (231). And in *Dubin's Lives*, the protagonist's father advises his son not to marry "somebody that she will take you away from the Jewish people," and Dubin's answer is, "How can a man be a Jew if he isn't a man?" (69), thus reversing and completing the author's belief, quoted earlier, that "all men are Jews, except that they don't know it." Similarly, in *Pictures of Fidelman*, the protagonist, a failure as an artist, is advised at the end of the novel to "think of love" and to invent life if he cannot invent art (199). As Fauconnier and Turner state, metaphorical thinking is not necessarily a one-way projection of meaning from one experiential domain to another; it may also be part of a complex integrated construct that radiates meaning through its components in all possible directions, giving an unpredictable dimension to thought, reason, belief, action, and creativity.

When all the concepts discussed so far are put together, they produce an allegorical conceptualization of humanity, whose elaboration builds on the metonymic process of identification of the Jewish man with Everyman. This identification is the fruit of the historical postwar context and embodies the writer's personal approach to his surrounding reality. Ihab Hassan views in Malamud's and other writers' responses to the hardships of the moment the repairing and regenerating power of creativity and the imagination: "Despite the culture of the postwar era, curiously violent and hedonistic, angry and apathetic, the American writer makes a place for his imagination in it. If he cannot escape the deep bemusement of his country—it amounts to a crisis of confidence in the 'American Way of life'—neither can he deny the enormous vitality that still throbs about him. Part of this energy sustains his creations, experiments, rebellions" (3).

Within this context, the salience that Malamud concedes to Jewish-ness and suffering in his regeneration proposal allows him to occupy a place in the U.S. literary canon that, as Hassan states, "is his own" (38), for the unique combination of moral qualities and extreme life experiences found in some of his work is not shared by other Jewish writers belonging to Goffman's "Golden Age of Jewish American Literature"; neither may it be considered a defining feature of North Americans' collective identity of the moment or of their way of conceiving and living life.

It is therefore important to address what makes Malamud's uniqueness unique. Lakoff and Turner contend that "great poets, as master craftsmen, use basically the same tools [metaphor, metonymy] we use; what makes them different is their talent for using these tools, and their skill in using them" (xi). Lakoff and his collaborators, in their studies on conceptual metaphor, have worked on the classification and analysis of conceptual metaphors that are at the basis of many ordinary language instances. They have investigated the conceptual mappings that underlie common expressions of everyday English and have found multiple basic projections that serve Americans and in some cases most of the Western world to conceptualize life. Among the most common metaphors they have found and discussed for life are "Life is a journey," "A lifetime is a year," "A lifetime is a day," "Life is a game of chance," "Life is a precious possession," "Life is a business," "Life is a commodity," "Life is fluid in the body," "Life is light," "Life is fire," "Life is a play," "Life is war" (with time/death), "Life is a struggle," "Life is a burden," and "Life is bondage" (Lakoff; Lakoff and Turner).

Out of all these ways of conceptualizing life, the four cited at the end of the paragraph—"Life is war," "Life is a struggle," "Life is a burden," and "Life is bondage"—surely contain the concept of suffering among the possible components that can be projected onto other domains and/or foregrounded and converted into central elements of attention in the author's fictional construction. We could investigate them all, but for the sake of brevity, let us focus on the description that Lakoff and Turner give of the metaphorical mapping "Life is bondage": "Life can be conceived of in terms of bodily bondage. The soul of a person leading the life is metaphorically a bound prisoner. Being embodied is metaphorically the chain or other physical device that binds the soul. Thus life can be said to imprison the soul in the body, and the body can be said to be a dungeon trapping the soul. The event of death is metaphorically the event of being released from imprisonment, as when the chains break, or as when the prisoner is released from prison" (23).

In actual fact, this representation of the "Life as bondage" metaphor runs in a way that sounds very similar to some of Malamud's writings, with the exception that Malamud does not contemplate death as freedom from any type of personal or human imprisonment. As has been seen, in Malamud's fiction, prisons of all types (physical or mental) are recurrent. For example, in *The Fixer*, the prison is real: "the fixer was chained to the wall all day, and at night he lay on the bedplank, his legs locked in the stocks" (263). In *The Tenants*, Willie Spearmint is not afraid of physical prisons: "I am out of it as much as I am in it" (63). But both he and Lesser are trapped to the point of imaginative death in their individualities, in their aspirations, in their struggle to produce art. In *A New Life*, Seymour Levin's prison is mental: "His doubts were the bricks of a windowless prison he was in. . . . The prison was really himself, flawed edifice of failures, each locking up tight the one before (362).

In "My Son the Murderer," the protagonist is a prisoner of his own fear: "My dear son Harry, open up your door. My son the prisoner" (448). In *Dubin's Lives*, William Dubin, the Jewish biographer who is used to living life through his writing of the life of others, experiences the peak of his midlife crisis as an "entrapment": "He lived within six sheets of glass, shouting soundless pleas for freedom. He could feel himself cry out but was encased in glass to his head. . . . He could not escape the imprisoning consciousness, the fixed self nailed to its past" (317). For Lakoff and Turner, metaphorical bondage is personal and emotional, while for Malamud, it may be personal and emotional or social and historical, and even true imprisonment acquires a metaphorical function.

CONCLUDING REMARKS

Having reached this point, it can be stated that all the situations depicted herein are understandable literally or figuratively and can be recognized in general terms as common. But what makes Malamud's metaphorical world creative and extraordinary is the configuration of concepts and the distribution of forces around them. There is, first, the presumption underlying the expressions used that any individual burden is that of all Jews as men and representatives of humanity; second, the expectations of redemption through and not from suffering; third, the cause-consequence relation established between suffering and positive life constituents such as freedom and love and art; and fourth, the value given to mere living as opposed to death. A thorough reading of Malamud's works makes it evident that suffering as a way of life needs to be considered a recurrent and explicit feature in his characters who suffer for themselves or for their children or for those whom they love or for their artistic creations or for freedom. Those are their reasons for living, and they are expected to do whatever it takes at any cost; but if the elements in this emotional structure fail, there is still bare life to fight for.

The persistent occurrence of this metaphorical thinking in Malamud's literary discourse makes its semantic load global and central instead of local and peripheral; it raises his writing to the status of an elaborate allegorical proposal and points at a way of conceptualizing life, art, and humanity that is his own but is meant for all. As a result of this, in his fiction, there is a multiplicity of new extended and interrelated metaphors: writing is life / painting is life / action is life / suffering is life / freedom of the mind is life / freedom of art is life. They all build around the idea that life is better than death; their basis is shared, but the combination and weaving of them is exceptional. Thus, in Malamud, suffering is a fact of life; it is personal and individual, but the metaphorical scope of its effects is universal and transcendental.

NOTES

1. "The Magic Barrel," "Man in the Drawer," and "My Son the Murderer" are included in Malamud, *Complete*. "Life Is Better than Death" and "Suppose a Wedding" are included in Malamud, *Idiots* (1975).

CHAPTER 8

"What's in a Name?"

Aptronyms and Archetypes in
Bernard Malamud's *The Assistant* and *The Fixer*

GUSTAVO SÁNCHEZ CANALES

UNIVERSIDAD AUTÓNOMA DE MADRID, SPAIN

And you shall no longer be called Abram, but your name shall be Abraham,

for I make you the father of a multitude of nations.
—Gen. 17:5

Was he, then, named Jacob that he might supplant me these two times?
—Gen. 27:36

According to the *Encyclopedia Britannica*, an aptronym is "a name that fits some aspect of a character, as in Mr. Talkative and Mr. Worldly Wiseman in John Bunyan's *The Pilgrim's Progress*, or Mrs. Malaprop in Richard Brinsley Sheridan's play *The Rivals*." Coined by the American journalist Franklin P. Adams, an aptronym—a blending of the adjective *apt* and the Greek noun νόμος (law, rule) that became *name* in English—typically gives a physical description and/or a psychological profile of its bearer. Some real-life examples of aptronyms include: the professor of psychiatry Jules Angst, who was famous for his works on anxiety disorders; the American advocate of prosperity theology Creflo Dollar; and the literary critic and novelist Francine Prose. Although the term *aptronym* is relatively new, the concept is as old as time. Charles H. H. Scobie explains that "in biblical thought a person's *name* is always closely linked with a person's *nature* and thus is regarded as highly significant" (108). According to Carol Meyers, "a name in the biblical world was not simply a means of identification but rather signified the essence of a person, the anthroponymic (name-giving) process meant establishing the vitality of a new life" (*Households* 43). The following two examples illustrate this point: Abram, whose name in Hebrew means "high, exalted Father," was renamed Abraham—"the father of a multitude of nations" (Gen, 17:5)—after he was called by Yahweh to leave his native Ur, to travel to an undesignated land and become the founder of a new nation. Abraham was accompanied by his barren wife, Sarai—etymologically, the name means "princess" in Hebrew. Yahweh, who had chosen Sarai to "give rise to nations" (Gen. 17:16), changed her name to Sarah.

Without abandoning the Old Testament world, I would like to go a little further by drawing on Carol Meyers's interesting difference between the concepts of "archetype" and "prototype." When she addresses the significance of some key female figures like Eve and Sarah, among others, she explains that "the characters in the creation story present the *essential* (archetypal) features of human life, not the *first* (prototypical) humans in a historical sense" (*Discovering* 80–81). This is precisely the purpose of addressing in this chapter the archetypal, not the prototypical, behavior of Malamud's Frank Alpine and Morris Bober in *The Assistant* (1957) and Yakov Bok and Raisl and Shmuel Rabinovitch in *The Fixer* (1966).

In the fiction of Bernard Malamud, considered "perhaps the purest story teller since Leskov" (Bloom, introduction 1), archetypes and aptronyms play a significant role. To give in chronological order examples of Malamudian heroes who are not analyzed in this chapter, first is Roy—*roi* in French means "king"—Hobbs. This new "king" in *The Natural* (1952) leads a second-rate baseball team ironically called The Knights to the first position. In "The Lady of the Lake"—included in *The Magic Barrel* (1958)—Henry Levin changes his name to Henry Freeman and shaves off his beard in an attempt to escape, or efface, his Jewish background. In *A New Life* (1961), S. Levin—S. indicates its bearer's wish to hide a part of his past, and Levin means "east"—is an easterner who tries to leave a traumatic past behind and start afresh. In *The Tenants* (1971), a key to understanding both protagonists' state of mind is found in the meaning of their names: Willie Spearmint—both names bear strong Freudian connotations—and Harry Lesser, whose surname points to the protagonist's inner self-degeneration in the decaying tenement block where he has been unsuccessfully trying to finish his third novel. In *Dubin's Lives* (1979), the protagonist's name, William, alludes to his masculinity—often referred to as "Will-yam" by his young lover, Fanny Bick—and his surname, Dubin (read as "dubbing") probably refers to the fact that for years he has not lived an authentic, genuine life of his own but a life through the lives of countless writers, musicians, and artists. And last but not least, in *God's Grace* (1982), the name of the protagonist, Cohn Calvin—whose surname coincides with that of the founder of the doctrine of predestination called Calvinism after him—reveals Malamud's hero's attempt to escape what seems to be a predetermined world.

By departing from Adams's concept of aptronym and Meyers's definition of archetype, this chapter focuses on the analysis of the names of Frank Alpine, Morris Bober, Yakov Bok, and Raisl and Shmuel Rabinovitch from a religious perspective in order to better understand their behavior.

Earlier I pointed out that the names of Old Testament figures like Abram/Abraham and Sarai/Sarah provide a lot of information about their bearers. In this sense, Richard S. Hess explains that "in the Bible's beginning, in the story of creation, names provide literary analogies and connections" (31). While the name Adam means "man" and "human being," the term *adam* sounds almost exactly the same as *adamah*, which means "ground." Hess also says that "understanding the meaning of biblical names also enriches our understanding of the whole text" (37). This is precisely why this chapter focuses on the interrelation between aptronyms and archetypes in Malamud's *The Assistant* and *The Fixer*.

When addressing the issue of Malamud's universality, Walter Shear explains that "often he seems to play with his role as 'artist' by deliberately blurring the distinction between the archetype, which has universal significance, and the literary cliché, a mode which has exhausted its significance" (208). Although Malamud seems to heavily draw on archetypal figures on which he models many of his heroes, he reshapes them with the intention of adapting them to his own artistic needs. This is the case with the characters in *The Assistant* and *The Fixer* analyzed here.

The Assistant—"originally called *The Apprentice*"—is the story of the Bober family (Davis 114). Loosely modeled on Malamud's Russian-immigrant parents, Morris and his wife, Ida, have almost given up their illusions for themselves, but they still expect their daughter, Helen, to have a better future thanks to a college education: "The store had been the prison from which Malamud had wanted to escape via his education; but now, in his very writing, he went back into it" (*The Assistant* 3–29, 115). Nat Pearl, a law-college undergraduate, is a shallow man who, as his surname indicates, epitomizes external beauty and an apparently promising future for Helen. Obsessed with the idea of improving his social class by prospering in line with materialist America, Pearl is antithetical to what Morris's family represents. Edward A. Abramson appropriately talks about the "law" to refer to people like Pearl and the "Law" to refer to people like Morris Bober (*Bernard* 26–27). To be sure, in *The Assistant*, there is a conflict between an old world of ancient wisdom (the Bobers') and a new, practical, materialist world (the Pearls'). Victoria Aarons addresses the significance of the concept of chiasmus in Malamud's fiction. According to her, chiasmus is "a figure of opposites, antitheses, because of the intrinsic reversal that defines the patterning of those phrases" ("Kind" 175).

Due to the similarity of the name of Morris Bober with that of Martin Buber, Malamud's hero has been compared with the Jewish philosopher (Shear 216; Abramson, *Bernard* 33–34; among others). Unwilling to diminish the importance of the parallel between Bober and Buber, I would rather focus on the similarity between Morris Bober and Job; the echo in the name of the suffering man par excellence and that of Bober might at first seem to be a bit distant, but it is clear to me. As the narrator explains, it seems that Morris's fate is written in his very name: "He was Morris Bober and could be nobody more fortunate. With that name you had no sure sense of property, as if it were in your blood and history not to possess, or if by some miracle to own something, to do so on the verge of loss" (*The Assistant* 18). Like Job, Morris has experienced many setbacks: first, when Karp, the owner of a drinks shop, confesses he fears a robbery, Morris is robbed (Job is dispossessed of part of his property—his livestock—as explained in Job 1:13–17); second, when Morris wants his store to be burned to receive the insurance indemnification (Job's house is pulled down in Job 1:19), Karp's business sets on fire. A *macher* proposes to burn Morris's house in a way that echoes Job's burning house. The *macher* wants to charge Morris $500, and Morris, in return, could receive up to $2,000 from his insurance company. The old man eventually refuses to carry on with this plan (*The Assistant* 254–56). Somehow, old Bober has been tested like Job.

Third, like Job, Morris has not offended God to deserve such disproportionate punishment. Like his biblical counterpart, Bober is resilient enough to suffer without giving up. He tells Frank Alpine, "I suffer for you" (150) and "The world suffers. *He* felt every schmerz" (5). Abramson refers to Morris Bober as "Frank's Job-like teacher and guide" (*Bernard* 33). Finally, as in the case of Job, Morris never loses his faith. He talks about the Jewish law as the Torah, although the basic principles he has chosen to live accordingly with are universal. It is in this sense, I believe, that Malamud's well-known comment that "all men are Jews except they don't know it" should be interpreted (Field and Field, introduction 11). Malamud considers that suffering, inherent to the human being, triggers self-knowledge.

A man like Morris is ready to suffer. Suffering, in Malamud's world, leads to commitment, and commitment is only possible if human beings love their neighbors. This step eventually enables Frank to conclude his learning process, his Alpine-like "ascension." Halfway through the novel, Helen sees Ida cry, and when she asks her mother why she is crying, Ida, echoing Morris's words, answers, "I cry for the world. I cry for my life that it went away wasted. I cry for you" (*The Assistant* 176).[1]

Ida's lamentation makes me think of one major difference between Bober and Job. Unlike Job, who sees his fortune amply reversed before his death, Morris pathetically dies shoveling snow off his store without seeing any of his dreams come true. Although Morris is a central character, Frank Alpine, the person who helps him and his family, is the real protagonist. Brought up in an orphanage where he heard about St. Francis of Assisi and developed a taste for the stories of his goodness, Frank owes his name to the Catholic saint. (Curiously, Frank spent a great deal of his childhood in San Francisco.) When asked by Sam Pearl what makes the monk so special, Frank answers that "he gave everything away that he owned, every cent, all his clothes off his back. He enjoyed to be poor. He said poverty was a queen and he loved her like she was a beautiful woman"

(34). This is the great lesson Frank learns in Morris's grocery. On the one hand, he stops being selfish and self-centered and focuses on assisting the Bobers; on the other, he loves a poor woman like Helen to the extent of eventually converting to Judaism. Frank's Assisian self-denial then starts when he lends a hand for free, makes Morris's business prosper, and after Bober's death, takes up the old man's store.

St. Francis of Assisi (1181/82–1226), founder of the Franciscan order, devoted all his life to living among his fellow men in fraternal charity. The saint renounced material goods and family ties to lead a life of poverty. His love of poverty is certainly a key characteristic of his spirit. Following the saint's footsteps, Frank has given up material things and looks for a more spiritual life. Daniel Walden refers to Frank Alpine as "a Franciscan in spirit" (169). Another important aspect of St. Francis's approach to life that connects him with Frank is that the monk considers nature as the mirror of God. He calls all creatures his brothers and sisters, and in his famous *Canticle of the Creatures* (1225), he uses terms like "Brother Sun," "Sister Moon," and even "Sister Death." This sense of brotherhood embraces all his fellow men as if all of them were equal. There are two well-known scenes in *The Assistant* that clearly echo St. Francis's love for creatures. The first one takes place early in the narrative. Frank is in Morris's grocery, and "his eye was caught by a picture in color of a monk. . . . He stared at the picture for five minutes" (33). The description of the picture Frank is looking at happens to be of St. Francis of Assisi: "The picture was of a thin-faced, dark-bearded monk in a coarse brown garment, standing barefooted on a sunny country road. His skinny, hairy arms were raised to a flock of birds that dipped over his head" (33). The other scene takes place later on. Helen has been looking for Frank Alpine, and she recognizes him in a park. Surrounded by birds, one inevitably thinks about his namesake: "Here people sat on benches during the day and tossed peanuts or pieces of bread to the noisy pigeons that haunted the place. Coming up the block, Helen saw a man squatting by one of the benches, feeding the birds" (142). At this stage of *The Assistant*, Frank has already started his inner transformation, and like the Catholic monk, he wants to slough off his old life and, in this way, to be able to see things from a different perspective. (A number of Malamudian characters—Roy Hobbs, Seymour Levin,

Yakov Bok, just to mention three—also want to change their old lives and start afresh in the hope of leading better lives.)[2]

For this transformation to be genuine, Frank, as in the saint's case, must get rid of his passions. In this sense, however, Frank cannot emulate his namesake, at least for a great deal of the time he spends with the Bobers. Unlike the saint, Frank has too many weaknesses of the flesh. He is a too earthly man who feels strongly attracted to Helen.[3] After unsuccessfully attempting economic progress at the expense of Morris, Frank's first attempt to ascend is probably when he climbs an elevator shaft to spy on Helen because he wants to see her naked. His second attempt, at a religious level, is when he becomes a Jew through circumcision. Frank's suffering in the grocery store may be interpreted "as a monastic training ground" (Abramson, "Zen" 72).

One day while Frank is reading about St. Francis in the library, he tells Helen that the monk "wakes up one winter night, asking himself did he do the right thing to be a monk. My God, he thought, supposing I met some nice young girl and got married to her and by now I had a wife and a family?" (*The Assistant* 114). This is most self-referential for Frank as, at this stage of the narrative, the assistant has seriously begun to try to establish a more "stable" relationship with Helen. Unlike the monk, who never got married and therefore never had a traditional family, Frank probably will.

Morris's grave-like store—defined as "a temporary haven-Canaan" (Sheres 73), as "Frank's monastery, and his tiny Spartan room, a cell" (Abramson, *Bernard* 31), and "as a Christian monastic cell" (Abramson, "Zen" 78), among others—eventually enables Frank's rebirth. Early in the narrative, Morris asks Frank about his nationality, and the assistant answers, "Italian. I am of Italian extraction. My name is Frank Alpine— Alpino is Italian" (*The Assistant* 40). As explained shortly, "Alpine" probably points to his gradual ascension, which culminates in his conversion to Judaism—his circumcision.

Prior to Frank's conversion, he slips and falls into the grocer's grave at Morris's funeral. His literal and metaphorical ascension starts at this point. Apart from the fact that "his descent into Bober's grave marks Frank's death as an uncommitted wanderer and his rebirth as Bober's spiritual son—one who lives by the Law," his surname "Alpine" perhaps symbolizes his attempt to climb up Mt. Sinai to fulfill the Covenant of the Mountain (Hays 219–20). As William Freedman points out, "Morris is the English equivalent for Moses, and the name Alpine may be intended to suggest that Frank too must climb a mountain to make his Covenant" (162).

Frank's ascension leads him to adopt a Morris-like attitude toward life—metaphorically he reaches the top of the mountain. In this way, Frank achieves something that the other characters fail to do: a certain reconciliation—a balance, rather—between both worlds. This balance has been achieved through suffering—physical, in Frank's case—which, in Malamud, typically involves improvement and redemption: "He had been one thing, low, dirty, but because of something in himself—something [Helen] couldn't define, a memory perhaps, an ideal he might have forgotten and then remembered—he had changed into somebody else, no longer what he had been. She should have recognized it before" (*The Assistant* 294).

Frank's inability to "open her eyes to his true self" (111) and Helen's own inability to see through Frank are eventually overcome. Once again, suffering is a great "instructor": "The pain enraged and inspired him. After Passover he became a Jew" (297). In this way, Helen's insult ("Dog—uncircumcised dog!" uttered after Frank's attempt to make love to her in the park) is forgotten (203). A renewed Frank has finally emerged. His sacrifice for the Bobers and all the suffering this entails leads to a moral, spiritual revelation of his true self. According to Abramson, Malamud chooses someone like St. Francis of Assisi for a person like Frank, who is also a Catholic, because "St. Francis, a paradigm of poverty and suffering for the sake of the soul, is his hero" (*Bernard* 36). Significantly, the stories Frank heard about the Catholic monk in the orphanage have been of great help to him in his final conversion to Judaism.

As typically happens in the Malamudian fictional world, the character's *hamartia* consists in trying to break up with—and hide—his past. In *The Fixer*, Yakov's *hamartia* starts when he drops his prayer bag in the Dnieper: "His bag of prayer things fell with a plop into the Dnieper and sank like lead" (*The Fixer* 28). He decides to abandon his faith, leave the *shtetl*, and travel to prerevolutionary Kiev.[4] His abandonment of Judaism entails his rebellion against God, whom he sees as a tyrannical being that turns a deaf ear to the suffering individual.

Yakov begins to live and work in an area forbidden to Jews. As happens with some Malamudian heroes—Roy Hobbs, Frank Alpine, and Seymour Levin immediately come to mind—Yakov Shepsovitch Bok fails to hide his identity. When Yakov, after saving the life of a retired anti-Semite called Nikolai Maximovitch Lebedev, introduces himself to the man and his daughter, Zina—her name is "Nazi" if read from right to left as in Hebrew—he says that his name is "Yakov Ivanovitch Dologushev." Later, when he is arrested and accused of the murder of a Christian boy following a presumably Jewish ritual, he is asked his name, and in order to pass for a Russian gentile, he lies and says that his full name is Yakov Ivanovitch Dologushev, whose initials are "Y.I.D." This is not accidental, and it becomes a leitmotif during his two-and-a-half-year stay in prison. Some prisoners start to address him as "Zhid, Zhid" and as a "mother fucking zhid" (*The Fixer* 72, 107). His surname—made up of the Latin *dolo*, which not only means "deceit" but also "pain," and *gushev*, meaning "abundance" in English—points to the fixer's ordeal throughout the story. Yakov's "self-incriminating" "Y.I.D." reveals his true background. When the narrator says that "we're all in history, that's sure, but some are more than others, Jews more than some," Yakov is presented as a dramatically predetermined man (314). (Malamud elaborates on this issue in *God's Grace*. As pointed out earlier, the very name of the protagonist, Calvin, alludes to the founder of the doctrine of predestination.)

Yakov has a redemptive role to play. He is the embodiment of the suffering Jew—the scapegoat, the sacrificial victim. "His first name, Yakov (Hebrew for Jacob), links him with the archetypical Jew of the Hebrew Bible. . . . His last name, Bok (Hebrew for goat), may be taken as an indication of his 'common' humanity as well as his role as scapegoat, which in fact the Jews were in Czarist Russia" (Dachslager 47). According to Alan Warren Friedman, "Yakov is kin to Job, that archetypal suffering Jew, who suffers because he exists—and because he is innocent" (122). I would add that his name Bok, like the name of Bober, echoes that of the suffering man par excellence. When addressing the composition of Malamud's *The Fixer*, Philip Davis acknowledges the novelist's indebtedness to *The Book of Job* in the following terms: "there was the Old Testament—the Psalms and the Book of Job—which stood resonantly at the back of the work like the dramas that lay behind *The Natural*, *The Assistant*, and *A New Life*" (240). Yakov symbolizes the Jewish people, like his namesake, and both come to embody the exiled Jew. Much the same as Jacob, who eventually marries Rachel after fourteen years of serving her father, Laban—this can be interpreted as Jacob's bondage to him—Yakov marries Raisl and accepts her as his true wife (Abramson, *Bernard* 71).[5]

Yakov Shepsovitch (son of the sheep; Abramson, *Bernard* 68) Bok—in German, it means "goat" (68); in Yiddish, it is a piece of iron, which epitomizes his resilience (68; J. Brooks 135); and in Russian, it is used to refer to Christ (Pinsker 66; I. Alter 165)—is a most revealing aptronym because the protagonist's name "is more than accidentally appropriate to the novel's major strategy" (Mellard 112).

Bok, a most suggestive aptronym, is a Christ-like figure who feels identified with Jesus Christ when, after a guard smuggles a copy of the New Testament to Yakov, he reads it for the first time and weeps for Christ. One of the most moving scenes pictures the fixer thinking that "Jesus cried out help to God but God gave no help" (*The Fixer* 232). Bok reads the four Gospels, and although at first he is reluctant to read the New Testament, what he learns eventually fascinates him. There is certain identification between the two: "In the end he was deeply moved when he read how they spat on him and beat him with sticks; how he hung on the cross at night. Jesus cried out help to God but God gave no help. There was a man crying out in anguish in the dark, but God was on the other side of the mountain" (232). Earlier in the narrative, just like Christ on the cross, Yakov "felt entrapped, abandoned, helpless" (155). Yakov cries because he sees Jesus Christ as a reflection of himself: he cries because, in spite of knowing that he is innocent, he has almost assumed that he will not be set free.

Much the same as Christ, Yakov Bok suffers outrageously unfair torment, humiliation, and unbearable suffering to the extent that, as in Jesus's case, it is rendered through blows and insults. Like his biblical counterpart, "he was unjustly accused" (104). Subsequently, Yakov bitterly complains about his fate: "What had he done to deserve this terrible incarceration, no end in sight? Hadn't he had more than his share of misery in a less than just world?" (153).

Later on, Kogin tells Yakov to read something from the New Testament, and Yakov reads about the ordeal Christ went through during his trial. This connects with the unbearable suffering Christ also experienced prior to, and during, his crucifixion: "He read him of the trial and suffering of Christ, as the yellow candle flame dipped and sputtered in the damp cell. When he came to where the soldiers pressed a crown of thorns on Jesus' head, the guard sighed" (234). In a conversation with Ruth Ingliss, this is what Malamud answered about Yakov's Jesus-like behavior in prison: "I know that some say Bok is a Christ figure . . . but anyone who is unjustly tormented becomes Jesus" (28). Also, like Jesus Christ, he comes to practice passive resistance. As in Christ's case, Bok's release might bring about a revolt, a pogrom. This helps substantiate the theory of those who believe that the poor fixer is not finally acquitted: "One of the results of this intense pressure is to make Yakov take upon his shoulders the historic destiny of the Jewish people" (Abramson, *Bernard* 60).

Toward the end of the novel, Yakov, who like Frank Alpine has learned what suffering is, is ready to be committed. The once selfish and self-centered Yakov eventually transforms into a selfless human being. He adopts a *Christi imitatio*–like behavior—"Live, Shmuel, he sighs, live. Let me die for you"—with his father-in-law, who has paid a pricey bribe to visit him (*The Fixer* 272). When the narrator says that "nobody suffers for him and he suffers for no one except for himself," one might think that Yakov's suffering is diametrically opposed to that of Frank Alpine's (240). This, however, is only true up to this point because after he is visited by his runaway wife, Raisl, and she asks for forgiveness and begs Yakov to father her illegitimate son, Chaim—a Hebrew word that etymologically means "life"—then he suffers for her and for his child. In a typically Malamudian fashion, he can reach commitment through love and selflessness.

After Yakov tells Shmuel, "let me die for you," one realizes that he has finally learned to suffer for others—in Malamud's world, this is essential before the character's redemption, as happens with Frank Alpine (272). In Martín Urdiales Shaw's timely explanation, *The Fixer* is "a tribute to the endurance of its protagonist and to his acceptance of his fate as a Jew" (*Ethnic* 14). Alan Friedman sees Yakov as "an archetypal victim," and in this sense, I think he turns into a Christ-like figure who, as explained earlier, eventually plays the role of scapegoat (119). In this way, he becomes a savior, a redeemer.

Gregor Gronfein, a Jewish prisoner whom Yakov meets in a cell, tells Yakov that he is "a martyr for us all" (*The Fixer* 157). Later on, during his indictment, Grubeshov, the prosecuting attorney, tells Yakov, "I have given thought to the possibility that you were once a virtuous man who became the expiatory victim of his co-religionists" (221). Yakov Shepsovitch, a scapegoat of the Jewish people, is told, prior to his conversation with the tsar, "One man is all they need so long as they can hold him up as an example of Jewish bloodthirst and criminality. To prove a point it's best to have a victim" (309). To be sure, the fact that the Russian authorities need a victim is confirmed when Warden Grizitskoy tells Yakov about a tailor in Odessa called Markovitch, accused of draining the blood of a nine-year-old child. Markovitch, who addresses Yakov as "Bok," summarizes the fixer's process extremely well: "I'll tell you this, Bok: if we don't convict one of you we'll convict the other. We'll teach you all a lesson" (323).

Another parallel that may be drawn between Yakov and Christ is to be found in these words: "Since the crucifixion the crime of the Christ killer is the crime of all Jews. 'His blood be on us and our children'" (273–74). Not only are these words self-referential, but they also seem to foreshadow what Yakov's death will imply not only for those who have unjustly sent him to prison but also for those who have done the impossible to prove him guilty of a crime he did not commit.

One final similarity between Yakov and the suffering Christ on the Cross is when Yakov says almost at the end of the novel, "When they try me it will be for the crucifixion" (297). The fact that "suffering is an integral part of the life of the main protagonist in *The Fixer*" suggests that the initials of his name, Yakov Bok (Y.B.), also echo the name of Job, the suffering man par excellence (Sheres 73).

Much the same as in Yakov's case, whose name, Yakov Shepsovitch Bok, or his fake name, "Yakov Ivanovitch Dologushev" (Y.I.D.), or even Yakov Bok (Y.B.) greatly helps understand the protagonist, his father-in-law's name, Shmuel, also helps us better understand him. Shmuel, a name that bears strong biblical overtones, alludes to Samuel, son of Elkanah who was born in answer to the prayer of his childless mother, Hannah (1 Sam. 19–20). Samuel's name has significant connotations: Hannah "named him Samuel, meaning, I asked the Lord for him" (1 Sam. 1:20). Similarly, Shmuel's daughter, Raisl, is a childless mother who, like Hannah, eventually bears her firstborn late in her life.

Second, Samuel, the founder of the monarchy in Israel, is a crucial figure in Jewish history because of his religious and prophetic leadership.

Likewise, it is precisely Shmuel who recommends Yakov not to leave his land or give up his faith because that could cause him—as it eventually does—many disasters. Even at the end of the novel, Yakov's father-in-law visits Yakov to tell him to go back to God. According to the old man, it is never too late to repent.

Third, Samuel is a doting father, a lovable husband, and a pious man fearful of God. Shmuel, a religious man, has always been good and patient with his daughter, Raisl, and very kind to Yakov. When the fixer decides to leave the *shtetl*, Shmuel talks to him about the dangers of living in Kiev, and above all, he begs him not to ignore his parents' faith. Just before Yakov leaves, the old man tells him that "that's all in the Torah" (*The Fixer* 12), that "blessed are they who put their trust in God" (17), and tells him, "don't forget your God!" (17). True, unlike Yakov, Shmuel, who "is a more common Jewish stereotype," remains faithful to his faith, complains but withstands all kinds of hardship (A. Friedman 123). Significantly, toward the end of the novel, the reader learns that the old man's full name is Shmuel Rabinovitch (the rabbi's son) Shmuel's is not Yakov's only visit in prison. His runaway "faithless wife," Raisl—for years, he has mistakenly believed that Raisl is "barren" (*The Fixer* 5, 6)—also visits Yakov in order to tell him that she has a son and expects him to father her child. Gerald Hoag explains that, in spite of Yakov's initial bout of anger, "in his most symbolically redemptive act, Bok writes out a declaration of his own paternity" (139). Yakov "also confirms his sense of oneness with his people, as [Raisl's] name is an anagram for Israel" (Abramson, *Bernard* 64). Raisl, "an anagram for Israel, is clearly identified with Judaism itself," and as such, she somehow behaves like Israel in Hosea (Mellard 104).

The prophet Hosea accuses Israel of "practic[ing] lechery" through its use of Canaanite rites and practices and temporarily suffers Yahweh's wrath (Hosea 4:10–11). However, Yahweh welcomes Israel like the husband who forgives his unfaithful wife. The account of Hosea's marriage to Gomer, a harlot, is symbolic as it represents Yahweh's love for Israel as well as his wish to renew his covenant with the chosen people despite their decision to break up with him after their participation in Canaanite rites. This reference, which turns out to be prophetic, anticipates the encounter between Yakov and Raisl. In both cases, after years of hard life and also after losing many lovers, Israel and Raisl go back to their respective husbands. This is how the prophet explains it: "And I will return to

My abode—Till they realize their guilt. / In their distress, they will seek Me / And beg for My favor. / Come, let us turn back to the Lord: / He attached, and He can heal us; / He wounded, and He can bind us up. / In two days He will make us whole again; / On the third day He will raise us up, / And we shall be whole by His favor. / Let us pursue obedience to the lord, / And He will come to us like rain, / Like latter rain that refreshes the earth" (Hosea 5:15–6:3).

Toward the end of the novel, in a scene that foreshadows Yakov's encounter with Raisl in prison, the fixer "turned often to pages of Hosea and read with fascination the story of this man God had commanded to marry a harlot. The harlot, he had heard it said, was Israel, but the jealousy and anguish Hosea felt was that of a man whose wife had left his bed and board and gone whoring after strangers" (*The Fixer* 242). Just before leaving the *shtetl*, Yakov complains to Shmuel that "she danced off with some dirty stranger," and a few pages later, on his way to Kiev, Yakov thinks about Raisl and imagines that "if she had been faithful he would have stayed" (11, 19). Raisl then goes back to Yakov like Hosea's harlot to her husband. As what happens in Hosea, in which the people of Israel ask for forgiveness, Raisl visits Yakov in the same hope: "Yakov, I didn't come here to fight about the past. Forgive me, forgive the past" (286). In Malamud's narrative, there are, however, two differences: first, Raisl tells her husband that she has an illegitimate son she would like Bok to accept as his own son. And second, unlike Hosea, Bok remains unfaithful to God. By now, Yakov has ignored his differences with his ex-wife, has accepted his fatherhood, and has forgiven her. He says, "I declare myself to be the father of Chaim, the infant son of my wife, Raisl Bok. He was conceived before she left me. Please help the mother and child, and for this, amid all my troubles, I'll be grateful. Yakov Bok" (292).

The name of Chaim is not accidental. As pointed out before, Chaim means "life" in Hebrew. This is the role the child plays in the story: he embodies Yakov's renewed spirit. In effect, Yakov has taken up his traditions again, and Chaim represents his return to the right path. Although whether Yakov is finally acquitted is not explicitly stated in the end, the fixer will probably join his wife, like Yahweh and Israel, and their son in order to start a new life together: "He felt an overwhelming hunger to be back home, to see Raisl and set things straight, to decide what to do. 'Raisl,' he said, 'dress the boy and pack the few things we need, we'll have to hide'" (330). Up to that moment, at least in my way of thinking, Yakov had not suffered for anyone. However, as a consequence of his two-year-plus imprisonment, his attitude toward others has changed: in accepting Chaim as his son—this is his way to forgive Raisl—and then when Ostrovsky, the fixer's new lawyer, tells him, "You suffer for us all" (305). Yakov, who has probably given up hope by the end of the novel, mistakenly thinks that his suffering has been pointless: "what suffering has taught me is the uselessness of suffering" (333). This is untrue because, like Morris, Yakov does not see the fruits of his suffering, but in both cases, it does finally bring its own reward.

At the outset of this chapter, I quoted Carol Meyers's approach to the concept of archetype as a way to show the "*essential* . . . features of human life." In line with this definition, Leland Ryken, James C. Wilhoit, and Tremper Longman III define the archetype as "an image or pattern that recurs throughout literature and life. Archetypes are the universal elements of human experience" (xvii). One way to see these "universal elements of human experience" is to show those universal experiences undergone by the human being, such as poverty, hunger, suffering, sadness, happiness, injustice, and so on. We have seen how in Malamud's fiction, through painful experiences, his protagonists may learn an invaluable lesson, which more often than not leads to their eventual salvation and redemption. For this kind of experience hides a lot of wisdom, which, among other things, puts the human being's strength and ability to the test. Arguably, Morris, Frank, and Yakov are Malamud's three archetypal suffering men par excellence.

NOTES

1. For a detailed study about the parallels between Morris Bober and Jesus Christ, see Beer.
2. In an interview with Malamud, E. H. Leelavathi Masilamoni alludes to the strong presence of Christianity in the novelist's works. Malamud answers, "Christianity as a theology does not interest me, but what is brought out in Christianity as a result of Jesus and St. Francis as men. I appreciate their response to human beings and the elements of nature (St. Francis responded to animals and birds). Any stimuli can be a force for the rest of a human being's life. I read the New Testament and found it stirred deep feelings in me" (Masilamoni 72).

3. "Helen, as her name suggests, comes to represent the beauty and love all the major characters seek, but she herself is too practical to accept this as an accurate description of what she is at the moment" (Shear 215). According to Peter L. Hays, Helen, etymologically *Helle*, is the "bright goddess of death and resurrection" (224). And Edward A. Abramson sees Helen as a "fertility goddess" (*Bernard* 41).

4. For an extended analysis of the historical facts in *The Fixer*, see Urdiales Shaw, *Ethnic* 51–64; J. Brooks; and Sánchez Canales, "Bernard."

5. For an analysis of the significance of the biblical Jacob, Rachel, and Job in *The Magic Barrel* and of the Old Testament figure of Isaac in *God's Grace*, see Zucker 160–64.

CHAPTER 9

Fixing Bernard Malamud's *The Fixer* through Translation

From *El hombre de Kiev* (1967) to *El reparador* (2011)

MARTÍN URDIALES SHAW

UNIVERSITY OF VIGO, SPAIN

This chapter traces the publication history of the three translations into Spanish of *The Fixer* (1966), Malamud's only novel based on historical facts.[1] Section 1 deals with the context of reception of *The Fixer* in America and the novel's layering of historical connotations, while section 2 focuses on the specific political and sociocultural circumstances faced by the early translation of *The Fixer* in late-sixties Spain. Drawing strands from both sections, section 3 will go on to comparatively assess the novel's translational challenges—Yiddish language and Ashkenazi legacy; Spanish culture and readerships—as these were successively negotiated in each of the three translations, from the 1967 text to the recent 2007 and 2011 versions.

1. THE AMERICAN LITERARY SCENE: *THE FIXER* AS HISTORICAL AND CONTEMPORARY NOVEL

Bernard Malamud's fiction underwent a significant reorientation from its beginnings in the 1950s to the 1960s. While Malamud's first novel,

The Natural (1952), completely sidestepped ethnicity, his second and subsequent works introduced Jewish identity as a pivotal theme. In *The Assistant* (1957), inspired by his immigrant father's life as storekeeper, Malamud developed a relationship between a Jew and a gentile that evolves toward a stress on the universality of Jewishness, and a number of stories of this period thematized redemptive visions of interpersonal relationships, often linked to Malamud's conceptualization of the suffering, struggling, and self-effacing Jew as "Everyman," embodied by Morris Bober in that novel.

The humanistic outlook and allegorical underpinnings started to fade from Malamud's work in the early sixties, as his writing took a distinct turn toward bleaker narratives. In grim tales like "The Jewbird" (1963) and "Black Is My Favorite Color" (1963), unrelenting anti-Semitism or unresolved prejudice govern interethnic relations in urban America, even though the former story retains folk-tale elements. As stories about anti-Semitism and black-Jewish relationships, respectively, these 1963 stories thematically prefigured two novels written in the latter part of the decade, *The Fixer* (1966) and *The Tenants* (1971), works that are closely connected in the author's recollection of this particular period of his writing career: "After [*A New Life*] I was sniffing for an idea in the direction of injustice on the American scene, partly for obvious reasons—this was a time of revolutionary advances in Negro rights—and because I became involved with this theme in a way that sets off my imagination. . . . I had hoped to portray an American experience, possibly concerned with a Negro protagonist" (Malamud, "Source" 88).

The "American experience" was deferred three years, when he started work on *The Tenants*, but at this time, Malamud looked back into world history, contemplating a number of causes célèbres of institutional injustice to be reworked fictionally (the Sacco-Vanzetti and Caryl Chessman death sentences in the United States, *l'affaire Dreyfus* in France) before finally settling on the Mendel Beilis case (Kiev, 1911–1914), a story he had heard in childhood from his father, Max, an immigrant Ukrainian Jew (Malamud, "Source" 88).

For some critics Malamud's best novel—the 1967 winner of the Pulitzer Prize and National Book Award—*The Fixer* (1966) adapts the historical conspiracy involving the major players, political circumstances, and social reality leading to the persecution and imprisonment of Mendel Beilis, named Yakov Bok in the novel. By happenstance, American readerships became fully conversant with the Beilis affair in 1966, since weeks before the publication of *The Fixer*, a nonfictional account of the case was published by the Zionist intellectual Maurice Samuel[2] under the title *Blood Accusation: The Strange History of the Beiliss Case*. While *Blood Accusation* was extensively researched, based on interrogation and trial transcripts, press reports, pamphlets, and diverse literature of the era, it shed little light on the figure of Beilis himself, as Leonard Shapiro, a contemporary reviewer, noted (quoted in Kessner 99). It thus functioned conversely to the novel, which, aside from the historical events and characters, was predominantly centered on Yakov's growing awareness of his exposure to historical circumstance and his moral endurance.

Although descendants of Beilis objected to Malamud's close use of the conspiracy account (see Beilis, Garber, and Stein), while not respecting the historical Mendel Beilis (unlike Yakov, a married father of five with a solid Jewish faith), Malamud always affirmed—and criticism concurs—that he was not interested in the man himself, because "[he had] to have room to invent" (quoted in Davis 240). He used the case, but he also drew from several other sources, including Russian-Jewish history, the Bible, and the Russian narrative tradition, in particular Dostoevsky (Davis 240; Abramson, *Bernard* 71; Langer 118) and Solzhenitsyn (Langer 118). Further, critics of Malamud's work have noted how the conceptualization of Yakov Bok as a character fully belongs in the "genealogy" of previous protagonists, questers who seek to "start over" in life and redefine their identity (Roy Hobbs, Frank Alpine, Sy Levin), while the imprisonment theme linked to Jewishness is relevant to the earlier *The Assistant* (R. Alter, "Jewishness" 33–35) and the store stories.

What sets *The Fixer* distinctly apart from the rest of the Malamud corpus is the writer's intention to make it resonate with history in a number of ways. The novel's direct historical background, the decay of Russia during the rule of Nicholas II (last tsar, 1894–1917), which finally led to the Bolshevik Revolution only three years after the Beilis case, was carefully adapted by Malamud into the novel's plot. The enforcement of the "Pale of Settlement" and the restriction of Jews to certain districts in large cities (Yakov leaves the *shtetl* and settles in a Kiev quarter forbidden to Jews) is grounded in strict historical accuracy (Service 33; Gitelman 2). Yakov's fateful encounter with Nikolai Maximovitch, the "Black Hundreds" member whom he assists, also employs historical circumstance, this being an actual (popular) name for royalist, ultranationalist, and anti-Semitic factions within the Union of Russian People, which enjoyed the tsar's unconditional support (Service 32). Through Yakov's interrogations (*The Fixer* 74–103), the news brought by his legal advisers (171–74, 303–10), and even public sermons (130–33), characters like Bibikov, Col. Bodyansky, Grubeshov, Father Anastasy, and Ostrovsky draw the larger canvas of Russian politics in the first two decades of the twentieth century: concerns about political parties, the tension between tsarist autocracy and the Duma (parliament), sociopolitical unrest, and the predicament of Jews in this agitated context. More specifically, they all address (in various ways) the ahistorical belief in the blood libel against Jews, established in the mind-set of a largely illiterate and superstitious Russian peasantry, less educated than German, Polish, and Jewish residents (Service 33). For Bibikov's ludicrous speech on "Jewish noses" (*The Fixer* 142), Malamud also draws explicitly on this era's pseudoscientific beliefs, "the racial theories of the Comte de Gobineau and Houston Stewart Chamberlain, both nineteenth-century anti-Semites who propounded racist theories that excluded Jews from membership in the 'Aryan race'" (Abramson, *Bernard* 60).

This leads in other future, yet past, historical directions as well. *The Fixer* is the first long work by Malamud to unmistakably evoke the Holocaust,[3] through the discourse of a ferryman who carries Yakov across the Dnieper toward Kiev. At suspecting Yakov's accent as that of a non-Russian, the anonymous boatman voices an anti-Semitic invective that conceptually climaxes in what the Nazi regime termed *Endlosung* ("final solution" in Nazi-Deutsch), namely, the scheme for the extermination of Jews from the motherland. The imagery employed in his envisioning of this event—"pil[ing] up the corpses," "light[ing] fires," "stinking ashes" (*The Fixer* 29)—is unambiguous and "demands an identification . . . between the deliberately shaped environment of Tsarist Russia and the actual history that is to come" (R. Alter, "Jewishness" 59; see also Brown 485; Abramson, *Bernard* 74). If this reference is inescapable, the critic Edward Abramson has also noted that Yakov's visual perception of the Kiev brickwork factory abounds in references to chimneys and smoke that foreshadow the death camps (*Bernard* 74). A strong advocate of the novel's symbolic evocation of the Holocaust was Robert Alter, who saw in Malamud's use of the Beilis case "a way of approaching the European Holocaust on an imaginable scale [that] transparently holds within it the core of cultural sickness around which the Nazi madness grew, representing a symptomatic junction of the medieval demonological conception of the Jew as satanic enemy to Christ and mankind, and the modern phobic vision of an international Jewish conspiracy" ("Jewishness" 38). Critics like Lawrence Langer, however, sidestepped the metonymical approach and have persuasively argued that, in spite of the imagery, the Holocaust is, in both scope and intensity, *experientially* removed from Yakov's imprisonment story, which takes up four-fifths of the text.[4]

In *The Fixer*, Yakov's identification with Jewishness, unlike that of earlier Jews in Malamud's fiction, is focused through the lens of the sociopolitical conditions of a specific historical moment but simultaneously evokes others. Although Yakov deliberately avoids Jewish milieus twice in the novel (first the *shtetl*, then the Podol district in Kiev) and claims, inspired by Spinoza's writings, to be a freethinker with no religion, the novel's bitter irony is that Jewish identity is forced on him in the most medieval and superstitious fashion, as a performer of mystical ritual. Gradually persuaded of the inevitability of history ("it snows history," "there's no such thing as an unpolitical man, specially a Jew"; *The Fixer* 314, 335), Yakov ultimately embraces a version of Jewishness that is militant and ideological and that points to the end of a regime (Russia 1917) and the birth of a new nation (Israel 1948). The novel closes with a daydream in which Yakov shoots a feeble tsar, followed by his thoughts, "Death to the anti-Semites! Long live revolution! Long live liberty!" (335), as it foreshadows the imminent Bolshevik uprising three years after the Beilis trial, in which the Romanov royal family was murdered. Just before Yakov's release from prison to attend the trial, he has signed a certificate in Yiddish consenting to father the baby boy Chaim (life), the son of another man, at the request of his ex-wife, Raisl. Her last words are, "Yakov . . . come home" (237), and her name is an anagram for Israel, in what emerges as a (patriarchal) regenerative archetype of Zionism.

American history is also clearly invoked. Yakov's westward journey from the *shtetl* to Kiev riding a wayward mule carries resonances of the nineteenth-century American westering epic and is a familiar trope in American culture. In reduced scale, the boat trip across the Dnieper toward the Kiev shore, besides its mythical implications,[5] parallels the American dream that was leading masses of European immigrants across the Atlantic in this very period (1880–1925). Like Yakov's crossing, their journey was a quest for prosperity and also usually entailed a relocation from country to city. In addition, more somber aspects of domestic history are evoked in *The Fixer*. When the law-abiding Magistrate Bibikov clarifies to Yakov that the blood libel against Jews was banned by nineteenth-century tsars and laments the current Russian regress since Emancipation,[6] he concludes, "There's something cursed . . . about a country where men have owned men as property" (142), a line that "permits the American reader to recognize and acknowledge a legitimate but devastating value judgement assessed against one aspect of his own national history" (I. Alter 162; Cohen 83). Indeed, *The Fixer*'s central theme "of a simple man against a corrupt state was eagerly received" (Ochshorn 141) in the late 1960s civil rights context when the novel appeared, since "anti-Semitic dehumanization translated well into the contemporary American effort to confront its own apartheid" (Malamud Smith, *My Father* 217).

Strikingly, on the centennial of Malamud's birth and fifty years after the novel's publication, the political backdrop of *The Fixer* is historically echoed by the geopolitics of eastern Europe, namely, in the conflict with Russian nationalists disputing regions of Ukraine's sovereign territory. In *The Fixer*, Ukrainian identity or sympathy for Ukraine are aligned with a compromise for justice, truth, and ethics (before becoming corrupt, Grubeshov was "a strong Ukrainophil"; Yakov's future lawyer at court is "an Ukrainian by birth"; *The Fixer* 171, 312), in sharp contrast to Russian nationalists like the Dnieper boatman or the Black Hundreds factory owner. Historically, the Black Hundreds and related turn-of-the-century Russian ultranationalist groups actively and violently disputed Ukraine's independence, like today's pro-Russian militia fighting the Ukrainian army on the east of the country, an ongoing conflict that, if not directly abetted, has not been defused by the Kremlin.

2. THE SPANISH SCENE: THE YEARS OF LATE CENSORSHIP AND THE FIRST TRANSLATION

In twentieth-century Spain, official censorship on cultural materials, both original and translated, was active for almost forty years, from the beginning of the Franco regime to the mid-1970s.[7] Censorship encompassed artistic creation across a wide variety of genres, including film, fiction, poetry, drama and theater, children's literature and comics, and all translations into Spanish thereof. Although the intensity and method of censorship was not absolutely invariable throughout the whole period (Santamaría López 211), still, any prospective publisher of a work to be translated into Spanish had to submit a form indicating the book's author and title, number of pages, format, print run, retail price, and details such as the publisher's series or if the work was children/youth oriented. This form was affixed to the manuscript with the proposed translation (the source text was absent) and was forwarded to the "readers" (*lectores*), as the official discourse named censors, who would report back with three possible outcomes: authorized as is, unauthorized, or authorized with the censor's amendments.

As the quirks of Spanish history have it, all files on the censorship of cultural materials during the regime are held today at the vast archival holdings in the Archivo General de la Administración (AGA) in the town of Alcalá de Henares, birthplace of Cervantes, who "for reasons of literary politics and irony, [claimed] that *Don Quijote* is actually a translation from . . . Cid Hamete, an Arab storyteller." Yet Cervantes lived in the Spanish Golden Age when a translation was called "an imitation of a classic" and was a "natural activity of a serious writer" (Barnstone 86); in Spain's twentieth-century cultural dark ages, the censors' reports were headed by a set of six questions, followed by a space to specify unacceptable pages. The questions, in this order, were elliptical, the verb and subject implied after question one: "Does [the work] attack Dogma [i.e., Catholic doctrine]? Morality? The Church [i.e., Roman Catholic] or its ministers? The regime or its institutions? People who cooperate or have cooperated with the regime?"[8] (CQ1 to CQ5). Question six was indirect and required particulars: "The passages to be censored, do they represent the overall content of the work?"[9] (CQ6). In the lower part of the form, a space was left for the censor to write a summary of the work or further remarks.

The priority given in these forms to religious concerns over political questions is patent: Catholic doctrine, sexual morals, and church hierarchy (CQ1, CQ2, CQ3) are prioritized over questions dealing with the political protection of the regime (CQ4, CQ5). Much has been written about the 1936 uprising as inextricable from the defense of the Catholic Church. Significantly, a central term coined by the insurgents (Franco's *nacionales*) to label the uprising against the established Spanish Republic was *cruzada* (crusade), a direct reappropriation of the term used in the military campaigns for the expansion of Christianity sanctioned by the Roman popes in the Middle Ages. The Franco regime was from its inception ideologically equated with what was broadly termed *Nacionalcatolicismo*, a designation unique to Spain that emphasized the great control of the Catholic Church on all aspects of social, political, public, and even private life. Consequently, many educational and cultural policies—including, centrally, censorship—during the period 1939–1976 were strongly influenced by ministers and government officials who were close to either conservative or ultraconservative sectors of the Catholic establishment.[10]

It is general consensus that the 1960s showed a "thawing out" of Spain in a variety of ways, which also brought about a loosening of the tight grip on culture. Economically, the early sixties witnessed the growth of industrial society, an unprecedented domestic immigration into industrial areas, a rapid—often anarchic—development of high-rise housing in cities (*desarrollismo*), and the consolidation of mass tourism from northern Europe, under the appeal of the renowned slogan "Spain Is Different" printed on large-format posters of beaches, landscapes, or historic sites. Culture, in all its facets, was directed, together with tourism, by the Ministry for Information and Tourism, established in 1951, an association of two areas of administration exclusive to the Franco regime, which ended in 1977. Since the inception of the agency, the first term of office had been held by Gabriel Arias-Salgado, an orthodox Catholic and a hardliner Falangist who had earlier held the posts of national vice secretary for education and delegate for press and propaganda for the Falange Española Tradicionalista, the only political party sanctioned by the regime. In June 1962, Arias-Salgado was replaced by Manuel Fraga Iribarne, who remained in office until 1969. Fraga Iribarne, a controversial figure who holds the (arguable) accomplishment of being the most versatile personality in Spanish twentieth-century politics,[11] is generally credited with coining the "Spain Is Different" tourism slogan but is also equally remembered, in his "Information" capacities, for endorsing the 1966 "Freedom of Press and Print" Law. While the first articles of this law have been justly critiqued by historians for their catch-22 rhetoric,[12] other articles did introduce significant changes, such as the ways in which the state implemented censorship. Article 3 decreed the termination of *censura previa* (prior censorship) of all printed material and its compulsory submission by publishers, a procedure that is replaced by what article 4 labels *consulta voluntaria*, or "voluntary assessment," whereby publishers are given the initiative of contacting the administration to request evaluation of a work.

This procedure was the one faced by the Barcelona publisher Plaza y Janés when the first translation of *The Fixer* was submitted in Spain in 1967, as I discovered in early October 2014 at the AGA in Alcalá. After registering as users, researchers at the AGA are assigned a working desk in a reading room. Examination of the physical files is requested from the head archivist, who looks up the entries in an internal catalog and calls forth the specific file boxes. Four censorship files (*expedientes*) turned up on the screen for translations of *The Fixer*, one for 1967, two for 1971, and one for 1975, matching the Biblioteca Nacional database, which records that the 1971 and 1975 entries are all reprints of the 1967 text. When the filing boxes were brought, and the thrill of locating the right manila envelope amid scores of other contemporaneous material inside each box had abated, the particulars of censorship policy became clearer. Publishers submitted the documentation for each single book to be printed and circulated, including reprints. But reprints, unless new paratexts had been added (prefaces, forewords, notes, etc.), were referred back by censors to the *expediente* containing the result of the first evaluation. As regards the translated text of *The Fixer*, this meant that the two 1971 files and the 1975 file were uninteresting, including only paperwork referring back to the original submission.

This material was in the large, bulging envelope marked "Expediente 5305/67," inside filing box (3)50 21/18242, which contained not only the publisher's submission forms but also the complete typewritten manuscript of the translation of *The Fixer* and the original censor's report on this manuscript. A significant finding here was that instead of the usual one, there were two submission forms, both attached to the same manuscript. The first, dated June 1967, referred to Malamud's *The Fixer* as *El remendón*, and this was also the typewritten title, in capitals, on the manuscript's first page. The second submission form, dated December 1967, indicates the title as *El hombre de Kiev* (The man from Kiev), and the original title, inserted parenthetically next to the new, is crossed out.

There is no conclusive way of knowing what determined this change of title—*not* censorship related—in a finished manuscript, but a strong clue points to France. During Francoism, partly for political reasons, French culture was a focal point for the Spanish literary establishment, particularly that based in Catalonia. Thus, it seems not accidental that the first French translation of *The Fixer*, by Éditions du Seuil, with the title *L'homme de Kiev* (The man from Kiev) was printed in November 1967, as specified on the back flap, thus leading the way for a last-minute editorial revision by Plaza y Janés of the Spanish title in imitation of the French.

Now one key challenge for Spanish translators of Malamud's historical novel—which I pursue in section 3—is how to render a term like *fixer* without loss of meaning: *fixer* has a wide range of connotation, derived from the polysemy of *fix*, which can literally mean "to repair" or "to mend" but also, more figuratively, to "(dishonestly) arrange" something and, in slang usage, "to punish," especially someone who has been unfair. As Sandy Cohen has noted (75), all these meanings were significant for Malamud in the construction of his character: in the *shtetl*, Yakov fixes broken things; in Kiev, he has to "fix" false residence papers, and after a long imprisonment, he "fixes" his marriage with Raisl by fathering her son; and in a fantasy sequence, he "fixes" Tsar Nicholas—by shooting him—for an unjust rule. The central theme, Yakov's endurance in prison and his demand for a fair trial, becomes a "fixing," a righting of justice in a corrupt state. The original Spanish title for the 1967 translation, *El remendón*, which is preserved within the novel as the regular equivalent for all occurrences of "the fixer," carries only the material implications of fix (repair, mend), but with an added complication. In Spanish, this term relates very specifically to the world of tailoring and shoemaking and not to general handyman work. Although it evokes a sense of poverty—fitting to the character's portrayal—*remendón* is a term that constrains meaning in a misdirected way. Yet by adopting the same wording for the title as the French Seuil, Plaza y Janés minimized the damage that the manuscript title would have caused; "Man from Kiev" is a graceful title that situated the novel geopolitically[13] for Spanish/French readerships, while it underlines the crux of Yakov's predicament, becoming a victim of the state for acting as a citizen within it.

Besides the change of title, the censorship documents yielded not much else. The typewritten manuscript contains no deletions, the set of six censorship questions is left blank (implying conformity), and the censor notes "to be authorized" below a personal, one-paragraph summary of the novel. In a novel in which "institutional religion does not fare well" (Ducharme 113), a passage that could face difficulties before inquiries like "Does the work attack Catholic doctrine?" (CQ1) is Yakov's discussion of the Gospel of John with his Russian guard Kogin. Here the fixer defends himself and the Jews from the blood libel, by quoting to Kogin that the blood and the body of Christ are instructed, in this Gospel, to be consumed by Christians, while the Old Testament explicitly forbids Jews from eating blood (*The Fixer* 233). The manuscript page examined at the AGA in Alcalá and the page in the published novel (*El hombre* 238–39) are identical, and a close reading of the Spanish translation next to Malamud's original text shows no toning down or abridging of the dialogue.[14] However, there is a specific alteration of language in the passage where the investigating magistrate Bibikov describes Father Anastasy, the instigator of the "blood accusation" against Yakov. In Malamud's novel, Bibikov exposes Anastasy as "a defrocked Catholic priest" (*The Fixer* 173). Significantly, and although the rest of the paragraph is left intact—including Anastasy's portrayal as an anti-Semitic pamphleteer and a fraudster—the term "defrocked" is not translated into Spanish but is replaced by the elaborate paraphrase "ecclesiastically downgraded": "*Era sacerdote católico . . . pero fue degradado canonicamente*" (*El hombre* 178). This precise alteration on the translator's part would be aimed at negotiating CQ3 in the forms ("[Does the work attack] the Church or its ministers?"), yet the result is amusingly paradoxical, since the term *sacerdote* (priest) makes no reference to a Catholic hierarchy to be "downgraded from," while the overall portrayal of Anastasy is just as damaging in the Spanish text.

The Fixer concludes with Yakov's cry "Long live revolution!" and "Long live liberty!" (335). This political climax, based on Spinoza's justification of the destruction of the state if it is inimical to human nature, could not have gone undetected by the Spanish censor, since the passage on the shooting of the tsar, immediately preceding these lines, is noted in the brief censor's report. Yet not a word was changed in the manuscript, and the published translation reads, "Viva la Revolución! Viva la libertad!" (*El hombre* 337). The relaxation of censorship procedure; the literalness of CQ4 and CQ5, which guided censors specifically to the "Régimen" in Spain; and ultimately, the perception that this was only a historical novel, safely removed in space and time and thus with no possible analogies to the dictatorship in Spain, must have safeguarded the preservation of Yakov's overtly radical discourse.

3. THE FIXING OF *THE FIXER*: THE FIRST TEXT (1967), THE REVISED TRANSLATION (2007), THE NEW TRANSLATION (2011)

The Fixer is Malamud's novel with the largest proportion of foreign languages, particularly Yiddish terms but also Russian and German. All the Yiddish in the novel is culturally bound, but while part of it specifically relates to the Judaic ritual that the conspirators want to impose on Yakov, another part is common usage in the *shtetl* world that Yakov abandons: *goy, Torah, shul, Hannukah*, and, indeed, *shtetl* itself. This occasional use of Yiddish, which recurs in other Malamud works and signposts much postwar Jewish American fiction, is not especially foreign to American readers. In contemporary metropolitan America, specially New York, a widespread familiarity with Yiddish has been cultivated by means of the extensive cultural influence of Ashkenazi Jewish descendants during the twentieth century. From the turn-of-the-century Yiddish music hall to Woody Allen's cinema, from Abraham Cahan to Adam Levin (*The Instructions*, 2010), filmmakers, entertainers, fiction writers, poets, and playwrights have infused Anglo-American language and culture with Yiddish. Dictionaries like the *OED* and *Merriam-Webster* contain today a large number of Yiddishisms, which have entered the English language via American usage, effectively becoming mainstream.

Such a familiarity with Yiddish and culturally bound Yiddish concepts, even those that are common, cannot be taken for granted in Spain. As Spain's modern history is quite dissimilar from that of its European neighbors, so also is its relation to Jewish history and diasporic identity, which might be best described as a discontinued legacy. The "visible" history of Jews in Spain came to an end with the 1493 edict by the Reyes Católicos, forcing Jews into either exile or conversion or, at worst, execution by the Inquisition. But even if the bygone Jewish culture of Spain had survived this period, Yiddish would not have been its vehicular language, since the Jews in Spain were of Sephardic lineage and not of the Ashkenazi branch of central Europe, where Yiddish originated and expanded from its core German component (Harshav 43). In the modern era, general knowledge of Jewish religious tradition and culture in Spain is limited. Franco reinstated freedom of faith in 1967 (*Boletín Oficial del Estado* 156 [1 July 1967]: 9191–94), ending thirty years of "National-Catholicism" as official creed, and the country has clearly become a more multicultural society; yet non-Catholic communities, although expanding, are still very small.[15] Among these, Judaism ranks particularly low simply because the Jewish population amounts to only twelve thousand people in a country of forty-seven million, a figure that has remained stable since the return of democracy in 1977, when Argentinian and Chilean Jews came to Spain fleeing the military regimes in South America. Predictably, the largest Jewish communities are metropolitan: Madrid and Barcelona make up around two-thirds of the total, while smaller communities are spread over the South and the Mediterranean, the Canary Islands, and the towns of Ceuta and Melilla, on the North African coast (Vigil 238–39).

The overall implication of these demographics is that a Spanish translation of *The Fixer* intended for a general readership in Spain[16] requires some degree of annotation of the Yiddish employed, to familiarize readers with Ashkenazi Jewish tradition and culture, as well as the situation of Jews in early-century Russia. It should be noted that Maurice Samuel's *Blood Accusation* was never translated into Spanish, so Spanish readers are more likely to be unfamiliar with the Beilis conspiracy. I now examine how this particular aspect, the familiarization of target readers with the Yiddish conceptual framework in Malamud's novel, was accomplished throughout the three existing translations into Spanish (Plaza y Janés, 1967; Sexto Piso, 2007; El Aleph, 2011), while I also look at the subsequent efforts (in the 2007 and 2011 versions) at rendering "fixer" in Spanish, a challenge that was first made evident, as discussed earlier, with the limitations of the term *remendón* and the last-minute revision of the 1967 title. Both centrally significant and challenging aspects of the novel's translation, their different handling in the 1967 first text, the 2007 revised version, and the new 2011 translation may be pictured as an ongoing process of "fixing" *The Fixer* for Spanish readerships from the late sixties until today.

At best, the 1967 translation by Ferrer Aleu, *El hombre de Kiev*, might be described as a text with a very inconsistent annotation of the culturally bound Yiddish language. The text opens promisingly with a few "translator's notes" but soon reveals a flagging interest in pursuing interpretation, as the more specific Yiddish related to the blood libel becomes more frequent in Malamud's novel. Thus, the first occurrences of *Vey iz mir!* ("Ay de Mi!"; *El hombre* 11), *shtetl* ("Asentamiento Judío"; 13), and *goy* ("Cristiano"; 15) are annotated at the bottom of the pages (although "pogrom" is not; 12), but after page 20, the text fails to provide any notes for "Torah," "Hanukkah," or "shul" (20–25). A significant example of inconsistency, with possible consequences, involves the rendering of "matzo." In *El hombre de Kiev*, this term is first transcribed as "mosot," the translator aptly providing an explanatory note here: "Pan sin levadura" (unleavened bread; 75). But when the term reappears in the context of the first hostile interrogation of Yakov by the Russian authorities, the spelling given is "massot" (and "massot shmuro"; 109) and remains so throughout the novel. Thus, the valuable translator's note on page 75 links to a term whose spelling occurs this once and is later abandoned, potentially generating confusion about the actual scope of this first note, particularly as the "matzo" is a key item in the fabricated evidence against the fixer and is crucial to the interrogation scene. Inconsistency is also apparent in clarifying aspects of Judaic practice: the translator annotates "hasid" (74) but neglects to annotate "misnogid" (107) or "tzadikim" (108), again terms that come up during the interrogation scene and that reveal the authorities' fixation with affiliating Yakov with ritual or mystical practice.

In addition, several translator's notes included in *El hombre de Kiev* involve problematic understatements. Although "hasid" is annotated, the curt definition of this term—"Secta Judía" (Jewish sect; 74)—sheds no light on the orthodoxy and ritual observance of Hasidim, later relevant to the interrogators' designs. The more serious understatement, however, relates to the boatman's invective. In Malamud's novel, this character, whose vision prefigures the Holocaust (see earlier), speaks of the extermination of "zhids" in their "zhidy quarters" (*The Fixer* 27–28), using an offensive Russian term loaded with anti-Semitic implications. But in *El hombre de Kiev*, the translator annotates "zhid" neutrally, simply as "Jewish" (Judío; *El hombre* 36), just as he has, also too neutrally, previously annotated "goy" as "Christian" ("Cristiano"; 15). In using this parallel, understated annotation, the translator encourages a reading that not only obviates the agency and subjectivity of ethnic labeling but also, problematically, conceals the anti-Semitic/prejudiced implications of the terms used. That translator Ferrer Aleu was eventually overwhelmed by the recurrence of specialized Yiddish denoting ritual is well illustrated by a gratuitous amendment of Malamud's text in an interrogation during Yakov's long imprisonment. Malamud writes, "the Prosecuting Attorney . . . asked the prisoner if he was related to Baal Shem Tov or Rabbi Zalman Schneur of Ladi, and whether there had ever been a shochet in his family" (*The Fixer* 226). The Spanish text begins accurately, but in the last clause, "shochet" is replaced by "rabbi": "el fiscal . . . le preguntó si estaba emparentado con Baal Shem Tov, o con el rabí[17] Zalman Schneur de Ladi, o si había habido algún *rabino* en su familia" (*El hombre* 231). Thus, the 1967 Spanish version has Grubeshov asking only about rabbis, yet Malamud's reference to the *shochet* (*shoykhet* in YIVO spelling), denoting the "kosher butcher" who slaughters cattle and fowl in the ritually prescribed way, is significant for readers in its implications that Prosecutor Grubeshov is obsessed with associating Yakov with sacrificial ritual.

The second version of Malamud's novel in Spanish appeared in 2007. Its publisher is Sexto Piso España, established in Madrid in 2005, a division of a press originally based in Mexico City, Sexto Piso Ediciones. The front matter of this edition contains the following note: "This press has been unable to contact the translator of the work at the time of publication. Should this translator come forward later and contact this publisher, all his rights will be fully acknowledged" (*El reparador* [2007] vi). An agent at Sexto Piso in Madrid confirmed to me that this is, substantially, a reprint of Ferrer Aleu's 1967 translation, revised by proofreaders who made occasional alterations and corrections to the text. The most visible of these is the replacement of *El hombre de Kiev* with a title seeking equivalence with the title word "fixer": *El reparador*. This word, signifying "repair man" or "handy man" and used for every occurrence of "the fixer," conveys a much fuller sense than the early *remendón*. Although perhaps not too common as an adjective in Spanish, *reparador* derives from the more frequent verb *reparar*, which, like "fix," has an extended polysemy, its many senses ranging from the physical to the figurative: it can mean to repair, renovate, adjust, rebuild, assemble, and so on, but it can also mean to remedy, compensate, satisfy, reward, help, amend, reimburse, among others (the only senses of "fix" that it cannot carry into Spanish are those of fraud and retribution). That editors at Sexto Piso were conscious of the need to translate "fixer" with a polysemic term like this, encompassing both literal and metaphorical domains, is made evident by the back-cover synopsis, which opens, "Yakov Bok . . . will be forced to be more than a *factotum*, he will have to fix his own life" (*El reparador* [2007] back cover).

While the new translation of "fixer" and its restitution as title word is a key enhancement, intervention in Ferrer Aleu's text is otherwise halfhearted. The occurrence of Yiddish is improved sometimes by using normalized Spanish spellings in terms like "la Tora," and the editors pertinently restore *shochet* (adapted to Spanish phonetics as "shojet"; *El reparador* [2007] 225) to Grubeshov's biased interrogation of Yakov. Unfortunately, no attempt is made at either refining or extending the body of translator's notes: the same six notes used by Ferrer Aleu in 1967, with those often understated definitions, are maintained. Thus, the restoration of *shochet* ("shojet") is a move in the right direction, but as it lacks annotation, the Spanish reader will be likely to miss its contextual significance. The remaining Yiddish, as in Aleu's version, is left unannotated. Moreover, in revising the Yiddish of Malamud's novel and the 1967 translation, the proofreaders have overlooked the inconsistent spelling of "matzoh," which persists from *El hombre de Kiev* into this edition (first occurrence: "mosot"; *El reparador* [2007] 72; subsequently spelled "massot"). Similarly, and although verbs and phrases are often rewritten in a more contemporary, updated Spanish, the proofreaders have kept "degradado canónicamente" (*El reparador* [2007] 173; *El hombre* 178) for Anastasy's "defrocking," perhaps unaware that the 1967 language would have been toned down in addressing Catholic hierarchy.

The third Spanish translation of *The Fixer* was published in 2011, by El Aleph Editores of Barcelona, with the same title as Sexto Piso, *El reparador*. This version is a totally new translation by Susana Rodríguez-Vida, whose distinguishing feature is a very decisive "fixing" of the annotation shortcomings of previous texts. With a body of forty-six consecutively numbered translator's notes, Rodríguez-Vida not only clarifies with precision all the Yiddish in Malamud's historical novel; she is also aware that a Spanish readership may require cultural interpretation of Jewish tradition even in the absence of Yiddish. In note 21, attached to Yakov's comment to Zina Nikolaevna that she is "unclean" (*The Fixer* 52), the translation ("Está usted impura!") links to a note in which Rodríguez-Vida clarifies that according to Jewish Law, a menstruating woman is "impure" for seven days (*El reparador* [2011] 80), a commandment that can be found in Leviticus 18:19. The specific clarification of this sexual taboo suggests the translator's awareness of the symbolic significance of blood in this novel in relation to Jewishness, which surfaces again in the biased interrogations concerning matzhos and in the fixer's discussion of the Gospel of John with Kogin. Annotation of Yiddish language, comprising twenty-five notes, is meticulous: for example, the plural "goyim" is annotated separately (184) from "goy" (30), a judicious choice as the terms are far apart and this type of plural is not self-evident for a Spanish reader. Occasionally, the notes specify the cultural or linguistic Ashkenazi source of terms, as in "shabbos" and "Jasidim" (41, 79), a point that is relevant when the readers' familiarity with Judaism is historically via the Sephardic tradition. Grubeshov's biased interrogation of Yakov (*The Fixer* 226), deficiently or problematically handled in earlier versions, becomes now clearer to contemporary Spanish readers than to English readers: not only is "shojet" (*shochet*) well annotated as the ritual slaughterer (*El reparador* [2011] 262), but the translator also identifies the roles of Baal Shem Tov and Zalman Schneur de Liadi, as respective founders of Hasidism and of Chabad (261), Orthodox Judaic movements.

Besides Yiddish, Russian and German are annotated. Specifically, the historical context is well served by the translator's notes in defining turn-of-the-century political parties and unions (Bund, Volkspartei, Seymist; 41, 126) even when these are translatable ("Nobleza Unida"; 204). Also referenced are some key historical events, like the battle that triggered the Russo-Japanese War (63), the Kishinev pogrom (339; this is an editor's note), and the 1861 Emancipation edict of Alexander II (203; see note 6), all of which have a certain bearing on the predicament of Yakov Bok / Mendel Beilis. It is finally worth noting that, in line with the precision in annotation, the term "zhid" used by the antisemitic boatman is pertinently "fixed" in Spanish as derogatory ("denomina *despectivamente* a un judío"; 52) and that Rodríguez-Vida even engages once in critical interpretation of Malamud's symbolic use of names, when in the course of Yakov's reveries on his fate as sacrificial victim, she pertinently clarifies, "Note that Bok, Yakov's surname, means 'he-goat' in yiddish"[18] (186).

One baffling aspect of this new version involves the translation of the term "fixer." While this edition maintains the Sexto Piso title (*El reparador*), the term used throughout the novel for "the fixer"—that is, the translator's choice—is *apañador*. I was unable to query Rodríguez-Vida on this issue, but my assumption is that editorial policy has prevailed in reprinting the 2007 title. The term *apañador* derives from the verb *apañar*, which belongs to a colloquial, often rural, register and has some polysemy in the Spanish language: to pick (as in "to harvest"), to take dishonestly, to dress or wash up, to season food, and, as the sixth and seventh entries in *Diccionario de la Real Academia Española*, respectively, to fix something that is broken and to solve in a precarious or interested way. Although *apañar* is not infrequent, the derived *apañador* is rare in contemporary peninsular Spanish, and the main connotations it takes from the verb, both literally and figuratively, do not ideally serve the portrayal of Yakov as a "righter" of wrongs, for a Spanish readership. As Rodríguez-Vida is originally Argentinian, her choice of the term could be related to informal Latin American usage, as for example the Chilean use of *apañador* to describe someone "who is there for you" or "helps you out."

The translation history of *The Fixer* into Spanish began with a last-minute revision of a title, *El remendón*, a title today hidden away inside a manila envelope in the depths of the General Archives in Alcalá de Henares. Fittingly, it ended with a superbly annotated text, which finally sheds light, for Spanish readers, on the Ashkenazi Jewish tradition and the predicament of Jews in early-century Russia. And yet, since it is in the very nature of literary translation that no individual translation can *fix* a text definitively, *el apañador* coexists within the pages of the 2011 edition with his own double, *el reparador*, presiding over the book's cover. Both are Yakov Bok.

NOTES

1. All translations of target texts, censorship documents, and names of Spanish institutions are mine. Likewise, all emphases within quotations are mine.

2. On the figure of Maurice Samuel and the reasons for undertaking this project, see Kessner 95–96.

3. On the treatment of the Holocaust in Malamud's earlier short fiction, see Watts.

4. Langer relates *The Fixer* primarily to the prison literature of Dostoevsky, Koestler, and Solzhenitsyn, as a "story of an individual whose moral sensibilities are assaulted by an external oppression which breeds internal resistance" (118). In that Yakov's endurance finally results in a

hope for real justice (the trial) and a moral triumph over the conspirators, his experience is incomparable to Holocaust narratives.

5. In Greek myth, Charon ferries the dead across the river Styx into the underworld. Yakov's trip involves a "passing" or symbolic death, as he sheds his Jewish *shtetl* identity by dropping the "prayer things . . . into the Dnieper" (*The Fixer* 28), scared by the boatman's antisemitic rant.

6. The term's implications are twofold. The Emancipation Edict (1861), decreed by Tsar Alexander II, freed peasants from serfdom, ending a predominant feudal system (Service 28). Abraham Lincoln's Emancipation Proclamation (1863), based on his constitutional authority as president, decreed freedom for slaves in all rebel states during the U.S. Civil War.

7. Two relevant studies of censorship in Franco's Spain are Abellán's *Censura y creación literaria en España*, with a focus on literature, and Román Gubern's *La censura*, with a focus on cinema.

8. "¿Ataca el Dogma? ¿A la moral? ¿A la Iglesia o a sus ministros? ¿Al Régimen y a sus instituciones? ¿A las personas que colaboran o han colaborado con el Régimen?" I deliberately use "attack" to translate the verb *atacar* (meaning "criticize") but in a martial language register, characteristic of the era's official rhetoric. Note that *Régimen* is derogatory in today's Spanish but was not during Francoism, when the term had an official status.

9. "Los pasajes censurables ¿califican el contenido total de la obra?"

10. For an overview of the stages and tensions in the development of a "national" culture, the shifts in university and educational policies, Arias Salgado's period of office as minister for education and tourism, and the rising influence of Opus Dei technocrats in policy making, see Paine, 434–39.

11. After having held several high-ranking positions with the Franco regime, Fraga played an active role in the *Transición* into democracy, as one of the "founding fathers" of the Spanish 1977 constitution. He was the founder and national head of the conservative party Alianza Popular (AP; later Partido Popular), but the poor results of AP in early general elections led him to successfully retreat into regional politics in his native Galicia, which he governed from 1990 to 2005.

12. "Ley 14/1966, de 18 de marzo, de Prensa e Imprenta," *Boletín Oficial del Estado* 67 (19 March 1966): 3310–15. Often quoted as "Ley de Libertad [freedom] de Prensa," the reference to freedom is not in the law's title. Article 1 broadly decrees "freedom of expression in print," yet article

2 itemizes as the "only restrictions" to article 1 "respect for truth and morality" and "compliance with all Fundamental Laws of the Movimiento Nacional," thus severely offsetting the law's rationale.

13. Counter to this translation strategy, the Portuguese translation of *The Fixer* adopted an overly didactic title that stresses the universality of the novel's antisemitic theme, *Será crime ser Judeu?* In English, this reads literally, "Is it a crime to be a Jew?"

14. Since censorship questions remained unchanged for a long period, editors and translators anticipated potentially "dangerous" passages or wording: official censorship was regularly preempted by carrying out self-censorship (*autocensura*), either through textual omissions or by toning down the language.

15. In decreasing order of population percentage: Episcopalian and Evangelical churches, Muslims, Buddhists, Greek Orthodox churches, and Jews. Altogether they account for only 3 percent of Spain's population (2008 data).

16. I do not focus here on how the Spanish translations might work for Latin American readerships.

17. Both *rabí* and *rabino* are used in Spanish: *rabí* is generally used as a title form, preceding a name.

18. Although this is an isolated example ("Raisl" as an anagram for "Israel" is not annotated), it proves the translator's meticulous scrutiny of this novel and possibly her familiarity with Malamud criticism.

CHAPTER 10

Dostoevsky, Lawrence, Malamud

Malamud's Heroes, Facing the Twin Rejection of Identity and Sensuality

RÉMI ASTRUC

UNIVERSITY OF CERGY-PONTOISE, FRANCE

Translated from the French by Alan Astro, Trinity University

Bernard Malamud's narratives seem to follow a cardinal rule whereby the heroes discover their identity by discovering sensuality. Two figures—woman and the "double" (at once mentor, rival, and image of the hero)—therefore emerge as privileged actors in the dramas of the slow discovery of love and self depicted in Malamud's novels. The quest for sensuality and the quest for self are quite obviously the twin pillars of his fictional universe. Likewise, they are, not surprisingly, at the heart of two novels key to understanding Malamud's oeuvre: Fyodor Dostoevsky's *The Double* (1846) and D. H. Lawrence's *Sons and Lovers* (1913).

The torments caused by uncertain identity and ambiguous sensuality are privileged themes in Malamud, starting with his very first works. Two of his mature novels present these motifs in a very particular manner insofar as they establish intertextual links with the two earlier writers and their novels that had historically laid the groundwork for such thematics.

AN AMERICAN JEWISH VERSION
OF *THE DOUBLE*

Indeed, Malamud's novel *The Tenants* relies quite explicitly on the "Saint-Petersburg poem" wherein the unfortunate Goliadkin, a lowly titular councillor, one fine day encounters a double, who is, to say the least, quite cumbersome. There are numerous common points between these two works, not only on the plot level but also regarding particular scenes and even their very structure.

However, in *The Tenants*, it is not exactly a "double," a physically identical being, who comes to haunt the writer Harry Lesser, the last occupant of an East Side tenement who is trying to compose the end of his novel. Rather, it is a fellow writer who has sneaked into the dilapidated building in search of the solitude and self-discipline that characterize Lesser. There is only one difference between them, but it is a major one: Lesser is Jewish, and the new arrival is black. Nonetheless, in their shared literary concerns, the two men clearly emerge as twins, before becoming bitter sibling rivals.

Even though Lesser is not faced with another Lesser exactly as Goliadkin finds a second Goliadkin, Lesser perceives his doppelganger as a sort of photographic negative of himself: is he encountering a "negative presence as though on film? The white figure of a black man haunting the halls?" (*The Tenants* 183). Moreover, the beginnings of the two novels are palpably similar. Harry Lesser, like Goliadkin, awakens one morning to start a new day of work and beholds his refection in the mirror: "Lesser catching sight of himself in his lonely glass wakes to finish his book" (1). Goliadkin does the same in *The Double*:

> It was a little before eight o'clock in the morning when Yakov Petrovitch Golyadkin, a titular councillor, woke up from a long sleep. He yawned, stretched, and at last opened his eyes completely. For two minutes, however, he lay in his bed without moving, as though he were not yet quite certain whether he were awake or still asleep, whether all that was going on around him were real and actual, or the continuation of his confused dreams. . . . From his bed he ran straight to a little round looking-glass that stood on his chest of drawers. (3–4)

In both works, the protagonists suffer from a difficulty in separating illusion from reality. Goliadkin confuses the world of dreams with real life, and Lesser imagines a stranger he meets on the stairs:

> Though he remembers none although his sleep is stuffed with dreams, Lesser reveries one touched with fear: Here's this stranger I meet on the stairs.
> "Who you looking for, brother?"
> "Who you calling brother, mother?"
> Exit intruder. (*The Tenants* 2)

Moreover, the appearance of both heroes' doubles seems linked to mental disorders producing pathological ideations: a "nervous condition" as diagnosed by Dr. Rutespitz in Goliadkin and a syndrome caused by lack of vitamin D in Lesser's case. For the latter, the malady is all the more important as his sole activity consists of composing fiction. In each work, the double is most of all similar to the protagonist, but they are also different and even complementary. Goliadkin No. 2 is everything that the first cannot or does not want to be: a smooth talker, a cajoler, a joker, one who knows how to gain favors from well-placed people in order to achieve his ends. In particular, he can charm his bureau chief, "His Excellency," as the hero himself only wishes he could. William Spearmint, in turn, possesses what Harry Lesser does not, and vice versa. Though both men are writers, they are incapable of producing a work: each one has what the other lacks. Lesser cannot come up with the raw experience that should make up the content of his novel, but he masters perfectly all the formal technical and literary aspects. Contrarily, Spearmint cannot compose perfect, pure form, because he is overflowing with the uncontrollable vitality of a rich, human experience that he tries to pour as such into his writing. The resultant prose can only be clumsy.

Hence, the rivalry between the two men, as in *The Double*, starts as something professional and social (Goliadkin dreams of a promotion as Lesser does of literary fame) and ends up as an amorous contest. In the earlier work, the love prize is Clara, whom Goliadkin wants to marry; and in the later work, it is Irene, who is already William Spearmint's girlfriend. What follows, in both cases, is an ever more overt struggle with a diabolical "other," which culminates in fatal hand-to-hand combat.

The very style of the two works offers striking similarities. In particular, Goliadkin expresses himself through repetitive, mirror-like formulae, of which the most recurrent is "There is this and that." Thus, he resembles the narrator himself, whose redundancies surprisingly reflect the scene itself and the invisible presence of the double:

> All at once Mr. Golyadkin broke off, his tongue failed him and he began trembling like a leaf; he even closed his eyes for a minute. Hoping, however, that the object of his terror was only an illusion, he opened his eyes at last and stole a timid glance to the right. No, it was not an illusion! . . . His acquaintance of that morning was tripping along by his side, smiling, peeping into his face, and apparently seeking an opportunity to begin a conversation with him. The conversation was not begun, however. They both walked like this for about fifty paces. All Mr. Golyadkin's efforts were concentrated on muffling himself up, hiding himself in his coat and pulling his hat down as far as possible over his eyes. To complete his mortification, his companion's coat and hat looked as though they had been taken off Mr. Golyadkin himself. (Dostoevsky 60)

Likewise, the very syntactic structure of *The Tenants* takes on a mirror-like quality. Sentences reverberate ad infinitum, as though carried by an echo: "As soon as he ends one he begins another. Now that the imagination is imagining Lesser imagines it done, the long labor concluded at last. . . . Ah this live earth, this sceptered isle on a silver sea, this Thirty-first Street and Third Avenue. This forsaken house. This happy unhappy Lesser having to write" (*The Tenants* 3).

Sometimes, an uncanny, bewitching symmetry resonates in a sentence—"The garbage of language become the language of garbage" (*The Tenants* 4)—and paragraphs almost always end on a phrase that is neutral in cadence, on a balanced chord, emphasizing the binary pattern on which the entire work is based. Some examples are "Home is where my book is"; "I don't know where's there but here I am writing"; "That was outside and he was in"; "A face is a face: it changes as it faces"; "He tests his fate: He lives to write, writes to live" (*The Tenants* 4, 7, 10, 11, 19).

It thus appears that Malamud executes a veritable macrostructural doubling of Dostoevsky's novel, bringing forth a relatively complex intertext wherein the questioning of identity not only exists on the plot level but also serves to explore differences between the work and its model, the hypotext *The Double*. The Malamudian theme of the double, buttressed by a relationship of intertextuality that reproduces it, allows the author to extend the scope of his novel with utmost skill. He adds to the internal mirror structure—concerning the identity of the protagonist—an external play of mirrors that moves the question onto the identity of the work itself, the status of fiction, and the writer's creativity. The specular dimension is transformed into a purely dizzying kaleidoscopic relationship, wherein the very *notion* of identity is subverted. That process is the hallmark of identity, according to Helga Schier's observations on the contemporary novel: "Although the novels present a character in search for a unified experience of self . . . the experience of time no longer leads to the experience of identity. What the novels describe instead is the division of self into various selves throughout discontinuous temporal moments" (90).

Indeed, the major thrust of *The Tenants*, which places this work squarely within the kind of modernity we are speaking of, lies in telling the story of a Goliadkin who is no longer a titular councillor but a writer. Harry Lesser's imagination, which is in large degree responsible for the appearance of his infernal double, William Spearmint, has also produced a novel that merges, at least in part, with *The Tenants* itself. This is suggested by ambiguous phrases such as "Lesser writes" and three "the end's" in the story, each of which is followed by more text. Thereby, Harry Lesser becomes one with the ultimate author, Malamud, in a final avatar of the phenomenon of doubling.

As the psychoanalyst Otto Rank reminds us, certain mythological traditions conceive of the universe as created through a god's admiring himself in a mirror, as Dionysus did in Hephaestus's looking glass. This is even truer of the double of the real universe constituted by the literary universe. Besides the part of himself that an author pours into his heroes, he is also a demigod in whose hands is placed his characters' fate.

If the novel is about a novelist looking for love—wherein doubles multiply themselves ad infinitum, as they do for Goliadkin in the grip of his paranoia—writing becomes a complex recursive structure that Lesser hopes will allow himself to change and acquire a new identity: "He will learn through some miracle of transformation as he writes, betrayal as well as bounty, perhaps a kind of suffering. . . . Thus Lesser writes his book and his book writes Lesser. That's what's taking so long" (Freese, "Trouble" 108).

However, rather than a god, the writer in *The Tenants* turns out to be a sorcerer's apprentice who plays with fire by attempting to flex divine attributes. Far from finding a reassuring image, he gets lost in the mirror. The double reflects not Narcissus's self-satisfaction but, instead, the demiurge's doubts and anxieties: he is a rival and a tormentor. Lesser's self-portrait thus takes on the anonymous, anguished-filled face of an identity crisis.

The Tenants is a proteiform work that extends itself in multiple explicit and implicit directions. It thus allows the author to revisit the problematics of identity and update them considerably. The appearance of the double is, as before, the manifestation of the protagonist's internal distress, but now it is linked to a precise social reality: the problem of tolerance and coexistence among ethnic communities in the modern world and, more particularly, in large American cities. The issue is thus taken directly out of contemporary history and transposed onto the artistic domain, where its terrible aspect is brought into critical focus. Alvin B. Kernan observes how this novel specifically marks the entry of a certain reality onto the literary field: "*The Tenants* is a carefully constructed parable in which every detail has meaning on at least two levels, and the tenement is not only a realistic depiction of the desperate state of much of New York City . . . but of the wasteland of modern western society and the incursion of this reality into literature toward the end of a terrifying century" (*Imaginary* 78).

Indeed, *The Tenants* illustrates how in 1970s American society, Jews and blacks are in the position of fraternal rivals. Although both communities have suffered from WASP hegemony, blacks consider the Jews—incomparably better integrated into the fabric of society—as being on the side of the white oppressor.

Additionally, the question of vexed identity is elaborated in *The Tenants* along a new axis: that of the conflict between art and life. Harry Lesser, alleging he cannot finish his novel in a place other than where he began it, wreaks havoc on the existence of his landlord by refusing to leave the tenement, despite all offers and supplications. The owner wishes to replace the building with a modern complex that would provide him with means to lead a decent life. He exclaims, "What's a make-believe novel, Lesser, against all my woes and miseries that I have explained to you? . . . For Christ's sake, what are you writing, the Holy Bible?" (*The Tenants* 18). Indeed, the identity crisis afflicting the modern Goliadkin—Lesser—has less to do with the position of Jews in American society of the 1960s and '70s than with the writerly condition, the alienation that keeps the novelist far both from normal life and from his contemporaries.

This modern American version of *The Double* permits the author to approach the second major theme of this work: sensuality. Lesser, absorbed in his art, is desensitized to love, which he nonetheless dreams of experiencing. Only by frequenting his double and his double's friends does Lesser succeed in opening up both himself and his art to the fresh sensations that life and love can offer. But to the detriment of such positivity, the amorous rivalry between the two writers ends up cutting each one off from the other and places them into selfish and deadly literary competition:

> One night Willie and Lesser met in a grassy clearing in the bush. The night was moonless above the moss-dripping, rope-entwined trees. Neither of them could see the other but sensed where he stood. Each heard himself scarcely breathing.
> "Bloodsucking Jew Niggerhater."
> "Anti-Semitic Ape."
> . . . They aimed at each other accurate blows. (*The Tenants* 211)

The hatred engendered by the rival is thus stronger than love. In fact, the two are led into a most complete kind of savagery, which cannot fail to remind us of the encounter and combat in *Sons and Lovers* between Paul Morel and Baxter Daws, his lover's husband: "They had met in a naked extremity of hate, and it was a bond. At any rate, the elemental man in each had met" (Lawrence 445).

SONS AND LOVERS IN VERMONT

Dubin's Lives, Malamud's work that immediately follows *The Tenants*, explores even further the theme of problematic sensuality and borrows much from D. H. Lawrence's final novel. The question of identity is posed by William Dubin's amorous roving. He loses sight of his true self as he writes the biographies of several "masters" and moves back and forth between his wife, Kitty, and his young mistress, Fanny. The resultant mental distress begins the process that led to doubling for Goliadkin and Lesser: "In one place he found himself in another. In the bathroom in the cellar. Lost self, selves" (*Dubin's Lives* 318).

But instead of being a new Goliadkin, William Dubin is a second Paul Morel, searching for sensuality and self-realization. Like Lawrence's hero, Dubin is imprisoned within a family tragedy that deprives him of the sexual fulfillment he seeks. Just as Paul Morel knows he cannot love properly and ends up hurting the women in his life, so William Dubin is cut off from experiencing any sexual or amorous plenitude in his marriage. Such sentiments are available for him solely in an adulterous relationship that he knows to be as destabilizing as it is inevitably ephemeral. Indeed, only in young Fanny's arms can he allow himself to be sensually awakened by the mystical communion of bodies—something that is revealed to him in D. H. Lawrence's novels and that he now attempts to make real in order the better to understand the writer whose biography he is composing. With Fanny, Dubin attempts to re-create the initiation to love experienced by Paul Morel and Miriam at Willey Farm. Together, they take a long walk through the countryside; Dubin teaches Fanny the names of flowers; and when they make love in the undergrowth, the discovery of pleasure is an epiphany: "He felt like a god" (*Dubin's Lives* 218).

Just as *The Tenants* sends us back to Dostoevsky's *Double*, the imbroglio of feeling is made all the more complex here through intertextuality: the explicit reference to *Sons and Lovers*, which climaxes in D. H. Lawrence's appearing to William Dubin in a dream. It is thus no longer a question simply of parallels between the works but rather of the effective presence of the source text's author taking the form of a fictional character. The British writer comes in person to reprimand a questionable biographer.

Thus, there is more than a simple relationship of intertextuality between *Dubin's Lives* and *Sons and Lovers*. Rather, we find an *intertextual variation*, according to Gérard Genette's definition of intertextuality as "the effective presence of one text within another" (8). The very figure of the author of *Sons and Lovers*—and no longer just his text—appears in Malamud's novel.

Dubin's life is thus afflicted with the ill so virulently denounced by Lawrence: an irreconcilable separation between mind and body that weighs down the corporeal with fatal inertia. The hero avows, "I was the waiter's true son, shared his inertia, fear, living fate—out of habit, compassion, impure love" (*Dubin's Lives* 87). Not reality but literature, for Dubin synonymous with vicarious living, is the sole area to which he can dedicate himself. In turn, Paul Morel, who likewise takes refuge in art in order to avoid life's demand that he compromise his principles, suffers a fragmentation of consciousness, manifested by invasive inner voices:

> "But you can go on with your painting," said the will in him. "Or else you can beget children. They both carry on her [Mrs. Morel's] effort."
> "Painting is not living."
> "Then live."
> "Marry whom?" came the sulky question.
> "As best you can." (Lawrence 412)

Similarly, Dubin's consciousness is splintered into interior dialogues, reinforcing the parallelism between the two works by extending it onto the formal level:

> Q. What makes a clown sad? A. Other clowns. . . .
> Q. Why did it happen? A. Who knows for sure? One day I took a chance, made a move, got involved. Life is to invest into life. (*Dubin's Lives* 87–88)

Malamud's hero, as victim of his own hesitation and weakness, sinks into a profound existential crisis that puts his marriage and entire life into question. Thus, William Dubin figures somewhere between Paul Morel and his mother, who made up for a failed existence—full of suffering and sacrifices in the company of a man whom she despised—by living through her children's experiences. Likewise, William Dubin compensates for his unhappy marriage and boring life by penning biographies of men who achieved both fame and personal thrill: "Everybody's life is mine unlived. One writes lives he can't live. To live forever is a human hunger" (*Dubin's Lives* 11).

However, even as Malamud carries on Lawrence's investigations into the difficulty of love and the ambiguous association of possessiveness and fear that perturbs desire, he uses his character Dubin to pose the problem of human relationships during a period when liberalization of behavior sometimes preceded that of consciousness. Thus, in the universe of *Dubin's Lives*, the characters are obsessed with the search for individual pleasure and have transformed egocentrism into a rule to live by. In the name of each one's quest for happiness that seems to justify the complete liberty of all to act as they will ("I am entitled to an open ordinary and satisfying life of my own," says Fanny; *Dubin's Lives* 268), the protagonists end up scorning the natural bonds of family, friendship, and love, which they now see as no more than obstacles. Dubin, attempting to live an intense experience with his young mistress, hopes to seize his last chance to escape the confinement and insipidness of his marriage as well as the self-denial involved in his work as biographer. However, he ends up lost in the twists and turns of a complicated sensuality that overtakes his family life as he deceives others and compromises himself. Indeed, the amorous fling with Fanny propelled by his pursuit of youth turns into a parody of sexual fulfillment and an ordeal that leads the hero to the point of physical and intellectual exhaustion. Premature sexual impotence comes as the result of a fatiguing double life wherein the hero is torn between two women: a wife for whom he feels, if not love, at least strong attachment; and a young, demanding mistress, passionate but capricious, with whom he pursues an extremely rocky romance.

Dubin has been led to seek a hedonism and freedom that are depicted in the poets he reads and are offered to him by modern society, which places an adventurous, "liberated" woman within his reach. The resultant experience fills the biographer Dubin's existence with successive disappointments that ultimately make him desire just one thing: the equilibrium he had known before. "I've had it with loneliness. I've had it with youth. I'll take only what I'm entitled to. . . . I'm an odd inward man held together by an ordered life" (*Dubin's Lives* 326).

Having become a "dangling man" (the title of a novel by Malamud's fellow Jewish American writer Saul Bellow), William Dubin discovers that psychological fragmentation and deep depression are the price to pay for the disorder he has contributed to creating in his own existence. Indeed, after he meets Fanny, it is impossible for him to return to his wife and family. He must find some balance between these two women, each of whom he loves in his own way; but he cannot bring himself to leave either of them. The final irony is that, as a father, William Dubin finds himself forced to reproach his daughter for acting in a way analogous to his own actions: at twenty, no older than Fanny, she is having an affair with a man her father's age. William Dubin is ever caught in the trap of his own contradictions.

Ultimately, the subject of *Dubin's Lives* is the difficulty faced by an American Jew in the 1970s as he tries to "be a man," to give meaning to that expression—an essential theme in *Sons and Lovers*. Malamud skillfully makes that motif emerge from the novel's backdrop, which includes Lawrence and his work *Sons and Lovers*. By basing his work on his predecessor's work and depicting a middle-aged Jewish American biographer's literary and sensual quest, Malamud establishes a parallel between contemporary American mores and the British author's theories of sexual liberation. We see a consequence of a way of life that developed in the United States in the 1960s and '70s. From it has resulted an all-devouring search for sensual fulfillment that poses the question of individual responsibility in the face of primordial family relationships—in a home where successive ordeals have moreover forged indestructible bonds. For that reason, the hero who starts seeking sensuality ends up searching for identity. As William Dubin's adventures conclude, he knows that his escapade with a woman who had barely entered adult life is neither a satisfying refuge from the failure of his own life nor an effective remedy for anxiety aroused by death slowly approaching: "I've had it with testing myself, he thought. Du bist Dubin. I know who I am. . . . I must act my age" (*Dubin's Lives* 323).

Moreover, as happened in *The Tenants*, Dubin's penchant for vicarious living opens an investigation into the novelist's craft and the discipline it demands. The autobiographical dimension can hardly escape the reader. William Dubin's double now takes on Malamud's own traits, in accordance with the autobiographical temptation that is yet another mark of the author's modernity.

In *Dubin's Lives* and *The Tenants,* issues of identity and sensuality merge into the main question on which Malamud's entire oeuvre is based: how to be an American Jew. In this regard, references to previous literary works permit the author to extricate themes he favors from their isolated cultural context and endow them with universality. Thus, two apparently very different works—*Dubin's Lives* and *The Tenants*—turn out to portray Malamud's very personal conception of Jewishness and what "being Jewish" in the United States can mean. At once serving as models and foils, *The Double* and *Sons and Lovers* allow the author to move beyond imitation of and distance from these works. He thereby lays a foundation for his own worldview, which reflects his era and the predicament of American Jews. The double literary and thematic forerunners help flesh out the complications of the author's Jewish American heroes, all of whom seem condemned to endless desire and perpetual exile from themselves and others.

CHAPTER 11

Writing on the Edge of Doom

Theological Reflections on Bernard Malamud's *God's Grace*

TILL KINZEL

TECHNISCHE UNIVERSITÄT, BERLIN, GERMANY

The American writer Saul Bellow notes in a letter to Bernard Malamud detailing his response to *God's Grace* that this book, written with a certain openness, "is unsettling": "I predict that it will invite an unusual diversity of interpretations" (*Letters* 388). Trying to answer the question "What sort of book is it?" he makes a number of observations that point to issues worth exploring: "The edge of doom, and over: the destruction of the planet, flood, apocalypse, the voice of God. Cohn is Noah, Cohn is Job, he is even Robinson Crusoe. The world's end can't put an end to Jewish wit. Your God is no humorist, however, and the novel is genuinely apocalyptic" (387). Bellow's prediction concerning the diversity of interpretations indeed proved correct. Malamud's novel is regarded by most critics as an abject failure. Joseph Epstein, writing in *Commentary* in 1982 and giving a complete overview of Malamud's career, compares Malamud unfavorably to Maimonides; and he notes that Malamud has become an "almost negligible figure" due to books like *God's Grace*. Epstein, it seems, does not enjoy what a less scholarly source calls a "witty fable" that can be recommended to book discussion groups (Reisner 121). As Epstein's comparison to Maimonides indicates, his critical frame of reference is somewhat odd, to put it mildly, even though the novel is steeped in Jewish references, leading David Mesher to the judgment that *God's Grace* is Malamud's "most Jewish novel" (111).

Harold Bloom's laconic reference to *God's Grace* as a "disaster" (introduction x) would seem to indicate that a closer study of the novel hardly merits the effort. In what follows, however, I explore the possibility that the novel was not in fact the disaster that Bloom thinks it is. A theological perspective on the book may well help us to see that Malamud offers not just a story to enjoy but food for thought about the most important issues for human beings—about God and the world, about the possibility of revelation and the possibility of understanding correctly this revelation. That Malamud's novel does offer food for thought was also noted by another reviewer, the novelist Alan Lelchuk (1982), although he seemed to regard this as more of an "extraliterary provocation" of doubtful literary or aesthetic value. The allegorical nature of Malamud's novel, its wealth of symbols and intertextual references, makes it a peculiar text for the postmodern age, because its manifest playfulness is in the service of a seriousness that betrays a decidedly nonpostmodern outlook. Decoding the novel's symbols has already been undertaken admirably by critics such as Peter Freese (*Apocalypse* 45–89), so there is no need to repeat this exercise here. Likewise, it does not make sense here to regurgitate all the intertextual references built into the novel or to explain in detail the readings that went into the making of the novel (see Davis 325). It should also be noted that *God's Grace* has not suffered a complete lack of scholarly attention, which luckily indicates that early reviewers' disparaging comments are not the last word—a different kind of "end"—on *God's Grace* (see, e.g., Cronin; Müller; Buchen; Wolford).

Malamud's story is a story about "the end." This is something that Malamud also addresses in connection with writing itself. Harry Lesser, in *The Tenants*, seems to produce a tentative "end of novel" early on in the book (23), but two pages on, he connects thoughts about the relationship between God and man to the end of the world and writing: "God since the dawn of man should have made it his business to call out names: Jacob meet Ishmael. 'I am not my brother's brother.' Who says? Back in his study he wrote hurriedly, as though he had heard the end of the world falling in the pit of time and hoped to get his last word written before then" (25).

Lesser's coupling the notion of the end of the world with his own situation as a writer who struggles "to get his last word written before then" creates the sense of a special urgency that is all the more troubling as it poses the question of why a writer writes. Does it really only come down to this: "He lives to write, writes to live," without any transcending ambition beyond that (23)? Later in the book, Lesser envisages the wrecking of the tenement building he alone inhabits with his book manuscript and again links the imagined loss of his book to the end of civilization itself: "End of book, era, civilization? Man's hasty fate?" (199). This hyperbolical link between the end of a novel and the end of the world is obvious enough in *The Tenants* but hardly prepares the reader for what is in store for him in *God's Grace*. This novel offers a truly disturbing picture not only of the fate of human beings in the world but also of the nature of God.

God is presented by Malamud as someone who makes mistakes, a notion that is already introduced on the very first page of the novel. In fact, this "minuscule" error on the part of God is the only reason that there is a story to tell in the first place (*God's Grace* 3). One might therefore say that storytelling, in this extreme case at least, presupposes the nonperfection of God's power. God only claims a sort of perfection for himself that goes as a matter of course, but this obviously only pertains to something internal, what one might call God's interiority (4). This internal perfection does not, it seems, spill over into the creation.

Telling a story about *the* end is, somewhat paradoxically, also a literary tradition within which this narrative conceit is repeated again and again, say, from Mary Shelley's *The Last Man* (1826) to the apocalyptic visions of Kurt Vonnegut's novels, Doris Lessing's *The Memoirs of a Survivor* (1974), or Cormac McCarthy's *The Road* (2006), to name just a few popular titles (see Freese, *Clown*; Maack; cf. Zamora). Apocalyptic scenarios differ widely and share distinct similarities with certain kinds of dystopian fictions. A narrator of apocalyptic developments faces particular problems in establishing reliability and authentification for what he or she reports, since the possible addressees are initially doubtful but then must presumably become aware of the apocalypse anyway. Whereas Cormac McCarthy's *The Road*, for example, circumvents this problem by employing a covert heterodiegetic narrator without any indications of hindsight knowledge, P. D. James, otherwise well known for her Adam Dalgliesh crime fictions, opts for an autodiegetic narrator who is also a trained historian, Theo Faren. In her novel *The Children of Men* (1992), she depicts a childless England under dictatorial rule, in which the last child was born twenty-five years ago, with human extinction looming on the horizon when the narrating time sets in. Further examples for writing the end might be those novels that tell about an end that happened a very long time ago, such as in Russell Hoban's *Ridley Walker* (1980) or Walter M. Miller's *A Canticle for Leibowitz* (1960) (see Horstmann, "Post-nuclear" 306). As Margaret Atwood points out, many writers imagine dystopias out of some moral concern: "Dystopias are often more like a dire warning than satires, dark shadows cast by the present into the future. They are what will happen to us if we don't pull up our socks" (104). This kind of moral approach would seem to be present in *God's Grace* as well. Malamud's scenario in *God's Grace* implies a very peculiar "pulling up our socks."

Malamud's story is a story about "the end." But it is an end that is primarily engineered by human beings, although no political analysis of the events leading to this catastrophic war is offered. Even though the novel features God as a character interacting with the last human being on earth, those who are directly responsible for "the end" are the human beings who started the nuclear war that instantly created the conditions pertaining in the novel (*God's Grace* 8). The fact that atomic missiles achieved this result links the novel not only to earlier literary attempts to depict "last men" but also to the political and philosophical literature on "the bomb." Thus, the German philosopher Karl Jaspers, in his best seller *Die Atombombe und die Zukunft des Menschen* from 1958, presented a thorough examination of the challenge to humanity posed by the existence of the atomic bomb. Jaspers expressed faith in the idea that human beings cannot stop being human beings and suggested that human beings cannot turn into apes or ants (see Wroblewsky 213). This kind of strict species boundary, however, can be ignored by novelists who want to confront the issues raised by the existence of the atomic bomb in the medium of storytelling. Jaspers linked his reflections on the atomic bomb to the problem that he called "Das Denken des Endes," that is, "thinking the end" (446–47). For even though thinking the end is an age-old question, there is a difference with regard to the twentieth century, namely, the fact that the human consciousness extends to the whole earth. What was regarded as "the end" in earlier times may only have been an end in one particular part of the world. But now that it is technically possible to explore every part of the earth and to know about it, a comprehensive end for human beings becomes thinkable. Thinking the end necessarily acquires mythic dimensions, as Jaspers notes, as in the theological tradition with its stories of the Flood or of the destruction of Sodom and Gomorrah (457). For even the vision of the destruction of life through the atomic bomb requires a kind of jumping toward an impossible knowledge of the whole that is a fiction (463). But precisely because it is a fiction, literature like Malamud's *God's Grace* can deal with an issue that even philosophy cannot deal with in purely analytical terms. "The end" understood comprehensively cannot really be understood.

In addition, the very possibility of annihilation through the atomic bomb implies theological consequences, as a contemporary of Jaspers, the nonacademic philosopher Günther Anders, indicated in a book first published in 1956. Anders suggests that the atomic bomb signals the fact that it is no longer God's power that can be considered absolute but rather our power (239). God's power to create something from nothing (*creatio ex nihilo*) is replaced, Anders argues, by the contravening power to annihilate (*potestas annihilationis*). The human power to kill each other off, to bring about "the end," radically unhinges God as God, for it is now human beings who are "masters of the apocalypse" (*Herren der Apokalypse*). This mastery however, is paradoxical, since it finally results in a complete loss of mastery.

Malamud's story world incorporates this twentieth-century state of things and of critical reflections by letting Calvin Cohn survive the nuclear holocaust. While this holocaust happened, Cohn was exploring the bottom of the sea, so that he was at a place located far away from the civilization that culminated in the complete annihilation of humankind. His survival can thus appear as the result of the fact that he was out of sight even of God himself. That he is indeed the only surviving human being is presented as an indubitable fact by the narrator in the beginning of "that story" (*God's Grace* 3). But this narrator cannot be a human being, nor can he properly address human beings. So the telling of the story cannot actually be told as a story is normally told, namely, after the fact, but rather must be told as a story that will happen, with a narrator pretending to tell something in the past, even though the "as if" nature of the story is occluded in order to make it more suggestive. This, of course, is the standard operating procedure of apocalyptic storytelling, as Jaspers suggests by noting that we are thinking Being after the doom (*Untergang*) as if we were still there ("Wir denken das Sein nach dem Untergang, als ob wir noch dabei wären, so wie wir den Kosmos denken und wie er vor allem Leben war"; 457). The "as if" nature of Malamud's story allows the author to explore so many issues in one book as if this were the last book written from which to extract everything there is to know about God and humanity. Freese's observations that the novel "is not only an exercise in theology but also one in anthropology" and that "the central issue of theodicy is intricately linked with that of evolution" point to this enormously wide "discursive field" spanning from the book of Genesis to Darwin and beyond (*Apocalypse* 73). Calvin Cohn is an inheritor and a representative of both these cultural forces that are in tension, even if various attempts at a synthesis have been undertaken. In Cohn, however, these divergent cultural forces sit uneasily side by side. On the one hand, he is a modern scientist; on the other, he does show religiosity and even reflects on the proper rules, such as those for saying kaddish. Cohn is also someone who not only listens to God but also thinks about what God says and argues with God about his statements.

The narrative of the novel presents Calvin Cohn in some kind of interaction with God, but the cognitive status of these interactions is not entirely clear. Malamud's intertextual playfulness in combination with a seemingly straightforward heterodiegetic narration poses problems of reliability. As Kurt Müller points out, Malamud occasionally uses a kind of narration also found in such texts by Nathaniel Hawthorne as "Young Goodman Brown," in which it remains purposefully unclear whether certain experiences are actual happenings in the world of material things or merely internal experiences (842–43). The prime exhibit is the following sentence: "He danced in a shower of rocks; but that may have been his imagining" (*God's Grace* 7). The sentence is framed by two references to God, first a reference to the creation of humans by God and second a reference to God's wrath or rather Cohn's fear of it. This casts some doubt on the reliability of the narration, at least concerning the source of God's words, words that are, strangely enough, presented in quotation marks, as Freese has pointed out (*Apocalypse* 87).

The God who speaks directly, or seems to speak directly, to the last surviving human being is a self-revealing God. He comments on his own nature, claiming that he is perfect, even though the world he set in motion is not. This God seems to have ordered in such a way that he does not have to be omniscient (*God's Grace* 4). A God who is not omniscient, however, may also not be in complete control of things. A God who can make errors, minuscule as they may be, is clearly not infallible. And even though God's speech is a kind of revelation, it is still a revelation that is not self-evident or that is not in need of interpretation. As the narrator presents Cohn's thoughts about God, he ascribes to God mysteriousness and, more significantly, adds that his "speech was silence" (23). At another place, God is explicitly mentioned as saying "nothing" (38). Silent speech is a paradoxical phenomenon, since it only increases the mystery, prompting the last man, Calvin Cohn, to wonder what God's plans actually are. The paradox involved here is that in spite of signals from God, it is still necessary to make sense of them, triggering the inescapable semiotic activity on the receiver's side. Semiotic decoding can be circumscribed by a system of codes that are incorporated into the very language and particularly the stories that have been transmitted from the most ancient times. The fact that Calvin Cohn owns a Bible and knows its stories makes him constantly read signs in light of these stories. This is equally true of the beginning of the story and its end. For in the beginning, Calvin Cohn sees "a faded rainbow" in the sky, traditionally interpreted as a sign for God's covenant with human beings (7). As a rainbow can be naturally explained, as the scientist Cohn surely knows, it is clear that he must have been influenced by the biblical stories to rejoice in face of the rainbow and to regard it as a "good sign" (7). The narrator adds the word "seemed" in order to make clear that reading the rainbow in this way is completely arbitrary. Cohn's mind is likewise suffused by biblical stories when he is finally killed in a sacrificial manner by Buz, the chimpanzee. Cohn and the ape reenact the story of Abraham going out into the mountains to sacrifice his son, Isaac. He wonders where the ram to be offered is, before he quickly realizes that he himself will be the burnt offering. The age-old stories lead him to expect a repetition of the old stories' content, although this is something that does not happen. Does that mean that the old stories are thrown into doubt? There is no naysaying angel to save him as Isaac was saved from being slaughtered. The whole

189

story of Abraham's challenge is one of the most provocative ones in the Old Testament and remains puzzling to many people who spend time thinking about it. Kierkegaard's *Fear and Trembling* (1843) is perhaps the book that presents the scandal of that disturbing story most memorably, though Malamud's gloss on it seems to turn everything on its head. Here, it is the "father" who is sacrificed, not the son, and there is no naysaying angel, no ram that miraculously replaces the intended victim of slaughter. Calvin Cohn seems to be more surprised by the fact that he is killed in old age than that he was chosen to be sacrificed in the first place. This can be read as reconciliation with God, even including some small ray of hope for a "world to come" (*God's Grace* 223). Whether God is in fact the power behind the monkey's actions remains doubtful, but perhaps the mere fact that the last act of the story, the ape's kaddish for Calvin Cohn, is a mimetic repetition, an "aping," of earlier rites enacted by Cohn himself should be read as a ray of hope. Cohn, at an earlier point in the story, is presented as imagining what God thought. God and his mercy are drawn into question precisely because men can and did come to "this dreadful end" (39). Cohn's reflections highlight the importance of the end for judging God's goodness, because the end, in this case, complete obliteration, is taken as the ultimate normative reference point for the evaluation of the meaningfulness or meaninglessness of God's creation. The creation that has to end in this way is a trial-and-error-creation: "Maybe next time" will there be a better hanging together of body and soul than in this dispensation, but even this "maybe" is less than certain. That the end intended by God might be just one end among many, turning out to be not "the" end, is indicated in the same passage that suggests everyone was his own story: God, it seems or seems plausible, likes "endings based on beginnings, and beginnings on endings" (39). The interchangeability of end and beginning, where every beginning is at the same time also an end and every end can be another beginning, amounts to a deconstruction of the very concepts of beginning and end. If creation is a beginning, it is also the end to chaos, and if Cohn can say a kaddish, which is also a sign for an end, the sound of the kaddish is carried over into a new world that will remember the old. Malamud's novel, in spite of the many passages in which God himself speaks, does not present God as beyond reproach. As a matter of fact, Cohn's quarrel with God, aiming proverbial arrows at him, is a pervasive theme of the novel that constantly directs readers' attention to a venerable theme, namely, how to justify the ways of God to men (135).

Alfred Hornung has noted that *God's Grace* affirms a "conservative tendency" (109) of Malamud's works that is connected to the use of myths in his fictions, in this case a dominating biblical frame of reference. Whether one should call this reference to and employment of myths "conservative" is open to question. As Malamud's novel exemplifies, even very old myths lend themselves to retellings and, hence, rewritings. Rewriting as such is neither progressive nor conservative but rather is creative and transcends merely political designations. *God's Grace* is a highly relevant case in point. This novel presents such an outrageously outlandish narrative constellation that it is difficult to conceive of any actual situation in which someone could tell the story to someone else. One might even be tempted to regard the whole novel as a lie of Swiftian proportions, inasmuch as Calvin Cohn lives among Yahoos with whose help he wants to start a new form of life—a new form of life that, however, does not promise to turn out better than the last time when human beings populated the earth. How rational is the hope to create a race of new hybrid beings that will populate the planet after the apocalypse? Only God knows. And Malamud perhaps. To claim that the novel is "dominated" by a biblical frame of reference has to be qualified, it seems to me, in light of the fact, noted by Müller, that both the formal and the thematic components of the novel are mutually parodic (841–42). In fact, the mutual deconstruction of all ingredients of the story presents not only a reretelling of old biblical stories about God, man, and beasts but also a sort of untelling, if that is possible. Robert Alter's criticism that Malamud's novel and its theological argument is "schematic, sketchy, lacking weight of experience and density of intellectual texture" does not invalidate the author's attempt to send his readers into a sea of weighty questions presented in a decidedly parodic manner ("Theological" 190). The effect of the seemingly incongruous mixture of narratives of various descriptions, of theological musings and references to scientific theories, especially concerning biological evolution, is to provoke wide-ranging reflections on "all things" on the part of the reader, the kind of reflection that includes God but does not imply an orthodox interpretation of God or theology. Calvin Cohn's continual engagement with God may have been crowned *for him* by God's mercy, but whether that is the case for the novel's reader is another matter (*God's Grace* 223). Here, God's grace appears more like a bad joke, with God refusing to explain his intentions to Cohn, and God appearing to be rather a selfish being who, at least according to one of the conversations reported in the book, created human beings in order to perfect himself (136–37). Cohn sees himself in the same position as Abraham and Job, taking them as models for his own questioning of God, but in the conversation he seems to have with God, God does not accept this analogy, even though it would seem that Cohn had even more reason than Abraham or Job to complain about the lack of God's mercy. For whereas Abraham suffered only a somewhat local bad fate, Cohn takes it upon himself to complain to God on behalf of all humankind. This is a much more comprehensive claim to justice than a mere complaint on behalf of oneself. That Cohn challenges God concerning (his) justice and mercy is theologically highly relevant. For it makes clear that the issues of theodicy have remained alive and well since the time of Abraham and Job and extend even beyond the end of the human race: justice is obviously a problem on which God and humanity cannot really (ever) agree.

The novel also presents farcical rewriting of other parts of the old Jewish texts, for example, when Cohn rewrites, and thus drastically changes, the Ten Commandments. He not only reduces them from ten to seven but changes "Commandments" into "Admonitions," a less severe concept (199, 204). This is odd, insofar the first Admonition explicitly refers to the end of the world that they have survived but seems to take this very survival as the normative ground for the rejection of killing each other. He also presents some Admonitions in such a way as to make them more enigmatic than the Commandments that were before. The rejection of a Christian interpretation of God, evident throughout the novel, is underscored by the explicit statement in the second Admonition that "God is not love, God is God," which in itself does not explain too much and is certainly beyond the apes who are meant to understand this (171; cf. 204).

Malamud's novel about God and humans, about grace and redemption, about the end and the beginning, about hope and bereavement, partakes of what the German literary scholar Ulrich Horstmann has called "apocalyptic imagination," a form of imagination that acquired its existential urgency after the detonation of the first atomic bomb (*Abschreckungskunst* 18). Surprisingly, however, Horstmann does not consider

Malamud's contribution to this "apocalyptic imagination." By calling the kind of art that results from this apocalyptic imagination *Abschreckungs-kunst*, that is, the "art of deterring," he suggests that art itself can function as a deterrent to nuclear war. However that may be, there can be little doubt that Malamud's novel *God's Grace* is a profoundly humane aesthetic meditation on the fate of humanity confronted with the possibility of apocalypse. What remains less clear is whether the image of God projected by the novel can be acceptable to believers. God, in this case, does not exactly prove to be a safe haven or a rock on which one can build. God remains enigmatic, if not idiosyncratic. If the end of the novel signifies a miracle, which it possibly does, as Cohn finally realizes that he will die as an old man, it is still disturbing that his kaddish is spoken by the gorilla George, an ape who is able to address God but whose own future is uncertain.

In addition, Malamud's strange book is itself a sort of kaddish for the failed opportunities to come to terms with the deepest questions that human beings face. The extreme case of the apocalypse, a nuclear holocaust, as presented in the novel, serves as a stark reminder for human beings that dystopian developments are always possible and that meditations on the end wonderfully concentrate the mind—on the "last" things in more than one sense. But in the same way that the last will be the first and the first will be the last, the ending portrayed in *God's Grace* may also be a beginning, even if it is only the beginning of a further retelling of ancient biblical stories. There is a paradox on another level: this possible beginning would itself be the result of the deconstruction of a tightly controlled concept of end and beginning. In the beginning is the word, and in the end is the word: "This is that story" (3). And there is always another story, even and especially after the end.

Short Stories

CHAPTER 12

Seeking the Man behind the Text or a Biographical Approach to Bernard Malamud's Short Stories

EMILIO CAÑADAS RODRÍGUEZ

UNIVERSIDAD CAMILO JOSÉ CELA, SPAIN

In "'The Tune of the Language': An Interview with Grace Paley," Victoria Aarons addresses her first question to the writer in the following terms: "I would like to begin the interview with some biographical information, not the usual date and place of birth, and the like, but with your sense of your formative years, the influence and circumstances of your family, your upbringing, your education and how these might have directed or formed your writing" (50). For years, establishing connections between a writer's life and a writer's work has been a major issue among scholars. The interrelation between biography and identity throughout Jewish American literature takes us back to the works of Mary Antin and Abraham Cahan. Mary Antin's *The Promised Land* (1912) and Abraham Cahan's *The Rise of David Levinsky* (1917) are, according to Alvin H. Rosenfeld, "the pattern to the art of autobiographical invention, more specifically, to modern Jewish autobiography." Furthermore, Rosenfeld maintains that both are "part of the broader literature of imagination" ("Inventing" 134). Hana Wirth-Nesher opens her article on Jewish American autobiography claiming that "autobiography is a widespread and characteristic form of American expression" (113). What is more, to Wirth-Nesher, there is an identification of autobiography in America with the essence of what America is.

Although Bernard Malamud's narratives are profoundly rooted in social matters, there is a close connection between literary identity and biography. Malamud's writing is built on experience, facts, and events, stories that follow an "autobiographical invention" and a "characteristic way of expression." Secrecy, an issue that is discussed in this chapter, is the only barrier to see through Malamud's life behind his texts. To be sure, the writer's concern about his own privacy comes through in Malamud's interviews and in the bio/critical studies of his work. Specifically, in Malamud's *Dubin's Lives* (1979), the interrelation between writing and life is at the center of the narration. What is more, this novel, which explores the relationship between self and character, presents a protagonist who cannot escape the shadow of Malamud's narrative philosophy. Although Dubin could have exercised any profession, Malamud's choice, however, bears a personal relationship: "When you write biography you want to write about people who will make you strain to understand them. . . . But the game is, I suppose, to make the reader think that's exactly what you have done, and maybe in a blaze of illumination even have outdistanced him. It's an illusionary farce that holds me by the tail" (*Dubin's Lives* 303–4). Dubin's character, for Malamud, might be thought of as what Mary Beth Pringle calls "a version of himself" (141). In Malamud's own words, "one must transcend the autobiographical detail by inventing it after it is remembered" (qtd. in Pringle 138). I definitely agree with Pringle when she suggests that "although Malamud invents and transcends, the reader can, without straining, detect biographical similarities shared by Malamud and his fictional characters" (138). As Paul John Eakin explains, "autobiographical truth is not a fixed but an evolving content in an intricate process of self-discovery and self-creation, and, further, that the self that is the center of all autobiographical narrative is necessarily a fictive structure" (3).

Criticism about Malamud's short stories has primarily focused on magical elements, Jewish identity, Jewish literary tradition, narrative construction, myth, and comedy. There is a deluge of scholarship that addresses the short story as genre (for instance, Abramson, *Bernard* 128–38; and Sío Castiñeira). There are not, however, many in-depth studies that explore the connection between Bernard Malamud's life and his short stories. And it is true that "[Malamud] was a more versatile writer than the fantasist who had become famous for his original variations on immigrant Jews themes" (T. Solotaroff, "Evening" 28). Indeed, this chapter explores "more than that," including an analysis of the central, defining biographical aspects of Malamud's work. If we accept Philippe Lejeune's definition of autobiography as "retrospective prose narrative written by a real person concerning his own existence, where the focus is his individual life, in particular the story of his personality" (4), we can find biographical traces and elements that provide the backdrop for Malamud's short stories, potentially opening new interpretive possibilities to his short fiction.

Writing short stories, for Malamud, provided the opportunity, in his words, "to breathe." Malamud defined his short stories in 1983 as "fictive biographies" and "biographed stories" (Giroux xiv). The interaction between Jewish identity and biography is quite clear. In Malamud's stories—especially, but not exclusively, in collections such as *The Magic Barrel* (1958) and *Idiots First* (1963)—autobiography exists even though the author somehow tends to hide behind "literary privacy." Malamud admitted that "all men are subjected to their history" (T. Solotaroff, "Evening" 29). But what do I really mean when I use the word "autobiography"? Do Malamud's works include fragments of his own life? If so, what fragments, and how were they incorporated into his fiction? In order to answer these questions, I focus on two exemplary stories: "Armistice" (1940)[1] and "The German Refugee" (1963).[2]

Various studies on Malamud's short fiction refer to the biographical elements in his works, including *Talking Horse* (1996) by Bernard Malamud; *Private Matters* (1997) and *My Father Is a Book* (2006), written by Janna Malamud Smith; and *Bernard Malamud: A Writer's Life* by Philip Davis (2007). Although *Conversations with Bernard Malamud* (1991; edited by Lawrence Lasher)—which covers a three-decade span of interviews granted by the novelist—does not offer a complete biographical sketch of Malamud's life, it sheds light on Malamud both as a fiction writer and as a human being. Malamud's narrative strength, brevity, and endless rewriting reveal the man behind the art. As an exacting author insisting on every detail—*le mot juste*—Malamud composed his stories bearing in mind what and who he best knew: "I write about Jews because I know them. But more important, I write about them because the Jews are absolutely the very *stuff* of drama" (Wershba 3). Elsewhere, Malamud is far more specific about who and what he usually wrote about: "I am an American, I'm a Jew, and I write for all men. A novelist has to or he's built himself a cage. I write about Jews, because they set my imagination going. I know something about their history, the quality of their experience and belief, and of their literature, though not as much as I would like" (Stern 63). And I would add that writing about Jews is a way to write of and about himself.

In *Talking Horse*, Malamud notes that "a short story packs a self in a few pages predicating a lifetime" (6). Indeed, Malamud often re-creates his own background in his stories. Malamud depicts recognizable Jewish Orthodox families and/or individuals who, like his own parents, came to America between 1905 and 1910. Malamud also writes about issues like identity, assimilation, and the Jewish family in the United States. It is interesting to analyze whether one can get to know Malamud, the author behind the scenes, by reading his short stories. Despite Malamud's insistence that the writer is distinct from the literary character, the framework of Malamud's own life often exists behind the pages of his fiction. Malamud's approach, however, seems to suggest that keeping his "fictional privacy" guides his authorial presence. Interviewed by Daniel Stern in 1975, Malamud was asked about "a little personal history" because "there's been little written about your life." His answer is straightforward: "That's how I wanted it. I like privacy and as much as possible to stay out of my books. I know that's disadvantageous to certain legitimate kinds of criticism of literature, but my needs come first" (Stern 55).

Due to that "need," some aspects of Malamud's biography remain hidden. Others remain available for the Malamud reader who wants to seek the man behind the text despite the writer's purported attempts to hide the personal, as if he had been custodian of his own truth. The two short stories that I analyze here seem to contradict this distanced position. Janna Malamud, in commenting on the issue of her father's privacy, opens *My Father Is a Book* addressing the early stories analyzed in this chapter: "When as an adult, I once asked about his childhood, he started telling me how he had relished going to the movies as a boy. When penniless, he sometimes half conned, half stole tickets to get into a local theater. Quickly embarrassed, he stopped himself midway through the recollection. I was in my thirties. Even then, he remained reluctant to talk about his early life, its pains and contradictions still unmanageable on his tongue" (2). The purpose of this chapter, which addresses "Armistice" and "The German Refugee," is not to explore those episodes of Malamud's life that "he remained reluctant to talk about" but rather to examine the portrait of families, not unlike Malamud's, who came to the United States during the mid- and late 1900s. Through a number of scenes in these two stories, I attempt to show some biographical aspects of the writer's family, including those of a young Bernard Malamud, and to show how they help form the basis of the unfolding narrative tensions.

Both "Armistice" and "The German Refugee"—set between 1935 and 1939—show the effects of the Depression years that culminated in World War II. The devastating consequences of the 1930s—war, suffering, and poverty—are themes that the Malamud reader is familiar with. On the one hand, in these two stories, the world of Malamud's characters seems to have been torn between those who win and those who lose, between what has been won and what has been lost. On the other, it is clear that reality and social history move into the writer's personal history. Both "Armistice" and "The German Refugee" reveal Malamud's autobiographical "essence," as Malamud suggests: "I prefer autobiographical essence to autobiographical history" (Stern 64). As Malamud puts it, "Events from life may creep into the narrative but it isn't necessarily my life history" (Stern 64).

Janna Malamud recalls that "in Dad's first published piece of fiction, 'Armistice' (1940), a Jewish grocer named Morris Lieberman becomes distraught when he hears reports of the rise of Nazism, which trigger his traumatic childhood memory of a pogrom" (11). The grocery store is a recurrent motif in Malamud's narratives, including "The Grocery Store" and "The Cost of Living," among other stories. As in the case of *The Assistant* (1957)—"a big book that arose out of the short stories" (Davis 23)—the grocery store is depicted for the impoverished Jew as a prison. Janna Malamud argues that "Armistice," "Spring Rain," and "The Grocery Store" epitomize the "prison motif," linking this backdrop to her father's life. At one point in her memoir, she recalls, "When Dad was five, Max and his wife, Bertha, lived in Borough Park in Brooklyn. Florence Hodes, my father's cousin, described this as a pleasant neighborhood of new houses, a mixed population (but mostly Jewish), and nice stores. Here, around 1920, Max and a partner named Ben Schmookler opened a grocery store described by

Florence as 'better than the usual grocery store around'" (13). The lives of immigrant Jewish parents like Max and Bertha Malamud are central to a story like "Armistice." Within the walls of a grocery store inspired by the novelist's father's precarious economic position, Malamud takes the reader to 1940, to the days of the Armistice—between France and Germany—and World War II. "Armistice," written by a twenty-six-year-old Bernard Malamud at the outset of the war, is clearly autobiographical. The protagonist, Morris Lieberman, for whom the prototype may have been Max Malamud, listening to the story from the front, feels melancholic. Lieberman had hoped that France would stop the Germans, believing that the fate of the Jews greatly depended on the French army. His eventual realization that the French could not actually save his people, however, soon made him despair. Philip Davis's biography *Bernard Malamud: A Writer's Life* begins with Max Malamud, on whom the characters of the grocers Morris Lieberman in "Armistice" and Morris Bober in *The Assistant* are based. Both the memories and the depictions of these groceries are inherent to the background and setting of these narratives. "Armistice," which mainly takes place in the protagonist's grocery store, connects Lieberman to the war through the radio waves.

"Armistice" opens interrelating past and present. The story deals with both the "here" and "there," with Europe and America, with France and New York, with the Nazis and Jews. The story illustrates the shaky situation of knowledge and information coming from the front, provided for the characters by a radio. The main character, Morris Lieberman—in German, "the preferred one"—is motivated by fear. This is, indeed, a story about fear, and the three main characters must contend with fear. The fourth character is the world, a world whose hostile climate increases the anxiety felt by both characters and readers. "Armistice" is the story of a Jewish widower and a Jewish son in New York—owners of a neighborhood grocery store visited by customers and providers during World War II—who suffer for their people. In effect, through the eyes of a young Bernard Malamud, this short story shows the worries and conflicts provoked by World War II and the way such conflicts affected the Jewish community. This is a story of dualities: suffering and identity, Russia and the United States, Morris's/Max's Russian background and Morris's/Max's and Leonard's/young Bernard's life in the States. Max Malamud was born in 1885, and at the time of the story, he would have been fifty-five. Bernard Malamud was born in 1914, and although the actual events depicted in the story must have taken place in 1927 or so, it is set in 1940. Autobiography, however, is not merely a question of providing exact dates, places, or settings.

The young Leonard/Bernard returns from school at three o'clock every day. This is the time when Morris turns off the radio, the same radio that keeps him updated with the latest war-related news. The radio is not only a window open to the war but also the last ray of hope for salvation. Morris, "listening . . . shares the woes inflected upon his race," eliciting "the same fear since the Nazis had come to power" ("Armistice" 103). As in the instance of the character of Leonard, children's daily routines in Malamud's stories seem to echo Malamud's experiences as a child. The reference, for example, to the adolescent son's return from school suggests several reasons for this interest in giving a detailed depiction of this event: first, because of the outstanding role that education plays in Malamud's writings; second, Malamud's insistence on presenting a young character like himself for whom the grocery store is at the center of his life; and third, the traumatic replay of the young Bernard Malamud coming back home at three o'clock to find his mother lying on the floor. Janna Malamud recalls the day when her father saw his mother on the floor after suffering a psychotic episode: "Dad was thirteen years old when he came home from school one day to find his mother, Bertha, alone, insane, sitting on the kitchen floor, an empty can of disinfectant ('something like Drano') in one hand, the poison foaming from her mouth" (17). Here Malamud masks the biographical data as an essential part of his narrative.

The young Malamud's traumatic discovery—"his mother frothing at the mouth on the clean kitchen floor, an empty can of disinfectant beside her. He had had to run for help to the local drugstore to save her. Bertha was hospitalized some time after the suicide attempt and never returned home" (Davis 5)—is a leitmotif in *Dubin's Lives*, again a suggestion of the connection for the writer between life and work:

> He rushed downstairs to the drugstore and afterward induced vomiting by getting her to swallow the contents of a bottle of citrate of magnesia he had bought in panic.
>
> Yes, she whispered, yes, yes. She drank from the bottle as though famished, as though she had wanted all her life to drink

the miraculous potion he served her. It would make her sane again, healthy, young—would restore her chance to have everything she hadn't had in her life. She drank her own everlasting hunger. When she recovered, her graying hair coiled in braids on her head, she promised she would never—never again.

Willie, don't tell Papa I am crazy.

Mama, don't say that. (68)

While William Dubin's mother's suicide attempt foreshadows the end, in "Armistice," life seems to come to an end when the radio stops playing. In other words, the fact that the radio stops playing seems to symbolize the grocer's metaphorical death. Had the radio stopped "vomiting" news—that is, should Max stop listening to the news about the French army's defeat—he would feel this defeat like his own. He would suffer the consequences of it, like the rest of the world. Davis recalls the existence of the radio in terms of its connection with another crucial person in Malamud's short stories: his mother—or, rather, her absence: "More refined than her husband, she became fanatically concerned with cleanliness. . . . She was scared of the radio that Max brought into the house, and often kept to the back bedroom, door locked, the household gradually deteriorating with her, though she still kept the children obsessively clean" (5–6). In "Armistice," Morris's sadness and incomprehension are acutely depicted while he is listening to the radio. The story, which sketchily describes the terrible events that occurred throughout the war, also represents the evolution of these events in Europe, ranging from the Belgians' surrender to Dunkerque's to the Germans' arrival in Paris. As the picture of the war becomes grimmer, so does Morris's/Max's state of mind. Morris/Max tries to hide his addiction to the war news, switching off the radio when his child comes back from school. He wants to spare his son the suffering taking place in Europe.

Jewish suffering and suffering for the other are characteristic preoccupations in Malamud's fiction. In *The Assistant*, Morris Bober—who shares Lieberman's first name—tells Frank Alpine, the young man who comes to work for him in the grocery store, "I suffer for you," and he refers to "Weltschmerz"—world pain (150). In "Armistice," Morris/Max suffers for his son, for his dead wife, for the Jews in Europe, and for the Jews and the world in general when he tries to hold his suffering back from his own child. Morris's/Max's neighbors find his suffering excessive. In this case, the customers and the store owners are puzzled by the way Morris behaves regarding the Jews' suffering. They are puzzled by Morris's inner pain. Increasingly, the grocery becomes a prison, "a real prison cell in a dungeon," a recurring metaphor central to Malamud's fiction: "Jewishness is the prison, a perfect symbol for the human and most particularly the Jewish condition. Metaphorically, the prison becomes an acceptance of life's limitations and responsibilities in this sense" (Field and Field, introduction 3).

This painful experience of suffering creates a feeling of imprisonment, which becomes a leitmotif in Malamud's works such as *The Assistant*, *The Fixer*, and *The Tenants*, among others. As Malamud suggests, the prison motif functions as "a metaphor for the dilemma of all men throughout history. Necessity is the primary prison, though the bars are not visible to all. Then there are the man-made prisons of social injustice, apathy, ignorance. There are others, tight or loose, visible or invisible, according to one's predilection or vulnerability" (Field and Field, "Interview" 12). Like Morris Bober in *The Assistant*, Yakov Bok in *The Fixer*, and Harry Lesser in *The Tenants*, Morris's and the young Leonard's lives are limited by the confines of the space of the grocery store, which makes them claustrophobic. Several references in the story correspond to events in Malamud's own life. The ages of the young Leonard and Bernard Malamud, an implied reference to Malamud's discovery of his dying mother, facing his father's anguish, and awaiting his bar mitzvah appear, too, in the story "The Lost Bar-Mitzvah" and in subsequent works like *Dubin's Lives*. Davis, in his discussion of *Dubin's Lives*, tells us that "in the drafts, Malamud gives the son's final reply as first, 'Don't tell me anymore. I'm only twelve, and then I'm not bar-mitzvahed yet.' There was never a proper bar-mitzvah, the ceremony that marks the coming of the age of the male Jew at thirteen, by reading a portion of the law in the synagogue" (7–8). Davis provides such details in his description of the story's previously unpublished manuscripts (7–10).

Furthermore, the sudden appearance of the third character in "Armistice" seems to make Morris's world—the father's world—crumble. Gus Wagner, the third man, "who delivered the delicatessen meats and provisions," "a heavy man," "a member of the AEF in 1918," is partly guilty for destroying Morris's world ("Armistice" 104). Gus, who enjoys causing trouble, addresses suffering and war-related issues as if he were talking about a Sunday soccer match. Malamud constructs him as one who admires the Germans and who believes them capable of ruling the world. Here we find a reflection of the world in the microcosm of the grocery, a place where Jews and Germanophiles meet in a battle of wills. Every time Gus Wagner comes to the store in order to make a delivery, he causes a battle between opposing feelings and points of view. Not only does Morris/Max have to deal with his wife's death against the weight of tradition—his people's defeat and the Holocaust—but he also has to deal with someone who reminds him of his Judaism on a daily basis and, moreover, of the position of the Germans' power as well as his own misery.

From a biographical perspective, there is a crucial moment in "Armistice" when Morris/Max dreams that he is chased by the Germans, and he fears they will arrest him. Later, in the daylight, the newspaper announces that the armistice has been signed. In the dream, Gus has taken advantage of that feeling of victory. As predicted, Gus comes to Morris and jokes about the fact that the grocer is not listening to the news that day. The last part of the story is an argument between the two characters. Gus makes Leonard cry. A crucial moment arrives when the child is listening to the conversation the adults are having and feels terribly upset. The men fight even when the boy is asking his father to stop arguing; he tries to intercede but is pushed down and begins to cry. Gus thinks he has gone too far. Morris and Leonard embrace each other, and Morris tries to calm him down, promising "[no] more" ("Armistice" 108). Gus leaves, and as the story comes to an end, each character is depicted as imagining his own triumph. Gus imagines Germany's victory:

> As he rode amid the cars on the avenue, he thought of the boy crying and his father holding him. It was like that with the Jews. Tears and people holding each other. Why feel sorry for them?
>
> Gus sat up straight at the wheel, his face grim. He thought of the armistice and imagined that he was in Paris. His truck was a massive tank rumbling with the others through the wide boulevards. The French, on the sidewalks, were overpowered with fear.
>
> He drove tensely, his eyes unsmiling. He knew that if he relaxed the picture would fade. (109)

In an interview with Phyllis Meras, Malamud refers to "The German Refugee" as his "last short story." Malamud describes the story as being "about a man who has suffered under Hitler and then comes to this country and finds it hard to adjust. It's a story that is both historically and politically centered" (Meras 16). "The German Refugee" is one of Malamud's most debated stories and one of the least studied from a biographical perspective. "Historically and politically centered," Malamud's story focuses on a refugee who comes to America during World War II and is instructed in the use of English by a tutor. As the story progresses, the focus is on both Oskar Gassner—the refugee—and Martin Goldberg (Malamud), the teacher. At that time, Malamud was interested in creating a story about "freedom, injustice" (Meras 16). In addition to the historical-political background and the emphasis on freedom and injustice, the story points to well-known episodes in the writer's life. In particular, the story's narrator is a university student who begins to teach before he completes his degree. The story is narrated in the first person, and Malamud's character defines himself as "a poor student [who] would brashly attempt to teach anybody anything for a buck an hour," admitting, "Mostly I gave English lessons to recently arrived refugees" ("The German Refugee" 93). Of Malamud's own early career years, Davis recalls that "after advertising on noticeboards, he began to tutor German-Jewish refugees in English" and, more to the point, that "the tutoring was serious and painful," as is the case in the story (48–49). What Goldberg/Malamud provides in fiction, Davis provides in the novelist's biography. Goldberg/Malamud, the narrator/writer of the story, points to the refugees as "Karl Otto Alp, the former film start; Wolfgang Novak, once a brilliant economist; Friedrich Wilhelm Wolff, who had taught medieval history at Heidelberg and . . . Oskar Gassner, the Berlin critic and journalist" (Davis 94). Davis recalls these "tutees" as "middle aged intellectuals who had had distinguished careers in Europe and were of a status, sophistication, and education far above Malamud's experience. But they were now exiles left fumbling for thoughts in a barely known language" (49). A significant parallel occurs in the story between the refugee's "loss of language" and identity-connected problems that Malamud might have suffered in the 1930s ("The German Refugee" 97). Davis explains that, at the time, "[Malamud] was not only a lonely man of words himself, struggling in the Depression, but also an equivocal fellow-Jew, without much in the way of Jewish knowledge, faith or identity, who now suddenly saw what being born Jewish might mean in the dangerous world of the thirties" (49).

The story's first-person narration and historical components—that is, real and factual—intersect: first, Goldberg refers to the Depression years—"Times were still hard from the Depression"—then to the 1935 crisis of Danzig, and finally to the beginning of World War II: "They were all over uptown Broadway in 1939" ("The German Refugee" 93–94). These elements clearly enable Malamud to set the framework for his own experience. Similar to "Armistice," "The German Refugee" takes place in the "here" and "there." Both stories are set in America and in Europe; in both, Malamud lives in America and suffers for Europe. Although in "Armistice" the radio is the leitmotif and in "The German Refugee" the leitmotif is Oskar's life, the emphasis is the situation in Europe: "across the ocean Adolf Hitler." Goldberg wonders, "Will I ever forget what went on with Danzig that summer?" (93), a question implicitly linked to "What will become of us?" in "Armistice" (106). "The German Refugee's" narrator introduces the displaced and discouraged character and his entrance into the United States: "He had come a month before Kristallnacht, when the Nazis shattered the Jewish store windows and burnt all the synagogues" ("The German Refugee" 95). Sometime later, after returning from Germany, Oskar works for the Institute for Public Services of New York, and he has to give a lecture in English that paralyzes him. In that moment, "his melancholy deepened" (95).

The fictional Goldberg is modeled on Malamud, who had also taught refugees with similar linguistic and situational problems. To be sure, Oskar Gassner's character is based on Dr. Friedrich Pinner—"the most memorable of all the pupils" and "an economist, aged fifty-five, who had been financial editor of the *Berliner Tageblatt*" (Davis 50). Davis concludes that "he remained in Malamud's mind, finally emerging in the transmuted account of a suicide" (50).

Both Gassner's learning process and the historical background develop simultaneously. Indeed, "When he gave up attempting the lecture, he stopped making progress in English" ("The German Refugee" 99). Both the preparation of the lecture and the historical events involving Germany seem to provoke an emotional breakdown in Gassner that leads to his suicide attempt: an interpretation of these melancholic episodes in fiction can be found in Davis's biography (49–50). At the end of the story, Gassner's suicide reveals his inability to write: it is a "paralyzis of my will," and "I have lozt faith. I do not—no longer possezz my former value of myself" ("The German Refugee" 102, 103). The invasion of Poland results in human loss in Europe and in America. It is September of 1939, and the historical element of the story resonates in Malamud's remark, "With me, the effects of Hitler have had some bearing, but I don't know about others. Hitler made me aware of the Jewish life of the past and the values the Jewish people tried to uphold (Meras 18). The history, time, and place depicted in "The German Refugee" suggest its autobiographical backdrop: a teacher tutoring German refugees in the United States in the 1930s; refugees who are going through a painful teaching and learning process in which language, communication, and close human relationships are crucial; and shared misery and depression—all of which contribute to an overview of the writer's biography and his place in history.

By analyzing the personal references in "The German Refugee" and "Armistice," I have attempted to approach Malamud's short stories from a biographical/historical perspective and to leave a door open for future interpretative accounts of Malamud's universe as seen through the lens of his short fiction. Malamud was a writer interested in Jewish suffering, in the way human beings feel for other human beings, a writer of deep empathy for others, imagining characters who internalize their lament and their pain. Thus, it is illuminating and brings a further dimension to his fiction to find the man behind his texts.

NOTES

1. "Armistice" is included in Malamud, *People* 103–9.
2. "The German Refugee" is included in Malamud, *Stories* 93–108.

CHAPTER 13

Malamud's Short Fiction

Angels and Specters

FÉLIX MARTÍN GUTIÉRREZ

UNIVERSIDAD COMPLUTENSE DE MADRID, SPAIN

> When in the normal course of history a traumatic break occurs, this break
> was termed by the rabbis *churban bayit*—destruction of the house—(mean-
> ing the Temple). In other words, when the entire existence of the commu-
> nity and thus of the individual is threatened, and life has lost all meaning
> (as on the night of the Destruction of the Temple), Jews internalize the
> experience and form the symbols which are to become the building blocks
> of the future.
>
> —Eveline Goodman-Thau, "Shoah and Tekuma"

I

"Can Jews haunt people?" This question opens Malamud's short story "Alma
Redeemed" (258).[1] As a general conjecture, such a query envisions an irradia-
tion of Jewish influence or its decline, although Gustav Mahler's ghost is
unique and appears to Alma two years after his death. One night, concludes
the story, Mahler's ghost appeared and asked Alma if she was finally moved
by his "classically beautiful music" (269). And as if he were reenacting the

apparition of Hamlet's ghost, Mahler's words voiced the haunting warning, "My time will come" (269). Yet Mahler was a renegade of Judaism, and the Jewish question would come between Alma and her lovers. The reader may suspect why she wrote in her diary that she would never "place a photograph of a living person next to someone who is dead" (269).

Revisionary proposals to revive collective memories or delve into the archives of history—Holocaust survival testimonies in the first place— may find spectral signs of critical and cultural filiations. Jewish cultural history and literary traditions have been deeply aware of their spectral refraction, and both continue to be haunted by questions of identity, religion, and transnational displacements. The shadows of social and political integration of Jewishness in America or of the configuration of its universalism still haunt the frontiers of new local geographies. At the time of Malamud's most productive years, for instance, American Jewish fiction found in the existential grounds of alienation, exile, or psychic dislocation the spectral mask demanded by its public acceptance. The postwar period was the time of the triumvirate—Bellow, Malamud, Roth—and it was the time when the prophetic vision of the cultural Jewish renaissance would shed new light on its own making. In the year that *The Fixer* came to life, 1966, Malamud would place these terms in their specific historical context, inviting readers to listen to Yakov Bok's haunting premonitions in his prison cell: "We're all in history, that's sure, but some are more than others. Jews more than some" (*The Fixer* 314).

History, observes Alvin H. Rosenfeld, "thickens around the Jews," and it remains a mystery to see why they continue serving "as a vehicle for history's doings," in spite of the fact that they have defied history "by refusing to succumb to it" ("Progress" 126). It is important to value this radical attitude and examine some of its effects, now that Jewish history, Jewish thought, and Jewish culture have been so meticulously diagnosed by the minds of Levinas, Freud, Benjamin, Derrida, Rosenzweig, and Yerushalmi so that spectrality seems a Jewish cultural construction. The discourse of moral responsibility, above all, its biblical foundations, the binding of the *akedah*, or the haunting revision of Judaism and its messianic redemption keep refashioning a self-reflexive discourse of spectrality.

In order to understand this self-reflexive discourse of spectrality, I will consider the role of the specter within the world of hauntology, in order to appreciate how the traces of the past that constantly question the present are filtered by the specter, inviting the living to perform revisionary thinking. Throughout this chapter, these two terms are used interchangeably, both producing the effect of something "fearfully and mysteriously strange or fantastic."[2] In Jacques Derrida's *Specters of Marx* (1994), the term "hauntology" is used to refer to the extraordinary. "Spectrality"—from the adjective "spectral" ("of, relating to, or suggesting a ghost")[3]—is used in critical discourse and has also been developed in *Specters of Marx*. Specters, who as in the case of Hamlet's father typically return because they feel they have had some unfinished business on earth, abound in Malamud's fiction. Curiously, this supernatural-related issue has remained unexplored in his work so far. Therefore, drawing on these two Derridean terms, I address the role that specters play not only in the aforementioned "Alma Redeemed" but also in a number of short stories, including "In Kew Gardens," "Man in the Drawer," "Pictures of the Artist," "A Lost Grave," and "Zora's Noise."

II

The phenomenon of spectrality, we are reminded, emerges precisely because reality presents itself as an incomplete process of symbolization. Perhaps, as Derrida has shown, we need the spectral activity to make sense of our existence, to understand history and culture. It is obvious that whether the specter is alerted by the anxieties of the postmodern condition or claimed as temporary partner in our daily lives, it has gained an extraordinary popularity, due perhaps, as Jonathan Gil Harris suggests, to the rituals of mourning and vengeance claimed by its messianic role. This fact should not ignore Lacanian psychoanalysis about the return of the dead[4] as the sign of some problem in the process of symbolization, since it dictates that once this process has been completed, the ghost could be sent away. If we listen to Derrida, on the other hand, the ghost would appear as a permanent other usually disguised as a familiar figure. Once he observed that those who wish Marxism dead were also haunted by his "dead" Marxism, Derrida implied that the specter had to point only to the future, though coming out of the past. The specter, he says, not only includes bodiless apparitions of the ghost "but also a spectral anticipation of the future," a "messianic" aspect or "demand for salvation," a "commitment to the event of what is coming" (167).

Malamud's short stories display a fascinating fictional mirage of depths and surfaces. A reading of *The Complete Stories*, published in 1997 and edited and introduced by Robert Giroux, offers splendid views of this intertextual landscape. The volume gathers fifty-five stories arranged in chronological order, a method that allows the reader to thread those stories—some of them "fictive biographies" and "biographed stories"—in the tapestry of Jewish history (Giroux, introduction to Malamud, *Complete* xiii). It is not easy to trace genealogical lines of artistic development in this volume or to diagnose ideological anxieties or interconnect political, social, or religious issues. The pleasures of reading channel any choice of literary interest. Each story keeps its own secrecy, its specific uniqueness and aesthetic call to artistic perfection, though several aesthetic transactions gravitate around the power of language, translation, and art, especially painting and music. As Victoria Aarons observes, a chiastic structure lies at the heart of the stories' textual articulation and channels their moments of recognition ("Kind" 175–86). It is worth recalling that the most popular stories selected by the author for his fine collection of 1983 masterfully reflected Malamud's belief that form "is the basis of literature" and that "the logic of language and construction" cannot tolerate any intrusion of thought (Malamud, introduction xi, x).

The "logic of language and construction" seems to many readers the proper habitation of spectral intimations or its visible architecture and narrative façade. Malamud has given voice to his aesthetic aspirations many times, and an examination of the short stories' self-reflexive structures and narrative motifs might unveil his philosophy of composition. It is indeed remarkable how the stories translate their own genealogy through narrative voice and verbal construction, especially the tales that might be said to form the aesthetic canon contained in *The Magic Barrel* (1958), *Idiots First* (1963), and *Rembrandt's Hat* (1973). If the influence of Hawthorne, James, Chekhov, or Bashevis Singer has compelled readers to filter the strands and twists of what Jonathan Lethem describes as "ecstasy of influence," Malamud's titanic compression of fictional form seems similar to Poe's transformation of the traditional "tales of effect" into formal unities of plot and effect. The search for formal perfection became a significant prospect for Malamud's creativity, and as he told Joel Salzberg, "I am enormously conscious of form, the right place for the right idea and it is form that I breed my ideas for; it is form, in a sense that gives birth to them" ("Rhythms" 46).

"What makes a miracle of reading," writes Maurice Blanchot in *The Gaze of Orpheus and Other Literary Essays* (1981), "is that here the stone and the tomb not only contain a cadaverous emptiness that must be animated, but they also constitute the presence—hidden though it is—of what must appear. . . . What responds to the appeal of literary reading is not a door falling or becoming transparent or even becoming a little thinner, rather, it is a rougher kind of stone, more tightly sealed, crushing—a vast deluge of stone that shakes the earth and the sky" (95, 96). Entrance into the world of Malamud's stories does not require pretextual invitations or special narrative incipits. It is a simple encounter with voices and characters that perform their own spectacles without breaking the rules of narrative credibility, and if they do, a higher rule of ethical nature will amend their final resolution. Each story performs the artistic miracle of "translating" multiple objects and voices of myth, folklore, biblical texts, social history, rituals, and dreams into a diagrammatic fictional mold. As brief narratives, the most popular stories depart from simple situations and follow a conceptual scheme intensifying their dramatic texture. Their final closure, however, takes us back to their haunting beginnings, a return that might not require the gothic settings described by Blanchot's exploration of Lazarus's tomb.

"Believe me, there are Jews everywhere," proclaims Manischevitz at the end of the story "Angel Levine" (166). Once in a while, fiction delivers wonderful blessings, a gift of God's grace to recover the theological aura in our reading experience. We might remember that a few years before the publication of this story in 1955, *The Eternal Light* campaign had already six million listeners receiving the ethical message of compassion and justice promoted by the Jewish Theological Seminary of America. The campaign was directed to a Jewish and non-Jewish audience and tried to explain "Jewishness" in its American context and universal projection. Among the many issues covered by the radio programs, Judaism was regarded as "the world's best secret," a religion that expressed faith in a universal God and a universal ethic. According to Markus Krah's description, religion helped to balance American integration and Jewish distinctiveness, responding to an idealized image of America (265–67).

The providential news announced by Malamud's protagonist Manischevitz would not only please theologians or historians of Judaism. It might attract the attention of linguists and rhetoricians, for the existential sentence implies that black Americans are part of the heavenly legion of new "incarnations" and at the same time conveys the assertive illocutionary force that makes Manischevitz responsible and guarantor of the truth expressed in the proposition "Believe me." In each case, Manischevitz's advice to his wife, Fanny, enlightens the whole story, clarifying its narrative logic and bringing his journey to a miraculous end. From the tailor's initial despair, or the apparition of Alexander Levine in his apartment, to the angel's trip to Harlem and his presumed flight to heaven, we are expected to come face-to-face with Levine's redemptive outcome and Manischevitz's consolation.

"There are Jews everywhere" admittedly enlarges the boundaries of narrative representation and leaves the specter of Jewishness free in the symbolic realm. Angel Levine's angelic nature displays absolute freedom of representation and belongs to the world of magic. We can therefore read the general statement as a conclusive revelation of the imperceptible regeneration of Jewishness in modern times. I use the word "imperceptible" on purpose, since narrative action and the theological debates on the Harlem synagogue do not offer clear plausibility of angelic saving mediation. On the contrary, narrative logic has magically played with uncertainty, in spite of Manischevitz's insistence on testing Angel Levine's Jewishness and his angelic power to perform miracles. The process of recognition is then essential, though as the story ends, Manischevitz is unable to see Angel Levine disappear but rather sees "through a small broken window" a dark figure borne aloft on a pair of strong black wings (166).

As I have introduced the story, the contrast between Manischevitz's disgraces and Angel Levine's disincarnated nature allows the ghost of Jewishness to inhabit very different worlds, one prefigured by Job's calamities (Job 1:16) and the other disfiguring racial differences in modern America. It is precisely in the fanciful interaction between moral conditions and the omnipotence of the imagination where we may come across specters in disguise. This is clear when Angel Levine and Manischevitz engage in a spectacle of recognition enigmatically exposed in Levine's "disincarnated" nature and affected by his temporal "condition of probation" (159,

160). Given the self-reflexive contour of pure fantasy and humor of the story, we can follow Malamud's favorite reading strategy of "active invention." What kind of transformations, within the realm of magical realism, do we expect from Levine's words "I am what I am granted to be, and at present the completion is in the future"? (159). A specialist on surrealist collages like Donald Barthelme would confess that the death of God had left the angels in a strange position.

Levine, however, engages in a redemptive mission magically justified, exhibiting his ethnic identity with unquestionable naturalness and dignity. His mediation between God and Manischevitz exerts a magisterial role carried out in familiar terms, confessing his Jewish identity and knowledge of Jewish traditions and rituals. It is this familiarity—"Touched by this sight from his childhood and youth"—that the climactic scene of instruction awakens in Manischevitz in the Harlem synagogue (163). And it is the final scene of specular projection experienced in this temple that brings him to the doors of acknowledged beliefs: "'I think you are an angel from God.' He said it in a broken voice, thinking. If you said it it was said. If you believed it you must say it. If you believed, you believed" (166).

If narrative endings are crucial to perceive fictional transactions, Manischevitz's list of conditional clauses pour the language of faith into a magical mold as narrative conclusion and inducted pretextual illustration, while Levine's "disincarnated" journey to save the tailor's oppressive life reaches its final redemptive outcome. This journey, however, mirrors an admission into the world of Jewishness that haunts Manischevitz's magical interventions. His pleading for divine help, his constant self-questioning about Levine's Jewishness, his feeling of alienation after traveling to Harlem, as well as his wondering "in the open dark world" mark several stages of his initiation into the territory of multiple racial Jewishness (161). The full integration into universal Jewishness would require complete "translation" of Angel Levine's identity, not only temporary disincarnation. However, the miracle saved Fanny's health, and Levine accomplished his mission.

Perhaps conventional notions of translation do not convey the complexity of transactions that Malamud's magical fiction performs. Beyond Angel Levine's surrealistic transmutation, literary translation channels Malamud's original visual and aesthetic transactions. Postmodern theories of translation seem to have reached a point of no return to meaning, challenging the source text as something fixed to be transferred to a system of signification. Malamud's translations, however, perform cultural, aesthetic, and ideological transactions that release language from its linguistic medium to generate analogical versions of original texts or to unsettle them. In a sense, those transactions could be read as Walter Benjamin's interlinear versions of literalness and freedom, drawn from the postwar history of Jewishness and its new contemporary politics of cultural self-identity.

One of the stories openly articulated as a process of translation and its textual doubles is "Man in the Drawer." The tale makes the confrontation and relation between Feliks Levitansky and Howard Harvitz an emblematic revision of Jewish survival as a self-conscious literary exchange of translation practices. Via translation, comments Kenneth Moss, the search for an authentic Jewish culture during the Russian Revolution of 1917 turned around language: "In practice, they conceived language as a kind of permeable membrane, . . . [and] it would provide a boundary within which an open-ended dialectic of particularity and universality, tradition and openness might play out as individuals wished" (283). Levitansky is a professional translator and writer who feels trapped in the process of cultural assimilation in Russia. The trip of the American writer Howard Harvitz to this country exposes the contradictions of surviving professionally under those political conditions. "I write presently for the drawer," states Levitansky. "You know this expression? Like Isaac Babel, I am master of the genre of silence" ("Man in the Drawer" 421).

As a master of the genre of silence, Levitansky introduces several literary pieces as expressions of his search for a true personal voice, free from political commitments, social pressure, and aesthetic prejudices. The search is staged by the American writer as a translational exchange, subtly disentangling literary matters as textual versions of cultural and moral issues. In fact, their dialogues generate teaching advice on aesthetic criteria, questions of style, fictional forms, representation, and other literary issues generally discussed in a classroom. But their multiple readings traverse the political horizons that had blurred Jewish cultural activism or repressed Jewish religious traditions. Added to that, political suspicion and repression permeate the pedagogical exchanges as haunting double, deepening the gap between literary device and real experience, literal translation and allegorical. It is after all a spectral activity—Althusserian readers would call it "specular"—carried out by tensions and physical displacements from cities, hotels, or airports, crucially activated by Harvitz's incident with the KGB with the poetry anthology *Visible Secrets* and his plan to smuggle Levitansky's short stories into the United States.

A close look at this pedagogical scene—paradigmatic in Malamud's fiction—may shed some light on the spectrality of cultural and religious translation. Levitansky's confessions about the fallacy of autobiographical readings of his short stories ("Don't confuse my story of writer, which you have read, with life of author"; 427) and his desire to translate truth without disguises, to eliminate ideological racial or religious references, and to face the nature of society ("I have faced up. Do you face up to yours?"; 434) and follow the dictates of the imagination outline an important program of cultural and ideological translations. Asked if his stories were the product of true experience, his answer, "Not true although truth," leaves secrecy suspended between moral criteria and the rules of narrative authenticity (427). No hypothetical equation will guarantee a perfect aesthetic analogy unless moral truth and fictional representation perform the spectacle mentioned by Harvitz a few pages before: "What they had to say was achieved as form, no telling the dancer from the dance" (424). The formal perfection evoked by this famous quotation stands as an ideal translation of Levitansky and Harvitz's exchange. As Irving H. Buchen declares, "When the artist aligns his aesthetic identity with that of the novel so that he is as refined into his form as the form is absorbed into his novelistic world, then the way he says what he says makes form and meaning one" ("Aesthetics" 103).

In spite of the clarifying process of literary appreciation carried out by Harvitz, the question of his responsibility toward Levitansky goes beyond conventional translation. It is through a process of tense interpellation that Harvitz's conscience comes to face the very limits and meaning of his engagement with Levitansky—"If I'm a coward why has it taken me so long to discover it?" ("Man in the Drawer" 437). The threat of political inspection does not prevent him from recovering the leaves of the manuscripts, and though Levitansky's ghost disturbs his dreams, he departs for the Moscow airport. Full translation of his commitment is postponed to the reading of a trilogy of stories in which fictive "truth" does not hide moral "truth," historically rooted in past cultural traditions. Their arguments and structures rewrite a very old script signed by repression during the Jewish Passover in Russia, political control of Jewish religious rituals, and the tragic death of a half-Jewish translator, Anatoly Borisovich, who burned his talent, his integrity, and his heritage. The return to that past would translate vivid memories of Jewish cultural activism and the perils of assimilation. It is no wonder that Anatoly Borisovich "had gone into translation" (445) when the Bolsheviks were taking over the Jewish cultural revolution.

Commenting on the problem of reading Holocaust narratives, Daniel R. Schwartz observes that there are important differences between how narratives are told and how they mean. "I see telling," he says, "as a crucial act, all the more crucial because of the trauma of the originating cause. Because we can never trust memory fully, in narration effects (how a teller presents himself or herself) sometimes *precede cause* (the explanation for why a narrator is the person he or she is)" (35; emphasis in the original). Bearing in mind the differences between testimonial narratives and narration, the perception of this original cause sheds light on the reading experience produced by the act of telling and its narrative transference as well as the translation of the interaction between teller and listener into the reader's cognitive position. Inevitably anxiety and the need to find its lost object or the attempt to overcome its absence play an important role in this process. The Holocaust, we will never forget, has severed the relation between reality and representation, radically decentering the subject and its narrative positions.

The fate of translation confronted in the short story "The German Refugee" causes the reader to witness the specific effects produced by the traumatic event and its memories. Oskar Gassner's situation as a German Jewish refugee living in New York is not able to provide a refuge in the new language to prepare his lecture "The Literature of the Weimer Republic," but instead he feels imprisoned in a spectral verbal house, inhabited by mental torture, paralysis, and loss of self-image: "I am left with myself unexpressed," he says, and as the narrator points out, "to keep from drowning in things unsaid he wanted to swallow the ocean in a gulp" ("The German Refugee" 360). Gassner's despair makes him a helpless victim—"a piece of bleeding meat . . . to the hawks" (362)—both of the Germans and of the Americans. His experience as an immigrant in exile and his battle with the language cannot match sense and meaning, psychic conflict and speech, literal translation and allegorical. The position he finds himself in of being between two worlds opens a haunting abyss of cultural transaction, linguistic incompatibility, and political confrontation, all inextricably connected in his personal and social spheres. Even the extract of Walt Whitman's poetical text that Gassner was preparing for his lecture passes untranslated, since he is unable to interpret Whitman's message in the context of his exiled transaction, tragically affected by the Germans' invasion of Poland and the slaughter of his wife, who had converted to Judaism. Such reactions should startle the reader, but as Dominick LaCapra declares in "Reflections on Trauma, Absence and Loss," "to the extent that someone is possessed by the past and acting out a repetition compulsion, he or she may be incapable of ethically responsible behavior" (191). The news from Germany and Gassner's suicide might be viewed through different analogical lenses, though the final tragic version comes from the knowledge of his wife's embrace of Judaism and the reading of the only sentence left untranslated in the story: "Ich bin dir siebenundzwanzig Jahre true gewesen" (I have been faithful to you for twenty-seven years; 363). The tragic irony of the story would probably compel readers to go beyond translation or accept an almost kabbalistic conception of it.

Of course, translation as the connecting thread of reflexivity not only has to face the ghostly return of the past, as Oskar Gassner's experiences reveal, but also open our eyes to the way this return restructures our present. The fictive world of the story "The Last Mohican" takes us back to that past and invites us to accept the burden of the necessity to mean with the aesthetic advantages of vision. The double perspective is quite relevant from the point of view of narrative focalization, and it is connected in structural layers, especially in a retrospective vision like this. But such a double vision is above all important for the introduction of a subjective gaze in the story. Formally, we recognize that narrative construction is analogous to the art of painting; and obviously the choice by the painter of the point of view is, as Vernon Lee affirms, the "most subtle choice of the literary craftsman" (37). The Italian setting of the story, for instance, opens a visual space framed by Arthur Fidelman's reaction to seeing himself as he was, a visual effect that reflects changing impressions of himself, an intense sense of being, and an "almost tri-dimensional reflection of himself" ("The Last Mohican" 201). The contemplation of Italian art in the Eternal City traces the stages of his artistic "rite de passage," initiated as a project to write a book on Giotto, to work as a critic, and to forsake his professional failures. Evidently the cultural conflict between the Italian history and his Jewish past is initially painted as an aesthetic choice, visually outlined by a shocking contrast between the Roman ruins, the Baths of Diocletian, and "the remembrance of things unknown" (204). It is in fact through the contemplation of the statues of Romulus and Remus that Fidelman perceives the "apparition" of a stranger. And it is through an intense visual exchange that the figure of a refugee comes to light.

The encounter between Arthur Fidelman and Shimon Susskind is then described as a visual fixation—"I knew you were Jewish . . . the minute my eyes saw you" (202), reveals Susskind, in an encounter that soon turns into an enigmatic refraction as Fidelman discovers the real condition of Susskind as a "luftmensch," a poor man who literally lives on charity. Susskind beseeches of Fidelman money and clothes and haunts his movements as a ghost. As Fidelman refuses to give the refugee his spare suit and Susskind reveals where he lives and how he lives—"I eat air" (207)—Susskind's figure appears and disappears as a phantom in the underworld of the ghetto, visiting the cemeteries or selling religious objects in front of St. Peter's, the same landscape that Fidelman will have to revisit. To the reader's amazement, Susskind seems to be flying or in the company of angels. Not only is his first visit to Fidelman's room described as an apparition—"the door opened, and instead of an angel, in came in his shirt and baggy knickers" (205)—but his provocative questions seem dictated by visionary knowledge or spectral wisdom.

The irruption of Susskind in the life of Fidelman stages a critical scene of instruction that is aggressively conducted by the refugee. As James Fenimore Cooper's Natty Bumpo in *The Last of the Mohicans* (1826) incarnates the real heroism of the frontiersman, Susskind forces Fidelman to confront his Jewish beliefs through the recognition of his artistic and critical capacity. This process exceeds the terms of a conventional pedagogical exchange, since the refugee follows Fidelman as a shadow, steals his manuscript, and exerts moral authority as a spiritual guide and interpreter: "The words were there but the spirit was missing," concludes Susskind, as he flees from the scene "light as the wind" (219). It is indeed a paradoxical and effective teaching experience, constantly brought to our attention by the staging of an inversion of pedagogical positions between teacher and students in order to produce real interaction. Susskind, however, goes much further and unsettles Fidelman's moral principles and attitudes, seeking close identification as a peddler and sharing religious experiences.

Susskind and Fidelman's exchange opens up a field of vision integrating dream landscapes and dark backgrounds, artistic references, and moral implications. The central scene exhibits the apparition of Virgilio Susskind in a dream, his guidance through the underworld of Jewish history, the vision of Giotto's painting, and the symbolic representation of Fidelman's artistic and religious dilemma. At the same time, the scene of St. Francis giving away his cloak adumbrates a visual prefiguration of Fidelman's moral responsibility toward the refugee, acting as mirror-stage of his effective transformation. Indeed, an allegorical reading probably underlies how Fidelman translates dreams into action, framing into an explicit fable of religious conversion his search for Susskind to give him the suit, his return to the ghetto or to the world of *yiddishkeit*. As S. Lillian Kremer states, "Only after he accepts the moral imperative of universal human responsibility can the art critic understand Giotto's interpretation of suffering humanity. . . . Having completed the task of directing the *schlemiel* to self-awareness and communal responsibility, Malamud's enigmatic spiritual guide, compound of the commonplace and mysterious, disappears, destined to keep on running, as the *lamed vov tzaddik* is to venture forth where he is needed" ("Reflections" 131).

But does the allegorical reading imply a radical option between art and moral commitment? Are aesthetic alternatives translated into moral alternatives? Since the publication of this story in *The Magic Barrel*, Susskind's apparitions were destined to enlighten *Pictures of Fidelman: An Exhibition*, a collection of six tales exposing surrealistic "pictures" presided over by the figure of Jesus/Susskind. This iconic figure reminded many readers of the aesthetic dilemmas faced by Jewish artists in the thirties and forties, particularly Marc Chagall's treatment of the image of Jesus in *The White Crucifixion* and other paintings, in which he openly Judaized the Christian symbols. Though some viewers may have interpreted those paintings as part of an American campaign to carry out a reinforcement of "Judeo-Christian values," his work decidedly answered the modernist attempt to place the visual definition of the Jews into the center of their cultural representation. Chagall's religious paintings can be interpreted as quasi-surrealistic works structured around historical motifs and patterns that play with objects, letters, places and family histories, and Yiddish language and folklore, as in his *Introduction to the Yiddish Theater* (1920) in Moscow. The case of Chagall is not the only one to introduce the viewer into surrealistic visions close to the absurd. Max Ernst, as we know, openly supported the ideas of an abstract surrealism. But the burning issue of modernist Jewish art was, as Barbara E. Mann points out, whether the question of self-representation was gaining force and cultural relevance. Quoting El Lissitsky's comments, she asks, "How does the Jew fit into an aesthetic tradition dominated by classical, pagan, and Christian motifs?" (676)

These remarks are not intended to read Fidelman's artistic journey in the "Pictures of the Artist" as a particular case of aesthetic isomorphism, though narrative textuality and visual representation go hand in hand with exposing Fidelman's artistic pretentions and their moral cost. Granted, it seems that in spite of the experimental texture of the "pictures," the sequel of dreams and their narrative hybridity must in the end preserve Susskind's magisterial vision and Fidelman's artistic instructions. But its dialogic structure opens new ways of reading the interaction between master and disciple, particularly if Susskind's interpellation plays the master's role invested with biblical authority. Susskind's sermon on the mountain performs a haunting ritual of moral instruction, mixing the authorial voice of the master with persuasive insinuations and questions. As might be expected, the paternal figure starts the sermon reminding Fidelman of the biblical law prohibiting the production of images or paintings, a command that generates a surrealistic chain of interrogations and ritualistic phraseology. Nonetheless, divine authority moves Fidelman to promise new fidelity—"I will never betray thee . . . / What happens will happen. . . . Follow me where I go, and we will see what we will see. This we will see. / Master, tis as good as done," and "burn everything, . . . papyrus, charcoal, a roll of canvas" (*Pictures of Fidelman* 163, 164).

Fidelman's absence from the final story, as Kremer has suggested, follows the traditional *tsaddik* role of disappearing presumably "to rematerialize when needed" once the salvational task is achieved ("Reflections" 135). Such transformation, we could suggest, "materializes" into words and images, in the surrealistic landscape where the marvelous may unveil the contradictions within the real. Jewish writing and art, states Gideon Ofrat, have manifested some reservations about surrealism. This might be due, he suggests, to the artists' awareness of Jewish history, to their transmission of the messages of memory. It is "the memories of history," he says, "the residues of historical catastrophes, and the remembrance of past Holocausts that prevent the Jewish and Israeli quasi-surrealist artists from becoming true surrealists" (110). And to emphasize this perception, he outlines a comparison of Marc Chagall's *White Crucifixion* (1938) with Salvador Dalí's *Christ of Saint John of the Cross* (1951) in order to show that the absence of memory and historical references in Dalí's Christ does not offer any hope, while Chagall's painting "remembers" from within a poetical and hallucinatory world.

As art historians would confirm, the Jewish historical past has found in expressionism a more congenial medium of representation than surrealism, though the transference of the subconscious and the logic of dreams invaded both worlds. Malamud's incursion in this fictional mode, on the other hand, created fantastical surrealistic mirrors in the novel *The Fixer*, enclosing Bok in a phantasmagorical space of oppression. His dreams, we can remember, made possible his new emergent identity and struggle for survival. Similarly, the gallery of texts and images collected in "Pictures of the Artist" interlace descriptive sections, verbal "collages," interior monologues, and biblical rhetoric, tracing hallucinatory detours that seem to follow historical continuity. But their structure is essentially phantasmatic, as Susskind's tour with Fidelman shows, in the final journey to the Crucifixion. Following Jesus's itinerary from Capernaum to the presence of the high priest Caiaphas to the Mount of Olives and its final "station" to mount Calvary, we visualize Susskind's crucifixion as a hilarious parody of Jesus's mystery of Redemption.

Obviously, the spectacle is essentially spectral, a burlesque ritual of symbolic mimicry. The reader is obliged to visualize the spectacle from Fidelman's point of view, following his vision of the crucifixion from behind the mask. Before the textual curtain is drawn, Fidelman paints three canvases of the Crucifixion, leaving the scene of the Resurrection blank, and the spectator is led to descend to an eschatological inferno. "*Je vous emmerde*. Modigliani" (*Pictures of Fidelman* 167). It belongs to the realm of fantasy or comic absurdity to see how the pictorial erection of Susskind's temple does not envision the Resurrection. And it seems clear that Susskind's preaching and Fidelman's artistic re-creation would provide a surrealistic mask for those performances of the *schlemiel* that, as Barbara Kreiger describes, is forced to suspend, to some extent, "his reliance on the redemptive nature of faith and adopt a purely ironic stance" (132). The literary transformations of the *schlemiel* figure may help to reconsider if Susskind's crucifixion and Fidelman's artistic rites make their role "unbearable," or at least inadequate to turn pain into laughter or vice versa. The general "picture" of this folk figure presented in the Fidelman stories, however, elicits "amused sympathy modified by satiric awareness," as Robert Alter has observed ("Jewishness" 31).

"Can Jews haunt people?" The itinerary followed in this detour has swerved between intertextual variations and forms of representation channeled by language, translation, and art. The seductions of biography, however, might induce readers to displace spectrality from the collective and historical landscapes glimpsed through those forms to individual subjects and their processes of identification. Indeed, Malamud displaced the trail of the specter in his last short stories from pictorial representation to musical interpretation, leaving Susskind's ghost in the background of artistic representation, projecting his shadow onto sporadic allusions, rhetorical formulas, puns, or conventional forms of address. In the short story "A Lost Grave," for instance, the specter's absence blurs Mr. Hecht's memory; in "Kew Gardens," Leonard Woolf projects his double consciousness as a British and Jewish character on the role of a Jewish mother; in "Alma Redeemed," Mahler's ghost betrays the spirit of Jewishness. "Jews," says Alma after meeting Frank Werfel, "have given us spirit but have eaten our hearts" ("Alma Redeemed" 267). And there is no doubt that "Jewishness" haunts these stories as a cultural emblem of residual history, as floating images in the literary landscape composed by Virginia's letter to Violet Dickinson in "In Kew Gardens," Dworking's cello in "Zora's Noise," or Mahler's mask in "Alma Redeemed."

But the question posed by "Alma Redeemed" does not imply a substitution of collective ghosts for personal biographies or of the representation of Jewishness for individual myths. Mahler's spectral influence, obviously, underlies the biographical portrait composed in "Alma Redeemed," particularly through the symphonic modulations of selected memories of his intolerant attitude toward Alma's musical taste, his conversion from Judaism to Catholicism, Alma's affairs and marriages, and his death. The conjectures surrounding Mahler's ghostly visitation invariably appear connected to the Jewish world, magnetically attracted by some mysterious cause or symptom: the crazy mystique of the artist, the father's shadow, the lover's "wild fantasies and burning desires" ("Alma Redeemed" 264) and its masks. As the story goes, Mahler becomes frightened of losing her, visits Freud in Leiden, and writes to his wife, "My darling, my lyre, . . . come exorcise the ghosts of darkness. They claw me, they throw me to the ground. I ask in silence whether I am damned. Rescue me, my dearest" ("Alma Redeemed" 261).

Mahler's cry for psychological restoration echoes his repeated gestures as a lecturer and spiritual guide to his wife, an impersonal preaching that Alma finds repellent and frightening: "He sounded more like a teacher than a lover," says the narrator (260). And indeed the search for the spiritual center turns into a voyeuristic tour around his musical ego and religious conversion. Both experiences make him a ghost, ignoring, on the one hand, his wife's artistic potential and, on the other, denying his past identity, a divorce that, as Siefried Mandel suggests, is tantamount to being dead (39). At the same time, Alma confronts Mahler's imposing presence, threatening to betray his musical genius and unmask his sexuality, even at the risk of incarnating the archetype of the fallen woman as Kokoschka's *Miss Julie* will show, transforming her corporeal body into a cosmic sound. Her phantasmatic world, however, centers on Mahler's figure, presided over by his iconic representation of death—"He looked like death masquerading as a monk"—and haunting her mind from the grave ("Alma Redeemed" 268). The reader wonders what kind of redemption might bring Mahler's ghost, unless the spirit of romantic love, religion, and art inhabiting musical composition and interpretation—evoked in the dedication of the Eighth Symphony to Alma or in Frank Werfel's last pieces—performs a liberating recognition of Alma's creativity: "How can one love Mahler if she best loves Wagner?" asks Alma (269). The question confirms her rejection of Mahler's proposal to make his melody hers, to share musical composition as true lovers, since she could not develop her experimental musical talent under his oppressive genius. There are also melodies prefiguring death or played at Werfel's funeral, melodies that she did not want to hear; rather, she refuses to attend Werfel's funeral and instead drinks Benedictine, a popular monastic "spirit" of restoration.

The orchestration of biographical consciousness and music performed in "Alma Redeemed" resonates in other short stories as a sign of women's creativity, a concern that had oriented Malamud's fiction in the seventies. However, its interpretation produces in "Zora's Noise," for example, a haunting alternation of discordant melodies between Dworkin's sublime vibrations of the cello—"an independent small Jewish animal" (231)—and Zora's earthy sounds, which characterize her ghostly living in the house she detests. It is really fitting that both Dworkin's personal constellation (the cellist) and Zora's noises are fused in "a living element of a ghostly constellation in the sky" (234), combining her utter misery with his cosmic sublimity, her "ghostly wailing" (241) for her lost baby with his "vibrations of the cello rise in his flesh" (244). If, as Vernon Lee states, "the construction of a whole book stands to the construction of a single sentence as the greatest complexities of counterpoint and orchestration stand to the relations of the vibrations constituting a single just note" (39), the duet played by Dworkin and Zora failed to produce a unisonant performance: "The noises cause the noises," Zora says ("Zora's Noise" 245).

It is precisely the "clamorous noises" in Virginia Woolf's head, or voices or words, that in the story "In Kew Gardens" drag her to the river Ouse to meet her death (257). In order to hear the choral counterpoints composed by Malamud's "In Kew Gardens," it is indispensable to enter Woolf's gardens and listen to her single note, because the joyful and introspective tone of "Kew Gardens" becomes in Malamud's story a haunting orchestration within her brain, a polyphonic composition of family affections and disaffections, maternal wounds, and sexual frustrations. It might be illuminating to read both stories as intertextual dialogue, contrasting Woolf's interior responses and impressions with Malamud's external frames and voices, the harmonious and episodic structure of "Kew Gardens" (1919) with the interlocking dialogues of "In Kew Gardens." The perception of memory and death in Woolf's story is grafted onto Malamud's sketchy montage of quotations, biographical confessions, and literary allusions, capturing Woolf's apparent "randomness" through iterative sentences and juxtapositions. While Woolf articulates narrative sketches through the force of language and voice, Malamud preserves the structures and interactive resonance of quotations, sentences, and statements as unique biographical objects, whether they belong to Woolf's narrative sketches, Quentin Bell's biography, the novel *Between the Acts*, or extracts from her diaries and letters.

Indeed, the dialogue we are suggesting between these two stories and their authors is essentially spectral, reflected through the textual recontextualization of "Kew Gardens" and its unveiling of the seductive transactions of Virginia Woolf's personal and literary life. It is worth recalling that Woolf had been Malamud's mysterious literary guide and that her narrative sketches—in the carefully sustained narrative transitions of "Kew Gardens"—helped him to mold his brief stories. In fact, her influence had been effective in the composition of *Dubin's Lives* and became an intimate source of inspiration when he decided to write fictional biographies. Additionally, the death of Woolf's mother brought Malamud's personal reverberations to this story, as he reveals in the memoir-lecture "Long Walk, Short Life" (1984) and his readings of Woolf's autobiographical essays. Thus, the interpellation opened in "In Kew Gardens" not only depicts the intimate canvas of Woolf's search for a room of her own—quoting Lily Briscoe's words in *To the Lighthouse* (1927)—but Malamud's fascination with autobiographical consciousness and its fictions.

Taking Virginia Woolf's autobiographical portrait as pretextual source, Malamud threads personal experiences mainly around Julia Stephen's death, its traumatic impact on Woolf, her mental instability, and her own death. Stephen's ghostly influence presides over Woolf's fragmentary pieces of psychotic discourse, vividly registered through citations, allusions to literary authors (Tennyson, James), exchange of narrative voices, or transcriptions from her novels. In spite of the traumatic wound caused by death, there is no room for deep melancholy or mourning, since Woolf's mental fertility melts fantasy, cold objectivity, and naked expressions. As her last dialogue with Leonard recites, "'Though you give much I give so little'. / 'The little you give is a king's domain.' At that time the writing went well and she artfully completed *Between the Acts*, yet felt no joy" ("In Kew Gardens" 257).

It might seem contradictory to bring Malamud's fascination with Woolf's fiction to those places where specters usually remain in the crypts. The textual crypts that Malamud erected for Virginia Woolf and Alma Mahler were mainly haunted by masculine specters. Perhaps Malamud's stories opened themselves to these visions when men, as "A Lost Grave" lets us see, had to calculate affective losses and nightmares or place marriage, conjugal love, divorce, and death as a drama of psychic reparation. It is significant that in "A Lost Grave," when Mr. Hecht goes to visit Mr. Goodman to inquire about the situation of the investigation, we hear the following plea:

> "Your young lady tried her computer in every combination but couldn't produce anything. What was lost is still lost, in other words, a woman's grave."
>
> "*Lost* is premature," Goodman offered. "*Displaced* might be better. In my twenty-eight years in my present capacity, I don't believe we have lost a single grave." (249; emphasis in original).

Dr. Goodman's ironic alternative marks a turning point in the story and insinuates that losses and displacements might refer not only to Mr. Hecht's lost grave but to twenty-eight years of Jewish history. Both terms articulate the dialectics of psychic restoration and mourning, and it seems that Malamud places these posthumous stories in psychoanalytic contexts, giving "Jewishness" its share of psychic rituals. The reader may follow the course of a thriller's investigation about a specific grave and its absurd discovery—"We have tracked your wife and it turns out she isn't in the grave there where the computer couldn't find her. To be frank, we found her in a grave with another gentleman" (251)—or depart from the specter of nightmares, reactivate memories, and obsessions until the material search of the grave frustrates the search: "Don't forget," Dr. Goodman tells Hecht, "you gained an empty grave for future use. Nobody is there and you own the plot" (251–52).

NOTES

1. "Alma Redeemed," "In Kew Gardens," A Lost Grave," and "Zora's Noise" are included in Malamud, *People*; "Angel Levine," "Man in the Drawer," "The German Refugee," and "The Last Mohican" are included in Malamud, *Complete*.

2. *Merriam-Webster Thesaurus Online*, s.v. "haunting," www.merriam-webster.com/thesaurus/haunting (accessed August 14, 2015).

3. *Merriam-Webster Dictionary Online*, s.v. "spectral," www.merriam-webster.com/dictionary/spectral (accessed August 14, 2015).

4. For a detailed analysis of the theme of "the return of the dead," see Harold Bloom's concept of *apophrades* in *The Anxiety of Influence: A Theory of Poetry* (139–55).

CHAPTER 14

Bernard Malamud's and John Updike's Art Stories

The Act of Creation in "Still Life" and "Leaves"

ARISTI TRENDEL

UNIVERSITÉ DU MAINE, FRANCE

Creativity and creation are not only explored by psychologists, art historians, and brain scientists but also by artists, who can have firsthand knowledge of their trade. Indeed, it is no wonder that Freud, in his ambivalence, trusted and admired this intimate knowledge and considered artistic insight into the act of creation most valuable, particularly in his essay "Delusions and Dreams in Jensen's *Gradiva*." Self-reflexivity is by no means the exclusive prerogative of postmodernism, and though a salient postmodern feature, it has also characterized fiction since its origin. Bernard Malamud is a case in point since artistic creation is a recurrent topic in his work. Unlike John Updike, who did not demonstrate the same amount of interest in exploring art in his fiction, Malamud's fiction is highly self-reflexive. However, Updike's "Leaves"[1] and Malamud's "Still Life"[2] juxtaposed appear complementary in their exploration of the act of creation. These two stories subtly display the creative act without any of the abrupt interruptions of narrative codes that we find in postmodern fiction. While Updike captures the creative process in a lyric story that stages the birth of a text, Malamud, from the labors of creation, attends to the reception of art, offering an astonishing image of art transmuting into life in a semicomic text. In addition, Malamud's story contributes significantly to the reception of art since this topic has been studied less in fiction than has creation. In spite of the stories' differences in scope and tone, "Leaves" and "Still Life" both inquire into the psychodynamics of creation and assert their authors' faith in the transformative power of art and their embrace of an art-and-life stance instead of an art-versus-life one.

I investigate the metafictional aspect in these two narratives, which involves the emergence of the creative process in "Leaves" and the reception of artistic creation in "Still Life." In both stories, art allows for a working through of guilt. The characters manage through art to resolve what has been tormenting them, providing, in this way, the resolution of an emotional conflict for the creative writer in Updike's story and the beholder in Malamud's. In both stories, repressed feelings are released and reintegrated into the personality of the characters.

Though it would be hard to decide which is Malamud's most metafictional work, Updike's most metafictional piece of fiction is certainly the Bech story cycle, in which in a comic-satiric vein, he tackles the act of creation through the fictional conceit of a writer's block. It is the release and relief of creation that "Leaves" brings into focus, pinpointing the narrow passage where life becomes art. In fact, Updike, in a period of great distress in his life, self-avowedly wrote this story "in a trance of misery" (De Bellis 293). Interestingly, he considered it "his best story," as Jack De Bellis reports (293), offering a marveled comment on his own story about the act of creation: "The way the leaves become the pages, the way the bird becomes his description, the way the bright and multiform world of nature is felt rubbing against the dark world of the trapped ego—all strike me as beautiful, and of the order of artistic 'happiness' that is given rather than attained" (Updike, *Hugging* 853). Updike's terse statement, which ushers the reader into the wings of the narrative, emphasizes the joy of artistic creation, the beauty of this new world, the natural gift of the artist, and ultimately the value of aesthetic experience. The author, both an insider and an outsider to his own work, pairs his self-conscious main text with an equally self-conscious paratext as if to guide the reader into this narrative, which features a suffering, guilt-ridden first-person narrator reflecting on his divorce and in the process of composing a text.

Nevertheless, critics have been both delighted with and quite puzzled by this brief short story whose metafictional tenor has eluded them. Robert Detweiler called the story "a prose-poem" (124), and Eileen Baldeshwiler included it in her discussion of the American lyrical short story to elucidate the category. Indeed, her definition of the category does describe, to a certain extent, this plotless, polished, meditative text: "Episodic in construction, few of the pieces revolve around a conventional plot; . . . the author gently leads us through an interlude of time depicted by means of minute, impressionist touches—not without occasional motifs or semi-symbolic figures—in such a way that the senses are alerted and the feelings softened and made reflective" (Baldeshwiler, qtd. in Luscher 199). It is precisely this reflective quality in the story that makes the shift to self-reflection appear smooth and unintrusive. In fact, the story engages the Freudian idea of the work of creation; just like the dream work and the work of mourning, the work of creation involves psychic operations that bring about a transformation. Moreover, "Leaves" depicts the stages of creation, which various scholars have attempted to define.

"Leaves" puts under the narrative spotlight a man in crisis facing a psychic upheaval and wrestling with inner turmoil while isolated in a marsh cottage deep in nature. Unlike Rev. Marshfield's prankish, forced retreat in Updike's novel *A Month of Sundays*, this narrator is grave and voluntary. The narrator in "Leaves" attempts to come to terms with a moral catastrophe of his own making—dangling between his initially abandoned wife and his currently abandoned wife-to-be, he reconsiders his divorce. The ferocity of moral offense and the siege of guilt that the narrator experiences cry out for a life sentence in a prison of perpetual pain. However, through the act of writing, he breaks the noose that is tightening around him, thus transmuting a subjective state of pain and guilt into a refined expression of an internal vision of humanity and nature that marks the passage to aesthetics and is therefore transmittable.

Updike's *mise en abyme* of the creative process in "Leaves" is built on metaphor and metonymy and calls for self-psychology's psychoanalytic perspective on creativity, which highlights the artist's search "to confirm and/or repair his or her sense of self" (Hagman, *Aesthetic* 68) In fact, the narrator's "sense of self" is deeply impaired by the wrong he feels he has committed in divorcing his wife, which is a recurrent theme in some of Updike's short stories such as "The Music School," "Death of Distant

Friends," and "Guilt-Gems." Significantly, in all these stories, the afflicted character develops different strategies to come to terms with guilt, but what distinguishes the narrator in "Leaves" is his leap into fiction and therefore the story's metafictional quality.

A master metaphor governs the text, one that rests on the natural process of photosynthesis; just like plants and other organisms that convert the sun into energy to fuel further activities, the narrator, "by some subjective photosynthesis" (Updike, "Leaves" 343), converts the inner "sun of guilt" (342) into the *élan vital* of prose to perpetuate life and restore man's lost innocence. Guilt is, indeed, pivotal and at the core of psychic processes that revolve around a major emotional conflict, one that is shaking and threatening the narrator's sense of being, as conveyed by this powerful image: "the inner darkness burst my skin" (342). This metaphorical wound reveals the violence of the mental one.

There are various models of the psychological processes that make artistic creativity unique. Freud stresses the unifying function of the artist's ego ideal. Though self-psychologists have criticized and gone further than Freud in their view of the creative act, they built on his basic premise of the intrapsychic dynamics.[3] George Hagman defines the work of creation as "the psychological processes of the artist that result in the creation of new, aesthetically legitimate works of art" (*Aesthetic* 61). Albert Rothenberg underlines that "psychodynamically, the inception of a poetic process and the inspirations that occur at the beginning or along the way are metaphorical embodiments of the poet's unconscious or pre-conscious emotional conflicts" (176). At the beginning of the story, "Leaves" intimates an emotional battle through "the long darkness of self-absorption and fear and shame in which [the narrator has] been living" (341) and presents the creative act as a movement from the obscure maze of the narrator's mind to the light of the text following certain stages.

Didier Anzieu distinguishes five phases in the work of creation and names the initial stage of inspiration "seizure" (*saisissement*), defined as "a mythic experience of the real that doubles, for that matter, the communication . . . with the . . . objective reality of things" (101; my translation). In "Leaves," the narrator's source of inspiration is nature, whose minute observation captivates him and triggers in him the desire to compose a text. The very first line of the narrative is a declaration of awe before the beauty of nature: "The grape leaves outside my window are curiously beautiful" (341). It is the beauty of nature, significantly defined by the narrator as "that which exists without guilt," that removes his attention from the inner fixation and makes him an eager reader of the Book of Nature, an enthralled beholder, and an aesthete (341).

Nature provides a sense of shelter from the moral homelessness of the ego: "The net effect, however, is innocent of menace. On the contrary, its intricate simultaneous suggestion of *shelter* and openness; warmth and breeze, invites me outward" (341–42; emphasis added). Gilbert Rose's concept of "rematriation" in the *Power of Form* seems quite relevant here. As Rose puts it, "By creating it, and loving it and being loved by the world for making it the artist is rematriated" (64). Therefore, the innocence of nature and its relational promise and "abundance of inventive 'effect'" not only put the text-in-progress in motion but also offer a model of composition ("Leaves" 341).

Indeed, there is more than the simple contiguity of inner turmoil with this composition. The narrator is precisely not a mere imitator of nature for he seems to be in the process of creating an aesthetic object with which the reader is encouraged to communicate. Actually, the reader is subtly addressed by the narrator, who, fascinated by a blue jay outside his window, invites the reader to witness this marvel of a bird transformed into an object of art: "See him? I do, and snapping the chain of my thought, I have reached through glass and seized him and stamped him on this page. Now he is gone. And yet, there, a few lines above, he still is, 'astraddle,' his rump 'dingy,' his head 'alertly frozen.' A curious *trick*, possibly useless, but *mine*" (341; emphasis added). This irrefutable evidence of self-consciousness could correspond to the second stage of creation, which Anzieu considers as the awareness gained thanks to a core of a symbolizing activity at work in the artist's preconscious (113). Nature's "inventive 'effect'" correlates with the narrator's "trick," which underlines the artist's originality.

Other metafictional signs stud the text, for example, "A spider like a white asterisk hangs in air in front of my face" ("Leaves" 343). This simile confounds the natural world with the written page and makes the spider a printing symbol, an attention-calling mark to the affinity of fear shared by the two creatures: "Across the gulf we feel only fear" (343). And just like the spider, the author spins the same gossamer web, but one of intricate emotions, whose hallmark is the splendor of language, which conveys the splendor of autumn in the narrative: "Wilt transmutes this lent radiance into a glowing orange, and the green of the still tender leaves . . . strains from the sunlight a fine-veined chartreuse. . . . The oak's [leaves] are tenacious claws of purplish rust; the elm's, scant feathers of a feminine yellow; the sumac's, a savage, toothed blush" (341–42). This vibrancy of color and the luminous effect of Updike's prose, based on a meticulously calculated regularity of narrative strokes, are reminiscent of a neoimpressionist rather than the impressionist technique suggested by Baldeshwiler.

Thus, the narrator creates his own literary leaves; he moves from an imitative stage to a truly creative one, which is the hallmark of art, according to James Sasso's model of the stages of the creative process. The narrative marks the passage from a "groping towards a more significant and meaningful arrangement of ideas and sensations which Graham Wallas identifies as the initial stage of genuine creativity" (Sasso 125) to a clear articulation of a literary creation: "And what are these pages but leaves? Why do I produce them but to thrust by some subjective photosynthesis, my guilt into Nature, where there is no guilt?" ("Leaves" 343). The text operates this transformation by holding out to the narrator and to the reader the possibility of "an experience of perfection or rather the reexperience of a lost, ideal self-state," which is, according to Heinz Kohut, "at the heart of creativity" (Hagman, *Aesthetic* 67). It depicts the narrator's experience and vision of the human being as an edge creature standing between the two kingdoms of innocence and sin, *and* it is free from guilt.

The narrator, then, may have reached the illumination stage of artistic creation, that is, the emergence of a new idea, according to Wallas's model or the third stage of "instituting and fleshing out a code" according to Anzieu's (116). His aesthetic and spiritual view of nature gives shape, meaning, and color to his vision, reinforced by another layer of leaves in the story, giving structure to the narrative. The narrator's creative endeavor during what Wallas calls the incubation period is prompted and strengthened by another literary work, Walt Whitman's *Leaves of Grass*, a celebration of the poet's philosophy of life and humanity. The narrator meaningfully refers to his readings of Whitman's poems during his retreat: "I went alone to bed and read . . . a few pages of an old edition of *Leaves of Grass* and my sleep was a loop, so that in awakening I seemed still in the book, and the light-struck sky quivering through the stripped branches of the young elm seemed another page of Whitman, and I was entirely open, and lost, like a woman in passion, and free, and in love, a shadow in any corner of my being" ("Leaves" 343). Nature and poetry offer the same type of aesthetic and spiritual experience to the narrator and help him to express his own. Updike provides his narrator with an artistic affiliation, that of Walt Whitman, a sine qua non condition to artistic endeavor, according to Anzieu. The American poet is the patron saint of the story.

Therefore, Robert Luscher unfairly denies a "Whitmanesque spiritual flight" to the story (50). "Leaves" *is* such a "flight," since the narrative offers the narrator the possibility to liberate himself from the prison of his condition and the reader the vision of the creative process and the value of the aesthetic experience. In addition, "Leaves" is a "genuflection"; though open-ended, the ending points to the narrator's way to recovery paved by the text-in-progress, providing closure to the story: "I imagine warmth leaning against the door, and open the door to let it in; sunlight falls flat at my feet like a penitent" ("Leaves" 343). As in other Updike stories, penitence seems to be the author's response to guilt. But here the specificity of "Leaves" is the story's metafictional foray into a "dynamic, integrative function . . . of creative activity," whose artistic labors Updike leaves out of this story and his work in general (Hagman, *Aesthetic* 63). "The Sea's Green Sameness," which features a writer in search of a subject, is a mild exception that confirms Updike's generally nonreflexive choices.

Contrary to Updike, Bernard Malamud gave particular attention to this aspect of creation, which he fully explored in *The Tenants*. On a much smaller scale, "Still Life" also reveals the labors of creation in the main character's efforts to become a painter, but the story's main interest and originality lie in the attention Malamud grants to the reception of art. The author's sensibility to the creative act could not possibly leave out its reception. The role of the beholder turns out to be the surprise that the narrative has in store for the common reader as it shifts its focus from the artist to the beholder to emphasize what Wolfgang Kempf calls "the most important premise of reception aesthetics: namely, that the function of the beholding has already been incorporated into the work itself" (181).

Though part of the story cycle *Pictures of Fidelman* (1969), composed as a sort of a comic bildungsroman that unfolds its picaresque hero's artistic progress (or regression) from critic to painter to craftsman, "Still Life" is a self-contained story. In this narrative, Arthur Fidelman, the expatriate Jewish American leading a bohemian life in wintry Rome, struggles with his creative potential as an aspiring painter and a thwarted lover. In the course of the narrative, Fidelman achieves a double recognition—his paintings win over his beloved Italian *pittrice*, as the story refers to the character of temperamental Annamaria Oliovino. The story's comic tone and quasi-farcical humor render much more complex and ambiguous Malamud's exploration of art, misleading some critics such as Sydney Richman, who partially read the story as a "sad-absurd sexual travesty" (127). Annamaria's final surrender to Fidelman's courtship, brought about by his self-portrait as a priest, though eminently comic, raises serious issues about the reception of art, which have not been sufficiently analyzed. As Allen Guttmann suggests, "This is a memorable conclusion but one is puzzled about what to conclude from it" ("All" 153–54). Unlike Guttmann, Thomas L. Rohner clarifies the necessity for the reader to contribute to the act of creation: "since the meaning behind Malamud's humor, satire, and irony is mostly concealed and thus creates an enigmatic aura, the reader has to detect the impact of the humorous, satirical or ironic tone himself" (221). Therefore, "Still Life," by incorporating the role of the beholder in the narrative, is ultimately a *mise en abyme* of the role of the reader, whose involvement is required to make sense of the story. This in and out between art and life creates a close association, an author-reader partnership that renders the act of creation a joint endeavor. Through such an enlarged perspective, the reader can step back into the story, which memorably ends with the tight embrace of the two characters, who exemplify the union of a man and a woman but also of an artist and a beholder. The narrative subtly prepares for this union by meandering through the different stages of the creative process and by the comic treatment of dramatic events, a delicate enterprise for Malamud, who deftly switches from one genre to another.

Both characters in "Still Life," deep in their artistic endeavors, are troubled, isolated, and weighed down by their past. Annamaria, an untalented painter, is tormented by guilt as the reader discovers at the end of the story. In a moment of confusion, she drowned her neonate, fathered by her uncle, in the Tiber. Fidelman, a former art student and Annamaria's tenant, is haunted by an acute sense of alienation from his surroundings as he struggles with his identity as a man and an artist. This double quest appears fruitless in his sketch of a "Figure of a Jew Fleeing," which not only does he draw and hide in panic, but then he also suffers a breakdown of inspiration ("Still Life" 48). Moreover, the characters' existential malaise, set "in the dead of winter" against a cold, rainy, windy Rome, whose center seems to be the menacing river, deepens their unease (41). As Herbert Leibowitz rightly observes, cold weather in Malamud is, characteristically, "a gauge of a person's spiritual discomfort" (38).

Yet this serious tableau is traversed by a comic element, Fidelman's caricatural acceptance of Annamaria's exploitation of him. Right from the beginning of the narrative, love at first sight makes him "a plucked bird, greased, and ready for frying" (41). Likewise, Annamaria's superstitious remarks, such as asking the painter "to touch his testicles three times to undo or dispel who knows what witchcraft," and his subsequent arousal, "although he cautioned himself to remember" that her request "was in purpose and essence theological," further introduce comic elements into the narrative (45–46).

However, Fidelman's pursuit of art remains serious and appears conjoined with the pursuit of love, thus a priori making the beholder part of the act of creation. When Annamaria rejects him, he cannot paint: "In fact he did not exist for her. Not existing how could he paint, although he told himself he must? He couldn't. He aimlessly froze wherever he went" (59). But the first "labor of love" and art had already been carried out (54). What appears to be the illumination stage (Wallas) of the creative process is highlighted in the narrative, as Fidelman recognizes, "struck by a thought: if you could paint this sight, give it its quality in yours, the spirit belonged to you. History become aesthetic!" (53–54). Though this insight is provoked by the contemplation of the city, it is Annamaria whom Fidelman then paints as the Virgin Mary holding baby Jesus, in this manner gaining access to her heart and, albeit inconclusively at this point of the narrative, to her bed. Here Christof Wegelin points to Malamud's insightful and undoubtedly serious exploration of the creative act interspersed with comic scenes: "With the aid of the traditional archetype, the Madonna and Child, the artist's imagination has discovered not only her beauty but also the guilt she has never dared tell the priest" (Wegelin 81).

Nevertheless, Wegelin focuses more on the production of art and less on its reception, which is remarkably the issue here. Annamaria's overwhelmed response to Fidelman's "Virgin with Child"—"You have seen my soul" (55)—points to the role of the artist as the seer and bard of the mind. As Dmitri A. Leontiev succinctly puts it, "The most distinctive property of art, its secret, consists in its ability to find the shortest way to the individual's soul, to exert a mighty, sometimes nearly hypnotic influence, to involve a person in such a degree *that he should weep for her*" (56; emphasis in original). The narrative demonstrates this property and investigates further the role of the beholder reenacting the myth of Pygmalion, already used by Malamud in "The Naked Nude," but significantly extended to include the viewer in "Still Life." Not only the creator but also the beholder brings the painting to life, as the ending makes clear. While Updike depicts how life becomes art, Malamud examines how art becomes life.

But the way to creation is long, and Malamud lingers on the creative process. The comic episode in Annamaria's bed, in which the painter turns out to be unable to satisfy the *pittrice* and is consequently dismissed, defers the fulfillment of desire and gives a new impetus to the act of creation. Annamaria is still the painter's muse and source of inspiration, a "major aspect of poetic creation," according to Rothenberg, "an intrinsically dramatic experience," but in a much more covert way (172–73).

Indeed, contrary to Edgar Allen Poe, who in his essays described a highly rationalistic approach to the creative act, Malamud seems to think that inspiration is difficult to pin down for an artist. Fidelman has no clues about the source of his inspiration as he pursues the labors toward an unforeseeable conclusion, whose goals Hershel Parker defines with the aid of Murray Krieger and Albert Rothenberg: "Krieger the literary theorist and aesthetician and Rothenberg the clinical psychiatrist are united in their depiction of the creative process as a struggle—toward growth to full size of a monster with a will of its own in Krieger's formulation, toward a psychological freedom in Rothenberg's" (105). Fidelman's headlong dive into the creative act results in his liberation from the ghost of the "Jew Fleeing," as he is transformed into a priest when he paints—like Rembrandt, the artistic affiliation in the narrative—his self-portrait in priest's clothes. His work then reflects Annamaria's liberation from guilt. The *pittrice*, overwhelmed by the painting, confesses to the painter, asks for absolution, and does penitence in his arms at his request. It is quite telling that where religion failed—since Annamaria abhorred priests—art succeeded. Edward A. Abramson's narrow view of the characters underestimates the interplay between the artist and the beholder, which this ending foregrounds (*Bernard Malamud* 4).

Indeed, E. H. Gombrich, commenting on Giorgio Vasari's account of the link between the imagination of the artist and that of his or her public, states that "an entirely new idea of art is taking shape, . . . an art in which the painter's skill in suggesting must be matched by the public's skill in taking hints" (165). Gombrich traces the emergence "of a psychological theory of painting that takes account of that interplay between the artist and the beholder" (167). It seems to be Fidelman's painting that has made Annamaria search in her tormented mind for the unexpressed and inarticulate. Through his work, the artist communicates to his viewer what is verbally not only ineffable but also ineffective. Where the man fails, since Fidelman is unable to seduce Annamaria, the artist succeeds. Richard Wollheim underlines the critical operation in process, which points to the fact or at least justifies the interpretative view that "meaning adheres to the work of art and derives from the original creative process (243). Annamaria's hidden crosses in her paintings first correlate with Fidelman's hidden Star of David and finally with the priest's attire. Her response, though spontaneous and unreflective, evokes the phenomena of "transmutation" and "transubstantiation," which Marcel Duchamp in his essay "The Creative Act" emphasizes: "The creative act takes another aspect when the spectator experiences the phenomenon of transmutation: through the change from inert matter into a work of art, an actual transubstantiation has taken place, and the role of the spectator is to determine the weight of the work on the esthetic scale" (139). Instead of an aesthetic analysis, the narrative offers Annamaria's telling act of surrendering to the all-seeing artist, who has the power to deliver her in his god-like or priest-like role. Like Pygmalion, she makes the work of art come alive. Thus, Annamaria fulfills the "beholder's share" (Gombrich's famous phrase) in the creative act, the lion's share in the narrative.

Nevertheless, in spite of such considerations, the reader must also examine the comic effect of the story's hilarious ending. Sheldon Hershinow underlines Malamud's intent and humorous exploration of art in "Still Life," emphasizing the stock figure of the schlemiel: "In presenting an 'exhibition of the artist as "schlemiel"' Malamud creates a humorous but probing exploration into the philosophy of art" (80). Yet the critic does not make clear what this philosophy is; the schlemiel role must be toned down since other critics have refuted it and Malamud disliked this characterization (Stern 59). Annamaria's gesture of grabbing the painter's knees and crying for help—"Help me, Father, for Christ's sake"—ambiguously substituting him for a real priest, triggers the comic effect and raises the issue of appearance or semblance discussed in aesthetic theory ("Still Life" 67). The concept of appearance marked by the tension between deception and truth goes back to Plato and Hesiod and is prominent in theories about the aesthetic phenomenon. Yet the position of aesthetic autonomy seems to be preserved in the narrative. As Annamaria, overpowered by the picture, throws herself to Fidelman's feet, uttering, "Forgive me, Father, for I have sinned," to initiate a confession, the painter is turned into a mock priest giving a mock absolution (66). However, neither Annamaria's most eloquent and forceful verdict nor the catharsis she experiences is a mock one. Karl Heinz Bohrer thus defines "suddenness" or the moment of the aesthetic appearance: "Suddenness establishes that pointlike quality which allows us to conceptualize the new, the entirely other of the cultural alternative in a purely static way, to disregard *the course of time* that is a necessary part of our consciousness" (120). The return to time also marks the passage from pathos to ethos in the narrative.

Significantly Malamud's compelling concern with the nature of the creative act seems to find relief in the comic mode, which allows him to offer his insights into the act of creation by adding another layer of creativity—humor. Arthur Koestler's characterization of creativity as "the spontaneous flash of insight which shows a familiar situation or event in a new light, and elicits a new response to it" is most relevant at the ending of "Still Life," where an explosion of comic energy occurs (45). The familiar situation is a couple making love, and the unfamiliar one is that the intercourse occurs under the auspices of art and religion. This clash points to Koestler's "bisociative pattern," mobilizing two "matrices of thought," secular and religious or moral (38). From pathos, the narrative moves to bathos, since Fidelman's taking advantage of the situation is morally objectionable or even blasphemous. At the same time, the joke is finally on the *pittrice*, who has taken advantage of the painter's love for her. Through humor, Malamud seems to encourage the reader to become ultimately detached from art and to reflect on its nature, refusing to let it become a fetish either for the author or for the reader, while deeply convinced that "narrative tries to find the way from one condition into another more blessed" (R. Solotaroff 156).

This "blessed" condition is anchored in the spirituality of art, as Wassily Kandinsky claimed in his 1910 essay *Concerning the Spiritual in Art*. Both "Leaves" and "Still Life" demonstrate this fundamental premise in their exploration of art as a liberator from guilt. Forming a diptych on the act of creation, the two stories constitute their creators' metafictional statement that art makes sense, thus taking up the gauntlet of "one of the most unguardedly problematic phrases in the grammars of creation" and winning a battle for hope in a despairing twentieth century (Steiner 36). Indeed, despite the story's title, Malamud's "Still Life" takes the reader back to a stirring, bustling life.

NOTES

1. "Leaves" is included in Updike, *Forty* 341–43.
2. "Still Life" is included in Malamud, *Pictures* 282–98.
3. For an overview of these developments, see Hagman, "Art."

CHAPTER 15

Arthur Fidelman's Aesthetic Adventures and Malamud's Poetics of Creativity

THEODORA TSIMPOUKI

NATIONAL AND KAPODISTRIAN UNIVERSITY OF ATHENS, GREECE

Published in 1969, *Pictures of Fidelman: An Exhibition* is, in the words of Bernard Malamud, "a loose novel, a novel of episodes, like a picaresque piece" (Ducharme 129). It consists of six stories woven into a novel that trace the adventures of a would-be artist, Arthur Fidelman, who takes a long journey to Italy, in pursuit of artistic greatness. Though the first story, "The Last Mohican," had been published twelve years earlier in *The Magic Barrel* and the next two, "Still Life" and "Naked Nude," in 1963 in *Idiots First*, Malamud insisted that he conceived the idea of writing the novel soon after he wrote his first story on Fidelman. As he himself put it in an interview, "Right after I wrote 'The Last Mohican,' . . . I worked out an outline of the other Fidelman stories, the whole to develop one theme in the form of a picaresque novel" (Field and Field, "Interview" 14). In a later interview, he expanded on his earlier comment:

> After I wrote the story in Rome I jotted down ideas for several incidents in the form of a picaresque novel. I was out to loosen up—experiment a little—with narrative structure. And I wanted to see, if I wrote it at intervals—as I did from 1957 to

1968—whether the passing of time and mores would influence [Fidelman's] life. I did not think of the narrative as merely a series of related stories, because almost at once I had the structure of a novel in mind and each part had to fit that form. (Stern 65)

Philip Davis, Malamud's literary biographer, concurs that the author intended it to be "a looser work, written occasionally, to make a picaresque comedy freed of the pressures of a continuous life or single-minded career" (265). Nevertheless, critical reception of *Pictures of Fidelman* diverged widely, partly because the book was considered as lacking the coherence and unity of a novel and partly because Fidelman's depiction departed significantly from the familiar Malamudian hero and the moral serious-ness he is characteristically endowed with. Thus, while most critics note that *Pictures* was "not precisely a novel, but rather a series of vignettes built around a single character" (Helterman 12), they also agree that, in the end, it was robbed "of the moral breadth, the grand lugubriousness, that distinguishes Malamud's best stories" (Broyard 5).

Taking heed from Peter Brooks's *Reading for the Plot*, I argue in this essay that Malamud employs ekphrasis[1] and ekphrastic models[2] as a pri-mary literary device that creates and sustains narrative movement toward narrative completion. I claim that in *Pictures*, Malamud's insertion—in absentia—of the visual element in the verbal text is used as a way to advance plot and achieve complex metonymic interconnections, working toward a sense of an ending. Indeed, ekphrastic narration serves, to para-phrase Brooks, as that which helps the plot "move forward" and "makes us read forward, seeking in the unfolding of the narrative a line of intention and portent of design that hold the promise of progress toward mean-ing" (xiii). Fidelman's obsessive desire to produce great art, described in the text vividly and often elaborately through the ekphrastic rendition of his artwork, is, employing Brooks's terms, the dynamic element of the plot that "connect[s] narrative ends and beginnings, and make[s] of the textual middle a highly charged field of force" (xiv). *Pictures*, then, does what all narratives do: "both tell of desire—typically present some story of desire" and "arouse and make use of desire as dynamic of signification" (37). The ekphrastic representation of the protagonist's creative desire is, then, the "motor force" that drives the text forward through repetition, postponement, and error (Brooks evoking Barthes's "dilatory space")[3] until its final resolution and cues the reader that a (mock) epiphany waits Fidelman at his journey's end.

At the same time, on a metanarrative level, *Pictures* is about the struggle involved in the creative process and the urge to penetrate the mystery of artistic greatness in relation to the visual arts as well as literature. Malamud spoke frequently, if obliquely, of his pestilential need to expand his writerly forces while he speculated on the art-life nexus. As he confided in a letter to Rosemarie Beck, his painter friend and confidante, "I . . . want to know the secret of great [artistic] strength" (Salzberg, "Rhythms" 52). Added to this, his engagement with art and aesthetic practice in *Pictures* articulates his own ambivalence toward art's romantic premise on disinterestedness[4] and the view of the artist-as-hero as virtually incompatible with contemporary society. In the midst of the most turbulent decade in American history, the 1960s, Fidelman's abandonment of his native country, his embrace of a bohemian life, followed by his frantic attempts to create great art inspired by the European Old Masters is indicative of Malamud's skeptical doubts with regard to the role of the artist-as-hero and the value of the arts of our times. *Pictures* suggests the author's preoccupation with the use of artistic talent and whether "this marvelous bit of magic" (52), as he calls it, could be employed any longer as a mode of human engagement with the world. In a revealing letter to Beck, Malamud attempts to give his definition of a "good" artist:

> When I say I want to be good, it is partly because good is beautiful; only thus may I become my own work of art. Many of us do too little with the self, starving it for art; but I think the art would be richer if the self were. The more the self comprises, in the sense of containing as well as understanding; in the sense of being able to "respond" to others, to their need for food of various kinds, as well as beauty, the richer the self is for life, for freedom, for the flight imagination takes from it, for the art it creates. Life, humanity, is more important than art. (53)[5]

Nevertheless, the fact that Fidelman remains confined within the limits of his destructive obsession over artistic perfection reflects Malamud's own loss of confidence in the power of art to effect or stimulate moral renewal. Not surprisingly, in exploring the aesthetic and ethical reaches of his artist's life and work, Malamud models Fidelman after Balzac's artist-hero Frenhofer, the fictional painter in "The Unknown Masterpiece" who was claimed as an influence by some of the greatest artists of the twentieth century.[6] Fidelman, like his legendary predecessor, is haunted by the ideal of absolute art, but unlike him, Fidelman is obliged to accept his artistic failure and become a deft craftsman of glassblowing in the final tale of *Pictures*. Though the tone of *Pictures* may be "largely comic" (Abramson, *Bernard Malamud* 78), the book puts into serious question Malamud's personal aesthetic goals and, in particular, the possibility of contemporary art to carry out its ethical imperative, given our persistently romantic notion of art as autonomous and isolated from society. In this sense, the use of ekphrasis in *Pictures* both exhibits Fidelman's artistic attempts and reflects on the nature of these attempts, or their "self-knowledge," as W. T. J. Mitchell would have it.[7] The representation in language of authentic and fictional paintings creates an intermedial text that not only makes possible a metonymic movement toward a satisfactory narrative resolution but also, on a metatextual level, challenges the idea of the artist (and by analogy of the writer) as creative genius and the reconcilability between life and art. To the extent that the visual and the textual complement each other to this effect, *Pictures* requires reading the relation between two arts and invites a larger reading public that goes beyond Malamud's (Jewish) American readership to include a transnational and interdisciplinary audience.

One might begin by examining the title of Malamud's novel, *Pictures of Fidelman: An Exhibition*: the term "pictures" of the title alludes to the artworks that the struggling, passionate artist composes (or fails to compose), or it may refer to the multifaceted aspects of Fidelman's subjecthood. Thus, on the one hand, relying on the lure of the visual, a virtual gallery of real or imaginary artwork is provided within the space of the novel, while on the other hand, each story presents us with a different life sketch of Fidelman's identity. The book's subtitle enhances this dual impression, as it relates to the ways in which the tales both depict an imaginary tour of Fidelman's artistic compositions and "exhibit" the hero's adventures, framed—literally and figuratively—by the artistic process. The title's duality encourages the reader to "read" the book as both a collection of pictures and a collection of narratives.

Interestingly, Arthur Fidelman, a Jewish American from the Bronx, is already "a self-confessed failure as a painter" (*Pictures* 3) when we meet him in the first story, "The Last Mohican." He arrives in Rome hoping that his exposure to "all this history" (52) will inspire him to complete a critical study of Giotto. Malamud's choice of Giotto is by no means accidental, as he is credited with being the father of the Renaissance "for his devotion to physical and emotional accuracy in portraying humans" ("Giotto"). Giotto's unparalleled grasp of human emotion is precisely what Fidelman seems to lack as a person and as an art critic. Paradoxically, Fidelman's uncanny encounter with one of the Italian painter's major frescos does not help him access "humanity." Instead, he attempts to possess Giotto's creative power for himself, as it were.

Upon Fidelman's arrival in Rome, he meets Susskind, an impoverished European Jew who challenges Fidelman's hollow belief in the autonomous artist and the authenticity of art. It should be noted, however, that despite the prevalence of the aesthetic in this and the subsequent tales of this multileveled novel, most critics emphasize the Jewish qualities of "The Last Mohican." For them, the story focuses on issues of Jewish identity, with Fidelman being the assimilated American Jew whose Adamic "innocence" and lack of appreciation of his Jewish inheritance is castigated by Susskind, a parodic version of the archetypal Wandering Jew, who stands for "the vital values" of a living ethnic culture (Ahokas 62). No doubt, the peddler's pursuit of the aspiring art critic aims at reuniting him with his own self and with his past, from which he has always been estranged. As Edward Abramson argues, Fidelman is forced "to come to a realization of what Susskind symbolizes—his own Jewishness and a needy recipient for his compassion" (*Bernard Malamud* 80).

But in my reading of the story, the "triumphant insight" (*Pictures* 37) that Fidelman experiences in the end of the story is not so much related to his reconciliation with his ethnic past as it is with the transmission of affect through Giotto's fresco. Thus, Susskind's provocative attitude in the course of the narrative does not seem sufficient to shatter Fidelman's naïve belief that he might find creative self-realization in art. Neither Susskind's claim to the American's second suit, made three times in the story, nor his theft of Fidelman's manuscript and its eventual destruction[8] prove enough to awake the hero to the affective/communicative dimension of art. Not even the insight and wisdom that canonical Western texts presume to offer and that both characters frequently reference seem to have the capacity to deepen Fidelman's self-understanding and human compassion (i.e., Dante's *Divina Commedia*,[9] Chekhov's "The Cherry Orchard,"[10] Tolstoy's "What Is Art?"[11]).

Carefully woven into the texture of "The Last Mohican," the ekphrastic depiction of Giotto's fresco is that which unexpectedly alters Fidelman's vision, its intensive quality opening up onto an artistic world that he wants to conquer. "The student" (i.e., Fidelman vis-à-vis the Old Master) "lay upon the stone floor, his shoulders keeping strangely warm as he starred at the sunlit vault above. The fresco therein revealed this saint in fading blue, the sky flowing from his head, handing an old knight in a thin red robe his gold cloak. Nearby stood a humble horse and two stone hills" (*Pictures* 46).[12]

The sight of Giotto's "San Francesco dona le vesti al cavaliere povero" (*Pictures* 36) brings about in Fidelman an instantaneous transformation that seems to culminate his ambition to become a Giotto critic. The fresco's expressive and lively narrative encourages him to turn his hand to active painting. He is now ready to part with his extra suit as well as the stolen manuscript in order to pursue his new (old) passion of painting and a life of a bohemian, autonomous artist.

Unlike critics who see Fidelman's revelatory experience as resulting in his acknowledgment of "Susskind's dismal present" and "the suffering experienced by European Jewry" (Urdiales Shaw 161) and as demonstrating "moral growth" (Abramson, *Bernard Malamud* 81), I read the protagonist's sudden change as his aesthetic response to his visual encounter with the Giotto fresco. The expectation roused by the look at the pictorial scene provokes a displacement of Fidelman's desire: from this narrative point onward, he embarks on a doomed hunt for an always already unfulfilled plenitude, translated as his pursuit of artistic perfection. In this sense, the ekphrastic description of the fresco operates as the locus where desire, having reached a state of intensity, as Brooks would have it, must move on and the fabula must go forward. Thus, the narrative power of the visual is reinforced as it actively structures and motivates the development of the plot.

Fidelman's transformation from an art student to an active painter initiates a new phase in his life, marked by four episodes. Each one of these is accompanied with an ekphrastic manifestation of the protagonist's artistic adventure, as if it were a complete pictorial image presenting itself in its entirety to the glance of the beholder, while, brought together, all episodes form a phantasmagoric gallery of actual and imaginary pictures. Each chapter/episode bears an appellation that stands as a caption to an imaginative picture, what Gérard Genette would term *le paratexte* of the intermedial composition: the space beneath (in this case, above) the main text that constitutes an access to the main text and its meaning.[13] "Still Life," "Naked Nude," "A Pimp's Revenge," and "Pictures of the Artist" all accurately describe each chapter's content while at the same time self-reflexively alluding to the protagonist's painterly efforts.

In the first of these episodes, Malamud uses the convention of the still life to explore Fidelman's artistic peregrinations intertwined with his sexual adventures in an attempt to assert his individuality as a man and an artist. Although there is no direct correspondence between a single ekphrastic rendition of a still life picture and the chapter's title, "Still Life" presumably acts as an indirect artistic self-portrait. In this way, the pictorial term *still life* is used to describe the stillness of the protagonist and his nonprogress. From assembled commonplace objects to abstract forms to conspicuous imitations of old masterpieces to a blank canvas, all Fidelman's painterly attempts ekphrastically reenacted are important as they convey both the artist's struggle for self-expression and his anxiety that each new creation be also novel. At the same time, his solipsistic self-absorption entraps him in a vicious circle that isolates him from his environment.

As expected, the ekphrastic representations tend to be brief and fragmentary, reflecting Fidelman's half-wrought compositions. When his desire to paint coalesces with his lust for Annamaria, his landlady and fellow artist, he claims her as his muse and finds in her a model to depict or represent. As he admits, "He would paint her, whether she permitted or not, posed or not—she was his to paint, he could with eyes shut. Maybe something will come, after all, of my love for her" (*Pictures* 54). On a narrative level, painting the visual becomes a way of possessing it,[14] but on a metanarrative level, describing the visual is an attempt to accommodate it within the linear dimension of textuality in anticipation of narrative closure. Thus, Fidelman's sexual desire awakens him to creative activity, which is ekphrastically rendered in the verbal representation of "Virgin and Child." "Annamaria, saintly beautiful, held in her arms the infant, . . . her face responsive to its innocence" (*Pictures* 54). Interestingly, the ekphrastic rendition of the painting "Virgin and Child" does not allude to a single artwork but to a pictorial type, a visual topos common to the Old Masters, which underlines Fidelman's antagonistic relation with the painterly aesthetic tradition. Seeing the painting so affects Annamaria that she decides to comply with Fidelman's sexual demands. She says, "You have seen my soul" (55), a statement that by now should not come as a surprise, given the affective force of pictures and the transformative power of the act of looking ekphrastically. As James Elkins observes, "Ultimately, seeing alters the thing that is seen and transforms the seer. Seeing is metamorphosis, not mechanism" (11–12).

Fulfillment of Fidelman's desire at this narrative moment, however, would lead to an abrupt ending of the tale without any of the protagonist's self-interrogations having been resolved or his lust for Annamaria having been appeased. In order for the narrative to continue unfolding, desire must be deferred. It is unsatisfied desire that sets Fidelman "on fire" to paint again, this time a self-portrait. He attempts to portray himself in priest's vestments, "envisaging another Rembrandt: 'Portrait of the Artist as Priest'" (*Pictures* 66). As a consequence, Fidelman "worked with smoking intensity and in no time created an amazing likeness" (66). Allusion to the work of the Dutch precursor may be regarded as a contentious act of competition, a representation of the artist's struggle to clear a space for himself by overcoming the precursor.[15] Nevertheless, the painterly simulation brings about the desired result, which is Fidelman's sexual possession of Annamaria, and in this way, the story reaches its most spectacular denouement. Note that Annamaria is profoundly affected not by Fidelman's impersonation, who stands in front of her wearing "a cassock and fuzzy black soupbowl biretta" (66), but by the representation of his impersonation as priest in the manner of Rembrandt. Added to this, the brief and unembellished ekphrastic transfer of the visual source allows a "free play" of the imagination, to Annamaria's story-making imagination (Louvel).[16] Which is to say that, with a detailed description of the narrative implications of the painting missing from the actual narrative discourse, Annamaria's unexpected sexual surrender comes to reinforce/accentuate the painting's mysterious power as site of alluring enigma and tantalizing desire.

Regarding the significance of the finale of "Still Life," the opinions of critics differ. For instance, Robert Solotaroff contends that it is "the beginnings of the sexual opportunist" (93), and Robert Ducharme notes that "the moral curve of Fidelman's progress . . . is downward" (136). Edward Abramson remarks that Fidelman "is a prisoner to his lust for Annamaria" (*Bernard Malamud* 83), and Martin H. Friedenthal regards the scene as "more punishment than an act of joy for either one" (qtd. in Shimazu 12). Sandy Cohen points out that the Malamudian hero ought to abstain from using "either art, religion, or life as means to reach each of the others. None should be the means to an end. This fact is what Fidelman must learn" (97). In reality, "Still Life" does not provide any atonement or cleansing, punishment or reward. Fidelman is entrapped in his vision of the alienated romantic artist who is dedicated to art and art alone and remains emotionally detached and socially isolated. This lack of character development is reinforced by the title of the story: "Still Life" articulates a "still movement" or "suspended moment" in Fidelman's artistic itinerary, captured by ekphrasis.

The same holds true for the next episode, to the extent that in "Naked Nude" the only change that takes place is Fidelman's geographical move-ment. Having abandoned Rome for Milan, he becomes involved in a bizarre scheme of two Italian villains to steal Titian's *Venus of Urbino*. In order to do so, he is asked to copy the Titian painting so that they can replace it for the genuine one. Fidelman's initial refusal but final sur-render to this odd demand results in his successful copying of the mas-terpiece, with which he subsequently becomes so enamored that he ends up stealing "his counterfeit creation" (*Pictures* 91). Accordingly, the text speaks directly to the aesthetic tropes of artistic integrity, authenticity and innovation, convention and representation that have concerned the fictional painter.

To begin with, unlike the previous (and the next) tale, which evokes "pictorial *cliché[s]*" (Yacobi 629) like the Madonna with Child, "Naked Nude" references ekphrastically a unique piece of artwork, namely, the famous Renaissance painting *Venus of Urbino*. Malamud's recourse to the particular Titian, rather than to the existing tradition of the reclining female nude, first and foremost pays homage to the Old Master's artis-tic talent, which is later displayed in the sensual ekphrastic rendition of the original painting. Added to this, his appeal to the old masterpiece, which the fictional painter is asked to make an exact copy of, raises seri-ous questions pertaining to mimesis, representation, and originality in literature and art at large. Concerns of "artistic direction, progress and frustrations" haunted Malamud throughout his writing career (Salzberg, "Rhythms" 44), becoming even more urgent in the late 1950s and with the advent of postmodernism. The new view of art employed playful reproduction and appropriation of old forms and styles, challenging modernist beliefs in purity, seriousness, and individuality in a direct correlation between liberal-humanist principles and moral conduct. It is no wonder that Malamud, an inveterate storyteller that he was, would feel torn and tormented between these alternative aesthetic approaches. As a result, the number of fictional artists in his work who are unable to finish their art product (novel or painting) and suffer from blockage proliferates.[17]

Fidelman is no exception in his affliction with self-doubt over the quality of his work, sparked by anxiety concerning the difficulty of originality. He paints first directly on canvas and scrapes it clean seeing "what a garish mess he has made" (*Pictures* 80). It is a distortion of the original that he carries "perfect in his mind" (81). He makes several drawings on paper of nude figures from art books, in vain. He goes back to a study of Greek statuary to compute the mathematical proportions of the ideal nude; he experiments with "Dürer's intersecting circles and triangles, and studies Leonardo's schematic heads and bodies" (82). As all his efforts go to waste, the copyist asks himself, "What am I, bewitched, . . . and if so by whom? It's only a copy job so what's taking so long?" (82).

In a letter to the author, Beck explains the fictional painter's failed painterly attempts as follows: "Fidelman's block might reside in his knowledge of Titian's process, his wishing to be true to it. His problem, poor nut, is insoluble, given time and conditions" (Salzberg, "Rhythms" 49).[18] Putting aside the issues of artistic technique that the epistolary exchange raises, it also reveals both the writer's and the painter's yearning for originality with regard to traditional painterly canons. Even more eloquent is Beck's response to an earlier admonition of Malamud that she paint like a master: "You say to me 'I hope you want to paint like a master.' What you should say to me is I should paint like myself (and that believe me is no small matter) and I should tell you the same. . . . Once we have gotten rid of all the mannerisms of a time and a style, the fear of losing face in the world of fashion; . . . then maybe we can shake hands with the masters, or at least, understand their humanity" (52). Beck's reaction is so Malamudian in spirit that I would think Malamud deliberately posed a provocative question to receive the expected response. Beneath this friendly exchange of artistic opinions, however, we recognize what Harold Bloom would characterize as the expression of filial struggle for creative autonomy from previous artists.

While "Naked Nude" ekphrastically depicts Fidelman's heroic efforts to literally paint like Titian, the visual artist at the same time finds himself pressured to compete with the master and to paint "as though he were painting the original" (*Pictures* 88). Paradoxically, he takes it upon himself to bring into life an "original copy," to create "a fake masterpiece." Thus, as he paints, Fidelman "seems to remember every nude that has ever been done. . . . He is at the same time chocked by remembered lust for all the women he had ever desired" (88). Scrupulous examination of the original painting is followed by submitting it to his erotic gaze and recognition of his desire to possess the painted nude and the masterful art of painting it. And as Peter Brooks reminds us after Lacan, "Desire necessarily becomes textual by way of a specifically narrative impulse, since desire is metonymy, a forward drive in the signifying chain, an insistence of meaning toward the occulted objects of desire" (84). Fidelman's desire desperately seeks visual expression on the canvas, while simultaneously its verbal articulation in the text performs a creative act of seeing. "Fidelman feels himself falling in love with the one he is painting, every inch of her, including the ring on her pinky, bracelet on arm, the flowers she touches with her fingers, and the bright green earring that dangles from her eatable ear" (*Pictures* 88–89). As the old myth of Pygmalion is revived, the ekphrastic moment coincides with the painting's completion in the text. Fidelman, having reached the climax of his achievement, triumphantly exclaims, "The Venus of Urbino, c'est moi" (89). As in the previous stories, the narrative proceeds through the "metonymic unpacking" of the ekphrastic rendering that "prolongs and formalizes the middle, and also prepares the end" (P. Brooks 320).

As in "Still Life," here, too, there seems to be no significant change in the protagonist's character or attitude. Nevertheless, even though, according to Abramson, Fidelman achieves "a sense of artistic elevation" (*Bernard Malamud* 84) in producing his best piece of work so far, his worship of his handiwork is an act of embrace of his own imaginative, artistic powers of creation. Indeed, Fidelman falls in love with his own performance and artistry and thus becomes trapped "by the notion of art as a form of autoeroticism" (I. Alter 136). The reader is asked to judge Fidelman's questionable achievement, taking into account the artist's psychic retreat from society. The result of this double reading is on the one hand to acknowledge Fidelman's serious commitment to his art and on the other to become aware of the dangers ensuing from his refusal to accept art as anything less than the romantic concept of perfection uncontaminated by the real world.

Malamud's ambivalent sketching of Fidelman is nowhere more unequivocally articulated than in "A Pimp's Revenge," thematically more ambitious and visually more compelling than the side stories. Through an ironic prism, this fourth story of *Pictures* and third episode of Fidelman's painterly adventures brings forward both Malamud's fascination with and frustration at the fundamental presuppositions underlying the belief in the artist as genius and the romantic vision of art: its imminent self-creativity, the guilt of belatedness, the indisputable value of the "eternal masterpiece." Put in narrative terms, after many trials and tribulations, the Malamudian hero reaches the apogee of his art in creating his "most honest piece of work" (*Pictures* 142), while he conspicuously neglects and maltreats everyone around him. From this standpoint, Fidelman can be seen as the embodiment of romantic genius who apprehends the world in aesthetic not moral perspectives. "If I'm not an artist, then I'm nothing" (124), he claims. "Art is my means for understanding life and trying out certain assumptions I have. I make art, it makes me" (128). And again, "In my art I am," he boastfully professes (110). At the same time, he may also be regarded as a total moral failure since he uses his girlfriend, Esmeralda, not only as a model for his painting but also for conveniently supporting him with her prostitution earnings. In the meantime, the more Fidelman agonizes to complete his masterpiece, the more arrogant and less invested—even disinterested—with real life he becomes. Although Malamud critics have been almost unanimous in their condemnation of Fidelman's egotistic conduct, his "moral bankruptcy" (Abramson, *Bernard Malamud* 86) and exploitation of others (I. Alter 139), it seems to me that Malamud's response to his artist hero is a lot more complicated.[19] He is at once fascinated and repelled by Fidelman's passionate devotion to art and insatiable thirst for absolute perfection. By this I do not mean to suggest that Malamud is insensitive to Fidelman's lack of moral fiber. But rather than have Fidelman reach a moral consciousness, Malamud stretches his artistic passion to its limits. In an unexpected narrative shift, Fidelman's

conviction of having achieved "a first-class work," one that would supposedly secure him a place in the history of the art canon, is fittingly punished: Ludovico, Esmeralda's former pimp, initiates a wave of insecurity
in Fidelman, undermining his artistic achievement with his remarks and
thus leading him to irrevocably ruin the picture. In this regard, Fidelman does not differ much from his literary predecessor Frenhofer. Like
Balzac's romantic painter in "The Unknown Masterpiece," Fidelman's
supreme confidence over his "grand oeuvre" is shaken by Ludovico's criticism.[20] As in the case of his legendary predecessor, Fidelman's obsessive
ambition for aesthetic perfection leaves no room for the imagination. His
intense effort to add more verisimilitude to the female portraiture, "to
make her expression truer to life" (*Pictures* 146), results in ruining his own
painting and precipitates his aesthetic downfall.

Interestingly, the germ of the painting that Fidelman has been trying to get on canvas for five years is an old photograph of himself as a
boy with his mother. The clichéd distinction between photography as an
"exact copy" of the subject and painting as an "interpretation" of it appears
here, only to underscore the superiority of painting and by extension of
literature over photography, because the first one nourishes imagination,
whereas the other involves merely mimesis.[21] In Fidelman's trouble to
capture his mother's image on the canvas, "to release her from the arms
of death" (122), as he characteristically puts it, he sets himself an impossible task. He says, "I always go back to 'Mother and Son'" (123), and as he
redoes the female figure endlessly, he finds it changed from "Mother and
Son" to "Brother and Sister" and finally to his masterpiece, "Prostitute
and Procurer."

As a matter of fact, since Malamud's *Pictures* depends on the defer-
ence of Fidelman's desire to visually create, as it has been argued, ekphrastic variation in "A Pimp's Revenge" is achieved with the completion of the
pictorial referent—even if only temporarily. In this story, Fidelman succeeds in extricating himself from the entrapments of the "family romance"
with masters of the past and the existing tradition (Bloom, *Anxiety* 8).
After endless frustrations of despair and self-doubt, he finally achieves
what he perceives as artistic excellence: "But the picture was, one day,
done. It assumed a completion: This woman and man together, prostitute
and procurer. She was a girl with fear in both black eyes, a vulnerable if
stately neck, and a steely small mouth; he was a boy with tight insides, on

the verge of crying. The presence of each protected the other. A Holy Sacrament" (*Pictures* 143). Although the finished picture still evokes a model image that corresponds to a genuine, historical art object (the Mother with Child topos), it nevertheless remains a fictional occurrence of visual art that owes its existence to ekphrasis. Like previous cases, the ekphrastic rendition functions in two ways: it motivates the plot, moving it forward with its dramatic force; and given the controversies of the description, it stimulates the reader's imagination to capture the visuality of the literary painting in the process of making sense of the narrative. Textually, however, ekphrasis does not stop with the verbal representation of Fidelman's masterwork-in-progress. It spills over the boundaries of ekphrastic description of the masterwork to include literary depictions of still lifes (Fidelman crossing the market, examines "a basket of figs," "pumpkins on hooks," "a bleeding dead rabbit"; 102), portraits (Esmeralda's "black eyes like plum pits," "small mouth," and "Modigliani neck"; 105), and landscape paintings (the "sunlight on the terraced silver-trunked olive trees"; 106). In fact, ekphrasis itself—being both "as narrative as it is descriptive," to recall Mieke Bal—far from stopping the "flow of time" (342), "generates narrative because it animates its environment" (369–70) and acts as a source of narrativity.

If "A Pimp's Revenge" represents Malamud's most intense efforts to address the agonies of creative life and its profound abysses, what happens with Fidelman's desire to create when he himself becomes a "murderer" (*Pictures* 147) of his own artwork, as is the case in this tale? Apparently, Fidelman's passion to realize his artistic vision has not exhausted itself in this self-inflicted punishment. As we have seen in Brooks, each text is "an exploration of the conjunction of the narrative of desire and the desire of narrative" (48). Subsequently, flouting bourgeois respectability, Fidelman embarks once again on a bohemian quest to seek individual expression and innovation, animated by his desire, which is also "the very motive of narrative" (48).

Yet "Pictures of the Artist," the fourth and final episode of Fidelman's adventures as artist, differs from the three previous ones. For one, Fidelman abandons representational art, though not painting, and moves onto more improvisational and expressive artistic styles. As if reflecting Fidelman's turn to aesthetic formalism, the tale, too, is "composed montage fashion" (Greenfeld 60) and uses "a neo-Joycean, comitragic, surrealistic stream-of-consciousness, visionary sequence" (Grebstein 43). The story's disjointed style offers Malamud the opportunity to explore the accusation against contemporary art as being opaque, difficult, and above all, "too focused on personal symbols and gestures" (Siegel 138). Although, as Salzberg argues, Malamud more often than not professed his attraction to nonrepresentational and experimental art, there were times he became highly critical of what was regarded as "the wasteland of contemporary art" ("Rhythms" 50). In a 1965 letter to Beck, having probably Fidelman in mind, Malamud condemns contemporary art's "hyperbolic offences" (50). As he half jokingly says, "The op-art shows are hard to take, I take little pleasure from them above the simplest, and trickiest esthetic satisfaction. I can't even call it satisfaction: it is that my eyes follow the command. To prove it they hurt and I come to the edge of nausea. Can I predict the next step in painting: more epater le viewer—the picture itself opens in the center, a mallet comes out and strikes the observer on the head" (50).[22]

Malamud's cause of dissatisfaction—"to the edge of nausea," as he puts it—was the eccentricity and individuality of some artistic practices in contemporary art. Although in many ways Fidelman is for Malamud the archetypal artist in his obsessive adventuring into his interior vision, he is also derided for his preposterous artistic experiments. For example, in a manner reminiscent of Claes Oldenburg's proto-earthwork *The Hole* (1967) and other conceptualist practices, "the sculptor," as Fidelman is now called, digs perfect holes in the ground "singly or in pairs according to the necessity of the Art" (*Pictures* 153). Like the conceptualist artists, Malamud's artist refutes the equation of expensive materials with aesthetic value and instead uses earth, soil, or dirt, material that is "unprocessed and unreinforced, thus producing a temporary form" (Boettger 8), left to change and erode under natural conditions.[23] He also repeats their chief claim that the articulation of an artistic idea suffices as a work of art and that concerns such as traditional forms, skill, and marketability are irrelevant standards ("Conceptual"). The increased emphasis on abstract form and rejection of representation naturally affects ekphrasis, which is called on to conjure with words the concrete visible image of site-specific art. Fidelman says, "I create my figures as hollows in the earth" (*Pictures* 151). And elsewhere, he would "dig a perfect square hole without measurement. He arranged the sculptures singly or in pairs according to the necessity of the Art" (153).

Nevertheless, Fidelman's "need to create and not to be concerned with the commerce of Art" (154) not only suggests the emphasis placed on the process of making art rather than the final product but also disregards viewers' response to it. Malamud's concern with contemporary art's removal from everyday experience, its incapacity to establish meaningful connection with viewers, is suggested through the reactions that Fidelman's new artistic tendencies provoke in its audiences. These range from mere curiosity to "amazement and disbelief" (154) to disappointment and hostility. On one occasion, the intense debate between the sculptor and a visitor of the exhibition/site over form and content in art ends with the stranger pushing Fidelman into the hole he himself had dug and filling it with earth. "So now we got form but we also got content" (160), says the stranger in response to Fidelman's insistence that "emptiness is not nothing if it has form" (159).

Brooks contends that "the desire of the text (the desire of reading) is hence desire for the end "but desire for the end reached" not "too rapidly—by a kind of short-circuit"—but through "the at least minimally complicated detour, the intentional deviance, in tension which is the plot of narrative" (102, 104). Following Freud's *Beyond the Pleasure Principle*, as "a dynamic-energetic model of narrative plot," Brooks argues that just as in life there is the danger of an "improper death," an "improper end" lurks throughout narrative, as well (108). "The organism must live in order to die in the proper manner, to die the right death. One must have the arabesque of plot in order to reach the end" (107). As has been demonstrated, Fidelman's artistic desire articulated through ekphrastic means serves as the "energy generated by deviance, extravagance, excess" (108) that binds together the tales that make up *Pictures*. Although the possibility of the premature discharge of energy, of short-circuit, has been a threat throughout the narrative—given Fidelman's repeated failures to achieve great art, which might have led him to abandon prematurely all effort to create art—the distance between beginning and end is finally maintained, and the collapse of one into the other is prevented through the detours and repetitions at play.

In the final tale of *Pictures*, titled "Glass Blower of Venice," Fidelman, now called "the ex-painter" (177), has turned into a boatman ferrying passengers across the canals of Venice, apparently overwhelmed by his artistic inadequacy. Later, and under the guidance of Beppo, a master glassblower and husband of his mistress, he learns the craft of glassblowing. He also becomes the homosexual lover of Beppo, whose counsel "If you can't invent art, invent life" (199) he takes at face value and starts following. After drifting for some time in Venice and apparently in a gesture of compassion toward Margherita (his mistress and Beppo's wife), who asks him to leave, he sails to America, where "he worked as a craftsman in glass and loved men and women" (208).

Critical accounts of the "Glass Blower of Venice" have almost unanimously concluded that in this final tale of *Pictures*, Fidelman loses his self-centeredness in his love for Beppo. For Tony Tanner, the use of the term "assistant" to describe Fidelman's new status is itself indicative of the hero's moral development, because "we recognize the term as honorific in Malamud's moral universe" (339).[24] Abramson claims that Malamud, in giving this ending to the novel, must have settled into believing that "'perfection of the life' is more important than the work" (*Bernard Malamud* 89),[25] while Howard Harper goes as far as to interpret Fidelman's love for Beppo as "less an acceptance of homosexuality than an affirmation of unselfish love for all humanity" (215).

Critics who emphasize Fidelman's moral growth and, as a consequence, privilege a moral reading of *Pictures* may be right in discerning Malamud's intentions, but the novel's intermedial form breaks through those intentions. The visual in the novel, which is textually present in the form of ekphrasis and thematically prevalent in the fictional artist's creative endeavors, seems to enact Malamud's own ambivalence toward art's moral imperative and its (ir)reconcilability with life. Although Malamud returned to a painfully serious exploration of the artist's responsibility and the conflict between art and life in *The Tenants* (1971) and numerous short stories,[26] in *Pictures* he does so in a playful yet ironic manner through ekphrasis. By incorporating into his novel the amazingly bizarre and whimsically odd pictorial descriptions of Fidelman's artistic endeavors conjointly with original works of art, Malamud creates a verbal text that mirrors the disenchanted writer's self-doubt and "throbs with frustration and rage" at engaging in meaningful creativity (King 22). At the same time as the ekphrastic descriptions propel the fabula, they also embody metanarrative reflection on the current status of art and its engagement with the present moment. Even though Malamud does not subscribe to the notion of art as a narcissistic venture of the artist's self-exploration, his equivocal depiction of Fidelman, along with his interpellation of the fictional painter's flawed work, reveals his deep apprehension about art's failure of communication and lack of social relevance. In short, the visual saturation that characterizes *Pictures* provides the opportunity for narrative cohesion, while it opens to multiple, even conflicting readings that raise wider questions without regard to disciplinary and national borders.

NOTES

1. The commonly accepted understanding of ekphrasis as a verbal representation of visual representation is applied throughout the text.

2. I use the phrase "ekphrastic models" interchangeably with Tamar Yacobi's "pictorial models," which she defines as "the ekphrasis of a visual model (as opposed to an ekphrasis of a single work of art)" (627).

3. The creation of a "dilatory space" concerns "the questions and answers that structure a story, their suspense, partial unveiling, temporary blockage, eventual resolution" (P. Brooks 18).

4. I use the term not with its Kantian connotations but to emphasize art's detachment from all pursuits that have any correspondence to a utilitarian purpose. I regard the condemnation of the commercialization of art along with the autonomy and authenticity of the artist as part and parcel of the romantic dream.

5. The letter was written on April 10, 1959, immediately after Malamud had won the National Book Award for *The Magic Barrel*, in which, as already mentioned, "The Last Mohican" makes its first appearance. The approximately three hundred letters that make up the Malamud-Beck correspondence range from 1958 to 1985. All references to their correspondence come from Joel Salzberg's article "The Rhythms of Friendship."

6. No critic to my knowledge has commented on Malamud's debt to Balzac's plots and characters and, in particular, to the many similarities between *Pictures* and "The Unknown Masterpiece."

7. In *Picture Theory*, Mitchell uses the term *self-knowledge* as "a metaphor" to define what he calls "a metapicture," that is "any picture that is used to reflect on the nature of pictures." Pictures are "objects that seem not only to have a presence, but a 'life' of their own, talking and looking back at us," but by doing so, they also "call into question the self-understanding of the observer" (57).

8. The destroyed manuscript is a recurrent theme in Malamud's fiction. See *The Tenants*.

9. In the last cemetery scene, the refugee, who has already assumed a symbolic role, is called "Virgilio Susskind" (*Pictures* 36).

10. "Call me Trofimov, from Chekhov," says Fidelman proudly when he first introduces himself to Susskind (*Pictures* 8).

11. In the last dream scene, Susskind and Fidelman have the following exchange: "Have you read Tolstoy? / Sparingly. / Why is art?' asked the shade, drifting off" (*Pictures* 36).

12. Characteristically, this dreamlike experience takes place in a cemetery "all crowded with tombstones" (*Pictures* 35), a site that is literally an access point to the other world. As has been pointed out by Urdiales Shaw, Malamud very effectively moves the fresco to this cemetery from its original place, on the nave of the Upper Church of San Francesco in Assisi (160n11).

13. More specifically, according to Genette, the paratext of the work consists of *peritext*, which includes "the title or the preface and sometimes elements inserted into the interstices of the text, such as chapter titles or certain notes," and *epitext*, which comprises "all those messages that, at least originally, are located outside the book, generally with the help of the media (interviews, conversations) or under cover of private communications (letters, diaries, and others)" (*Paratexts* 5).

14. This constitutes a perfect example of Brooks's "erotic nature of the tension of writing" (103).

15. In "Rembrandt's Hat" (1973), a mediocre sculptor, Rubin, wants to become as great as Rembrandt. We have yet another example of Harold Bloom's idea of the "anxiety of influence."

16. Liliane Louvel calls "double fiction" this fiction that runs parallel to the text, adding "a critical fictional effect to the text being read" (46).

17. The struggles of Fidelman to copy the painting resemble Harry Levin's (*The Tenants*) travails to finish his unfinished novel.

18. Malamud enjoyed Beck's astrological speculations and was not averse to using them "as a recourse to invent the character of Arthur Fidelman." In a July 2, 1962, letter to Beck, he writes, "Can you get me Fidelman's horoscope[?] . . . He has been having a miserable painter's block—can't get the Venus right. What do you see in his Venus from June 16 to 30[?] When is a more propitious time for him? Why is he having trouble[?] . . . Give me the business" (Salzberg, "Rhythms" 49).

19. Robert Scholes observes, "Even the artist's name in this tale dwindles from Fidelman to F" (34).

20. Frenhofer in "The Unknown Masterpiece," after ten years of trying to complete his would-be-masterpiece, yields to his friends' demand to see the painting. When they tell him they see nothing but "confused masses of colour and a multitude of strange lines, forming a dead wall of paint," Frenhofer is devastated. The following morning he is found dead in his studio, with all of his canvases burnt (Balzac).

21. Indeed, Fidelman can begin to capture pictorially the density and profundity of the model only after Esmeralda destroys the old photograph and releases him from medium specificity.

22. The reference is to *épater la bourgeoisie*, which means "to shock the middle classes." The phrase became a rallying cry for the French Decadent poets of the late nineteenth century.

23. Although the term was first used in the mid-1970s, the starting point of earthworks, according to Suzaan Boettger, is the year 1967, with Claes Oldenburg's *Placid Civic Monument* (aka *The Hole*). As Boettger explains, the term *conceptual art* was applied to a variety of vanguard forms, and Oldenburg corroborates the use of conceptual art for his excavation. The critic goes on to describe the impact of this negative sculpture, which was dug (and then filled by professional diggers) under the artist's supervision in Central Park. "Oldenburg dug into the park soil to create a sculpture that consisted of a recession into the ground instead of a projection upward from it" (8).

24. The reference is to Malamud's second novel, *The Assistant* (1957), in which Frank, the assistant, learns to find grace and dignity through his contact with his employer.

25. Abramson here refers to the epigraph for *Pictures* which is from Yeats: "The intellect of man is forced to choose perfection of the life or of the work."

26. Short stories included in *The Magic Barrel* and *Rembrandt's Hat*, among others.

ANNOTATED WORKS CITED

PRIMARY SOURCES

Malamud's Works of Fiction in English

The Assistant. New York: Dell, 1957; repr., 1974.

The Complete Stories. New York: Farrar, Straus and Giroux, 1997.

Dubin's Lives. New York: Farrar, Straus and Giroux, 1979.

The Fixer. New York: Farrar, Straus and Giroux, 1966.

God's Grace. New York: Farrar, Straus and Giroux, 1982.

Idiots First. Farrar, Straus and Giroux, 1963. Repr., New York: Pocket Books, 1975.

The Magic Barrel. New York: Farrar, Straus and Giroux, 1958.

The Natural. New York: Farrar, Straus and Giroux, 1952.

A New Life. New York: Farrar, Straus and Giroux, 1961.

The People and Uncollected Stories. New York: Farrar, Straus and Giroux, 1989.

Pictures of Fidelman: An Exhibition. New York: Farrar, Straus and Giroux, 1969.

Rembrandt's Hat. New York: Farrar, Straus and Giroux, 1973.

The Stories of Bernard Malamud. New York: Farrar, Straus and Giroux, 1983.

The Tenants. New York: Farrar, Straus and Giroux, 1971.

Malamud's Works in Translation (French, German, Greek, and Spanish)

Bilder einer Ausstellung. Köln, Germany: Kiepenheuer & Witsch, 1975.

Cuentos. Barcelona: Plaza & Janés, 1987.

Cuentos reunidos. Barcelona: El Aleph, 2011.

Das Zauberfass und andere Geschichten. Köln, Germany: Kiepenheuer & Witsch, 1962.

Der Fixer. Reinbek, Germany: Rowolht, 1971; Berlin: Verlag Volk und Welt, 1989.

Der Gehilfe. Reinbek, Germany: Rowohlt, 1969.

Der Unbeugsame. Munich: DTV Deutscher Taschenbuch, 1984.

Die Leben des William Dubin. Köln, Germany: Kiepenheuer & Witsch, 1980.

Die Mieter. Berlin: Volk und Welt, 1979.

Ein neues Leben. Munich: DTV Deutscher Taschenbuch, 1988.

El barril mágico. Barcelona: Seix Barral, 1962.

El dependiente. Barcelona: Seix Barral, 1984.

El hombre de Kiev. Barcelona: Plaza y Janés, 1967.

El mejor. Barcelona: Plaza & Janés, 1984.

El reparador. Madrid: Sexto Piso, 2007.

El reparador. Barcelona: El Aleph, 2011.

El sombrero de Rembrandt. Barcelona: Destino, 1979.

Η τελευταία χάρη. Athens: Psychoyios, 1983.

Ενοικιοστάσιο. Athens: Viper, 1974.

Idiotas primero. Barcelona: Seix Barral, 1969.

La grâce de Dieu. Paris: Flammarion, 1983.

La gracia de Dios. Barcelona: Plaza y Janés, 1984.

Las vidas de Dubin. Barcelona: Plaza & Janés, 1981.

La vie multiple de William D. Paris: Flammarion, 1980; Paris: Le livre de poche, 1990.

Le commis. Paris: Gallimard, 1960; Genève: Éditions Métropolis, 2006.

Le meilleur. Paris: Rivages, 2015.

Le people élu. Paris: Rivages, 1992.

Les idiots d'abord. Paris: Éditions du Seuil, 1965.

Les locataires. Paris: Éditions du Seuil, 1976.

Le tonneau magique. Paris: Gallimard, 1967.

L'homme dans le tiroir. Paris: Flammarion, 1992.

L'homme de Kiev. Paris: Éditions du Seuil, 1967.

Los inquilinos. Barcelona: Destino, 1975.

Ο βοηθός. Thessaloniki, Greece: ASE A.E. 1979.

Pluie de printemps. Paris: Rivages, 1992.

Portraits de Fidelman. Paris: Éditions du Seuil, 1971.

Rembrandts Hut: Erzählungen. Berlin: Volk und Welt, 1980.

Retratos de Fidelman. Barcelona: Lumen, 1981; Buenos Aires: Raíces, 1988.

Schwarz ist meine Lieblingsfarbe: Kurzgeschichten. Köln, Germany: Kiepenheuer & Witsch Verlag, 1971; Berlin: Verlag Volk und Welt, 1977; Munich: DTV Deutscher Taschenbuch-Verlag, 1981.

Será crime ser judeu? Lisbon: Minerva, 1968.

Το μαγικό βαρέλι. Athens: Grammata, 1983; *Η Φυλακή*. Athens: Roes, 2008.

Una nueva vida. Barcelona: Lumen, 1966.

Une nouvelle vie. Paris: Gallimard, 1964.

Works of Fiction by Other Authors

Antin, Mary. *The Promised Land*. Boston: Houghton Mifflin, 1912.

Baldwin, James. *The Fire Next Time*. 1962. New York: Harcourt Brace, 2000.

Balzac, Honoré de. "The Unknown Masterpiece." 1845. Project Gutenberg ebook 23060. 2007. www.gutenberg.org/ebooks/23060 (accessed 4 February 2015).

Baraka, Imamu Amiri. *Transbluesency: The Selected Poetry of Amiri Baraka / Leroy Jones (1961–95)*. New York: Marsilio, 1995.

Cahan, Abraham. *The Rise of David Levinsky*. 1917. New York: Harper and Brothers, 1960.

Chaucer, Geoffrey. "The Prioress's Tale." *Canterbury Tales*. *The Blood Libel Legend: A Casebook in Anti-Semitic Folklore*. Ed. Alan Dundes. Madison: University of Wisconsin Press, 1991. 91–98.

Cooper, James Fenimore. *The Last of the Mohicans*. 2 vols. Philadelphia: H. C. Carey and I. Lea, 1826.

Dostoevsky, Fyodor. *The Double: A Petersburg Poem*. 1846. Trans. Constance Garnett. University Park: Pennsylvania State University, 2006.

Ellison, Ralph. *Invisible Man*. New York: Random House, 1952.

———. *Three Days before the Shooting*. Ed. John F. Callahan and Adam Bradley. New York: Modern Library, 2010.

Hoban, Russell. *Ridley Walker*. 1980. London: Picador, 1982.

James, P. D. *The Children of Men*. 1992. London: Faber and Faber, 2000.

Lawrence, D. H. *Sons and Lovers*. 1913. London: Penguin Books, 1995.

Lessing, Doris. *The Memoirs of a Survivor*. 1974. London: Flamingo, 1995.

McCarthy, Cormac. *The Road*. New York: Knopf, 2006.

Miller, Walter M., Jr. *A Canticle for Leibowitz*. 1960. New York: Bantam, 1997.

Shelley, Mary. *The Last Man*. 1826. Ware, UK: Wordsworth, 2004.

Updike, John. *Forty Stories*. London: Penguin Books, 1987.

———. *Hugging the Shore*. New York: Knopf, 1983.

———. *A Month of Sundays*. 1974. London: Penguin Books, 2007.

Vonnegut, Kurt. *Galápagos*. London: Flamingo, 1985.

Woolf, Virginia. "Kew Gardens." 1919. *The Penguin Book of English Short Stories*. Ed. Christopher Dolley. Harmondsworth, UK: Penguin, 1974. 201–7.

———. *To the Lighthouse*. London: Hogarth, 1927.

SECONDARY SOURCES

Malamud-Related Works

Aarons, Victoria. "'In Defense of the Human': Compassion and Redemption in Malamud's Short Fiction." *Studies in American Fiction* 20.1 (Spring 1992): 57–73. Taking as a point of departure Mendel's well-known "you bastard, don't you understand what it means human," this essay demonstrates that in Malamud's world, compassionate and merciful acts, which do not come from God but from human beings, help us achieve redemption.

———. "A Kind of Vigilance: Tropic Suspension in Bernard Malamud's Fiction." Avery 175–86. This chapter focuses on the term "chiasmus"—a group of words balanced by their reversed order and arranged spatially around an implied center—in order to explore the implications of this figure of speech in Malamud's fiction.

Abramson, Edward A. *Bernard Malamud Revisited*. New York: Twayne, 1993. This comprehensive book-length study follows the development of Malamud's themes and techniques through a chronological study of his novels and a thematic discussion of his short stories.

———. "Zen Buddhism and *The Assistant:* A Grocery as a Training Monastery." Avery 69–86. This chapter analyzes *The Assistant* in light of the impoverished grocery store that, according to the author, can be regarded as a training monastery in the tradition of the Soto Zen school of Buddhism.

Ahokas, Pirjo. "Through the Ghetto to Giotto: The Process of Inner Transformation in Malamud's 'Last Mohican.'" *American Studies in Scandinavia* 19 (1987): 57–69. By drawing on Freudian and Jungian psychology, this essay shows that from the protagonist's viewpoint, the long journey in Italy is, in the critic's phrase, "a protracted integrative individuation process."

Allen, John Alexander. "The Promised End: Bernard Malamud's *The Tenants*." Field and Field, *Malamud: A Collection* 104–16. Although the title of this essay points to Malamud's 1971 novel—and as such addresses the Jewish-black troubled relationship during the second half of the 1960s, the figure of the Malamudian antihero, and the like—it also analyzes the behavior of other schlemiel-like characters such as Morris Bober and Yakov Bok.

Alonso, Pilar. *Tres aspectos de la frontera interior*. Salamanca, Spain: Ediciones Universidad de Salamanca, 1987. One-third of the book is devoted to addressing the issue of suffering throughout Malamud's novels and short fiction. The other two-thirds explore the same theme in the fiction of two other key Jewish American novelists, Saul Bellow and Philip Roth.

Alter, Iska. *The Good Man's Dilemma: Social Criticism in the Fiction of Bernard Malamud*. New York: AMS Press, 1981. In order to analyze Bernard Malamud's novels and short stories, the author of this volume starts from the so-called social criticism and explores issues such as responsibility, compassion, and goodness in Malamud—referred to as the "humanistic spokesman."

Alter, Robert. "Jewishness as Metaphor." Field and Field, *Malamud and the Critics* 29–42. This essay provides an in-depth analysis of the figure of the *shlemiel-shlimazel* that plays a key role in novels such as *The Assistant* and *The Fixer*.

———. "A Theological Fantasy." Bloom, *Bernard* 187–91. This is a review of *God's Grace* in which the critic addresses the biblical elements in Malamud's apocalyptic novel.

Astro, Richard. "In the Heart of the Valley: Bernard Malamud's *A New Life*." Field and Field, *Malamud: A Collection* 143–55. Defining *A New Life* as a roman à clef, this essay provides the key autobiographical/historical background in order to better understand the novel, set in the fictional Cascadia (Corvallis, Oregon).

Avery, Evelyn, ed. *The Magic Worlds of Bernard Malamud*. Albany: State University of New York Press, 2001. This book is divided into three parts. The first part, "The Author," focuses on an analysis of the writer from a human(e) perspective; the second part, "Individual Works," addresses some Malamud novels and short stories; and the last part, "Thematic Threads," explores the writer's fiction from a thematic standpoint.

Beer, Brian. "Bernard Malamud's Religious Duality: Frank Alpine and Morris Bober." *Explicator* 70.2 (2012): 78–82. This essay establishes parallels between Jews and Christians in *The Assistant*. Just as Frank Alpine represents in the initials of his name and in his actions the person of Saint Francis of Assisi, Morris represents not only Martin Buber but also Jesus, the Jew who sought to bring the faithful into an I-Thou relationship with the deity.

Beilis, Jay, Jeremy S. Garber, and Mark S. Stein. "Pulitzer Plagiarism: The Malamud-Beilis Connection." *Cardozo Law Review de novo* 225 (2010). This essay demonstrates that in writing *The Fixer*, the novelist did not plagiarize from Mendel Beilis's memoir and, therefore, the novel was not an attempt to debase the memories of Beilis nor his wife.

Bellman, Samuel Irving. "Women, Children and Idiots First: The Transformation Psychology of Bernard Malamud." *Critique* 7 (Winter 1964–65): 123–38. This article addresses what the author calls "the great Malamud mystery," that is to say, the writer's literary success despite the sorrow, misery, and weirdness of the characters that populate his work. Bellman discusses much of Malamud's work and its place in the contemporary literary scene, focusing especially on his then-last collection of stories *Idiots First*. He concludes that the key to Malamud's acceptance by the public is "his reconstructionist view of society and man's position in it."

Bellow, Saul. "In Memory of Bernard Malamud." Bellow, *Letters* 435–36. This is a letter in which Saul Bellow answers Malamud's criticisms of his 1953 novel *The Adventures of Augie March*.

———. *Letters*. Ed. Benjamin Taylor. New York: Viking, 2010. This book collects Bellow's letters sent to fellow writers (William Faulkner, Ralph Ellison, and Philip Roth, among others), wives, lovers, and friends.

Benedict, Helen. "Bernard Malamud: Morals and Surprises." Malamud, *Conversations* 130–38. This interview appeared originally in *Antioch Review* (1983) after the publication of *God's Grace*.

Bloom, Harold, ed. *Bernard Malamud*. New York: Chelsea House, 1986. This book gathers a collection of essays arranged in the chronological order in which they were originally published. The essays range from *The Natural* to *God's Grace*, and some of them also address the writer's short stories.

———. Introduction. In Bloom, *Bernard* 1–4.

Briganti, Chiara. "Mirrors, Windows and Peeping Toms: Women as the Object of Voyeuristic Scrutiny in Bernard Malamud's *A New Life* and *Dubin's Lives*." Salzberg, *Critical* 174–86. This essay, which focuses on *A New Life* and *Dubin's Lives*, shows that the Malamudian protagonist's search for identity engages in a sentimental education. In the process of self-knowledge, women typically serve to precipitate the hero's crisis.

Brooks, Jeffrey R. "Stranger than Fiction: Historical 'Truth' in Malamud's The Fixer and Samuel's Blood Accusation." *CLIO* 31.2 (2002): 129–50.

Brown, Michael. "Metaphor for Holocaust and Holocaust as Metaphor: *The Assistant* and *The Fixer* of Bernard Malamud Reexamined." *Judaism* 29.4 (Fall 1980): 479–88. This essay analyzes the setting of the writer's 1957 novel, focusing on the idea that the place the Bobers inhabit is reminiscent of Holocaust Europe.

Broyard, Anatole. "Review of *Pictures of Fidelman*." *New York Times* 4 May 1969: 5. This review compares *The Assistant* and *Pictures of Fidelman* on the basis of the Italian-Jewish background of Frank Alpine and Arthur Fidelman, respectively.

Buchen, Irving L. "Malamud's *God's Grace*: Divine Genesis, Mortal Terminus." *Studies in American Jewish Literature* 10.1 (1991): 24–34. This essay analyzes the themes, motifs, symbolism, and so on of Malamud's most apocalyptic novel—the end of civilization—departing from the statement that the writer's 1982 novel caps his work with "a worrying and often angry resentment" of some of his concerns.

Cohen, Sandy. *Bernard Malamud and the Trial by Love*. Amsterdam: Rodopi, 1974. This book explores the theme of self-transcendence, in connection to a myth-based literary technique, as an ideal that drives the development of the protagonists of Malamud's novels. The author argues that Malamud's central characters, from Frank Alpine in *The Assistant* to Yakov Bok in *The Fixer* (and, arguably, Roy Hobbs in *The Natural*) "begin as egocentric, frustrated individuals with an insecurity-dominated need for success and status" and evolve toward self-transcendence through intense suffering and an "elaborate and ritualistic trial by love" (9).

Cronin, Gloria L. "The Complex Irony of Grace: A Study of Bernard Malamud's *God's Grace*." *Studies in American Jewish Literature* 5 (1986): 119–28. This essay demonstrates that Calvin Cohn can only win the knowledge of grace through ironic twists and reversals, fact and fantasy that take place in a setting where terror and humor are alternating all the time.

Dachslager, Earl L. "'Hateful to Crist and to His Compaignye': Theological Murder in 'The Prioress's Tale' and *The Fixer*." *Lamar Journal of the Humanities* 11.2 (1985): 43–50. This essay is partly devoted to exploring the implications of the figure of the Christ-like Yakov Bok in *The Fixer*.

Davis, Philip. *Bernard Malamud: A Writer's Life*. New York: Oxford University Press, 2007. This first full-scale account of Bernard Malamud's life and works sheds light on one of the finest twentieth-century Jewish American writers. This valuable biography includes exclusive interviews with Malamud's family, friends, and colleagues and reproduces extracts of his journals, letters, and manuscripts.

Ducharme, Robert. *Art and Idea in the Novels of Bernard Malamud: Toward "The Fixer."* The Hague, Netherlands: Mouton, 1974. This book-length study addresses Bernard Malamud's novels (from *The Natural* to *The Tenants*) from different perspectives, including his use of irony, father-son relationships, and suffering.

Epstein, Joseph. "Malamud in Decline." *Commentary* 74.4 (1982): 49–53. www.commentarymagazine.com/article/malamud-in-decline. Although this is a review about *God's Grace*, it also addresses the artist's previous works.

Field, Leslie A., and Joyce W. Field. "The Art of Fiction: Bernard Malamud." Malamud, *Conversations* 54–68.

———, eds. *Bernard Malamud: A Collection of Critical Essays*. Englewood Cliffs, NJ: Prentice Hall, 1975. Published five years after *Bernard Malamud and the Critics*, this collection of essays continues where the 1970 volume stops. Among other chapters, it is worth reading the well-known "Interview with Bernard Malamud," granted to the editors of the book.

———, eds. *Bernard Malamud and the Critics*. New York: NYU Press, 1970. This collection of essays not only approaches Malamud's fiction from a thematic viewpoint but also addresses specific novels (*The Assistant*, *A New Life*, and *The Fixer*) and short stories ("The Magic Barrel").

———. "An Interview with Bernard Malamud." Field and Field, *Malamud: A Collection* 8–17. This is one of the most well known and frequently cited interviews granted by the novelist; in it, he addresses characteristic Malamudian themes like the imprisonment motif and suffering.

———. "Introduction: Malamud, Mercy, and Menschlechkeit." Field and Field, *Malamud: A Collection* 1–7.

Fisch, Harold. "Biblical Archetypes in 'The Fixer.'" *Studies in American Jewish Literature* 7.2 (Fall 1988): 162–76. In order to explore the writer's use of myth and archetype as marks of virtuosity, this essay focuses on the analysis of *The Fixer*.

Fishman, Boris. "Seeking Bernard Malamud on His 100th Birthday: A Young Novelist Explores the Anxieties of Influence." *Jewish Daily Forward* 25 April

2014. forward.com/culture/196989/seeking-bernard-malamud-on-his-100th-birthday/. On the occasion of Malamud's one hundredth birthday, the author of this article—in charge of hosting the centennial celebration of the artist at the Center of Fiction in Midtown Manhattan, takes a very personal approach to the novelist's life and work.

Freedman, William. "From Bernard Malamud, with Discipline and with Love (*The Assistant* and *The Natural*)." Field and Field, *Malamud: A Collection* 156–65. This essay shows that the Malamudian character, who prepares mainly through education, endures and waits, and although he complains about the yoke of his endurance, he eventually demonstrates that his renunciation leads (him) to higher spirituality.

Freese, Peter. "Trouble in the House of Fiction: Bernard Malamud's *The Tenants*." *Self-Reflexivity in Literature*. Text & Theorie 6. Ed. Werner Huber, Martin Middeke, and Hubert Zapf. Würzburg, Germany: Verlag Köningshausen and Newmann, 2005. 99–112. This book chapter not only explores the troubled relations between Jews and blacks in New York as presented in *The Tenants* but also serves as a reflection about different types of literature and how they may affect the writing process.

Friedman, Alan Warren. "The Hero as Schnook." Bloom, *Bernard* 113–28. This essay focuses on Yakov Bok (*The Fixer*) as schnook—a gullible Jew who is distinguished only by misery and his sense of victimization. Bok inhabits a meaningless, arbitrary world, which, in spite of his own feebleness and irrelevance, he confronts and eventually triumphs because he endures.

Furman, Andrew. "Revisiting Literary Blacks and Jews." *Midwest Quarterly* 44 (2003): 131–47. This essay addresses *The Tenants*, and in order to analyze the troubled relations between Jews and blacks at that time, the author responds to Ozick's well-known essay "Literary Blacks and Jews."

Giroux, Robert. Introduction. Malamud, *Complete* ix–xv.

———. Introduction. Malamud, *People* vii–xvi. In this introduction, the author recalls his first encounters as editor with Bernard Malamud.

Grebstein, Sheldon Norman. "Bernard Malamud and the Jewish Movement." Field and Field, *Malamud: A Collection* 18–44. This essay takes as its point of departure suffering as a major and recurrent theme of the Jewish movement, focusing on the analysis of this dominant issue in Malamud's *The Natural*, *The Assistant*, and *The Fixer*.

Greenfeld, Josh. "The Six Lives of Fidelman." *New York* 12 May 1969: 58, 60. This review of *Pictures of Fidelman* shows why its author views Malamud as "the most Jewish of the significant American-Jewish writers."

Guttmann, Allen. "All Men Are Jews." Bloom, *Bernard* 151–58. This essay explores the theme of Jewishness in some of Malamud's works, like *The Natural*, *The Assistant*, and *The Fixer*, among others.

Hays, Peter L. "The Complex Pattern of Redemption." Field and Field, *Malamud and the Critics* 219–33. This essay explores *The Assistant* in terms of the complexity with which Malamud's realistically presented pattern is reinforced with myth and symbol. The last part of the article studies the novel's philosophy in light of Martin Buber's I-It, I-Thou relationship.

Helterman, Jeffrey. *Understanding Bernard Malamud*. Columbia: University of South Carolina Press, 1985. This volume, which is part of a series titled Understanding Contemporary American Literature, caters to university students and nonacademic readers interested in an analysis of the writer's use of language and symbolism, among other relevant themes.

Hershinow, J. Sheldon. *Bernard Malamud*. New York: Frederick Ungar, 1980. This monograph, which includes an analysis of Malamud's novels from *The Natural* to *Dubin's Lives*, examines *Pictures of Fidelman* as a novel. The book focuses on the novelist's style, humor, and moral vision, among other patterns.

Hoag, Gerald. "Malamud's Trial: *The Fixer* and the Critics." Field and Field, *Malamud: A Collection* 130–42. Almost five years after the publication of *The Fixer*, this essay is a reassessment of the reviews about this novel written until then.

Hornung, Alfred. "Zwischen Realismus und Anti-Realismus: Malamud—Roth—Hawkes." *Der zeitgenössische amerikanische Roman: Von der Moderne bis zur Postmoderne, Vol. 2: Tendenzen und Gruppierungen*. Ed. Gerhard Hoffman. Munich: Fink, 1988. 102–45. This comprehensive essay situates Malamud's fiction, together with that of Philip Roth and John Hawkes, between modernism and postmodernism and points out the diverging concepts of reality of these writers.

Ingliss, Ruth. "The Book-Makers." Malamud, *Conversations* 27–28. Originally published in *Nova* (1967), this interview appeared after the publication of *The Fixer*.

Kellman, Steven G. "*The Tenants* in the House of Fiction." *Studies in the Novel* 8 (Winter 1976): 428–67. This essay explores the turbulent mid- and late 1960s in light of the novelist's 1971 novel.

Kernan, Alvin B. "*The Tenants*: 'Battering the Object.'" In Bloom, *Bernard Malamud* 193–206. This essay analyses Malamud's novel as a confrontation of text and society and, as such, argues that *The Tenants* portrays the romantic beliefs about the reality of a literary text and the breakdown of these beliefs when confronted by social realities.

Kessner, Carole S. "Two Views of Jews: Bernard Malamud, Maurice Samuel and the Beilis Case." *Studies in American Jewish Literature* 29 (2010): 90–101. This is a comparative analysis of the Beilis trial (1913) from two points of view: Maurice Samuel's historical account and Malamud's fictional narrative.

Kremer, S. Lillian. "Reflections on Transmogrified Yiddish Archetypes in Fiction by Bernard Malamud." Avery 123–38. This essay presents Malamud as the most successful contemporary writer who incorporates into fiction stock figures from Yiddish literature and folklore, such as the *tzaddik* and the *schnorrer*.

Langer, Lawrence. "Malamud's Jews and the Holocaust Experience." Salzberg, *Critical* 115–25. This essay examines what its author calls "the gift of suffering" in characters like Morris Bober (*The Assistant*) and Yakov Bok (*The Fixer*) and proposes how an exposure to physical anguish or deprivation enriches the human being's inner self.

Leibowitz, Herbert. "Malamud and the Anthropomorphic Business." Bloom, *Bernard* 37–39. This essay looks at the behavior of a Malamudian character like Mendel in "Idiots First" as an idiot—that is, a fool, clown.

Lelchuk, Alan. "Malamud's Dark Fable." *New York Times* 29 August 1982. www.nytimes.com/1982/08/29/books/malamud-s-dark-fable.html. This review of *God's Grace* partly addresses the presence of biblical elements in the novel.

Malamud, Bernard. *Conversations with Bernard Malamud*. Ed. Lawrence Lasher. Jackson: University Press of Mississippi, 1991. This volume, which collects twenty-eight of Malamud's best interviews, includes the last one the writer granted before his death.

———. "Imaginative Writing and the Jewish Experience." Malamud, *Talking* 184–90. In this essay, the novelist addresses key themes in his writing such as Jewishness, suffering, and the like.

———. Introduction. In Malamud, *Stories* vii–xiii.

———. "Source of *The Fixer*." Malamud, *Talking* 88–89. This two-page piece written by the novelist gives the reader keys to the composition of *The Fixer*.

———. *Talking Horse: Bernard Malamud on Life and Work*. Ed. Alan Cheuse and Nicholas Delbanco. New York: Columbia University Press, 1996. This book includes a number of the novelist's previously unpublished interviews, essays, lectures, and notes.

Malamud Smith, Janna. *My Father Is a Book: A Memoir of Bernard Malamud*. New York: Houghton Mifflin, 2006. On the occasion of the anniversary of Malamud's death, the novelist's daughter analyzes his unpublished letters and journals as a tribute to him.

———. *Private Matters: In Defense of the Personal Life*. Reading, MA: Addison-Wesley, 1997. In this book, Bernard Malamud's daughter addresses the concept of private life or at least what can be considered private life.

Mandel, Siegfried. "Bernard Malamud's 'Alma Redeemed': A Bio-Fictional Meditation." *Studies in American Jewish Literature* 14 (1995): 39–45. This essay, which starts from the idea that Malamud's preoccupation with redemption has been present throughout his career, attempts to demonstrate Malamud's fascination with biography by the early 1980s. His short story "Alma Redeemed" provides a case study.

Marshall, John. "Author of *A New Life* Likes Coming Back." Malamud, *Conversations* 76–79. This interview, which originally appeared in the *Gazette Times* (1977), was granted on the occasion of the novelist's visit to Corvallis (i.e., Cascadia in *A New Life*) sixteen years after the publication of this novel.

Masilamoni, E. H. Leelavathi. "Bernard Malamud—An Interview." Malamud, *Conversations* 69–73. This interview originally appeared in the *Indian Journal of American Studies* (1976).

Mellard, James M. "Four Versions of Pastoral." Bloom, *Bernard* 101–12. This essay analyzes the pastoral mode—according to this critic, Malamud's greatest strength as a fiction writer—in *The Natural*, *The Assistant*, *A New Life*, and *The Fixer*.

Meras, Phyllis. "An Interview with Its Author [*The Fixer*]." Malamud, *Conversations* 16–18. This interview originally appeared in the *Providence Sunday Journal* (1966) just after the publication of *The Fixer*.

Mesher, David. "Gorilla in the Myth: Malamud's *God's Grace*." Avery 111–19. The first part of the title points to the presence of a kaddish-reciting gorilla at the end of Malamud's 1982 novel. The author of the article uses this image to underscore his attempt to argue for an optimistic reading of the book.

Müller, Kurt. "Biblische Typologie im zeitgenössischen jüdisch-amerikanischen Roman: E. L. Doctorow's *The Book of Daniel* und Bernard Malamud's *God's Grace*." *Paradeigmata: Literarische Typologie des Alten Testaments. Zweiter Teil: 20. Jahrhundert*. Ed. Franz H. Link. Berlin: Duncker and Humblot, 1989. 831–51. This book chapter explores biblical archetypes in Jewish American fiction, focusing on Doctorow's *The Book of Daniel* and Malamud's *God's Grace*.

Nisly, L. Lamar. "'What about God?': Evidence of Bernard Malamud's Beliefs," *Studies in American Jewish Literature* 21 (2002): 39–45. Drawing on the writer's interviews, essays, letters, and the like, the author of this essay sheds light on a number of key Malamudian themes such as his approach to Jewishness, suffering, and so on.

Ochshorn, Kathleen. *The Heart's Essential Landscape: Bernard Malamud's Hero*. New York: Peter Lang, 1990. This book-length study, which focuses on the Malamudian protagonist's character, places an emphasis on his flawed nature. The volume addresses major themes such as basic dignity and humanity of the writer's characters.

Ozick, Cynthia. "Judging the World: Library of America's Bernard Malamud Collections." *New York Times Sunday Book Review* 13 March 2014. www.nytimes.com/2014/03/16/books/review/

library-of-americas-bernard-malamud-collections.html. The author of this
article gives some keys to the novelist's creative powers and craftsmanship.

———. "Literary Blacks and Jews." Field and Field, *Malamud: A Collection*
80–98. Reprinted in Cynthia Ozick, *Art & Ardor*. New York: Knopf, 1983.
90–112. This essay analyzes *The Tenants* in light of Irving Howe's well-known
"Black Boys and Native Sons," which triggered a debate with Ralph Ellison
about an issue similar to that addressed in Malamud's novel.

———. "Remembrances: Bernard Malamud." Avery 25–27. A telephone conversation held with Malamud in 1976 elicits the author's remembrances.

Pinsker, Sanford. "Bernard Malamud's Ironic Heroes." Field and Field, *Malamud: A Collection* 45–71. This essay examines the significance of the figure of
the *schlemiel* in *The Magic Barrel*, *The Assistant*, *A New Life*, and *The Fixer*.

Pringle, Mary B. "(Auto)biography: Bernard Malamud's *Dubin's Lives*." *International Fiction Review* 9.2 (Summer 1982): 138–41. This review of the novelist's 1979 novel *Dubin's Lives* establishes parallels between the lives of two
writers, William Dubin and Bernard Malamud.

Rajagopalachari, M. *Theme of Compassion in the Novels of Bernard Malamud*.
New Delhi, India: Prestige Books, 1988. This monograph, which offers an
overview of Malamud's novels and short stories, revolves around the theme
of compassion, a core issue in the novelist's fiction.

Richman, Sidney. *Bernard Malamud*. New York: Twayne, 1966. This seminal
study of Malamud's early novels and short stories places an emphasis on the
writer's craftsmanship.

Rohner, Thomas L. "Enigmatic Humor in the Novels of Bernard Malamud."
Ph.D. dissertation, Zurich, 1985. This dissertation addresses the use of irony
in the novelist's novels.

Salzberg, Joel, ed. *Critical Essays on Bernard Malamud*. Boston: G. K. Hall, 1987.
This book is a compilation of reviews, book chapters, and essays about different themes connected with the artist's fiction.

———. "The Rhythms of Friendship in the Life of Art: The Correspondence
of Bernard Malamud and Rosemarie Beck." Avery 43–58. This chapter,
which provides extracts of Malamud's correspondence with Rosemarie Beck,
aims to show how seriously the novelist took friendship.

Sánchez Canales, Gustavo. "Bernard Malamud's Russian Background in *The
Fixer*." *Mundo Eslavo* 5 (2006): 55–62. This essay establishes a comparison
between the historical context of the Beilis case and the fictional world as
presented in the writer's 1966 novel.

Scholes, Robert. "Portrait of the Artist as 'Escape-Goat.'" *Saturday Review*
10 May 1969: 32–34. www.unz.org/Pub/SaturdayRev-1969may10-00032. In
this review of Malamud's collection of six short pieces, *Pictures of Fidelman*,
Scholes argues for the way in which Malamud comically paints the Six

Stations of the Cross. In this way, Fidelman attempts to navigate his way through this shifting landscape.

Shear, Walter. "Culture Conflict." Field and Field, *Malamud and the Critics* 207–18. This essay looks at *The Assistant* as a novel of culture—i.e., it examines the ambiguities in the relationship between individuals and their values.

Shenker, Israel. "For Malamud, It's Story." *New York Times* 3 October 1971. www.nytimes.com/books/97/09/28/reviews/malamud-talk.html. This is an interview the novelist granted to the *New York Times* after the publication of *The Tenants*.

Sheres, Ita. "The Alienated Sufferer: Malamud's Novels from the Perspective of Old Testament and Jewish Mystical Thought." *Studies in American Jewish Literature* 4.1 (Spring 1978): 68–76. This essay explores the significance of the story of Abraham's sacrifice (*akedah*) as the first and main key to the understanding of Malamud's fiction.

Shimazu, Atsuhisa. "Numbers in 'Still Life.'" *Kobe International Communication Center Journal* 7 (2010): 7–14. Kobe University Repository. www.lib.kobe-u. ac.jp/handle_kernel/81002798 (accessed 17 March 2015). This essay examines the relationship between Annamaria and Fidelman in "Still Life" through the use of the numbers 2 and 3.

Sío Castiñeira, Begoña. *The Short Stories of Bernard Malamud: In Search of Jewish Post-immigrant Identity*. New York: Peter Lang, 1998. In this book-length study of Malamud's short fiction, the author attempts to capture an instance of identity by denouncing the isolation caused by extreme Jewish orthodoxy and by brutal assimilation.

Solotaroff, Robert. *Bernard Malamud: A Study of the Short Fiction*. Boston: Twayne, 1989. This volume, which focuses on Malamud's short stories, addresses Malamud's most significant short fiction, including biographical data and style. This book-length study includes a chronology of the writer's life and works and a small but representative selection of critical responses until the late 1980s.

Solotaroff, Theodore. "Bernard Malamud: The Old Life and the New." *Red Hot Vacuum and Other Pieces on the Writing of the Sixties*. Ed. Theodore Solotaroff. New York: Atheneum, 1970. 71–86. This book chapter addresses the fiction of Malamud and is included in a collection of essays that explore some key figures in American letters, such as Saul Bellow, Irving Howe, Isaac Rosenfeld, and James Purdy.

———. "An Evening with Bernard Malamud." *New England Review* 24.2 (2003): 27–31. The author of this article recalls the writer's visit to Oregon State upon receiving the National Book Award for his 1958 collection *The Magic Barrel*.

Stern, Daniel. "The Art of Fiction: Bernard Malamud." Malamud, *Conversations* 54–68. Originally published in *Paris Review* 61 (Spring 1975): 40–64, www.theparisreview.org/interviews/3869/the-art-of-fiction-no-52-bernard-malamud. This is an interview that Malamud granted to the literary critic in his Bennington (Vermont) house on the occasion of the novelist's sixtieth birthday.

Stevenson, David L. "The Strange Destiny of S. Levin." *New York Times Book Review* 8 October 1961: 1–2. This is a review of *A New Life*.

Tritt, Michal. "Mendel Beilis's *The Story of My Sufferings* and Malamud's *The Fixer*: A Study of Indebtedness and Innovation," *Modern Jewish Studies* 13.4 (2004): 58–78. This essay establishes parallels between the life of Yakov Bok, the protagonist of *The Fixer*, and Mendel Beilis, the man whose life inspired Malamud to write the novel.

Urdiales Shaw, Martín. *Ethnic Identities in Bernard Malamud's Fiction*. Oviedo, Spain: Universidad de Oviedo, Servicio de Publicaciones, 2000. The author of this volume refers to the term "ethnic identities" to approach Malamud's fiction from the point of view of race, nationality, cultural conditioning, attitude to heritage, and other related relevant issues. The chapter "Historical Source: The Beilis Case" is a comparative analysis of the historical and fictional elements in the writer's 1966 novel *The Fixer*.

Walden, Daniel. "Bernard Malamud and His Universal Menschen." Avery 167–73. This essay examines the concept of the *mensch*—the idea that the Malamudian character can create a new life for himself through moral obligation with others—in *The Natural*, *The Assistant*, and *The Fixer*.

Watts, Eileen H. "Not True Although Truth: The Holocaust's Legacy in Three Malamud Stories: 'The German Refugee,' 'Man in the Drawer,' and 'The Lady of the Lake.'" Avery 139–52. One of the major points made by the author of this chapter is that, in contrast to the grotesqueness of the Holocaust experience, Malamud underscores the significance of the individual's intrinsic value and dignity.

Wegelin, Christof. "The American Schlemiel Abroad: Malamud's Italian Stories and the End of American Innocence." *Twentieth Century Literature* 19.2 (April 1973): 77–88. This essay addresses the behavior of Malamud's schlemiel-like characters in Italian contexts, such as Fidelman's in Rome, and the implications of their European tour.

Wershba, Joseph. "Not Horror but Sadness." Malamud, *Conversations* 3–7. Originally published in the *New York Post* (1958), this interview appeared one year after the publication of *The Assistant*.

Wolford, Donald L. "Calvin Cohn: Confidence Man Interpreting Bernard Malamud's 'God's Grace' as a Parody of Herman Melville's 'The Confidence-Man.'" Master's thesis, Youngstown University, 2009. This study, which addresses *God's Grace* from a parodic perspective, establishes parallels between Calvin Cohn and Melville's *The Confidence Man*.

Zucker, David J. "Malamud as Modern Midrash." *Judaism* 43.2 (Spring 1994): 159–72. This essay focuses on the idea that Malamud's fiction serves as a figurative parallel to the rabbis' use of the midrash.

Other Works

Aarons, Victoria. "'The Tune of the Language': An Interview with Grace Paley." *The Changing Mosaic: From Cahan to Malamud, Roth and Ozick*. Ed. Daniel Walden. *Studies in American Jewish Literature* 12 (Albany: State University of New York Press, 1993), 50–61. In this interview, Paley speaks to the influence of her early life and the lives of her immigrant parents on the narrative voices in her short fiction.

Abellán, Manuel. *Censura y creación literaria en España: 1939–1976*. Barcelona: Península, 1980. This book addresses the theme of censorship in Spain during Francisco Franco's dictatorship (1939–75). Among other issues, the author explores how books and films underwent censorship in the course of those years.

Anders, Günther. *Die Antiquiertheit des Menschen, Vol. I: Über die Seele im Zeitalter der zweiten industriellen Revolution*. Munich: Beck, 1994. This volume addresses the idea that a gap has developed between humanity's technologically enhanced capacity to create and destroy. The author reflects on the human being's ability to imagine that destruction.

Anzieu, Didier. *Le corps de l'oeuvre: Essais psychanalytiques sur le travail créateur*. Paris: Gallimard, 1981. This volume starts from the idea that not only is a given work of art deeply influenced by a creative piece of work, but its originality and the power it exerts over us is greatly due to its shape and style. The body of the work of art (not just the text itself) is the work of art itself.

Arlow, Jacob A. "Aggression and Prejudice: Some Psychoanalytic Observations on the Blood Libel Accusation against the Jews." *The Spectrum of Psychoanalysis: Essays in Honor of Martin S. Bergmann*. Ed. Arlene Kramer Richards and Arnold D. Richards. Madison, CT: International Universities Press, 1994. 283–94. This essay examines the reasons that may account for the appeal of anti-Semitism to some people, a psychological predisposition associated with unconscious fantasies and reactions to primitive, irrational, and childhood wishes, among others.

Atwood, Margaret. *Moving Targets: Writing with Intent, 1982–2004*. Toronto: House of Anansi, 2004. This book collects Margaret Atwood's nonfiction covering the years indicated in the second part of the title. Among other writings, it is composed of autobiographical essays, book reviews, and introductory pieces.

Bal, Mieke. "Over-writing as Un-writing: Descriptions, World-Making, and Novelistic Time." *Narrative Theory: Critical Concepts in Literary and Cultural Studies*. Ed. Mieke Bal. London and New York: Routledge, 2004. 341–88. This chapter, included in a volume that offers a brief history of the applicability of narrative theory, develops a view of narrative as generated by what the author calls "a descriptive motor."

Baldeshwiler, Eileen. "The Lyric Story: The Sketch of a History." *Studies in Short Fiction* 6 (1969): 443–53. By making a distinction between two narrative modes—the lyrical and the epical—the author of this essay gives a general overview of the history of the lyrical short story in which she addresses major writers who have made a significant contribution to it.

Barnstone, Willis. *The Poetics of Translation: History, Theory, Practice*. New Haven, CT: Yale University Press, 1993. This book gives an overview of the history and theory of literary translation as an art form and argues that literary translation, which goes beyond the transfer of linguistic information, has imaginative originality not only in the translation but also in the source text.

Belluscio, Steven J. *To Be Suddenly White: Literary Realism and Racial Passing*. Columbia: University of Missouri Press, 2006. This is an in-depth study about the relationship between literary passing and literary realism, the dominant aesthetic motivation behind the late-nineteenth- and early-twentieth-century ethnic texts.

Blanchot, Maurice. *The Gaze of Orpheus and Other Literary Essays*. Ed. P. Adams Sitney. Trans. Lydia Davis. New York: Station Hill, 1981. The editor of this book has carefully collected a number of excerpts from Blanchot's most influential works.

Bloom, Harold. *The Anxiety of Influence: A Theory of Poetry*. New York: Oxford University Press, 1973. This well-known book is a first attempt made by its author to advance a new "revisionary" ("antithetical") approach to literary criticism.

Boelhower, William. *Through a Glass Darkly: Ethnic Semiosis in American Literature*. New York: Oxford University Press, 1987. The author of this volume, in questioning current ideas about the American literary canon, applies semiotics to the study of American ethnicity.

Boettger, Suzaan. *Earthworks: Art and the Landscape of the Sixties*. Berkeley: University of California Press, 2003. This is a comprehensive history of the Earthworks movement in the United States, providing an in-depth analysis of the forms that initiated the broader genre of Land Art.

Bohrer, Heinz Karl. *Suddenness: On the Moment of Aesthetic Appearance*. New York: Columbia University Press, 1994. This book, which takes as its point of departure the term *suddenness* as an expression of discontinuity and rupture, resists aesthetic integration. The essays included in this volume explore a romantic (and modernist) literary phenomenon and trace its textual appearance in the works of early German Romantics such as Schlegel, Schleiermacher, and Kleist through Nietzsche.

Brooks, Peter. *Reading for the Plot: Design and Intention in Narrative*. Cambridge, MA: Harvard University Press, 1992. This volume addresses the idea that plot reflects the patterns of human destiny, and as such, it aims to impose a new meaning on life.

Buber, Martin. *I and Thou*. Trans. Walter Kaufmann. 1970. New York: Touchstone, 1996. Originally published in German as *Ich und Du*. Köln: Verlag Jakob Hegner, 1962. This book focuses on the premise that the human being's life is meaningful in relationships. Humans' relationships are defined by two word pairs: I-It and I-Thou.

Buchen, Irving H. "The Aesthetics of the Supra-Novel." *The Theory of the Novel: New Essays*. Ed. John Halperin. New York: Oxford University Press, 1974. 91–108. This chapter sets forth the structural, stylistic, formalistic, and epistemological aspects of the theory of the novel.

Buhle, Paul, and Robin D. G. Kelley. "Allies of a Different Sort: Jews and Blacks in the American Left." *Struggles in the Promised Land: Towards a History of Black-Jewish Relations in the United States*. Ed. Jack Salzman and Cornel West. New York: Oxford University Press, 1997. 197–230. This book chapter examines new ways to think about the American Left and those Jewish and African American radicals who played a key role in it.

"Conceptual Art Movement." The Art Story. www.theartstory.org/movement-conceptual-art.htm (accessed 21 May 2015). This article offers a synopsis and some key ideas about "conceptual art."

De Bellis, Jack. *The John Updike Encyclopedia*. Westport, CT: Greenwood, 2000. This encyclopedia includes a chronology that summarizes the major events in Updike's career, as well as an introductory chapter that examines his progress as a writer and entries summarizing Updike's books, all his major characters, allusions, images, and symbols, and it includes the most significant scholarship on the novelist.

Delbo, Charlotte. *Auschwitz and After*. Trans. Rosette C. Lamont. New Haven, CT: Yale University Press, 1995. Narrated in first person, this trilogy gives an account of Delbo's life and survival in Birkenau, the concentration camp.

Derrida, Jacques. *Specters of Marx*. New York: Routledge, 1994. Originally published in French one year before the English version appeared, this book collects a series of lectures during "Whither Marxism?," a conference on the future of Marxism that Derrida gave at the University of California in 1993.

Des Pres, Terrence. "Excremental Assault." *Holocaust: Religious and Philosophical Implications*. Ed. John K. Roth and Michael Berenbaum. New York: Paragon House, 1989. 203–20. This book chapter is an in-depth study of problems like dysentery and diarrhea that afflicted prisoners in concentration camps.

Detweiler, Robert. *John Updike*. 1972. Rev. ed. New York: Twayne, 1984. Starting from the term "secular baroque," this is a seminal book-length study of the novelist that focuses on Updike's use of mythic patterns in his novels published until the late '60s and early '70s.

Duchamp, Marcel. "The Creative Act." *The Writings of Marcel Duchamp*. Ed. Michel Sanouillet and Elmer Peterson. New York: Da Capo, 1989. 138–40. This collection of essays brings together two essential interviews and two statements about Duchamp's art that underscore the serious side of the writer. In "The Creative Act," Duchamp explains what he understands by this concept.

Dundes, Alan. "The Ritual Murder or Blood Libel Legend: A Study of Anti-Semitic Victimization through Projective Inversion." *The Blood Libel Legend: A Casebook in Anti-Semitic Folklore*. Ed. Alan Dundes. Madison: University of Wisconsin Press, 1991. 336–38. This essay examines the theme of "blood libel" or "false accusation" and attempts to demonstrate the power of folklore to influence thought and history.

Eakin, Paul J. *Fictions in Autobiography: Studies in the Art of Self-Invention*. Princeton, NJ: Princeton University Press, 1985. This book argues that autobiographical truth is not a fixed but an evolving content in a process of self-creation through an analysis of the writing of Mary McCarthy, Henry James, Jean-Paul Sartre, Saul Friedlander, and Maxine Hong Kingston.

Elkins, James. *The Object Stares Back: On the Nature of Seeing*. New York: Simon and Schuster, 1996. The author refers to drawings, paintings, diagrams, and photographs to order to raise new questions about the nature of vision.

Ellison, Ralph. *The Collected Essays of Ralph Ellison*. Ed. John F. Callahan. New York: Random House, 1995. This book includes posthumously discovered reviews, interviews, and criticism. There are also a number of essays that address the theme of race and explore literature and folklore, jazz and culture.

———. *Trading Twelves: The Selected Letters of Ralph Ellison and Albert Murray*. Ed. John Callahan. New York: Modern Library, 2001. This volume includes a collection of letters that span a decade in the friendship of two writers who discuss literature, race, and identity.

Encyclopedia Britannica Online. s.v. "aptronym." www.britannica.com/EBchecked/topic/30911/aptronym (accessed 30 May 2014). Definition of the term "aptronym," first coined by the American journalist Franklin P. Adams.

Fauconnier, Gilles, and Mark Turner. "Rethinking Metaphor." *Cambridge Handbook of Metaphor and Thought*. Ed. Ray Gibbs. Cambridge: Cambridge University Press, 2008. 53–66. ssrn.com/abstract=1275662. This book chapter explores the metaphor of time as space.

———. *The Way We Think*. New York: Basic Books, 2002. This book focuses on the creative aspects of the mind, arguing that all learning and thinking consist of blends of metaphors based on simple bodily experiences.

Fiedler, Leslie A. *Fiedler on the Roof: Essays on Literature and Jewish Identity*. Boston: David R. Godine, 1991. Although the author of this book addresses the theme of Jewish identity, he extends his analysis to the works of writers such as James Joyce, I. B. Singer, William Styron, and Bernard Malamud, among others.

Freese, Peter. *The Clown of Armageddon: The Novels of Kurt Vonnegut*. Heidelberg, Germany: Winter, 2009. This volume gives an account of the novelist's development from a neglected "hack" writer to an international celebrity and analyzes his fourteen novels, explaining how each one is related to the others by recurring characters and settings as well as by the themes and motifs that haunt Vonnegut's fictional cosmos.

———. *From Apocalypse to Entropy and Beyond: The Second Law of Thermodynamics in Post-war American Fiction*. Essen, Germany: Die Blaue Eule, 1997. The author ponders the idea that in contemporary fiction, scientific theory has replaced metaphysical speculation.

Freud, Sigmund. "Delusions and Dreams in Jensen's *Gradiva*." *The Standard Edition of the Complete Psychological Works of Sigmund Freud*. Ed. James Strachey. Stanford, CA: Stanford University Press, 1997. 3–86. Freud analyzes from a psychoanalytic perspective the behavior of a young archaeologist called Norbert Hanold—Jensen's protagonist—who realizes his love for a childhood friend through a complex process.

Friedman, Saul S. *A History of the Middle East*. Jefferson, NC: McFarland, 2006. This history covers the Middle East from its ancient beginnings to the present. The confluence of events that produced civilized society is discussed in detail, along with the establishment of Judaism, Christianity, and Islam.

Genette, Gérard. *Palimpsestes: La littérature au second degré*. Paris: Éditions de Seuil, 1982. Translated as *Paratexts: Thresholds of Interpretation*. Cambridge: Cambridge University Press, 1997. The term *palimpseste* (paratext), coined in this book for the first time, has been used since then to study the relationships between two or more texts and defines their hypertextual relationships.

Gibbs, Robert. "Suspicions of Suffering." *Christianity in Jewish Terms*. Ed. Tikva Frymer-Kensky, David Novak, Peter Ochs, David Fox Sandmel, and Michael A. Signer. Boulder, CO: Westview, 2000. 221–29. This book chapter, included in a collection of essays that explore a specific aspect of Christian thought from a Jewish standpoint, focuses on the issue of suffering.

"Giotto di Bondone." Artble. www.artble.com/artists/giotto_di_bondone (accessed 21 May 2015). This webpage analyzes the figure of the Italian painter Giotto, focusing on his life, works, style, and influences, as well as the reception of his work.

Gitelman, Zvi. *A Century of Ambivalence: The Jews of Russia and the Soviet Union, 1881 to the Present*. Bloomington: Indiana University Press, 2001. This volume traces the historical experience of Jews in Russia in the second half of the nineteenth century through the paradoxes posed by the post-Soviet era.

Goffman, Ethan. "The Golden Age of Jewish American Literature." *Proquest Discovery Guides* (March 2010). didattica.uniroma2.it/files/scarica/insegnamento/38823-Letteratura-Anglo-americana-1-Lm/6186-Saggio-The-Golden-Age-of-Jewish-American-Literature-Mod.-B. This essay examines the legacy of some Jewish American writers such as Bernard Malamud, Philip Roth, and Cynthia Ozick who exemplify the tension between tradition and assimilation in a context of increasing acceptance and material comfort. The trajectory of Jewish American literature in the second half of the twentieth century is explored.

Gombrich, Ernst H. *Art and Illusion: A Study in the Psychology of Pictorial Representation*. Oxford, UK: Phaidon, 1959. This volume examines the history and psychology of pictorial representation in the light of present-day theories of visual perception information and learning. The author revisits many ideas concerning the imitation of nature and the function of tradition.

Goodman-Thau, Eveline. "Shoah and Tekuma—Jewish Memory and Morality between History and Redemption." *Studia Universitatis Babes-Bolyai, Studia Europaea* 4 (2009): 5–30. This essay focuses on three key issues: (1) the Jewish contribution to the Western tradition in the age of secularization; (2) the clash of different cultures; (3) and the search for a united Europe.

Gottlieb, Dovid. "Providence and Suffering." Torah.org. www.torah.org/features/spirfocus/suffering.html (accessed 25 May 2015). This article—which opens with the question "Why do the innocent suffer?"—gives an account of the possible reasons for the existence of suffering.

Gubern, Román. *La censura: Función política y ordenamiento jurídico bajo el franquismo (1936–1975)*. Barcelona: Península, 1981. This book is an in-depth study of the theme of censorship during Francisco Franco's dictatorship (1939–75). For example, it explores the origin, motives, and consequences of censorship in Spain throughout those years.

Guttmann, Allen. *The Jewish Writer in America: Assimilation and the Crisis of Identity*. New York: Oxford University Press, 1971. This is a brief literary history of Jewish American fiction that partly focuses on assimilation and identity.

Hagman, George. *Aesthetic Experience: Beauty, Creativity and the Search for the Ideal*. New York: Rodopi, 2005. This book addresses psychoanalytic ideas about art and beauty through the lens of current developmental psychology. The author of this volume revisits theorists such as Freud, Ehrenzweig, Kris, Rank, Winnicott, and Kohut, among others.

———. "Art and Self: A New Psychoanalytic Perspective on Creativity and Aesthetic Experience." *Self and Systems.* Ed. William J. Coburn and Nancy P. VanDerHeide. Hoboken, NJ: Wiley, 2009. 164–73. In this essay, the author, who provides a contemporary self-psychological perspective on aesthetic exprcience, art, and creativity, argues that aesthetics is as important to human life as are sex, hunger, aggression, love, and hate.

Handy, William J. *Modern Fiction: A Formalist Approach.* Carbondale: Southern Illinois University Press, 1971. This book examines the terms and methods used by the New Critics in their approach to poetry. The works analyzed in this volume include James Joyce's "The Dead," Theodore Dreiser's *Sister Carrie*, William Faulkner's *As I Lay Dying*, Ernest Hemingway's *The Old Man and the Sea*, Bernard Malamud's *The Fixer*, and Saul Bellow's *Seize the Day.*

Harper, Howard M. "Trends in Recent American Fiction." *Contemporary Literature* 12.2 (Spring 1971): 204–29. www.jstor.org/stable/1207737?seq=1#page_scan_tab_contents. This essay analyzes the factors that help explain why the literary and cultural climate at the end of the 1960s and early 1970s was very different from that of the previous decades.

Harris, Jonathan Gil. "Four Exoskeletons and No Funeral." *New Literary History* 42 (2011): 615–39. This essay examines the term *exoskeleton* as a metaphor through which to understand the untimely duration of the past within the present and in a manner different from Harold Bloom's "apophrades" and Jacques Derrida's "hauntology."

Harshav, Benjamin. *The Meaning of Yiddish.* Stanford, CA: Stanford University Press, 1990. This is an in-depth study of the major aspects of Yiddish language and culture.

Hassan, Ihab. *Contemporary American Literature: 1945–1972.* New York: Frederick Ungar, 1973. This is a brief study of American literature, ranging from the mid-1940s to the early 1970s. Among others, there are sections devoted to Jewish American writers like Bernard Malamud, Saul Bellow, and Philip Roth.

Hersey, John. "A Completion of Personality: A Talk with Ralph Ellison." *Conversations with Ralph Ellison.* Ed. Graham Maryemma Graham and Amritjit Singh. Jackson: University Press of Mississippi, 1995. 272–301. Originally published in *A Collection of Critical Essays*, edited by John Hersey, this is an interview with the novelist.

Hess, Richard S. "Getting Personal: What Names in the Bible Teach Us." *Bible Review* 6 (December 1997): 31–37. This article looks at the role biblical names such as Abram/Abraham and Sarai/Sarah played in the ancient world.

Hobbs, Allyson. *A Chosen Exile: A History of Racial Passing in American Life.* Cambridge, MA: Harvard University Press, 2014. This book explores the challenges and possibilities that racial indeterminacy presents to men and women living in a country obsessed with racial distinctions.

Horstmann, Ulrich. *Abschreckungskunst: Zur Ehrenrettung der apokalyptischen Phantasie.* Munich: Fink, 2012. The author of this volume, who asks why the Third World War has not started (yet), reflects upon the role that apocalyptic fantasy plays in contemporary literature.

———. "Post-nuclear Dystopia: Russell Hoban, *Riddley Walker* (1980)." *Dystopia, Science Fiction, Post-apocalypse: Classics, New Tendencies, Model Interpretations.* Ed. Eckarts Voigts and Alessandra Boller. Trier, Germany: WVT, 2015. 303–16. This is a model interpretation of a major postnuclear novel, presented by a professor of English who is also one of the most radical apocalyptic thinkers, suggesting that postapocalyptic fictions may have contributed to the actual nonoccurrence of the nuclear apocalypse during the Cold War.

Jacobs, Joseph. "Little St. Hugh of Lincoln," *The Blood Libel Legend: A Casebook in Anti-Semitic Folklore.* Ed. Alan Dundes. Madison: University of Wisconsin Press, 1991. 41–71. This is an in-depth study about an English boy (1246–1255) whose death prompted a blood libel during the second half of the thirteenth century.

Jaspers, Karl. *Die Atombombe und die Zukunft des Menschen: Politisches Bewußtsein in unserer Zeit.* Gütersloh, Germany: Bertelsmann, 1988. This is a CD that includes a 55-minute speech given in 1956 by Karl Jaspers. The speech is about the effects of the A-bomb in the future.

Kandinsky, Wassily. *Concerning the Spiritual in Art.* 1914. Toronto, ON: Dover, 1977. This is an in-depth study that explores the most genuine reasons for creating art. One of Kandinsky's key ideas is that there is an "internal necessity" that leads artists to create as if they were impelled by a spiritual force. That same "internal necessity" makes their audiences admire art as a spiritual hunger.

Kawash, Samira. *Dislocating the Color Line: Identity, Hybridity and Singularity in African-American Narrative.* Stanford, CA: Stanford University Press, 1997. This book, which explores the meaning of racial identity, shifts the focus of analysis from understanding differences to analyzing division.

Kempf, Wolfgang. "The Work of Art and its Beholder: The Methodology of the Aesthetic of Reception." *The Subjects of Art History: Historical Objects in Contemporary Perspective.* Ed. Mark A. Cheetham, Michael Holly Ann, and Keith Moxey. Cambridge: Cambridge University Press, 1998. 180–94. This book chapter analyzes the beholder's relationship with the object—that is, the work of art—according to what the author calls "conditions of its appearance."

Kernan, Alvin B. *The Imaginary Library: An Essay on Literature and Society.* Princeton, NJ: Princeton University Press, 1982. This volume explores the inability of contemporary writers to maintain a literary vision in a society that denies their values and methods.

Kierkegaard, Søren. *Fear and Trembling.* 1843. Ed. C. Stephen Evans and Sylvia Walsh. Cambridge: Cambridge University Press, 2006. In this well-known book, the Danish thinker reflects on the biblical story of God's command to Abraham from a philosophical standpoint. Kierkegaard also elaborates on the idea that Abraham's determination to sacrifice his son, Isaac, was a test of faith.

Kifner, John. "Echoes of a New York Waterloo," *New York Times* 22 December 1996. This article discusses Albert Shanker, a former local union chief and later a national educational leader who played a significant role in Brooklyn's Ocean Hill–Brownsville district.

King, Francis. "Perfectionist." *Spectator* 15 January 1983: 22. archive.spectator.co.uk/issue/15th-january-1983. The author of this article about *Pictures of Fidelman* establishes parallels between Arthur Fidelman and Bernard Malamud.

Kirsch, Sharon J. *Gertrude Stein and the Reinvention of Rhetoric.* Birmingham: University of Alabama Press, 2014. By departing from the idea that rhetoric and literature still have a vexed relationship, the author of this book moves forward in an attempt to broaden the reader's understanding of Gertrude Stein's influence and impact on the field of rhetoric.

Klein, Marcus. *After Alienation: American Novels in Mid Century.* New York: World, 1964. This volume, which starts from the concept of "alienation" in order to move onto that of "accommodation," looks at the novels of Saul Bellow, Ralph Ellison, James Baldwin, Wright Morris, and Bernard Malamud as epitomes of the mood of comic social accommodation, which the author sees as central in post-1950 American literature.

Koestler, Arthur. *The Act of Creation.* London: Hutchinson, 1964. This is a study of the processes of discovery, invention, imagination, and creativity in humor, science, and the arts in an attempt to develop an elaborate general theory of human creativity.

Krah, Markus. "Role Models or Foils for American Jews? *The Eternal Light,* Displaced Persons, and the Construction of Jewishness in Mid-Twentieth Century America." *American Jewish History* 96.4 (December 2010): 265–67. This essay shows that *The Eternal Light*'s answer to the question of meaningful Jewishness, and by extension to the larger question of Jewish integration and distinctiveness in America, is closely connected with the reality of the post-Holocaust Jewish world.

Kreiger, Barbara. "The Jewish Literary Hero: Political Transformation in America," *Response* 17 (Spring 1973): 131–38. In this article, the author analyzes the figure of the *schlemiel*—the typical Jewish (anti)hero. One of her arguments revolves around the idea of the *schlemiel's* reliance on the redemptive nature of faith as a key way to come to terms with him- or herself.

Kremer, S. Lillian. *Witness through the Imagination: Jewish-American Holocaust Literature*. Detroit: Wayne State University Press, 1989. This volume offers a critical reading of themes and stylistic strategies of major American Holocaust fiction.

LaCapra, Dominick. "Reflections on Trauma, Absence and Loss." *Whose Freud? The Place of Psychoanalysis in Contemporary Culture*. Ed. Peter Brooks and Alex Woloch. New Haven, CT: Yale University Press, 2000. 178–204. The author, who establishes a distinction between the concepts of "absence" and "loss," offers a general overview of contemporary trauma theory.

Lakoff, George. "Contemporary Theory of Metaphor." *Metaphor and Thought*. Ed. Andrew Ortony. Cambridge: Cambridge University Press, 1993. 202–51. This essay is an in-depth analysis of the metaphor, focusing on the connection between conceptual metaphor and linguistic metaphor.

Lakoff, George, and Mark Johnson. *Metaphors We Live By*. Chicago: University of Chicago Press, 1980. This groundbreaking study of metaphor shows this trope to be a key mechanism of the mind that allows individuals to use what they know about their physical and social experience to provide understanding of other individuals.

Lakoff, George, and Mark Turner. *More Than Cool Reason: A Field Guide to Poetic Metaphor*. Chicago: University of Chicago Press, 1989. This volume addresses the idea that poetic metaphor is not very different from everyday language or thought processes.

Langmuir, Gavin J. "Thomas of Monmouth: Detector of Ritual Murder." *The Blood Libel Legend: A Casebook in Anti-Semitic Folklore*. Ed. Alan Dundes. Madison: University of Wisconsin Press, 1991. 3–40. This is a detailed analysis of the Benedictine monk Thomas of Monmouth, who published a controversial book titled *The Life and Miracles of St. William of Norwich*, commonly believed to be the origin of the blood libel against Jews.

Lee, Vernon. *The Handling of Words and Other Studies in Literary Psychology*. London: John Lane, The Bodley Head, 1923. This groundbreaking work, which was a first attempt to design the method of close empirical analysis of texts, anticipates some of the developments in contemporary criticism such as the role of the reader as cocreator.

Lejeune, Philippe. *On Autobiography: Theory and History of Literature*. Minneapolis: University of Minnesota Press, 1989. The author of this book, addressing what he calls the "autobiographical contract," attempts to examine literary texts as a "thing-in-itself."

Leontiev, A. Dmitri. "What's Hecuba to Us? Basic Propositions for a Psychological Theory of Art." *Emotions and Art: Problems, Approaches, Explorations*. Ed. Leonid Ya. Dorfman. Perm, Russia: Perm Institute for Arts and Culture, 1992, 45–65. This essay offers an analysis of art as a counterweight to a theoretical-normative approach.

Lethem, Jonathan. "The Ecstasy of Influence." *The Best American Essays*. Ed. Adam Gopnik. New York: Houghton Mifflin, 2008. 105–33. This volume is a collection of essays—memoir, fiction, and criticism, among others—that cover everything from major novels to old films, including graffiti and cyberculture. The chapter is inspired by Harold Bloom's concept of "the anxiety of influence."

Levin, Edmund. "The Last Blood Libel Trial." *Slate* October 2013. www.slate.com/articles/news_and_politics/history/2013/10/mendel_beilis_and_blood_libel_the_1913_trial_in_kiev_russia.html. This article examines the well-known "Beilis Case" on which *The Fixer* is loosely based.

"Ley 14/1966, de 18 de marzo, de Prensa e Imprenta." *Boletín Oficial del Estado* 67 (19 March 1966): 3310–15. This makes reference to an Act passed in 1966—10 years before the end of Franco's dictatorship—about freedom of the press and censorship.

"Ley 44/1967, de 28 de junio, regulando el ejercicio del derecho civil a la libertad en materia religiosa." *Boletín Oficial del Estado* 156 (1 July 1967): 9191–94. This act, which was passed in 1967, almost a decade before the end of Franco's dictatorship, makes reference to freedom of worship.

Louvel, Liliane. "Photography as Critical Idiom." *Poetics Today* 29.1 (Spring 2008): 31–48. By focusing on the photography-text relationship, this essay examines how photography has renewed fiction and continues to do so through its specific properties.

Luscher, Robert M. *John Updike: A Study of the Short Fiction*. New York: Twayne, 1993. This book-length study on Updike focuses solely on the writer's short fiction and explores each of Updike's story collections separately and in approximate chronological order.

Maack, Annegret. "'Aus dem Chaos eine neue Form der Stärke': Doris Lessing's *Memoirs of a Survivor*." *Apokalypse: Weltuntergangsszenarien in der Literatur des 20. Jahrhunderts: Materialien*. Ed. Gunter E. Grimm, Werner Faulstich, and Peter Kuon. Frankfurt/M.: Suhrkamp, 1986. 168–86. This book chapter sketches the theme of catastrophe and the search for possibilities of survival in a number of works by Doris Lessing, a writer who is equally concerned with the physical survival of humankind as with the psychological survival of the individual.

Mann, Barbara E. "Visions of Jewish Modernism." *Modernism/Modernity* 13.4 (November 2006): 673–99. Taking as point of departure the tension between text and image in modernism, this essay shows that Jewish writers and artists had a special relation to this tension, given the history of European Jewish culture and its prohibition on visual representation.

Marcus, Mordecai. "The Unsuccessful Malamud," *Prairie Schooner* 41 (1967): 88–89. This short book review considers *The Fixer* an ambitious but flawed novel. It claims that while the novel contains familiar characters, themes, and techniques, they are not handled well. The ineffectual character of Yakov Bok is seen as emerging from a failure of sensibility on the part of Malamud rather than a quality that the character himself possesses. The themes are recalcitrant, and the technique is inept. All of this contributes to the failure of the novel.

Meyers, Carol L. *Discovering Eve: Ancient Israelite Women in Context.* New York: Oxford University Press, 1988. This book depicts Israelite women not as submissive chattel in an oppressive patriarchy but rather as strong actors within their families and the society of their time.

———. *Households and Holiness: The Religious Culture of Israelite Women.* Minneapolis, MN: Fortress, 2005. This volume provides an overview of the role women played in ancient Israelite religion and shows the diversity of religious practices in ancient Israel.

Mitchell, W. J. T. *Picture Theory: Essays on Verbal and Visual Representation.* Chicago: University of Chicago Press, 1994. This volume looks at the interplay between the visible and the readable across culture, from literature to visual art and to the mass media.

Montefiore, C. G., and H. M. J. Loewe, eds. *A Rabbinic Anthology.* New York: Cambridge University Press, 1938. The two authors/editors of this anthology have selected and arranged with comments the entire manuscript, and all the texts are translated.

Moss, Kenneth. *Jewish Renaissance in the Russian.* Cambridge, MA: Harvard University Press, 2009. This is a comprehensive study of the period ranging from 1917 to 1921, a five-year time span crucial in Jewish and Russian history. Numerous would-be cultural revolutionaries such as El Lissitzky and Haim Nahman Bialik are examined in relation to their implication for a new Jewish culture.

Myrdal, Gunnar. *An American Dilemma: The Negro Problem and Modern Democracy.* 1944. Repr., 2 vols. Piscataway, NJ: Transaction, 2009. In order to explore the contradictions of American democracy, the author of this book examines the moral contradiction of a country that moves between allegiance to its highest ideals and awareness of the realities of racial discrimination.

Ofrat, Gideon. "Why Is There No Jewish Surrealism?" *Shofar* 32.3 (2014): 102–19. This seminal essay addresses the reasons for the lack of true surrealism in Palestinian-Israeli art and literature, while all the other major trends of twentieth-century literature and art have found echoes in Palestinian-Israeli culture.

Paine, Stanley. *The Franco Regime (1936–1975)*. Madison: University of Wisconsin Press, 1987. This volume offers deep insight into the career of Francisco Franco, a complex figure, and the enormous changes that shaped Spanish history during his regime.

Parker, Hershel. "The Determinacy of the Creative Process and the 'Authority' of the Author's Textual Decisions." *College Literature* 10.2 (Spring 1983): 99–125. This essay examines not only the way authority is infused into a literary text but also how this process comes to an end. The author refers to Herman Melville as an archetypal example to illustrate his point.

Pfeiffer, Kathleen. *Race Passing and American Individualism: A Literary Study of the Ambiguities of Racial Identity in American Culture*. Amherst: University of Massachusetts Press, 2010. This volume explores the implications of the dilemma that black characters experienced in the late nineteenth century and early twentieth century when they passed for white, through an analysis of the fiction of Jessie Fauset, Frances E. W. Harper, William Dean Howells, Nella Larsen, Jean Toomer, and James Weldon Johnson.

Podair, Jerald E. *The Strike That Changed New York: Blacks, Whites, and the Ocean Hill–Brownsville Crisis*. New Haven, CT: Yale University Press, 2002. This volume is an in-depth study of the Ocean Hill–Brownsville crisis—a watershed in modern New York City race relations.

Rampersad, Arnold. *Ralph Ellison: A Biography*. New York: Knopf, 2007. This volume is an in-depth study of the life of a writer who is well known for his important work *Invisible Man* but, as the author of this biography shows, a writer who also produced influential essays on race, literature, and culture.

Reisner, Rosalind. *Jewish American Literature: A Guide to Reading Interests*. Westport, CT: Libraries Unlimited, 2004. This volume covers a wide range of genres and literary works in Jewish American letters. Among others, there are chapters devoted to Holocaust literature and to biography/autobiography.

Rose, Gilbert J. *The Power of Form: A Psychoanalytic Approach to Aesthetic Form*. New York: International Universities Press, 1980. Although it seems that Freud never psychoanalyzed a living artist or wrote outside the context of analysis, the author of this volume has explored aesthetics from a Freudian perspective.

Rosenfeld, Alvin H. "Inventing the Jew: Notes on Autobiography." *The American Autobiography*. Ed. Alfred E. Stone. Englewood Cliffs, NJ: Prentice Hall, 1981. 133–56. This book provides a wide selection of texts that deal with personal narratives from different perspectives, as is the case with Rosenfeld's article. Rosenfeld explores the theme of autobiographical invention in modern Jewish autobiography.

———. "The Progress of the American Jewish Novel." *Contemporary Jewish Review* 7 (1973): 115–30. Rosenfeld argues that themes of legitimate concern to Jewish writers—especially immigrant writers—have largely lapsed since the early literature in America as a response to assimilation and to the changing focus on other minority cultures.

Roth, Philip. "Pictures of Malamud." *New York Times* 20 April 1986. In this sketch, Roth recalls how he met his fellow writer in Corvallis (Oregon) in February 1961.

———. "Writing American Fiction." *Reading Myself and Others*. 1975. New York: Viking Penguin, 1985. 173–91. In this essay, the novelist analyzes the prose of Jewish American writers such as Saul Bellow, Bernard Malamud, and Grace Paley, among others.

Rothenberg, Albert. "Inspiration, Insight and the Creative Process in Poetry." *College English* 32 (November 1970): 172–76, 181–83. This essay offers preliminary findings from the author's research, including interviews with both prominent and novice writers, in order to explore the poetic creative process from a psychiatric and psychological perspective.

Ryken, Leland, James C. Wilhoit, and Tremper Longman III. *Dictionary of Biblical Imagery*. Downers Grove, IL: InterVarsity, 1998. This reference work is dedicated to exploring the images, symbols, motifs, metaphors, and literary patterns found in the Bible.

Samuel, Maurice. *Blood Accusation: The Strange History of the Beiliss Case*. New York: Knopf, 1966. Appearing the same year as *The Fixer*, this book is an in-depth study of the Beilis case, on which Malamud's 1966 novel is loosely based.

Sánchez Canales, Gustavo. "Alienation and Marginality in Saul Bellow's Early Novels." *Evolving Origins: Transplanting Cultures*. Ed. Laura Alonso and Antonia Domínguez. Huelva, Spain: Universidad de Huelva, 2002. 177–88. This article explores Saul Bellow's first novels, *Dangling Man* and *The Victim*, from an existentialist perspective.

———. "The Significance of Martin Buber's Philosophy of Dialogue and Suffering in the Overcoming of 'Core-to-Core Confrontation' in Chaim Potok's *The Chosen*." *Estudios Ingleses de la Universidad Complutense* 18 (2010): 53–65. revistas.ucm.es/index.php/EIUC/article/view/EIUC1010110053A. This article focuses on how Martin Buber's philosophy of dialogue facilitates the mutual understanding between two opposing worlds in Potok's novel *The Chosen.*

Santamaría López, José Miguel. "La traducción de obras narrativas en la España franquista: Panorama preliminar." *Traducción y censura inglés-español: 1939–1985.* Ed. Rosa Rabadán. León, Spain: Universidad de León, 2000. 207–25. This essay looks at how literary works went through censorship during Franco's dictatorship in Spain.

Sasso, James. "The Stages of the Creative Process." *Proceedings of the American Philosophical Society* 124.2 (29 April 1980): 119–32. This essay analyzes the structures of the stages of the creative process as manifested in artistic production, taking the overlapping issues concerning cognitive development into account.

Schier, Helga. *Going Beyond: The Crisis of Identity and Identity Models in Contemporary American, English and German Fiction.* Tübingen, Germany: Max Niemeyer Verlag, 1993. This study is an overview of the issue of identity crisis from a literary standpoint.

Schwartz, Daniel R. *Imagining the Holocaust.* New York: St Martin's, 1999. This book addresses Holocaust narratives that have shaped the way we understand and respond to the events of that time, including analyses of first-person narratives such as Elie Wiesel's *Night* and Primo Levi's *Survival at Auschwitz.*

Schwarzschild, Steven S. "On Sufferings." *Encyclopedia Judaica.* 2nd ed. Detroit: Macmillan Reference, 2007. xxviii. The Rabbinic attitude toward sufferings is one of humble resignation to the will of God. The convinced faith in a blessed future enabled the Rabbis to face sufferings with fortitude and even joy, because it was seen as a pathway to heaven. The old view of sufferings as punishment never entirely disappeared; it was better to be punished by sufferings on earth so as to ensure happiness in the world to come.

Scobie, Charles H. H. *The Ways of Our God: An Approach to Biblical Theology.* Grand Rapids, MI: Eerdmans, 2003. This book addresses the nature and task of biblical theology and some major themes such as God's order, God's servant, and God's people.

Service, Robert. *Historia de Rusia en el siglo XX.* Barcelona: Editorial Crítica, 2000. This book provides an overview of the history of Russia from its beginnings until Boris Yeltsin's office.

Siegel, Katy. *Since '45: America and the Making of Contemporary Art.* London: Reaktion Books, 2011. The year 1945 was not only when the center of the art world moved significantly from Paris to New York but also the year of the A-bombs dropped on Hiroshima and Nagasaki. This book addresses the influence of history on art.

Silberman, Lou H. "Compassion." *Encyclopedia Judaica*. 2nd ed. Detroit: Macmillan Reference, 2007. 122–23. This article gives a brief account of the theme of compassion as addressed in the Bible and in Rabbinic literature.

Sollors, Werner. *Neither Black nor White yet Both: Thematic Explorations of Interracial Literature*. Cambridge, MA: Harvard University Press, 1999. In order to explore the issue of race, this book analyzes recurrent motifs in scientific and legal works as well as in fiction, drama, and poetry.

Stein, Gertrude. "Portraits and Repetition." *Lectures in America*. Boston: Beacon, 1985. 165–208. In this essay, the author defends herself against the criticism that her literary portraits of fellow artists are full of repetition. She insists on the difference between emphasis and repetition.

Steiner, George. *Grammars of Creation*. London: Faber and Faber, 2001. This book addresses the various "nothingnesses" that contemporary individuals live with. Not only are individual lives haunted by absence, but every work of art is influenced by what Steiner calls "a two-fold shadow": that of its own possible or preferable inexistence and that of its disappearance.

Tanner, Tony. *City of Words: American Fiction, 1950–70*. New York: Harper and Row, 1971. This volume gives an overview of the most prominent literary figures in American letters of the 1950s and 1960s.

"Top Hamas Official: Jews Use Blood in Their Passover Matzos." *Israel National News* 31 July 2014. www.israelnationalnews.com/News/News. aspx/183541#.VcokwrJViko. This article deals with the idea that the "matzah blood libel," traditionally used by some Muslims, was used by a top Hamas representative in Lebanon, Osama Hamdan.

Turtel, Chasia. "Beilis, Menahem Mendel." *Encyclopaedia Judaica*. 2nd ed. Detroit: Macmillan Reference, 2007. 267–68. This article gives a biographical sketch of M. Mendel Beilis, on whom Yakov Bok, the fictional character of *The Fixer*, is modeled.

Vigil, Barbara. "The Jewish Communities." *Multilingualism in Spain: Sociolinguistic and Psycholinguistic Aspects of Linguistic Minority Groups*. Ed. M. Teresa Turell. Clevedon, UK: Multilingual Matters, 2000. 235–53. This book, which starts from the idea that multilingualism in Spain explores the sociolinguistic and psycholinguistic aspects of established and new migrant minority groups in Spain, covers three key areas: language, migration, and discrimination. The reference here is to Jewish communities in Spain.

Wasserman, Eric. "An Interview with Ehud Havazelet." *Bosewell Magazine* (online) October 2000. www.ericwasserman.com/docs/EHUD%20 HAVAZELET-interview.pdf. According to the interviewer, Israel-born Ehud Havazelet continues the tradition of storytellers such as Malamud. During the interview, in which the writer is asked about his work *Eight*

Rabbis on the Roof, he talks about his writing habits and the themes that are of interest to him, among other things.

Wirth-Nesher, Hana. "Jewish-American Autobiography." *Prooftexts* 18 (1998): 113–20. This essay gives a general overview of the theme of autobiography in Jewish American writing. Interestingly, *Prooftexts* devoted one special issue (18.2–3, 1998) and the *Jewish Quarterly Review* another one (95.1, 2005) to this question.

Wollheim, Richard. "Art, Interpretation and the Creative Process." *New Literary History* 15.2 (Winter 1984): 241–53. The author of this essay proposes a method of criticism in the arts through what he calls "the Scrutiny thesis."

Wroblewsky, Vincent von. "Jaspers, Sartre, Camus und die Atombombe." *Karl Jaspers und Jean-Paul Sartre im Dialog: Ihre Sicht auf Existenz, Freiheit und Verantwortung*. Ed. Anton Hügli and Manuela Hackel. Frankfurt/M.: Peter Lang, 2015. 209–33. The author of this chapter reflects on philosophical issues such as existence, freedom, and responsibility in light of the effects of the dropping of the atomic bomb. In order to find an answer, he establishes a dialogue between Jaspers, Sartre, and Camus.

Yacobi, Tamar. "Pictorial Models and Narrative Ekphrasis." *Poetics Today* 16.4 (Winter 1995): 599–649. ncadjarmstrong.com/ma--art-through-a lens-/ pictorial_models.pdf. Taking the term *ekphrasis* as a point of departure, this essay analyzes two neglected forms—pictorial models and narrative ekphrasis.

Zamora, Lois Parkinson. *Writing the Apocalypse: Historical Vision in Contemporary U.S. and Latin American Fiction*. Cambridge: Cambridge University Press, 1989. This is a comparative literary study of apocalyptic themes and narrative techniques in the contemporary North and Latin American novel. The author, demonstrating that there are symbolic tensions inherent in the apocalyptic myth with special meaning for postmodern writers, focuses on the works of Gabriel García Márquez, Carlos Fuentes, Julio Cortázar, Thomas Pynchon, John Barth, and Walker Percy.

CONTRIBUTORS

Victoria Aarons holds the position of Mitchell Distinguished Professor of Literature in the English Department at Trinity University, San Antonio, Texas, where she teaches courses on American Jewish and Holocaust literatures. Her many publications include *A Measure of Memory: Storytelling and Identity in American Jewish Fiction* (1996) and *What Happened to Abraham: Reinventing the Covenant in American Jewish Fiction* (2005), both recipients of the Choice Award for Outstanding Academic Book, and the coedited volume *The New Diaspora: The Changing Landscape of American Jewish Fiction* (2015), a finalist for the 2015 National Jewish Book Award. She is a contributor to the two-volume *Encyclopedia of Holocaust Writers*, and she was an invited speaker at the eightieth birthday celebration/symposium for Elie Wiesel. She is a judge of the Edward Lewis Wallant Award, a prize awarded each year to a rising American Jewish writer of fiction. She has published well over seventy articles and book chapters, and her work has appeared in a number of scholarly venues. She is on the editorial board of *Philip Roth Studies, Studies in American Jewish Literature*, and *Women in Judaism*. She is the recipient of the Piper Professor Award for Outstanding Scholarly and Academic Achievement and the Z. T. Scott Faculty Fellowship for Outstanding Achievement in Teaching and Advising. Aarons has been invited to speak at a number of public venues, including Florida Atlantic University's Center for the Study of Values and Violence after Auschwitz and Purdue University's seventh annual Larry Axel Memorial Lectureship in Religion. She is currently editing the *Cambridge Companion to Saul Bellow*, and her book on third-generation literary representation of the Holocaust is forthcoming.

Pilar Alonso is an associate professor of English linguistics in the English Department at the University of Salamanca, Spain. Her main fields of research are discourse analysis and discourse coherence and cognitive linguistics with a special interest in literary discourse analysis. She has published numerous articles on semantic, pragmatic, and cognitive aspects of literary works by North American and British authors; among them are "The Conceptual Integration Network Model as a Paradigm for Analysis of Complex Narrative Discourse" (2004), "A Cognitive Approach to Short Story Writing" (2012), and "The Role of Cognitive Coherence in Non-expert Processes of Literary Discourse Reception" (2014). She is the author of *A Multi-dimensional Approach to Discourse Coherence: From Standardness to Creativity* (2014) and has coedited *Aspects of Discourse Analysis* (2002) and translated and edited I. B. Singer's book *Un amigo de Kafka y otros relatos* (1990).

Alan Astro is a professor of modern languages and literatures at Trinity University, San Antonio, Texas. He is the author of over thirty articles on writers as diverse as Bashevis, Baudelaire, Beckett, and Borges; a recent piece, published in *Partial Answers*, is a new reading of Elie Wiesel's *Night* in its English, French, and Yiddish versions. Astro is the editor of *Yiddish South of the Border: An Anthology of Latin American Yiddish Writing*; and his translation of Éric Marty's *Radical French Thought and the Return of the "Jewish Question"* has recently been published.

Rémi Astruc is a professor of comparative and Francophone literature at the University of Cergy-Pontoise, France. He is codirector of the research group Agora (literature and social sciences) and founding member of CCC (community of scholars working on community). After completing his Ph.D. thesis on identity in Jewish American contemporary novels and films (Bellow, Malamud, Roth, and Woody Allen), he has specialized in the analysis of different forms of humor, writing two essays and many articles on the grotesque. His research currently focuses on the question of community and its contemporary expressions in art.

Emilio Cañadas Rodríguez teaches English and literature at the Faculty of Social Sciences and Education at Camilo José Cela University in Spain, where he is also the director of the International Education and Bilingualism master's program. Since 2010, he has served as head of the English Studies Department. His research focuses on the American contemporary short story, and he has published book chapters, articles, and essays on Truman Capote, Tim Gautreux, Bernard Malamud, and

Raymond Carver, among others. He is also literary coeditor of *Verbeia: Journal of English and Spanish Studies*.

Leah Garrett is the Loti Smorgon Research Professor of Contemporary Jewish Life and Culture at Monash University. She has published four books and numerous articles on Jewish literature. Garrett's scholarship has been devoted to understanding how Jewish authors in an array of languages use their literary discourse to enact, reimagine, and subvert conventional ideas about the relationship between Jews and the modern world. Her most recent book, *Young Lions: How Jewish Authors Reinvented the American War Novel*, was a finalist for the 2015 National Jewish Book Award.

Andrew M. Gordon is a professor emeritus of English at the University of Florida. His publications include *An American Dreamer: A Psychoanalytic Study of the Fiction of Norman Mailer*, *Psychoanalyses/Feminisms*, coedited with Peter Rudnytsky; *Screen Saviors: Hollywood Fictions of Whiteness*, coauthored with Hernan Vera; and most recently, *Empire of Dreams: The Science Fiction and Fantasy Films of Steven Spielberg*. He also has eighty-five essays and thirty-five reviews on Jewish American writers such as Bellow, Roth, Malamud, Ozick, and Kosinski; on other contemporary writers such as Barth and Pynchon; and on American science-fiction novels and films.

Till Kinzel received his Ph.D. (2002) and habilitation (2005) from the Technical University of Berlin. He has published books on Allan Bloom (*Platonische Kulturkritik in Amerika*, 2002), Nicolás Gómez Dávila (2003, 4th enl. ed. 2015), Philip Roth (*Die Tragödie und Komödie des amerikanischen Lebens*, 2006), and Michael Oakeshott (2007). Most recently, he has edited a number of writings and translations by Johann Joachim Eschenburg and coedited *Imaginary Dialogues in English* (2012) and *Imaginary Dialogues in American Literature and Philosophy* (2014; both with Jarmila Mildorf), as well as *Johann Joachim Eschenburg und die Künste und Wissenschaften zwischen Aufklärung und Romantik* (2013) and a book on the reception of Edward Gibbon in Germany (2015; both with Cord-Friedrich Berghahn).

Jessica Lang is an associate professor of English and the Newman Director of the Wasserman Jewish Studies Center at Baruch College, CUNY. Her primary areas of interest are in Holocaust literature and Jewish American fiction.

Holli Levitsky is the founder and director of the Jewish Studies Program and professor of English at Loyola Marymount University in Los Angeles. Her research and scholarship focus on Holocaust representation and questions of (Jewish) identity, especially as it relates to exile and displacement. Most recently, she is the coeditor of *The Literature of Exile and Displacement: American Identity in a Time of Crisis* (2013) and *Summer Haven: The Catskills, the Holocaust and the Literary Imagination*, an edited collection of literature and essays on the experience of the Holocaust in the Catskill mountain resorts, hotels, and bungalow colonies in upstate New York (2015).

Paul Malamud was born in 1947 in New York City to Ann and Bernard Malamud and grew up in Corvallis, Oregon, and Bennington, Vermont. He attended the Cambridge School of Weston and Yale College and received a Ph.D. in British literary studies at Columba University. After 1980, he lived in Washington, D.C., and worked as a writer and editor. His poems and translations from French and Latin have appeared in magazines.

Félix Martín Gutiérrez is a professor of English and American literature at the Complutense University (Madrid, Spain). As a Fulbright scholar in Austin, Texas (1972–75) and visiting professor at Yale (1984) and Stanford (1987), he was able to concentrate his research interests in literary history and critical theory, mainly applied to American literature and American studies. His latest book, published in Spanish, *Retorno a la historia literaria norteamericana* (2014) surveys recent speculations on literary history and critical pedagogy in the States. As specialized topics, he has published essays on Edgar Allan Poe, Herman Melville, Walt Whitman, Hart Crane, W. H. Auden, Margaret Atwood, Grace Paley, Adrienne Kennedy, and Arthur Miller.

Timothy Parrish, a professor of English at Virginia Tech University, is the author of *Walking Blues: Making Americans from Emerson to Elvis* (2001), *From the Civil War to the Apocalypse: Postmodern History and American Fiction* (2008), and *Ralph Ellison and the Genius of America* (2012). He is also the editor of *The Cambridge Companion to Philip Roth* (2007) and *The Cambridge Companion to American Novelists* (2013). He has published widely on contemporary American literature in such journals as *Modern Fiction Studies*, *Contemporary Literature*, *Studies in Jewish American Literature*, *Texas Studies in Literature and Language*, *Shofar*, and *Prospects*.

Gustavo Sánchez Canales teaches English at the Faculty of Teacher Training and Education at the Universidad Autónoma de Madrid, where he is also vice dean for research and innovation. He served as vice dean for international relations between 2011 and 2013. From 1999 to 2010, he taught English and U.S. literature at the Universidad Complutense de Madrid. His research focuses on contemporary Jewish American literature. He has published book chapters, articles, and essays on Saul Bellow, Philip Roth, Bernard Malamud, Cynthia Ozick, Chaim Potok, Rebecca Goldstein, Allegra Goodman, and Michael Chabon, among others. He has coedited with Victoria Aarons a thematic volume on Philip Roth titled *History, Memory, and the Making of Character in Roth's Fiction*. He has also coedited with Victoria Aarons a forum titled "Saul Bellow as a Novelist of Ideas" in *Partial Answers*.

Aristi Trendel is an associate professor at the Maine University, Le Mans, France, where she offers courses in American civilization. She has taught American literature and creative writing for several years at the School of Management of Strasbourg. Her doctoral dissertation focused on John Updike's short fiction. She has published articles on American writers (John Updike, Philip Roth, Flannery O'Connor, Henry James, Jeffrey Eugenides, Rikki Ducornet, Djuana Barnes, and others) in the *Psychoanalytic Review*, the *John Updike Review*, *Philip Roth Studies*, the *Columbia Journal of American Studies*, the *Journal of the Short Story in English*, the *EJAS*, and the *Baltic Journal*, among others; book reviews; and fiction in literary magazines. She is the author of four books of fiction.

Theodora Tsimpouki is a professor at the Faculty of English Studies, University of Athens. She studied at the University of Athens, the Sorbonne, and New York University, from which she received her Ph.D. Her essays have appeared in English and Greek in numerous journals and edited collections, including *Post-Exceptionalist American Studies* (2014), *States of Emergency / States of Crisis* (2011), *Philip Roth and World Literature* (2014), *East-Central European Traumas and a Millennial Condition* (1999), *Women in Dialogue: (M)uses of Culture* (2008), *On the Road to Baghdad, or, Travelling Biculturalism* (2005), and *Revisiting Crisis / Reflecting on Conflict: American Literary Interpretations from WWII to Ground Zero* (2008). Her published works also include *Culture Agonistes: Debating Culture, Re-reading Texts* (coeditor, 2002), *Conformism, Non-Conformism and Anti-Conformism in the Culture of the US* (coeditor, 2008), and *Our America: American Culture in Greece* (2010, in Greek). She has been book reviews editor of the *Journal of the European Association for American Studies (EJAS)* since 2000.

Martín Urdiales Shaw is an associate professor in the Department of English, French and German at the University of Vigo, Spain, where he has been teaching since 2000. He belongs to the NETEC research group (Textual and Cultural Negotiations), which is part of the network Rede de Investigación en Lingua, Literatura inglesa e Identidade, funded by the Galician autonomous administration (Xunta de Galicia). He has specialized in the fields of Jewish American narrative, 1930s urban fiction, and more recently, graphic novels and Holocaust studies. His main publications include a monograph on Bernard Malamud's work (*Ethnic Identities in Bernard Malamud's Fiction*, 2000) and articles on the works of Malamud, Henry Roth, Michael Gold, Clifford Odets, and Tillie Olsen, among others. His more recent research has focused on Art Spiegelman's graphic novel/memoir *Maus*, both in relation to the artist's reinscription of the survivor's discourse and as regards the translation of Vladek's foreignized English into Spanish and other Romance languages. He has also worked on the visual in Spiegelman's *Maus* and *In the Shadow of No Towers*, arguing the relational nature of the cartoonist's representational strategies and the conceptual indeterminacy of Spiegelman's post-9/11 book.

INDEX

Specific works are listed under the author, except for those of Bernard Malamud, whose works are listed separately. In the index BM stands for Bernard Malamud.

303